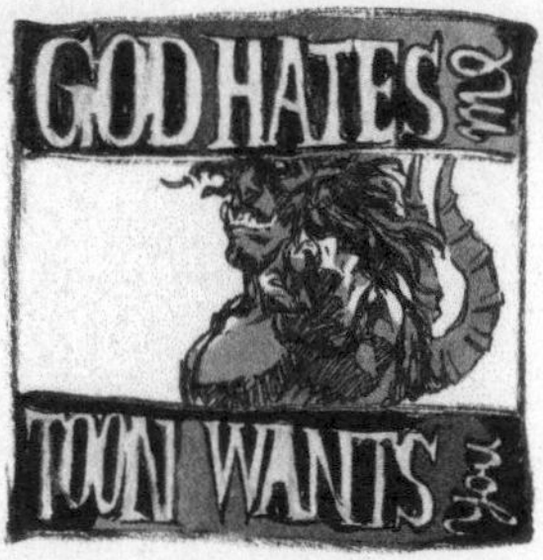
GOD HATES me
TOON WANTS you

Recently I've been meeting other manga artists so frequently I can't even believe it. It's fun. We meet and talk about manga. It's a lot of fun. Could it be that I actually like manga? I don't read too much of it though.

-Tite Kubo

Bleach is author Tite Kubo's second title. Kubo made his debut with *ZOMBIEPOWDER.*, a four-volume series for *Weekly Shonen Jump*. To date, *Bleach* has been translated into numerous languages and has also inspired an animated TV series that began airing in the U.S. in 2006. Beginning its serialization in 2001, *Bleach* is still a mainstay in the pages of *Weekly Shonen Jump*. In 2005, *Bleach* was awarded the prestigious Shogakukan Manga Award in the *shonen* (boys) category.

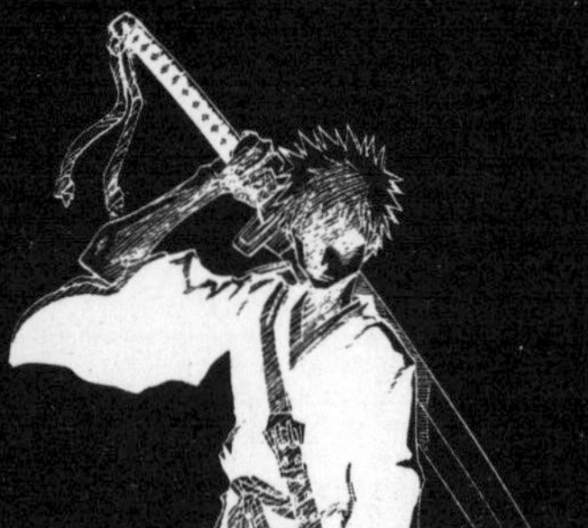

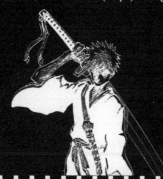

BLEACH
Vol. 34: KING OF THE KILL
SHONEN JUMP Manga Edition

This volume contains material that was originally published in English
in SHONEN JUMP #95–98. Artwork in the magazine may have been
altered slightly from what is presented in this volume.

STORY AND ART BY
TITE KUBO

English Adaptation/Lance Caselman
Translation/Joe Yamazaki
Touch-up Art & Lettering/Mark McMurray
Design/Sean Lee, Yukiko Whitley
Editors/Alexis Kirsch, Yuki Takagaki

BLEACH © 2001 by Tite Kubo. All rights reserved. First published
in Japan in 2001 by SHUEISHA Inc., Tokyo. English translation rights
arranged by SHUEISHA Inc.

The rights of the author(s) of the work(s) in this publication to be so
identified have been asserted in accordance with Copyright, Designs and
Patents Act 1988. A CIP catalogue record for this book is available from
the British Library.

Printed in the U.S.A.

Published by VIZ Media, LLC
P.O. Box 77010
San Francisco, CA 94107

10 9 8 7 6 5 4 3 2 1
First printing, March 2011

PARENTAL ADVISORY
BLEACH is rated T for Teen and is recommended
for ages 13 and up. This volume contains
fantasy violence.
ratings.viz.com

www.viz.com

THE WORLD'S
MOST POPULAR MANGA
SHONEN JUMP
www.shonenjump.com

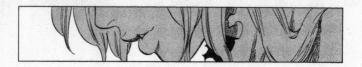

If you were to give me wings
I would fly for you

Even if this entire land
were to sink underwater

If you were to give me a sword
I would stand up and fight for you

Even if this entire sky
were to pierce you with its light

BLEACH 34 KING OF THE KILL

STARS AND

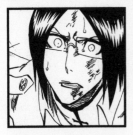

柝木ルキア

Rukia Kuchiki

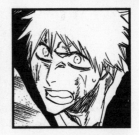

Uryû Ishida

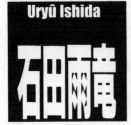

石田雨竜

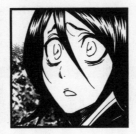

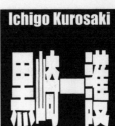

Ichigo Kurosaki

黒崎一護

plot

When high school student Ichigo Kurosaki meets Soul Reaper Rukia Kuchiki his life is changed forever. Soon Ichigo is a soul-cleansing Soul Reaper too, and he finds himself having adventures, as well as problems, that he never would have imagined. Now Ichigo and his friends must stop renegade Soul Reaper Aizen and his army of Arrancars from destroying the Soul Society and wiping out Karakura Town as well.

Having penetrated the enemy's stronghold Las Noches to rescue Orihime, Ichigo and his allies must face the powerful Espadas. Ichigo is able to defeat the Espada Grimmjow, but soon afterward he is attacked by a new enemy, Nnoitora. Just when things look hopeless, Nel steps in and transforms into a powerful warrior!

BLEACH ALL

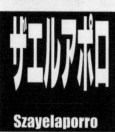

ザエルアポロ

Szayelaporro

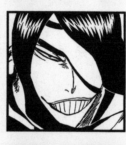

ネリエル

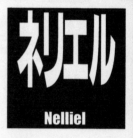

Nelliel

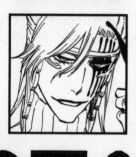

Nnoitora

ノイトラ

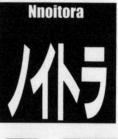

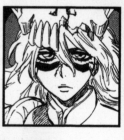

STORIES

BLEACH 34

KING OF THE KILL

Contents

296.	Changed Again And Again	7
297.	King of the Kill	27
298.	INTRUDERZ 3	47
299.	The Verbal Warfare	71
300.	Curse Named Love	91
301.	Nothing Like Equal	111
302.	Pride on the Blade	135
303.	Dumdum-Dummy-Dumbstruck	155
304.	Battle of Barbarians	175
305.	The Rising Phoenix	195

296. Changed Again and Again

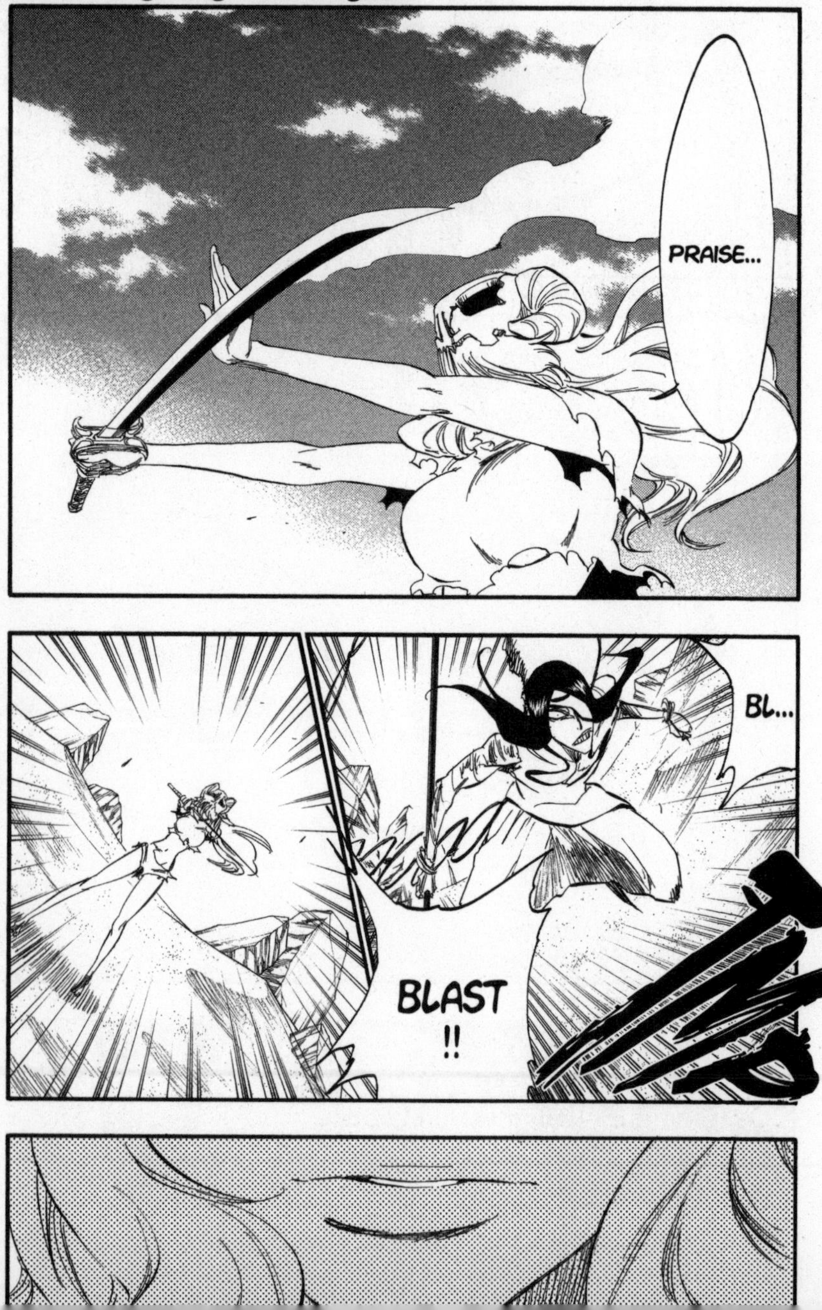
PRAISE...
BL...
BLAST !!

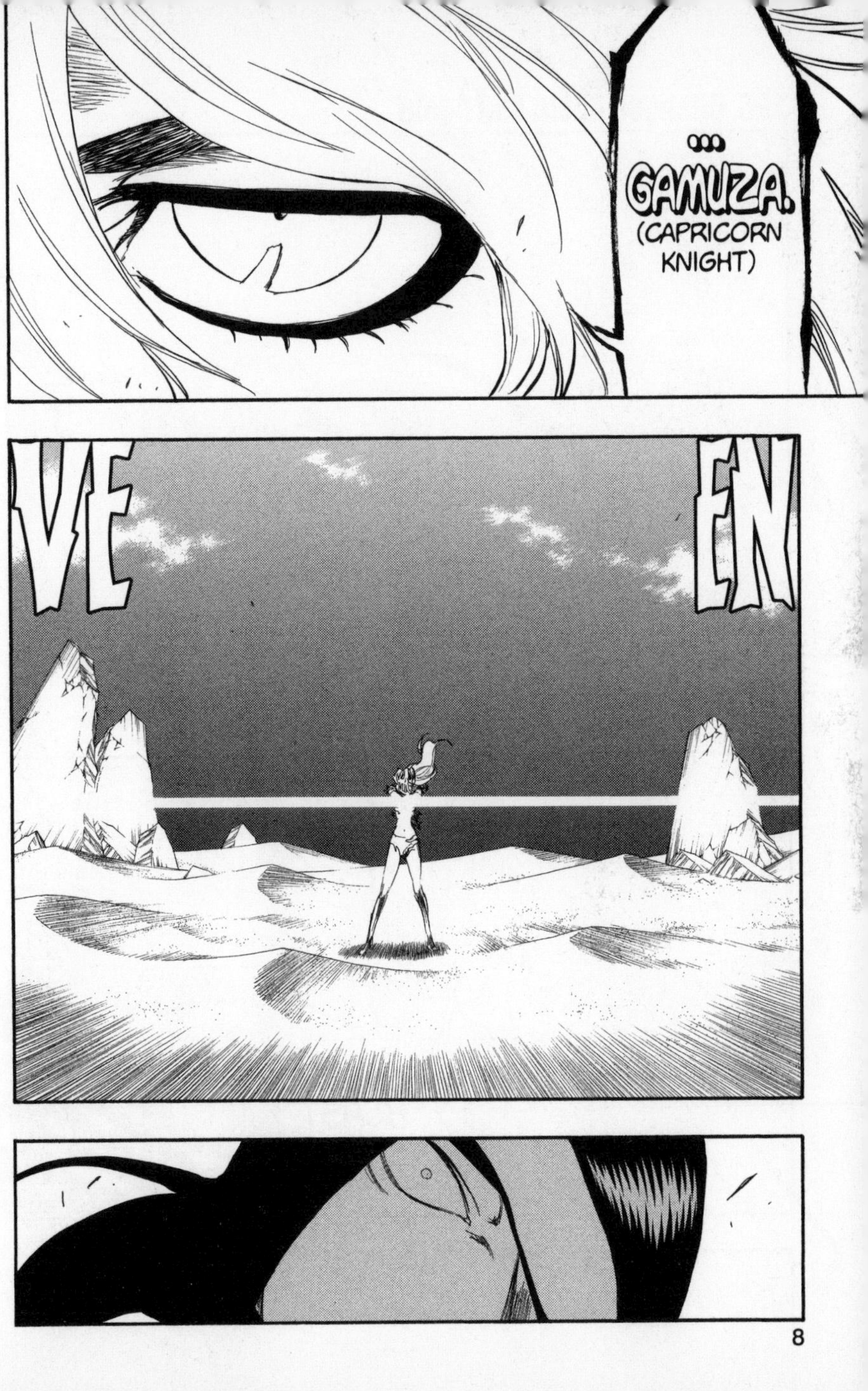
...
GAMUZA.
(CAPRICORN KNIGHT)
VE
EN

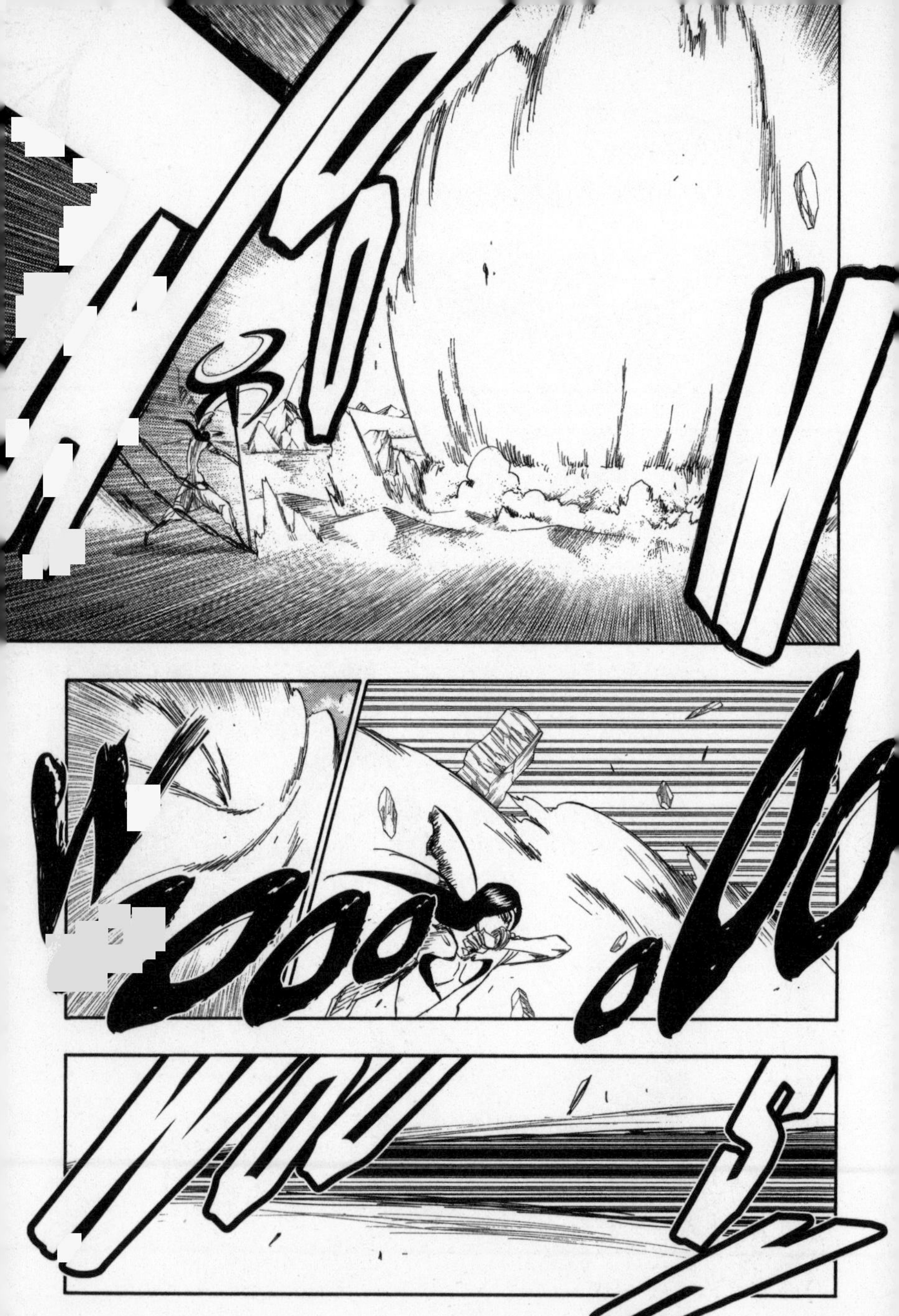
WOOSH

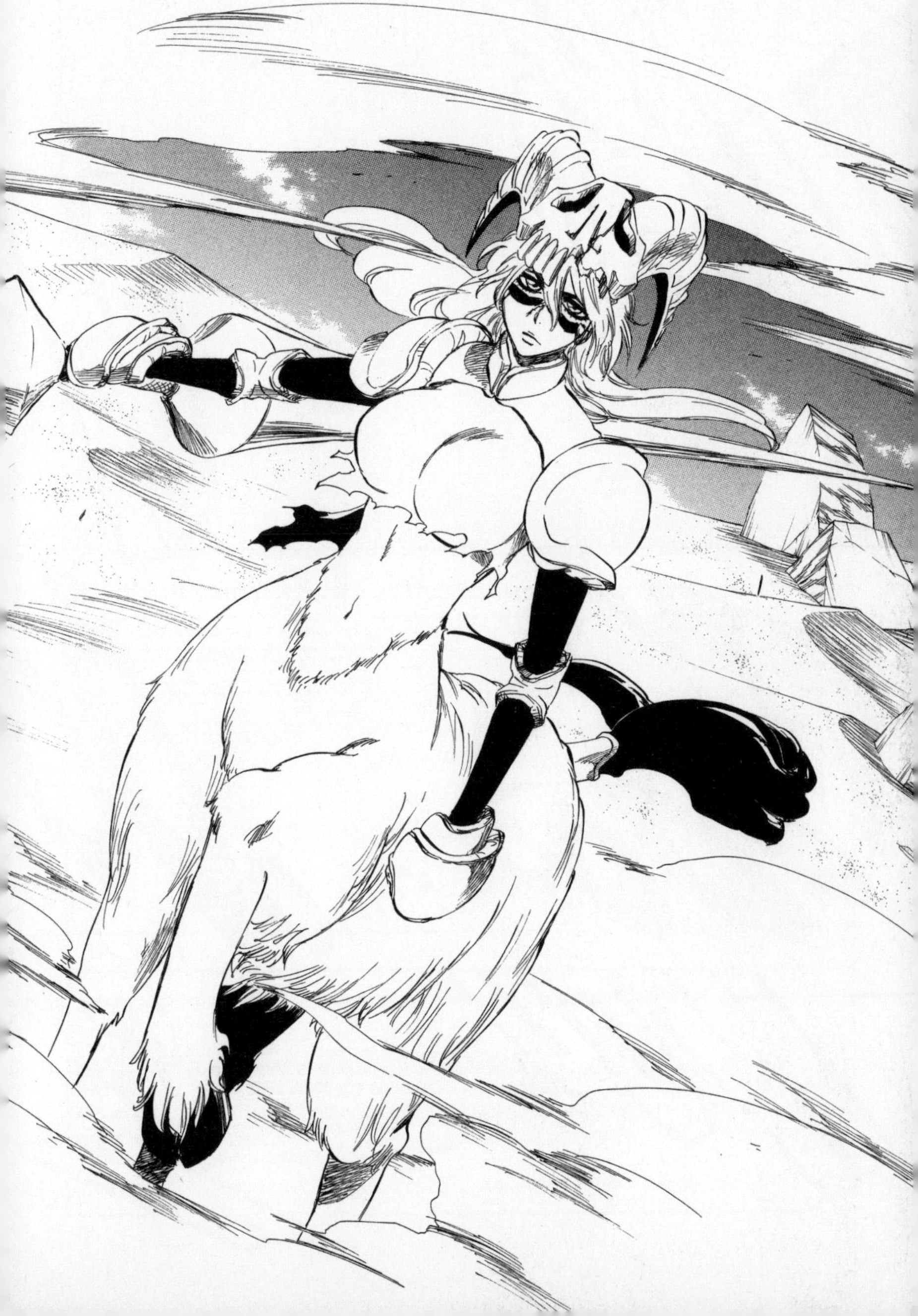

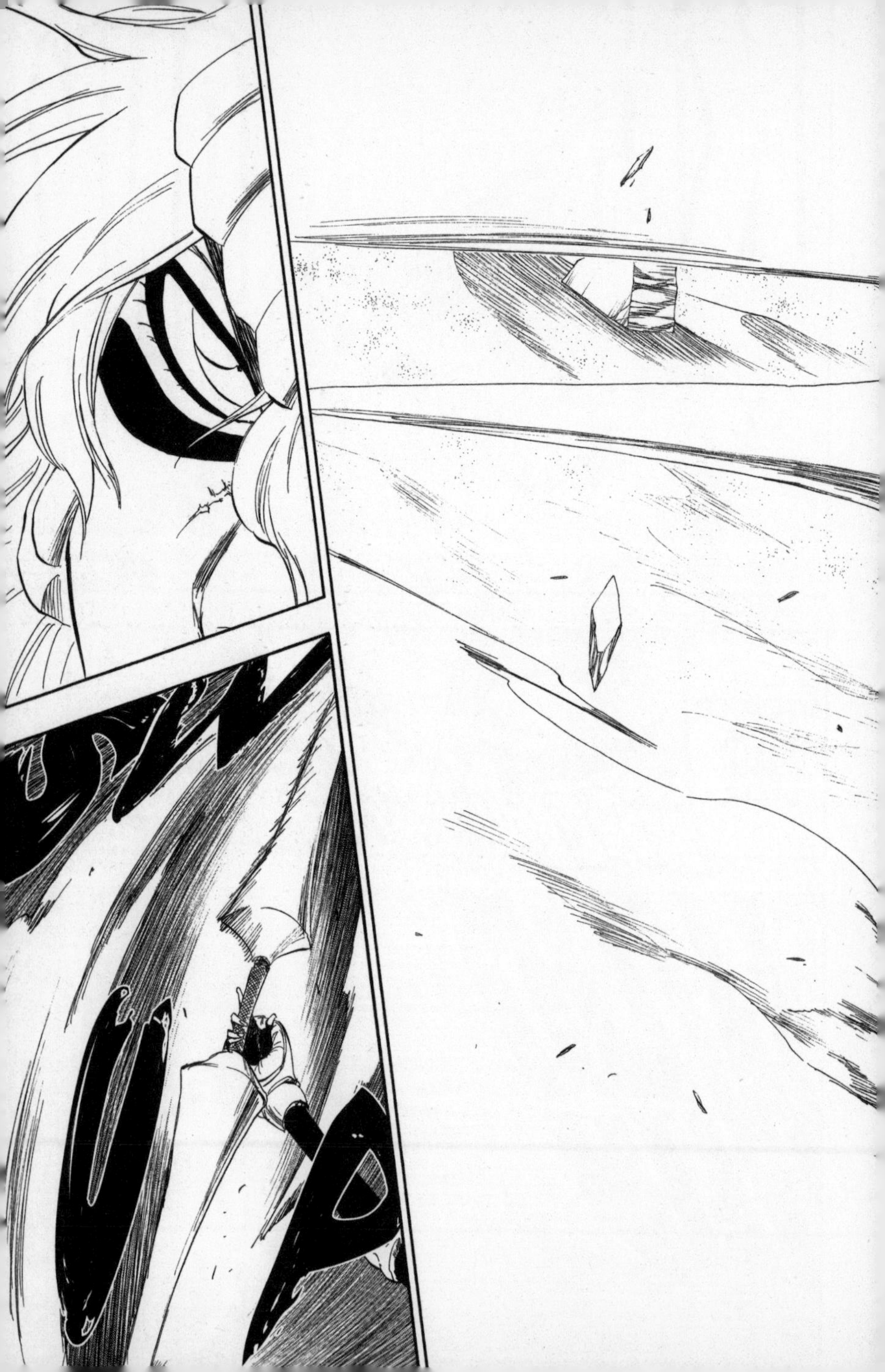

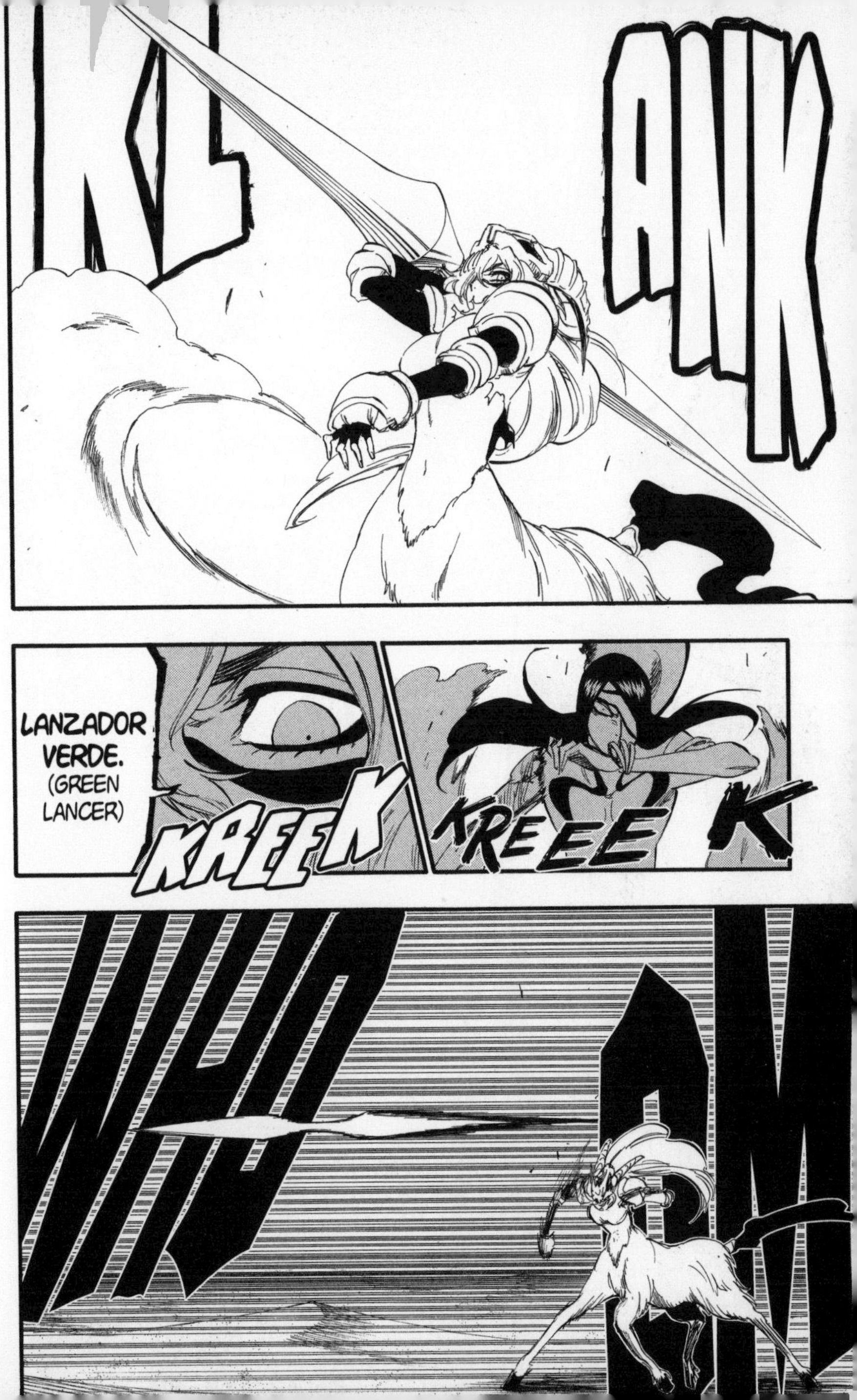
KLANK
KREEEK
LANZADOR VERDE.
(GREEN LANCER)
KREEK
WHAM

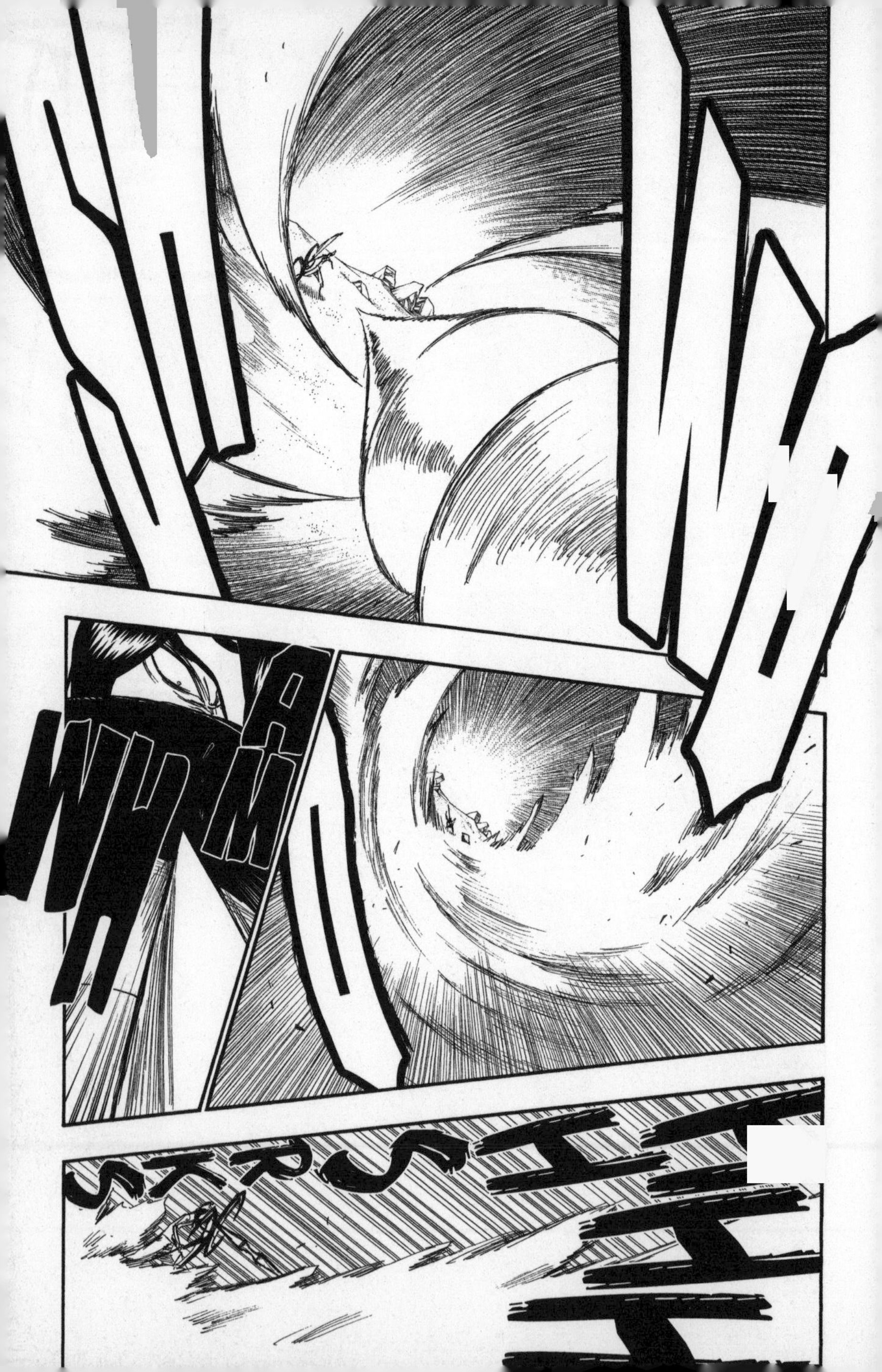
WHAM

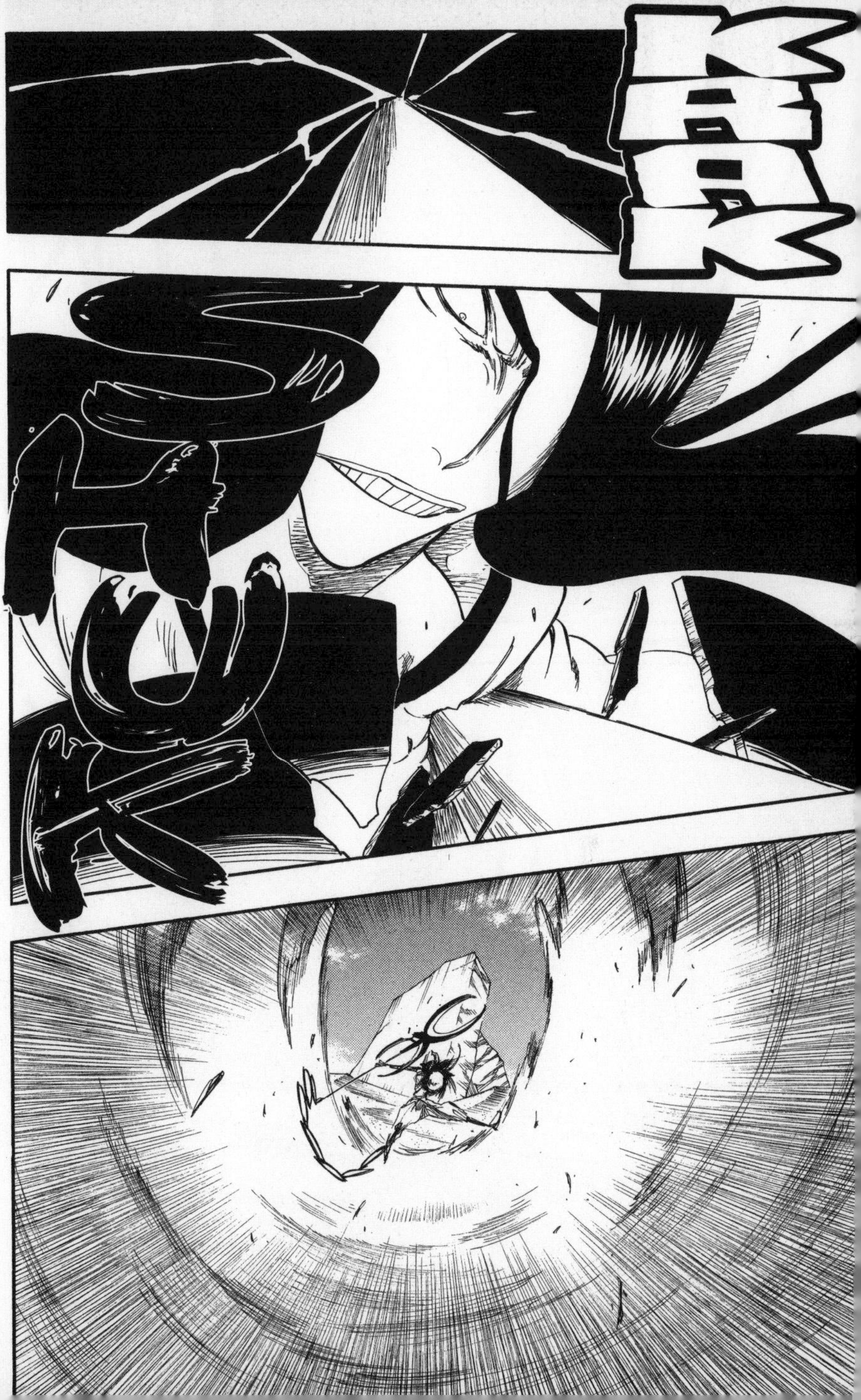
KRAK

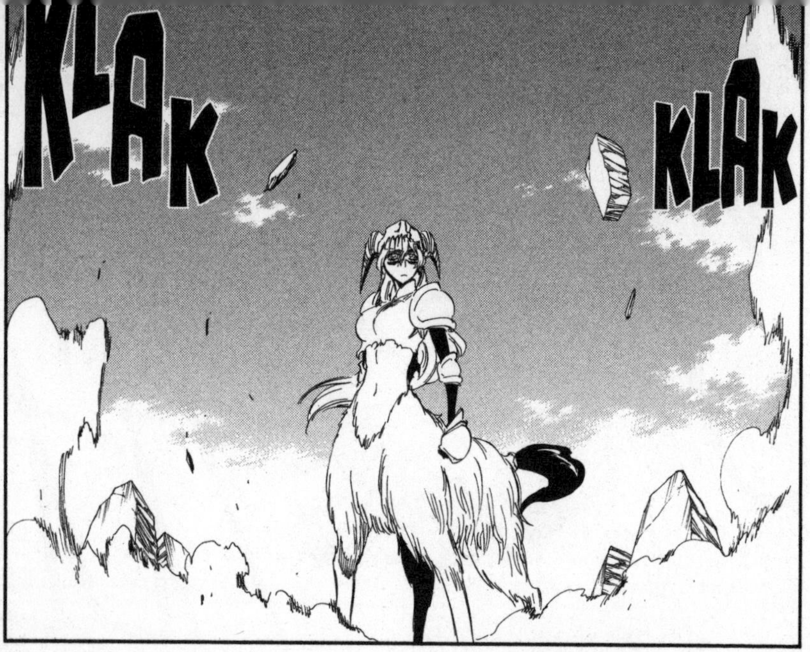
KLAK
KLAK

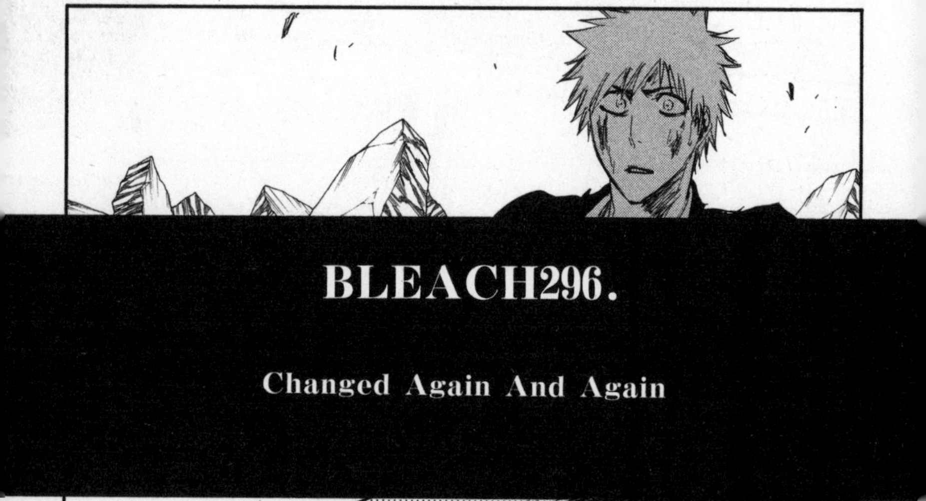

BLEACH296.

Changed Again And Again

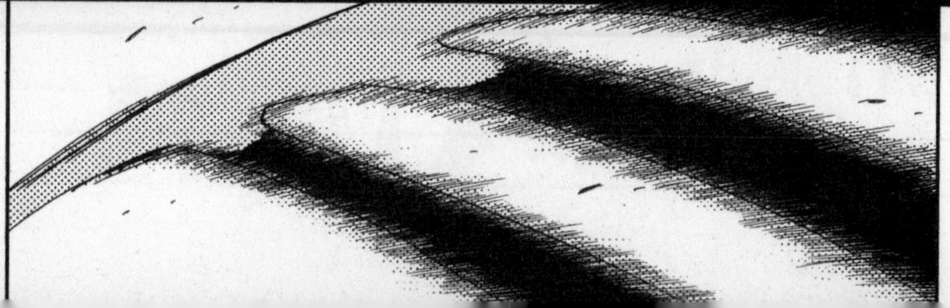

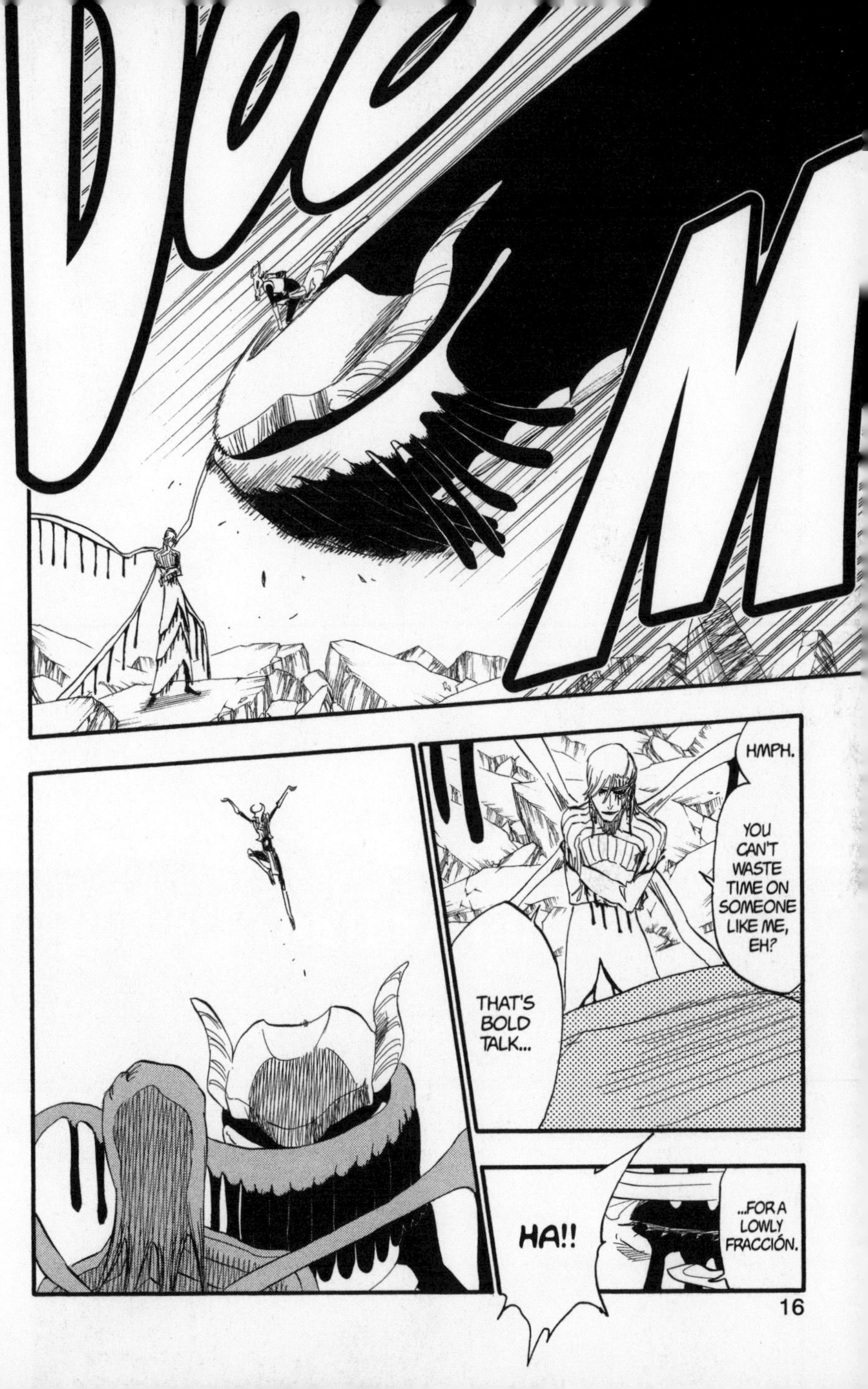
HMPH.
YOU CAN'T WASTE TIME ON SOMEONE LIKE ME, EH?
THAT'S BOLD TALK...
...FOR A LOWLY FRACCIÓN.
HA!!

READ THIS WAY

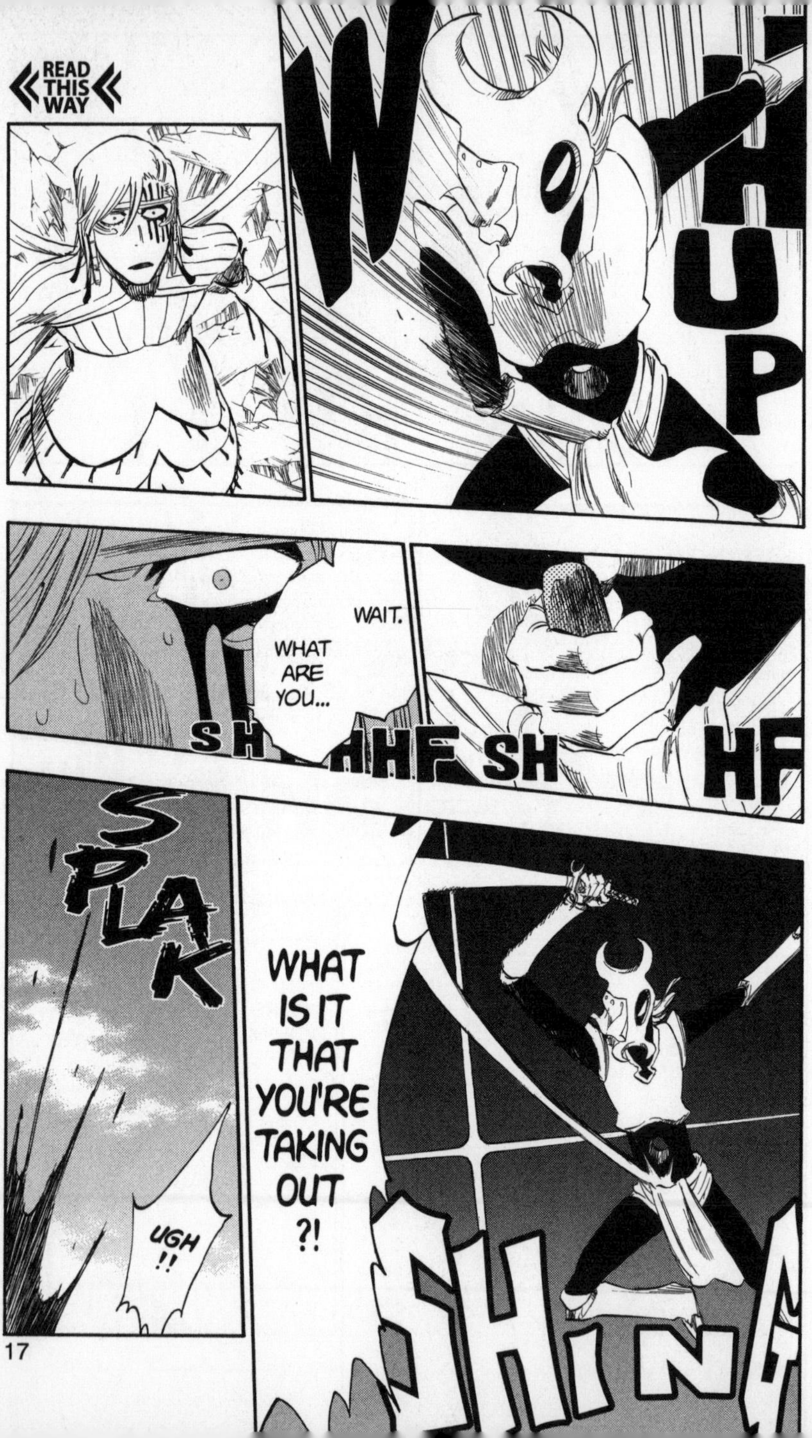
WHUP
WAIT.
WHAT ARE YOU...
SHHHF SHHF
WHAT IS IT THAT YOU'RE TAKING OUT ?!
SHING
SPLAK
UGH !!

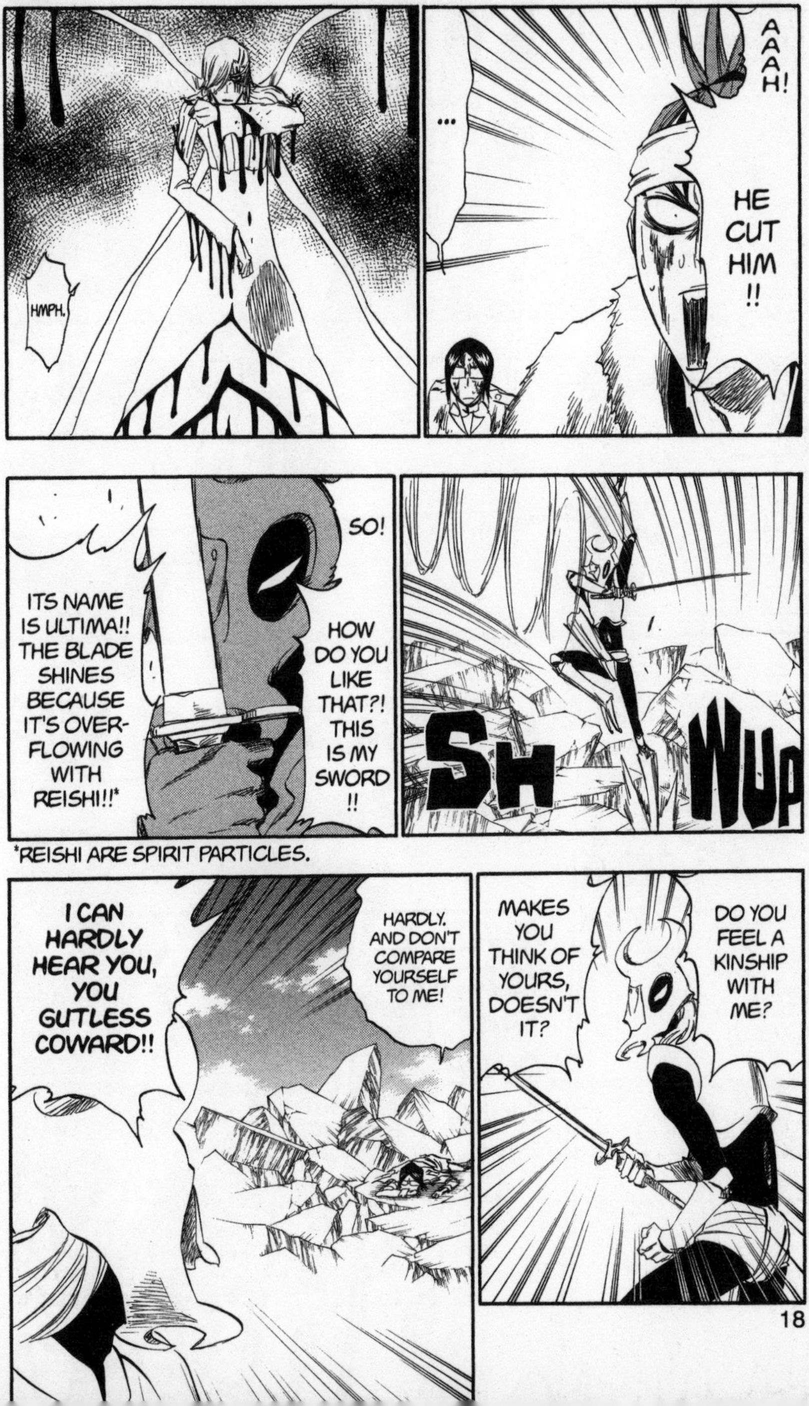
AAAH!
...
HE CUT HIM!!
HMPH.
SHWUP
SO!
HOW DO YOU LIKE THAT?! THIS IS MY SWORD!!
ITS NAME IS ULTIMA!! THE BLADE SHINES BECAUSE IT'S OVERFLOWING WITH REISHI!!*
DO YOU FEEL A KINSHIP WITH ME?
MAKES YOU THINK OF YOURS, DOESN'T IT?
HARDLY. AND DON'T COMPARE YOURSELF TO ME!
I CAN HARDLY HEAR YOU, YOU GUTLESS COWARD!!

*REISHI ARE SPIRIT PARTICLES.

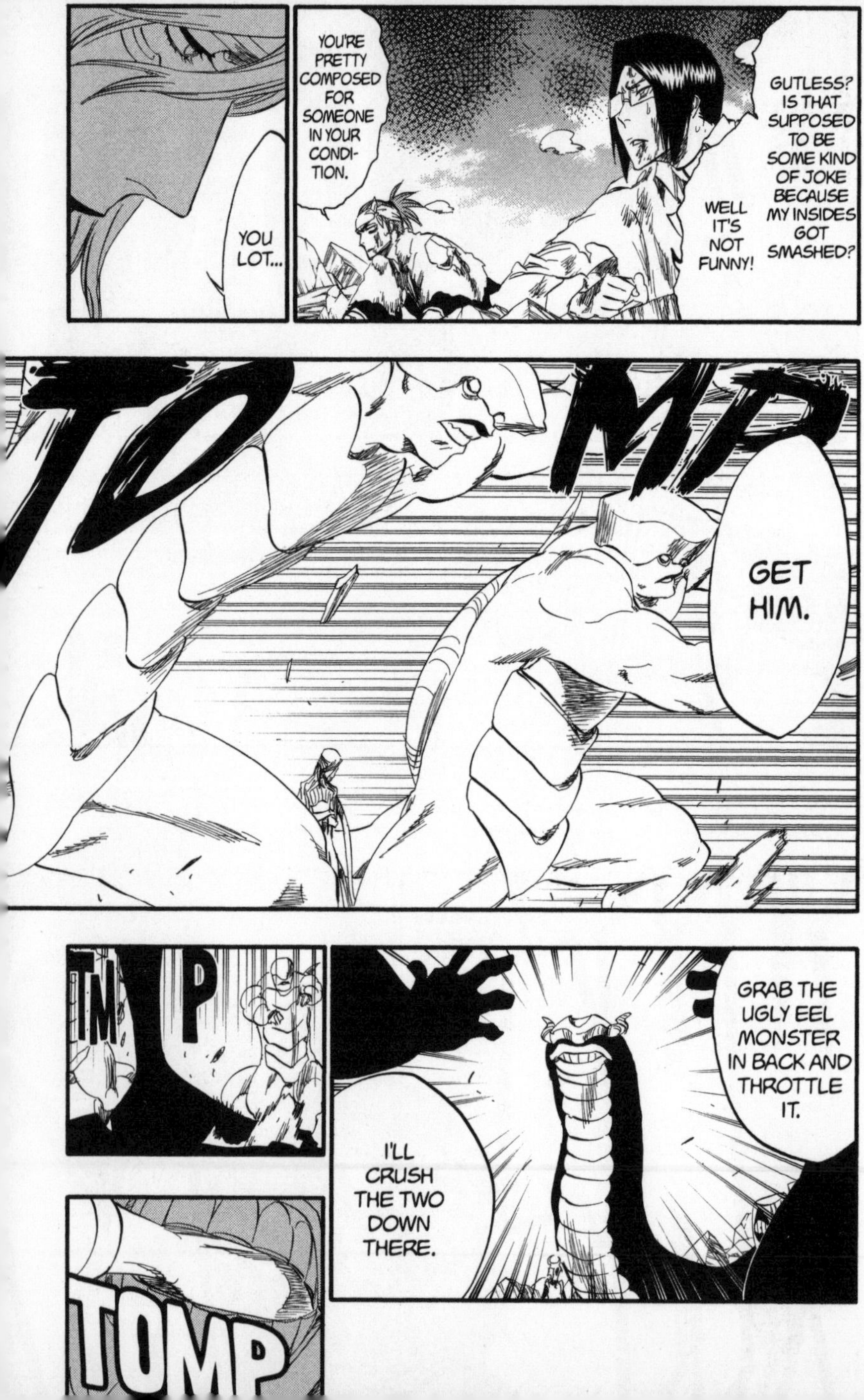
GUTLESS? IS THAT SUPPOSED TO BE SOME KIND OF JOKE BECAUSE MY INSIDES GOT SMASHED?
WELL IT'S NOT FUNNY!
YOU'RE PRETTY COMPOSED FOR SOMEONE IN YOUR CONDITION.
YOU LOT...
TO MP
GET HIM.
GRAB THE UGLY EEL MONSTER IN BACK AND THROTTLE IT.
I'LL CRUSH THE TWO DOWN THERE.
TM P
TOMP

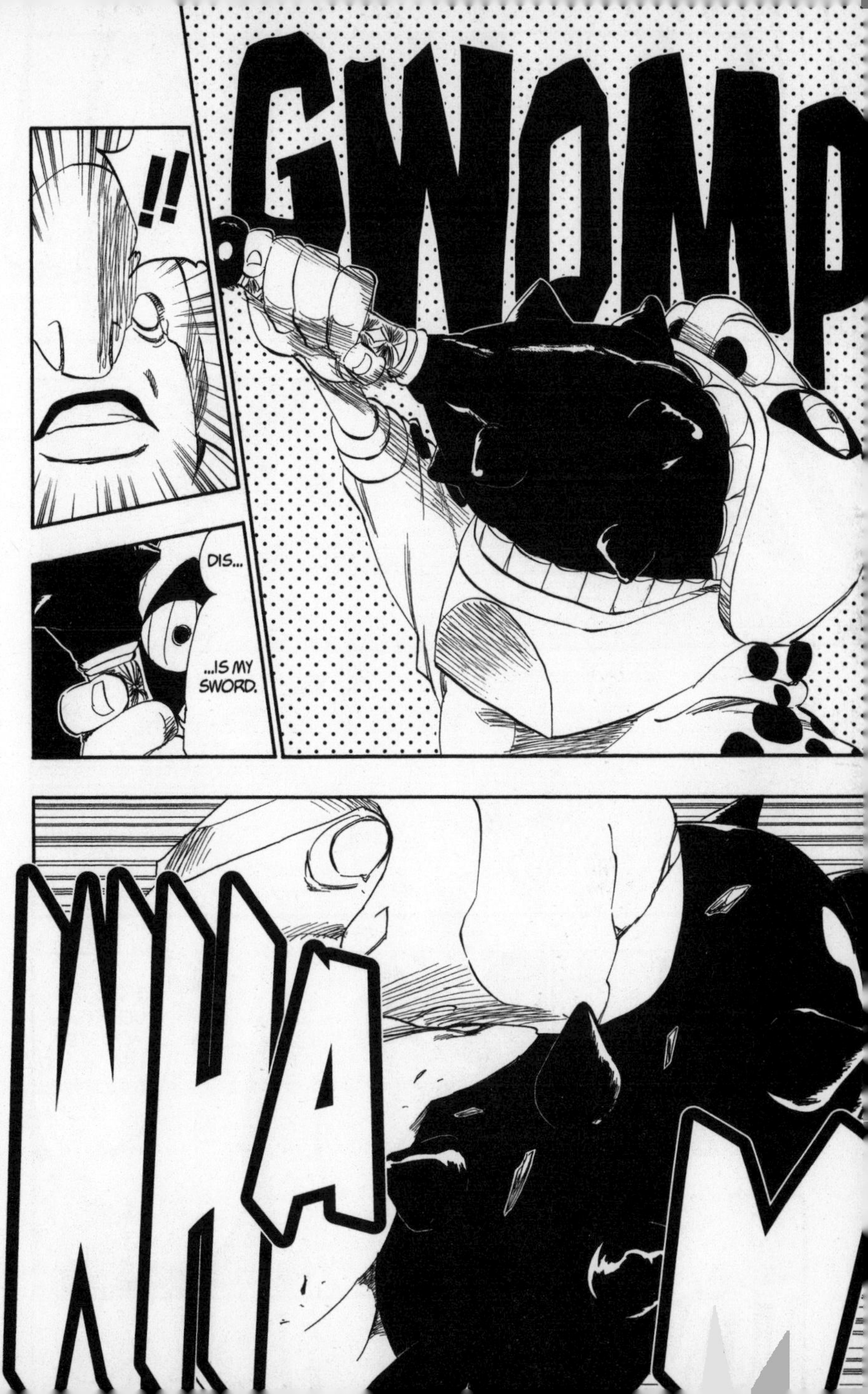
GWOMP
!!
DIS...
...IS MY SWORD.
WHAM

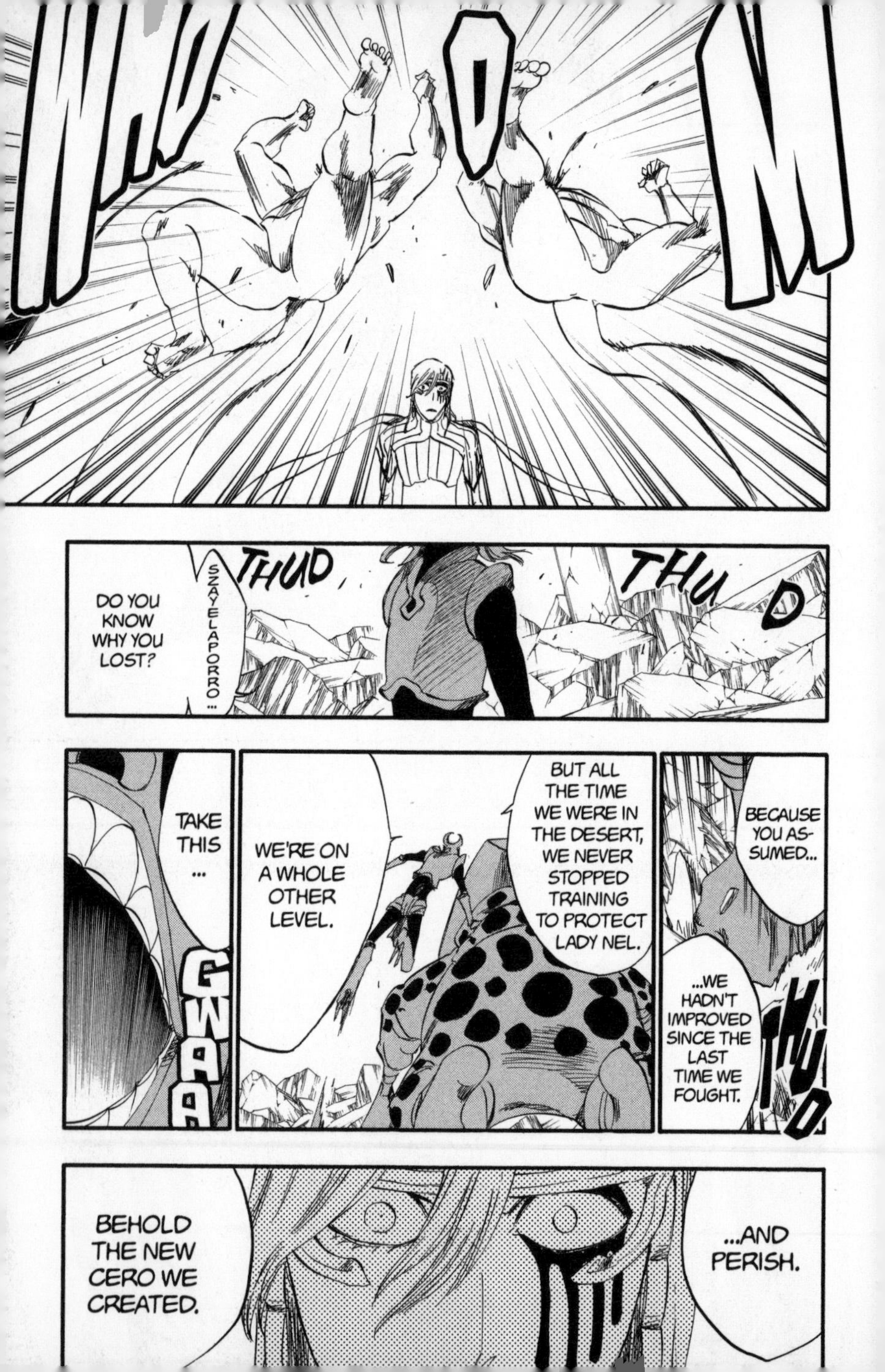
WHOOM
THUD
THUD
SZAYELAPORRO...
DO YOU KNOW WHY YOU LOST?
BECAUSE YOU AS-SUMED...
...WE HADN'T IMPROVED SINCE THE LAST TIME WE FOUGHT.
THUD
BUT ALL THE TIME WE WERE IN THE DESERT, WE NEVER STOPPED TRAINING TO PROTECT LADY NEL.
WE'RE ON A WHOLE OTHER LEVEL.
TAKE THIS ...
GWAA
BEHOLD THE NEW CERO WE CREATED.
...AND PERISH.

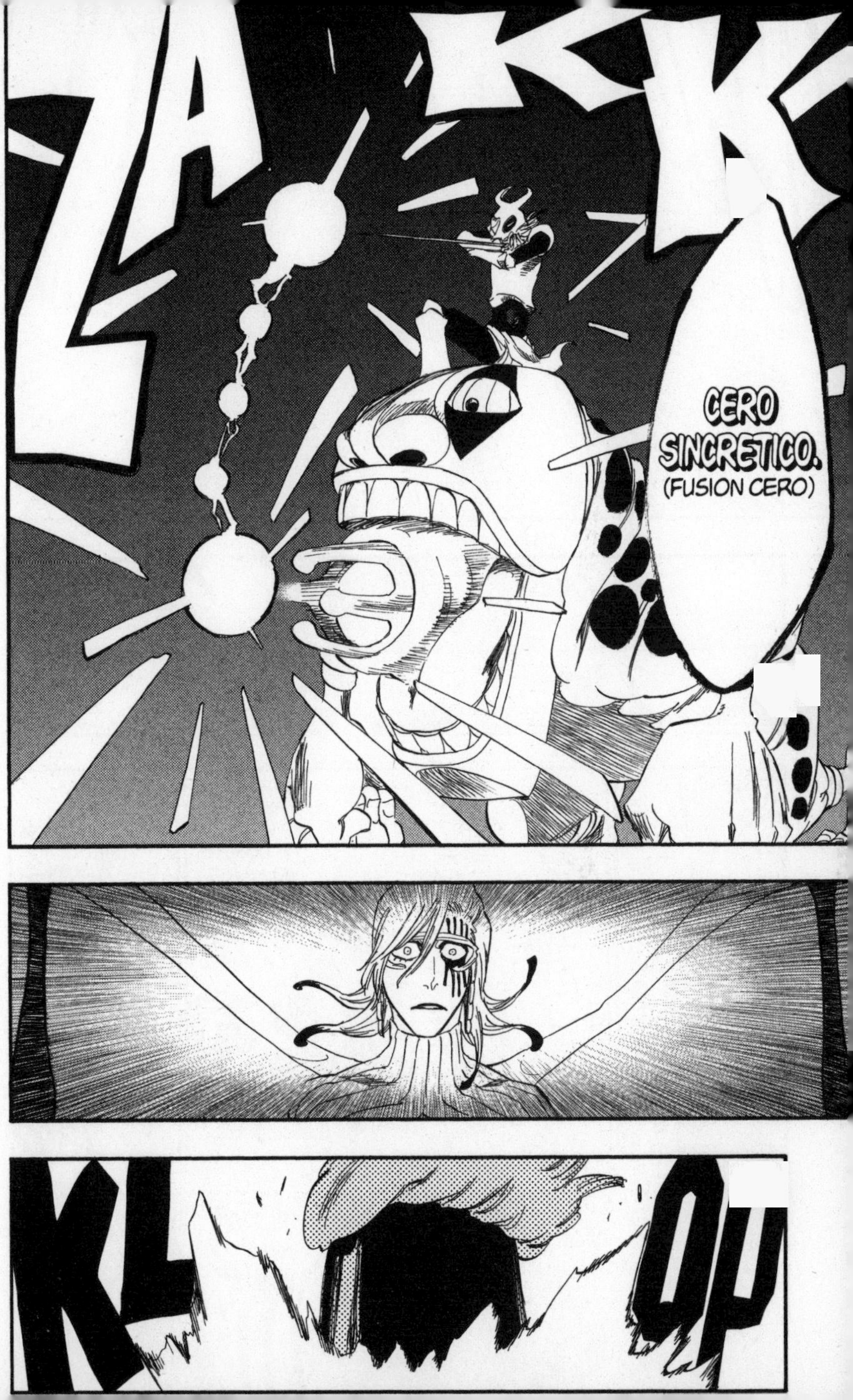
ZA-K-K
CERO SINCRETICO.
(FUSION CERO)
KL-OP

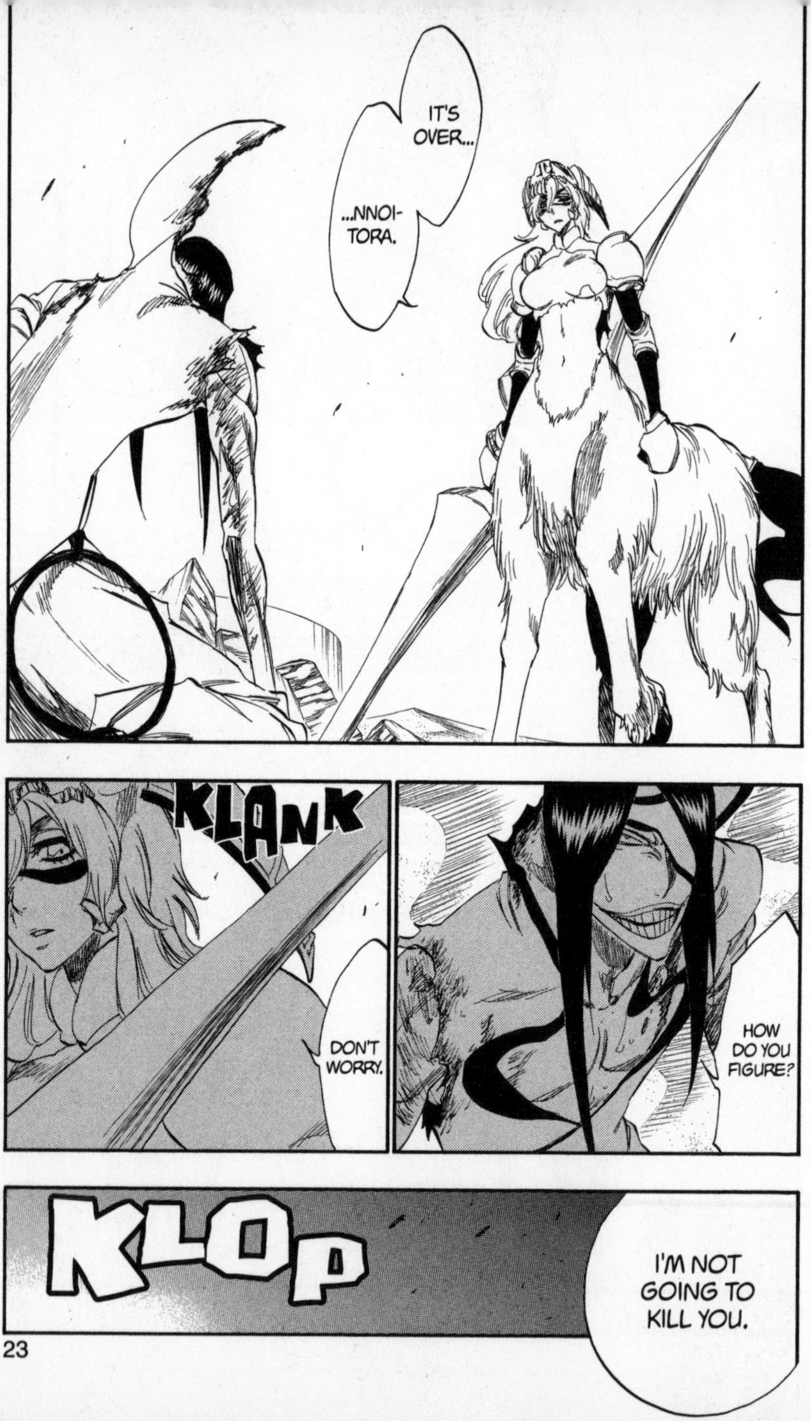
IT'S OVER...
...NNOI-TORA.
HOW DO YOU FIGURE?
KLANK
DON'T WORRY.
I'M NOT GOING TO KILL YOU.
KLOP

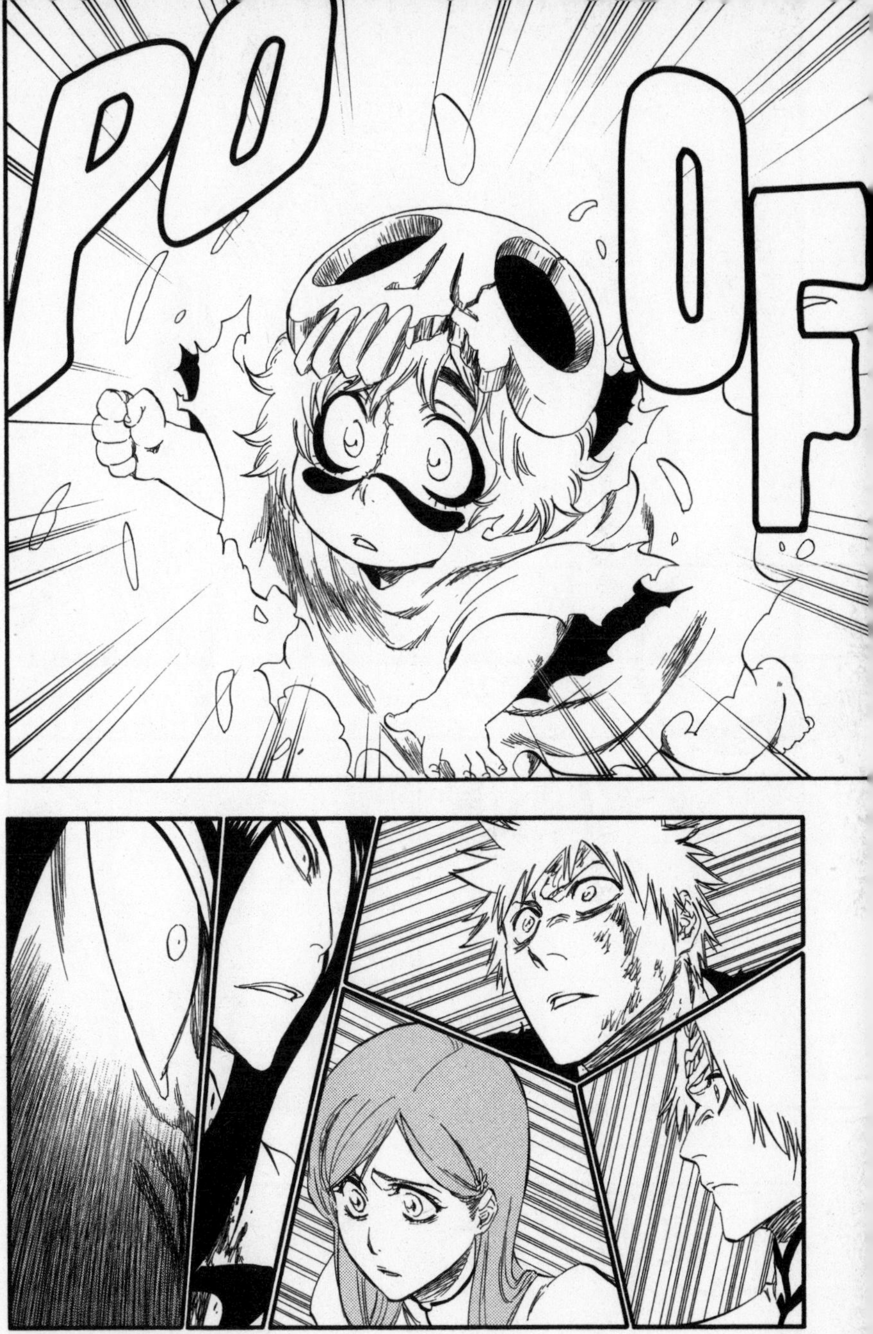
POOF

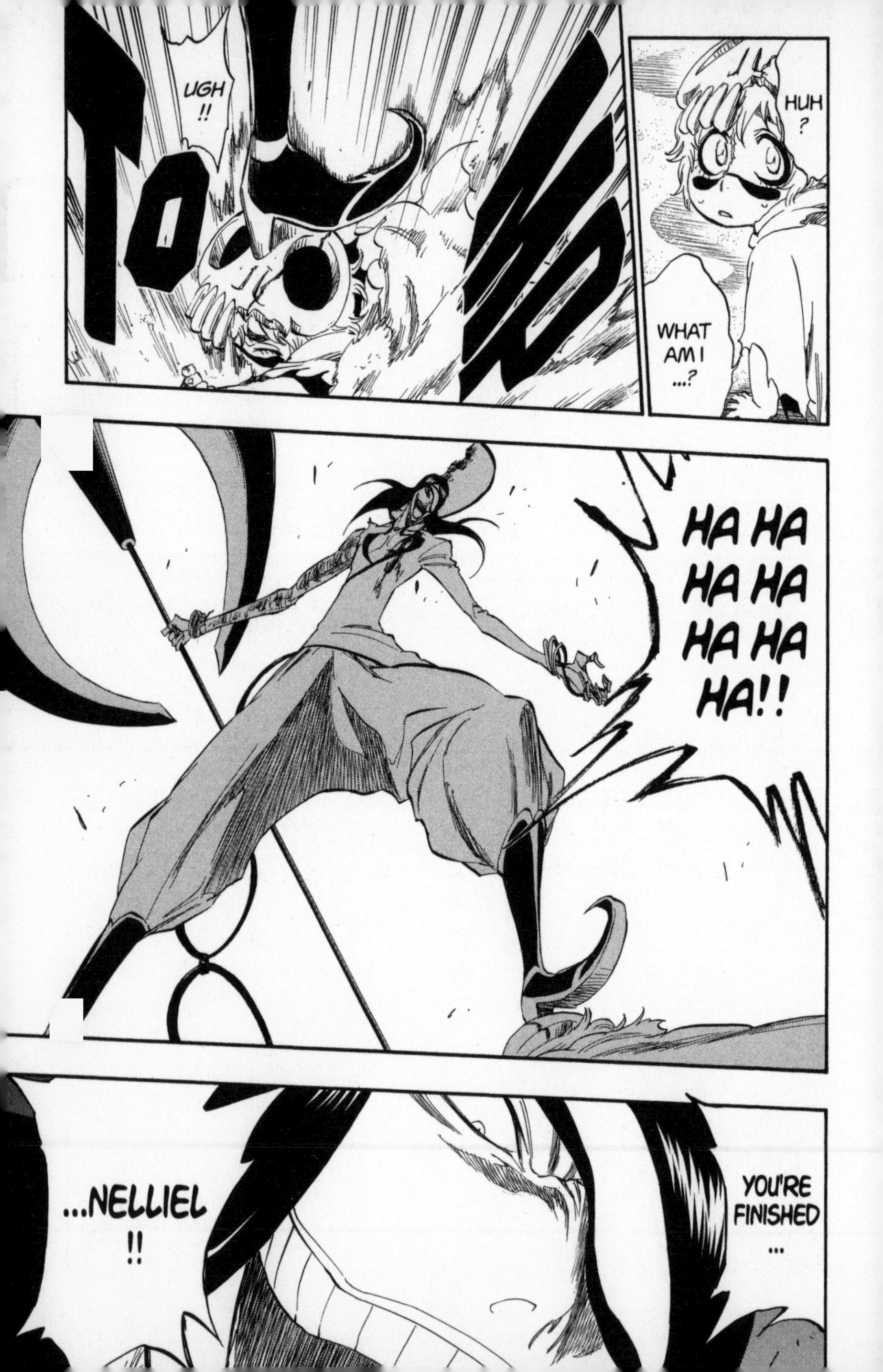
HUH ?
WHAT AM I ...?
UGH !!
HA HA HA HA HA HA HA!!
YOU'RE FINISHED ...
...NELLIEL !!

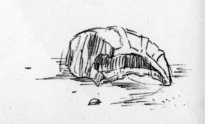

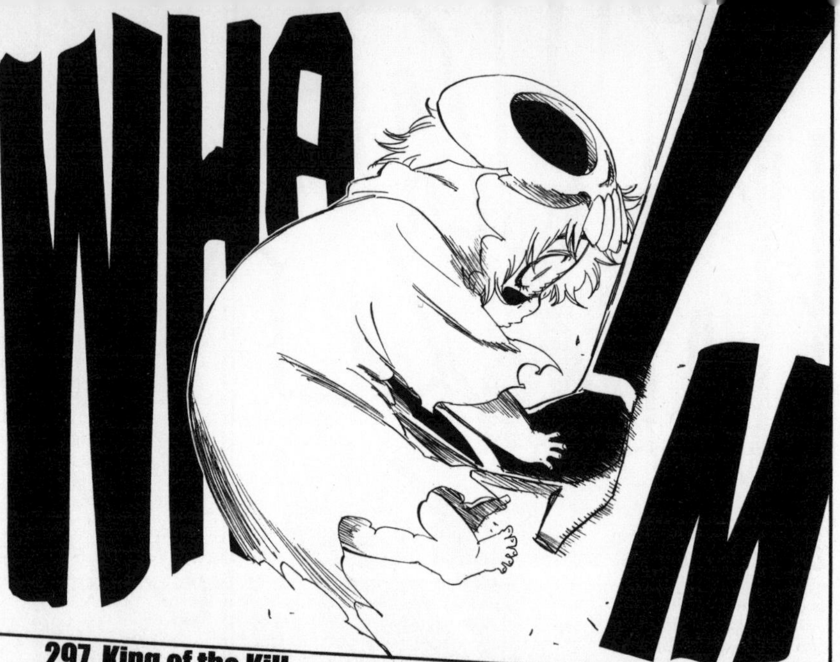
WHAM

297. King of the Kill

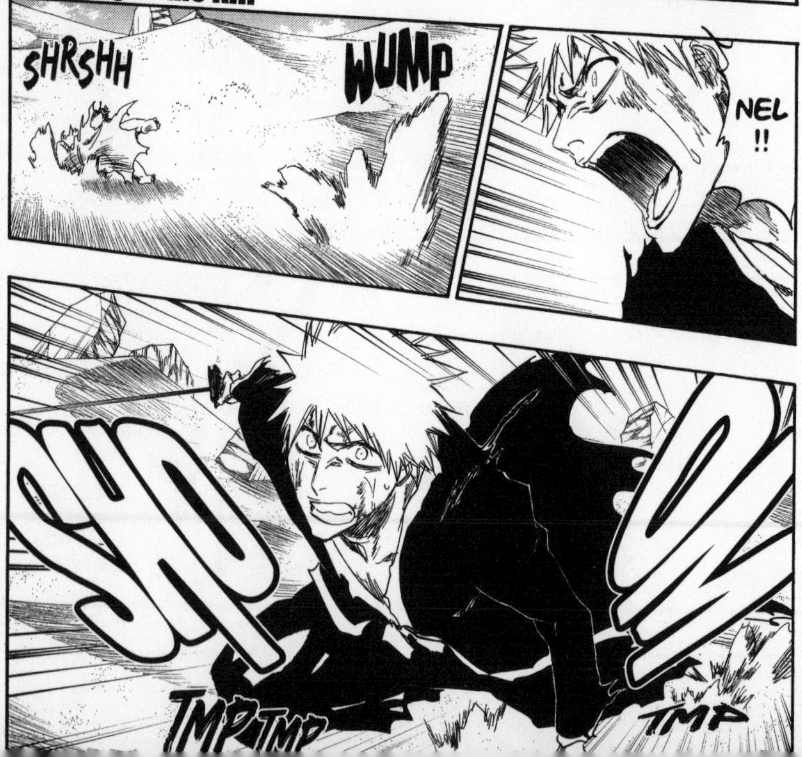
NEL
!!
SHRSHH
WUMP
SHO
OM
TMP
TMP TMP

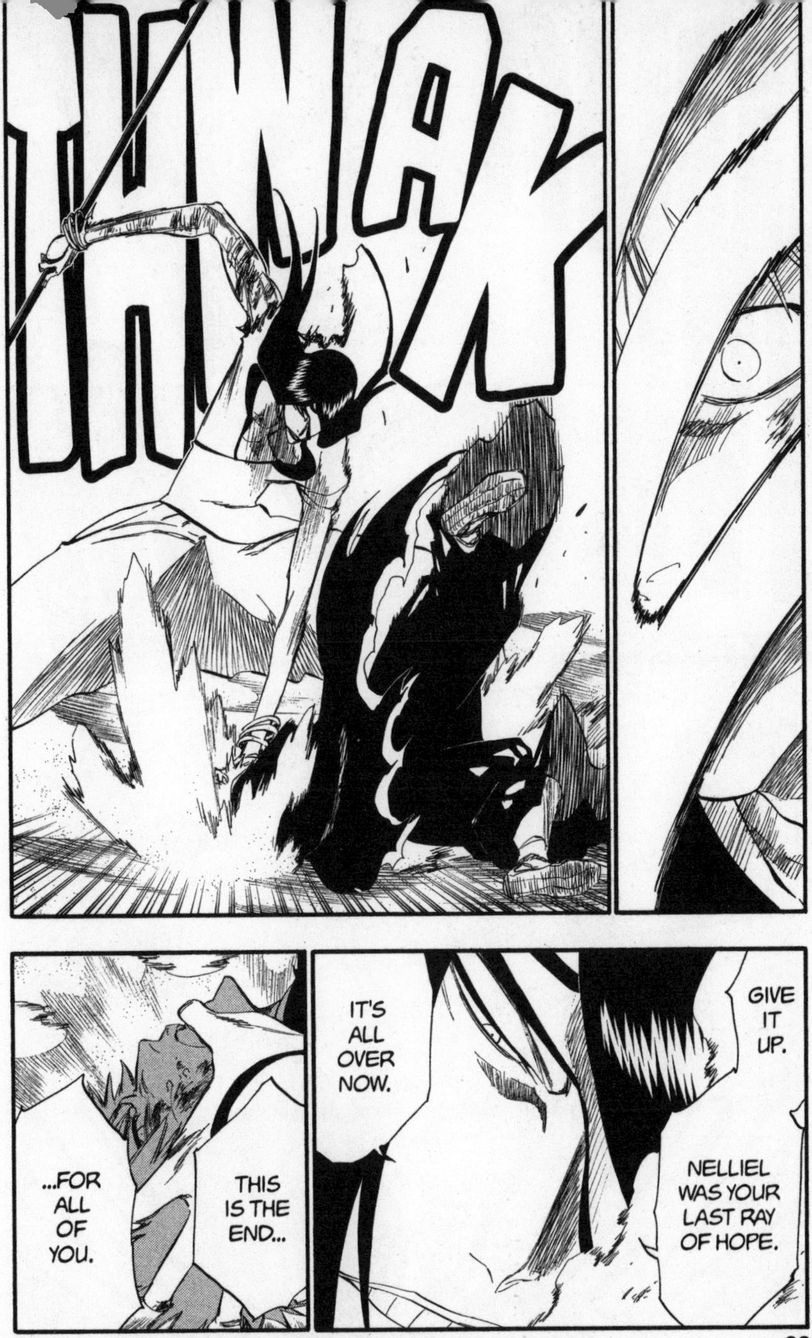
THWAK
GIVE IT UP.
NELLIEL WAS YOUR LAST RAY OF HOPE.
IT'S ALL OVER NOW.
THIS IS THE END...
...FOR ALL OF YOU.

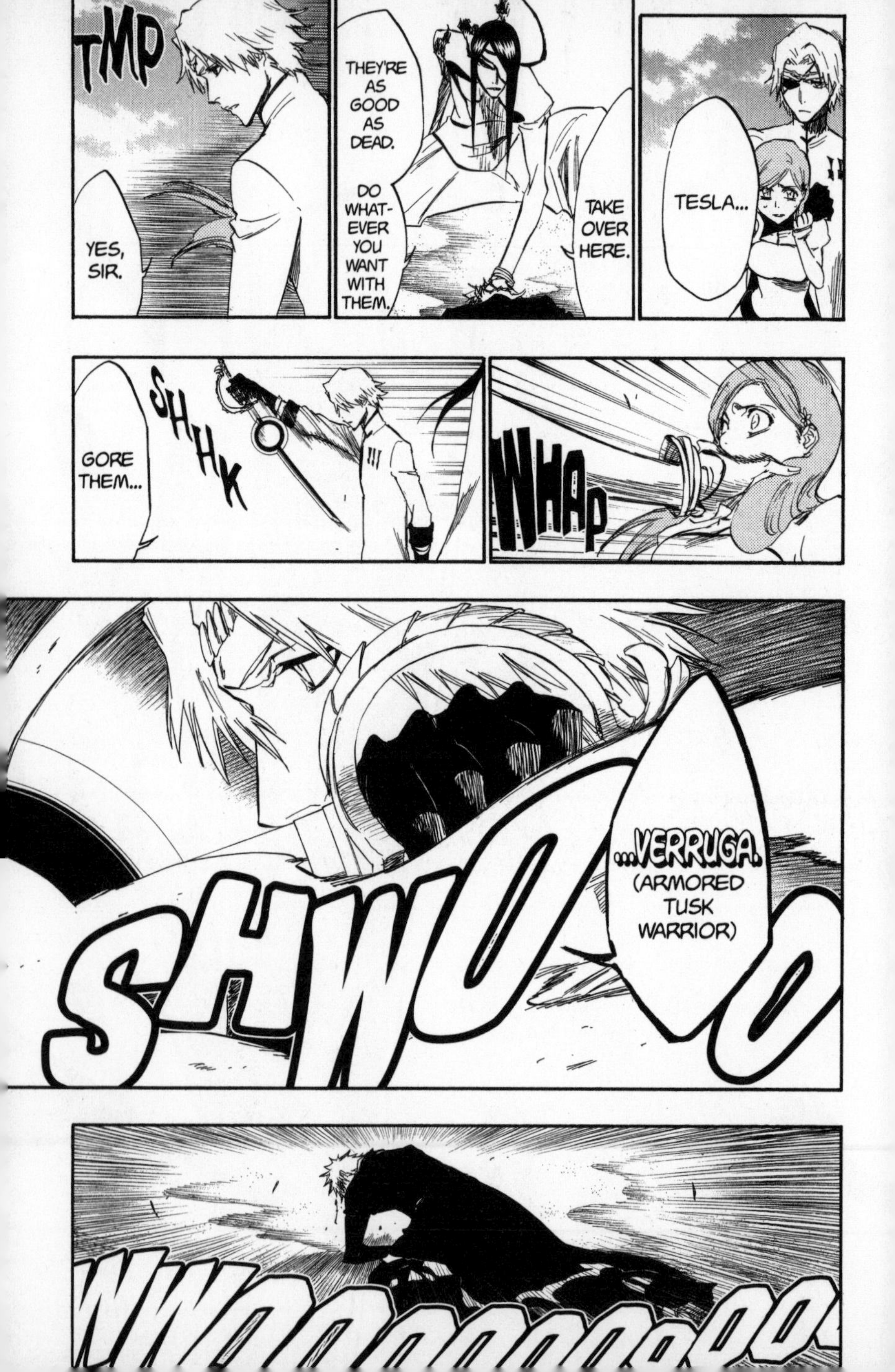
TESLA...
TAKE OVER HERE.
THEY'RE AS GOOD AS DEAD.
DO WHATEVER YOU WANT WITH THEM.
TMP
YES, SIR.
WHAP
SHHK
GORE THEM...
...VERRUGA.
(ARMORED TUSK WARRIOR)
SHWOO

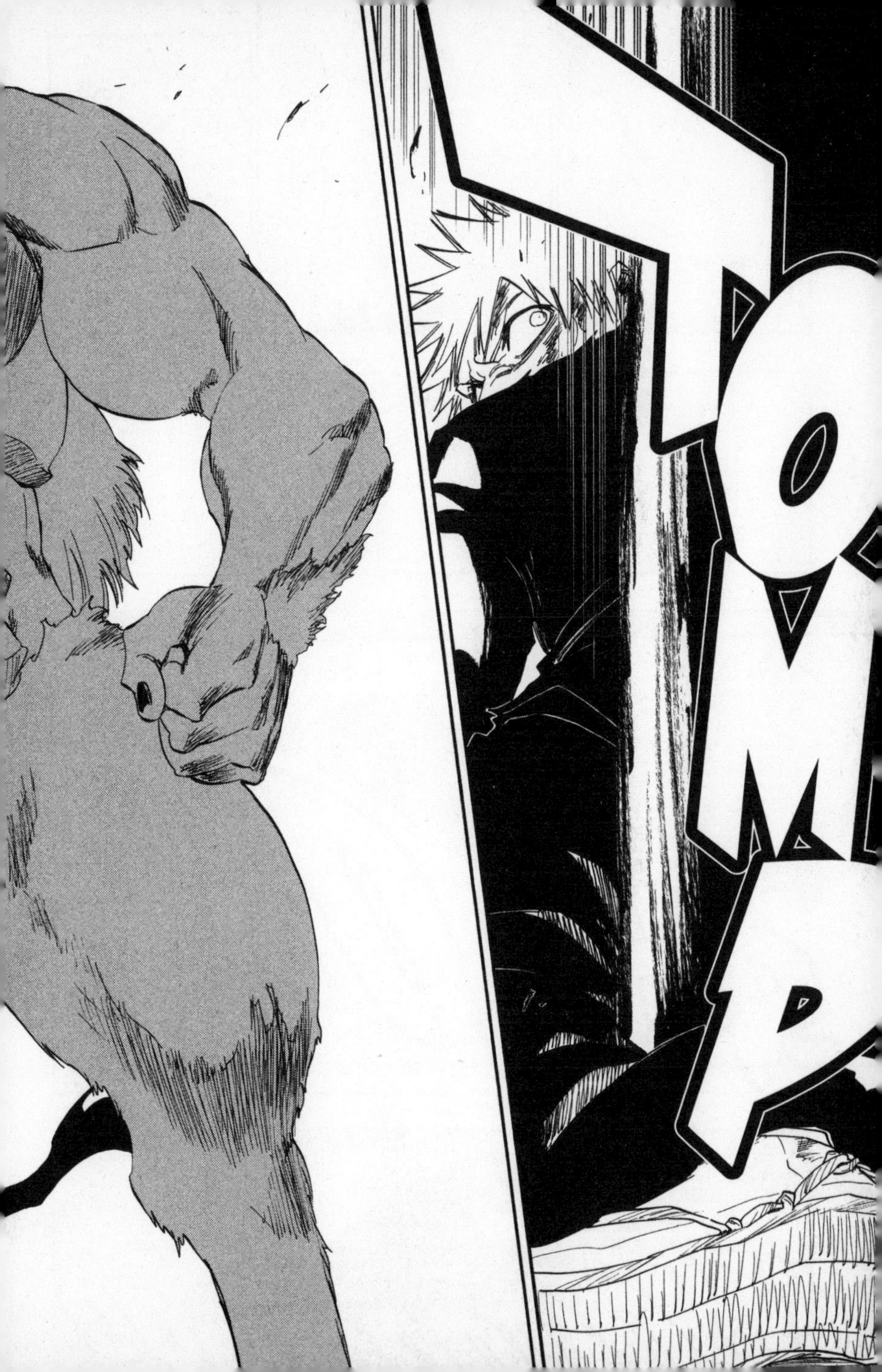
TOMP

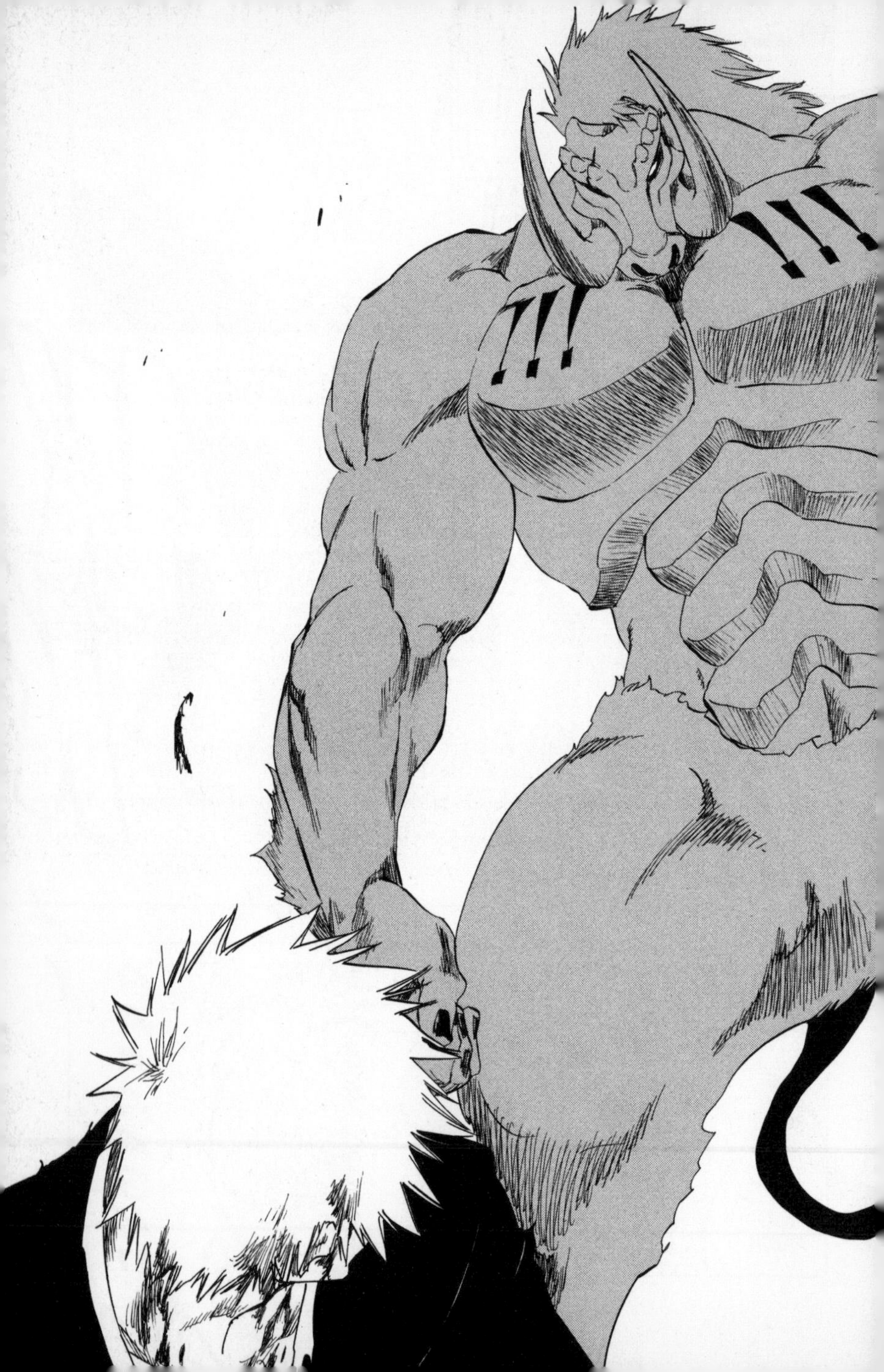

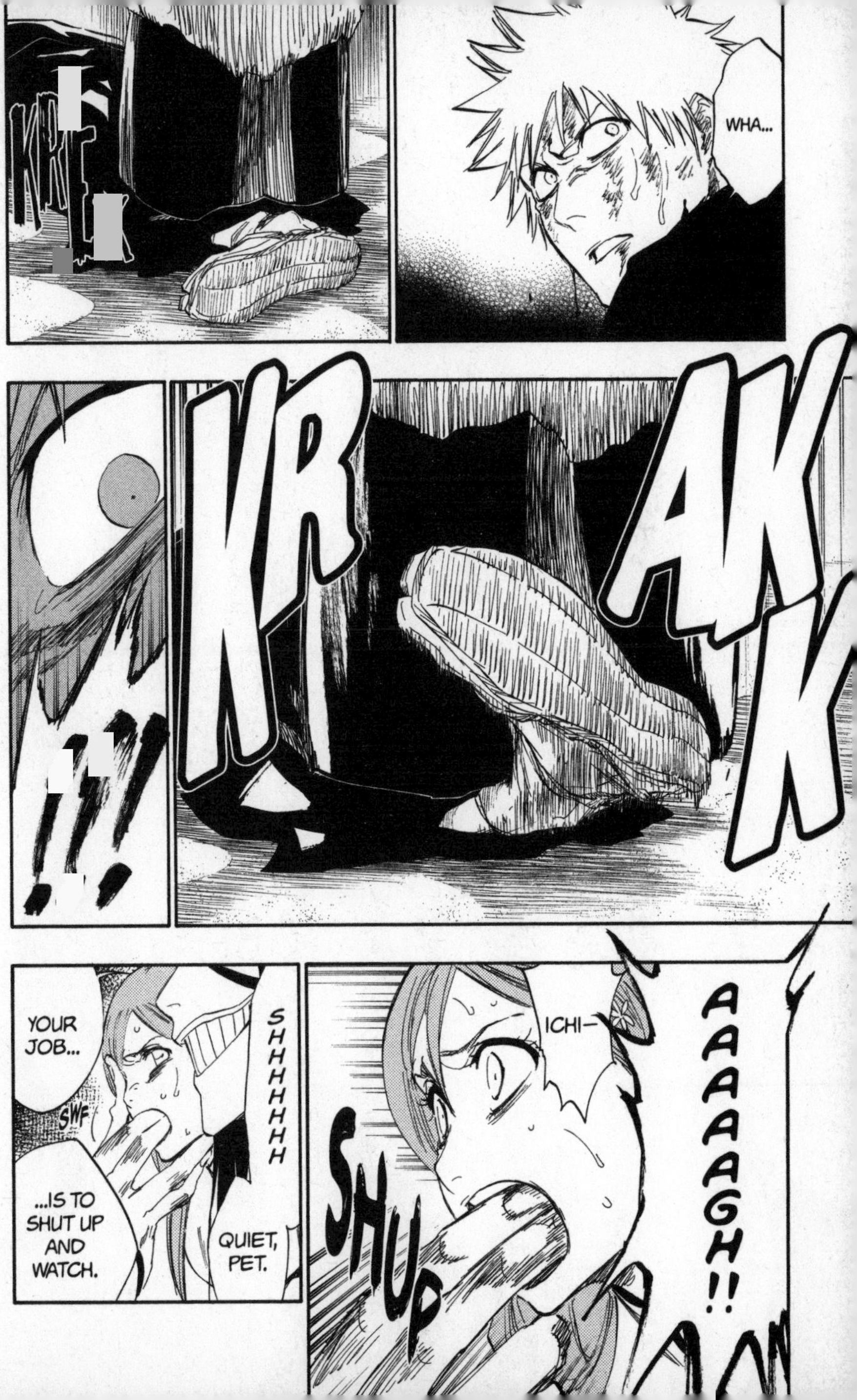
WHA...
KRAKK
ICHI—
AAAAAGH!!
SHUP
SHHHHHHHH
QUIET, PET.
YOUR JOB...
SWF
...IS TO SHUT UP AND WATCH.

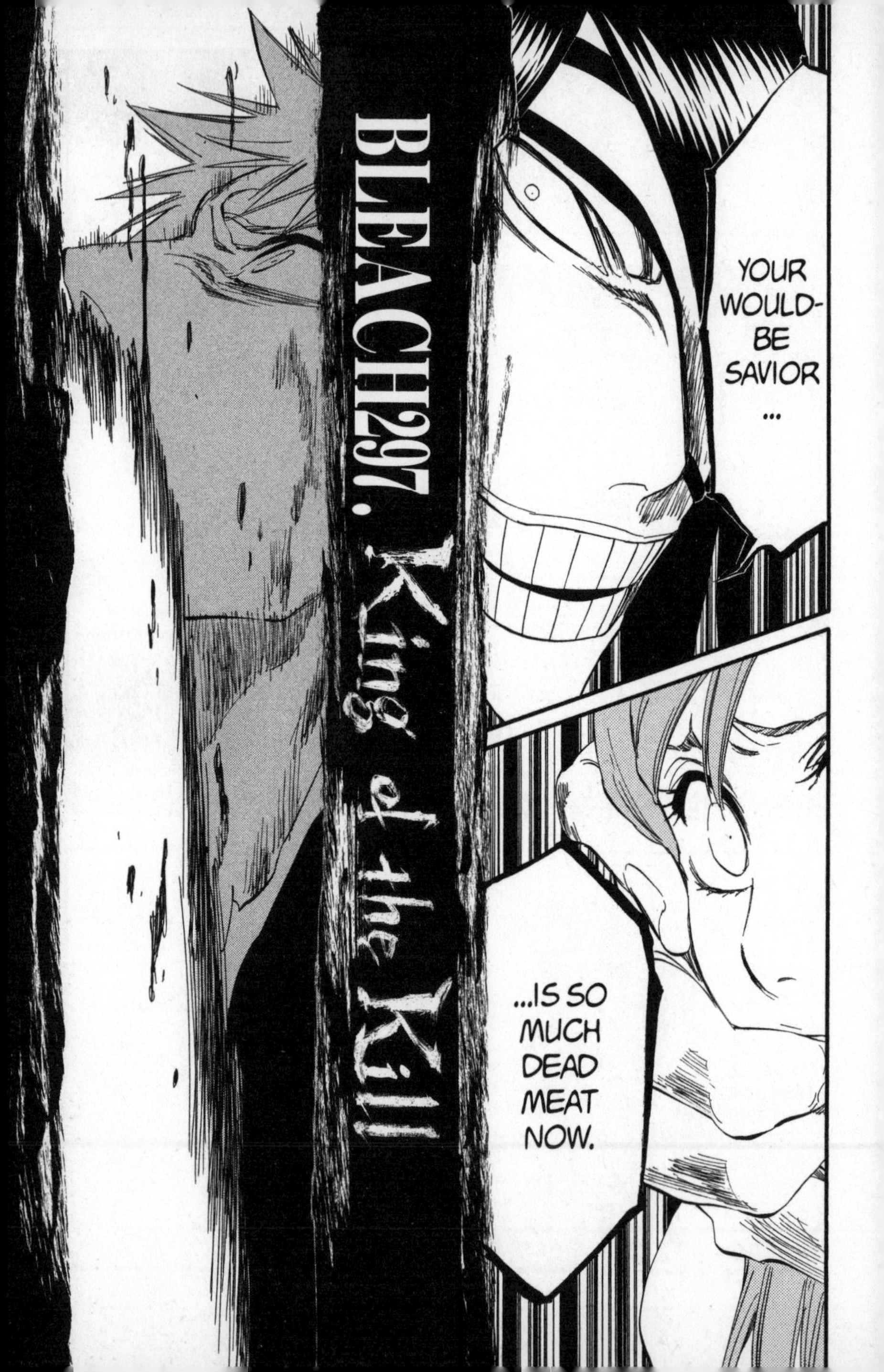
YOUR WOULD-BE SAVIOR...
...IS SO MUCH DEAD MEAT NOW.
BLEACH297. King of the Kill

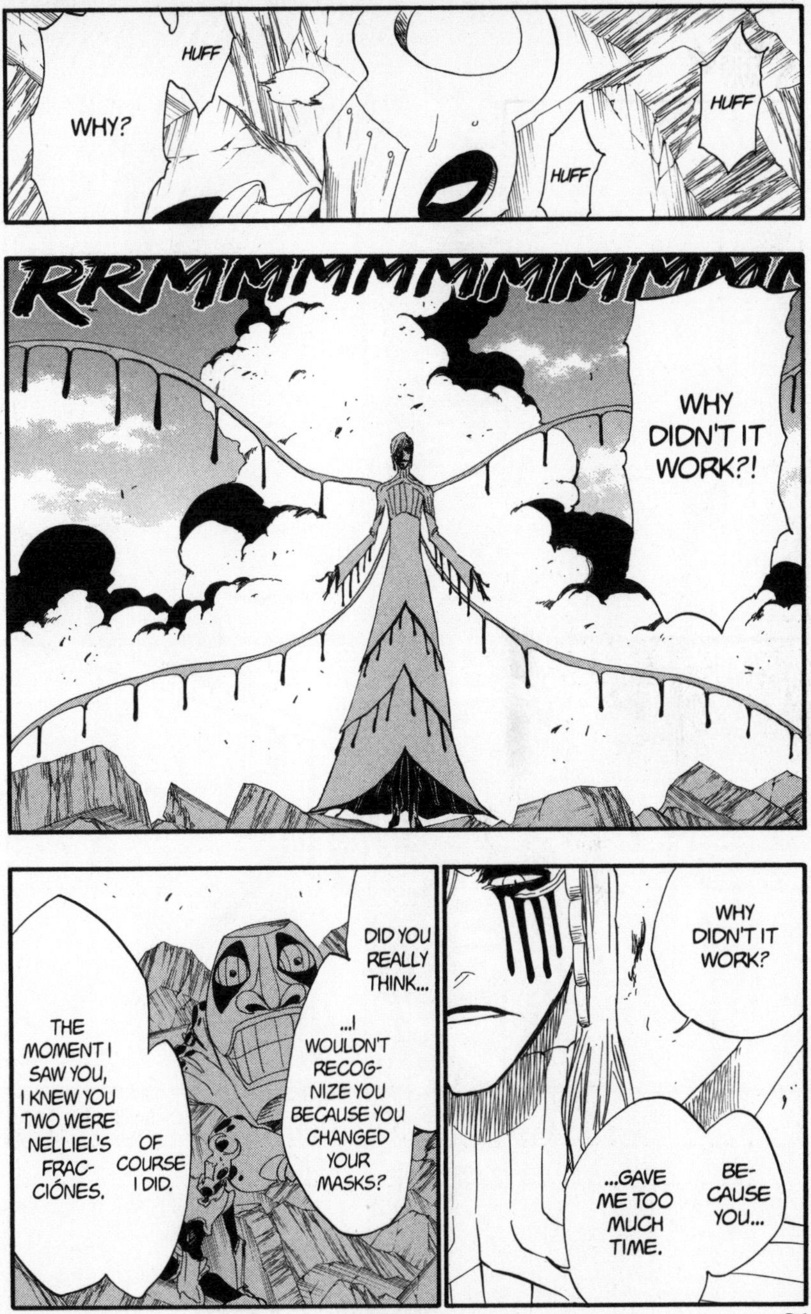
HUFF
HUFF
HUFF
WHY?
RRMMMMMMMMMMM
WHY DIDN'T IT WORK?!
WHY DIDN'T IT WORK?
BE-CAUSE YOU...
...GAVE ME TOO MUCH TIME.
DID YOU REALLY THINK...
...I WOULDN'T RECOG-NIZE YOU BECAUSE YOU CHANGED YOUR MASKS?
OF COURSE I DID.
THE MOMENT I SAW YOU, I KNEW YOU TWO WERE NELLIEL'S FRAC-CIÓNES.

READ THIS WAY

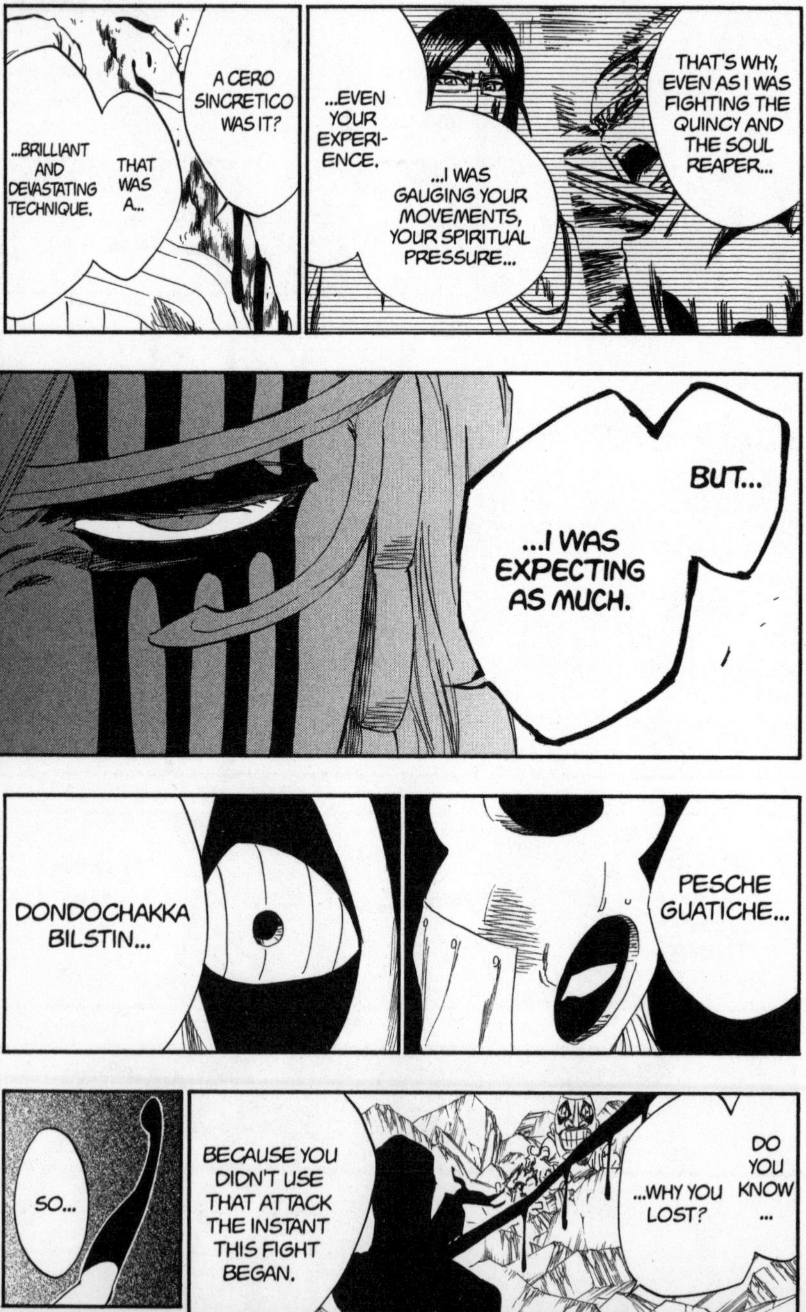
THAT'S WHY, EVEN AS I WAS FIGHTING THE QUINCY AND THE SOUL REAPER...
...I WAS GAUGING YOUR MOVEMENTS, YOUR SPIRITUAL PRESSURE...
...EVEN YOUR EXPERIENCE.
A CERO SINCRETICO WAS IT?
THAT WAS A...
...BRILLIANT AND DEVASTATING TECHNIQUE.
BUT...
...I WAS EXPECTING AS MUCH.
PESCHE GUATICHE...
DONDOCHAKKA BILSTIN...
DO YOU KNOW...
...WHY YOU LOST?
BECAUSE YOU DIDN'T USE THAT ATTACK THE INSTANT THIS FIGHT BEGAN.
SO...

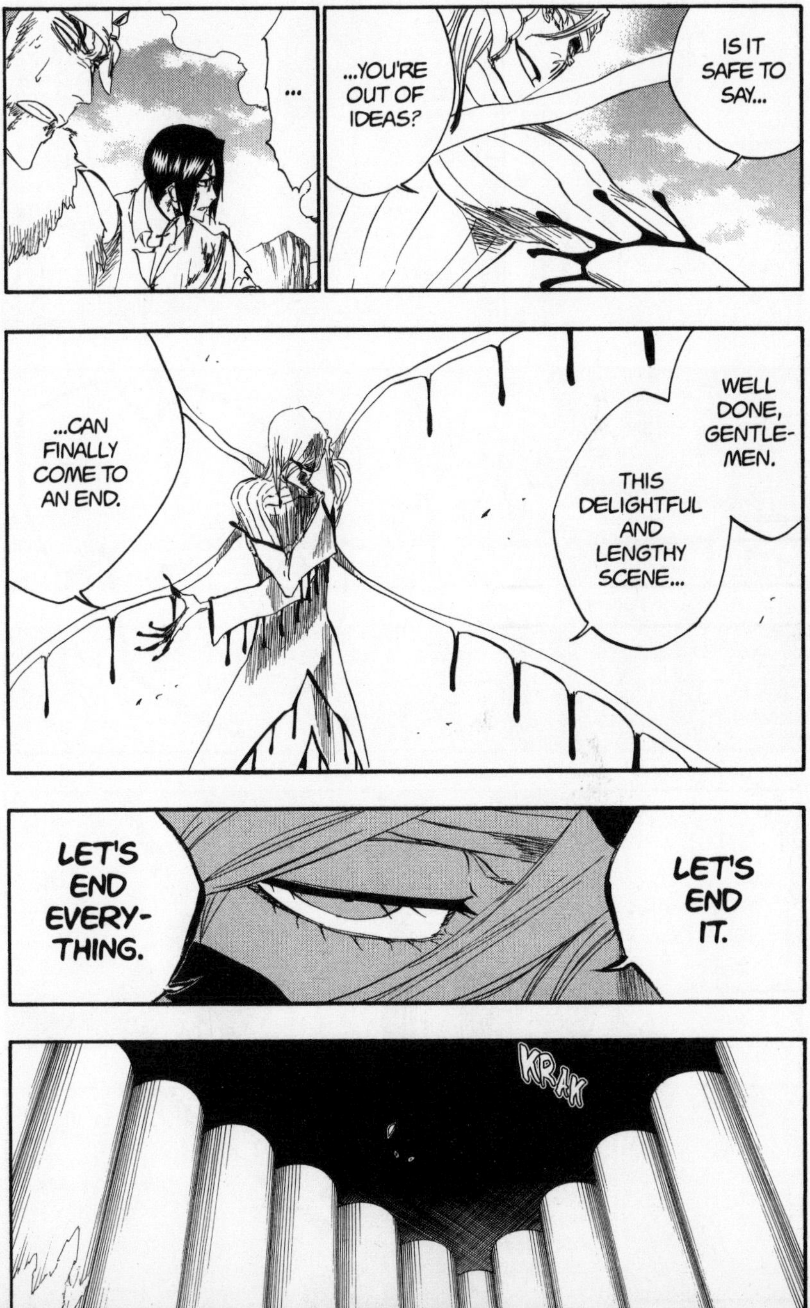
IS IT SAFE TO SAY...
...YOU'RE OUT OF IDEAS?
...
WELL DONE, GENTLE-MEN.
THIS DELIGHTFUL AND LENGTHY SCENE...
...CAN FINALLY COME TO AN END.
LET'S END IT.
LET'S END EVERY-THING.
KRAK

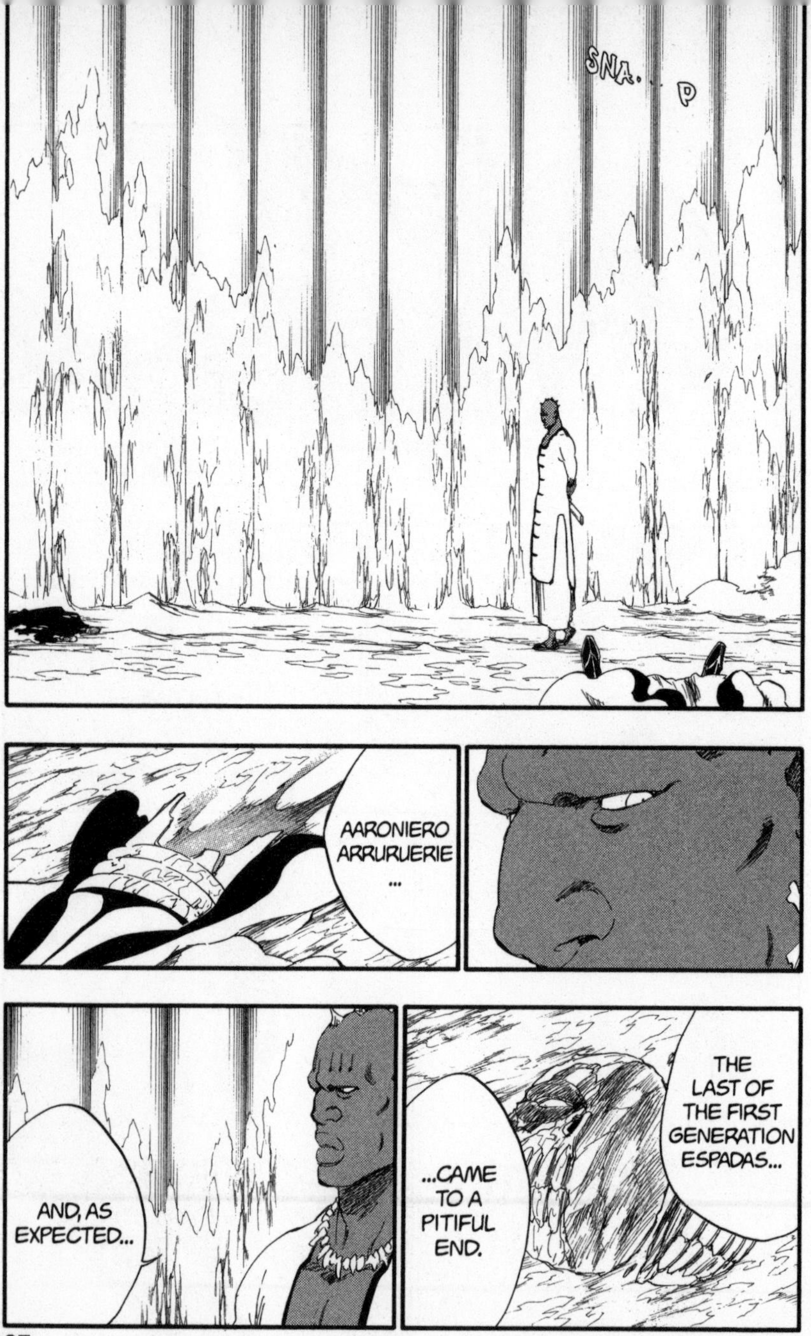
SNA... P
AARONIERO ARRURUERIE ...
THE LAST OF THE FIRST GENERATION ESPADAS...
...CAME TO A PITIFUL END.
AND, AS EXPECTED...

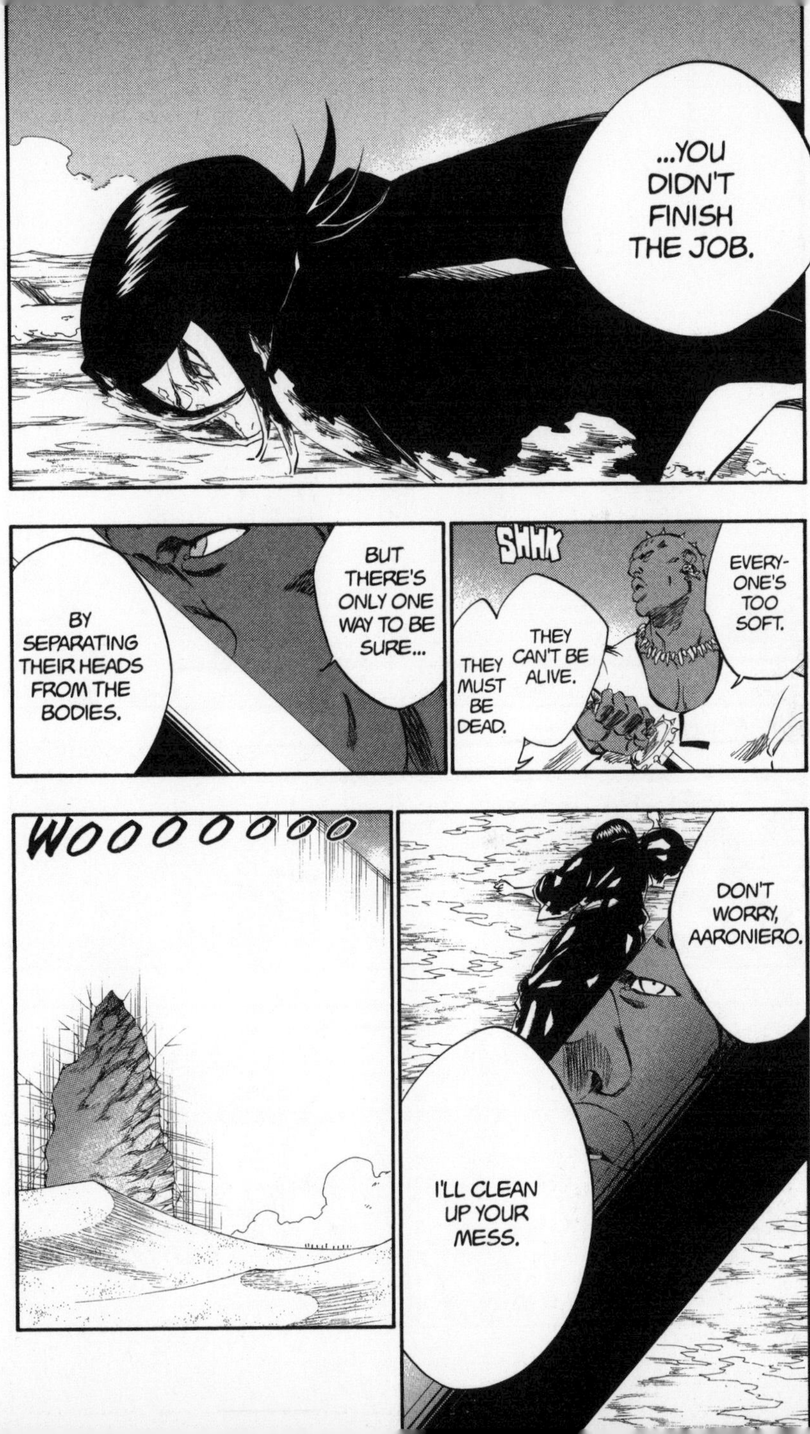
...YOU DIDN'T FINISH THE JOB.
SHHK
EVERY-ONE'S TOO SOFT.
THEY CAN'T BE ALIVE.
THEY MUST BE DEAD.
BUT THERE'S ONLY ONE WAY TO BE SURE...
BY SEPARATING THEIR HEADS FROM THE BODIES.
DON'T WORRY, AARONIERO.
I'LL CLEAN UP YOUR MESS.
WOOOOOOOO

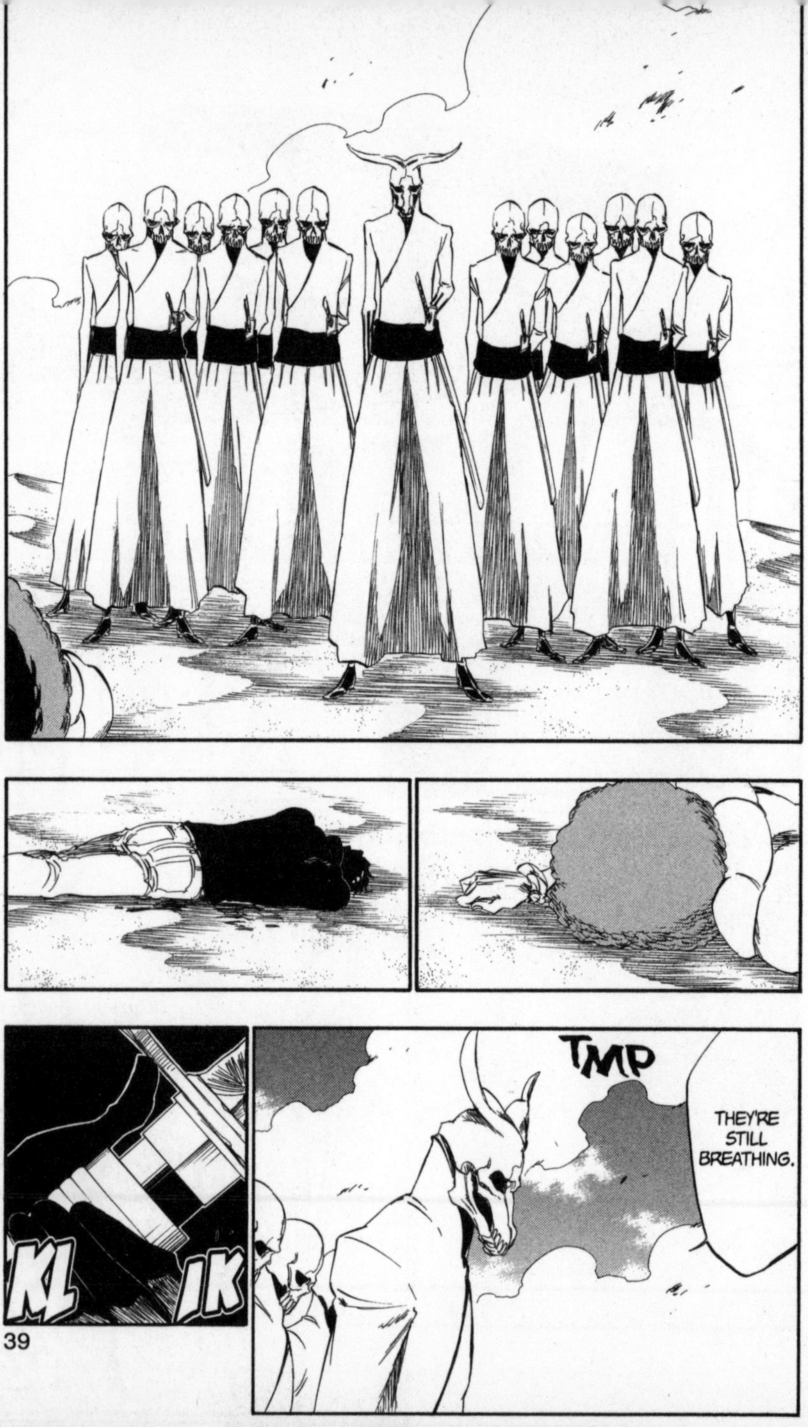
TMP
THEY'RE STILL BREATHING.
KLIK

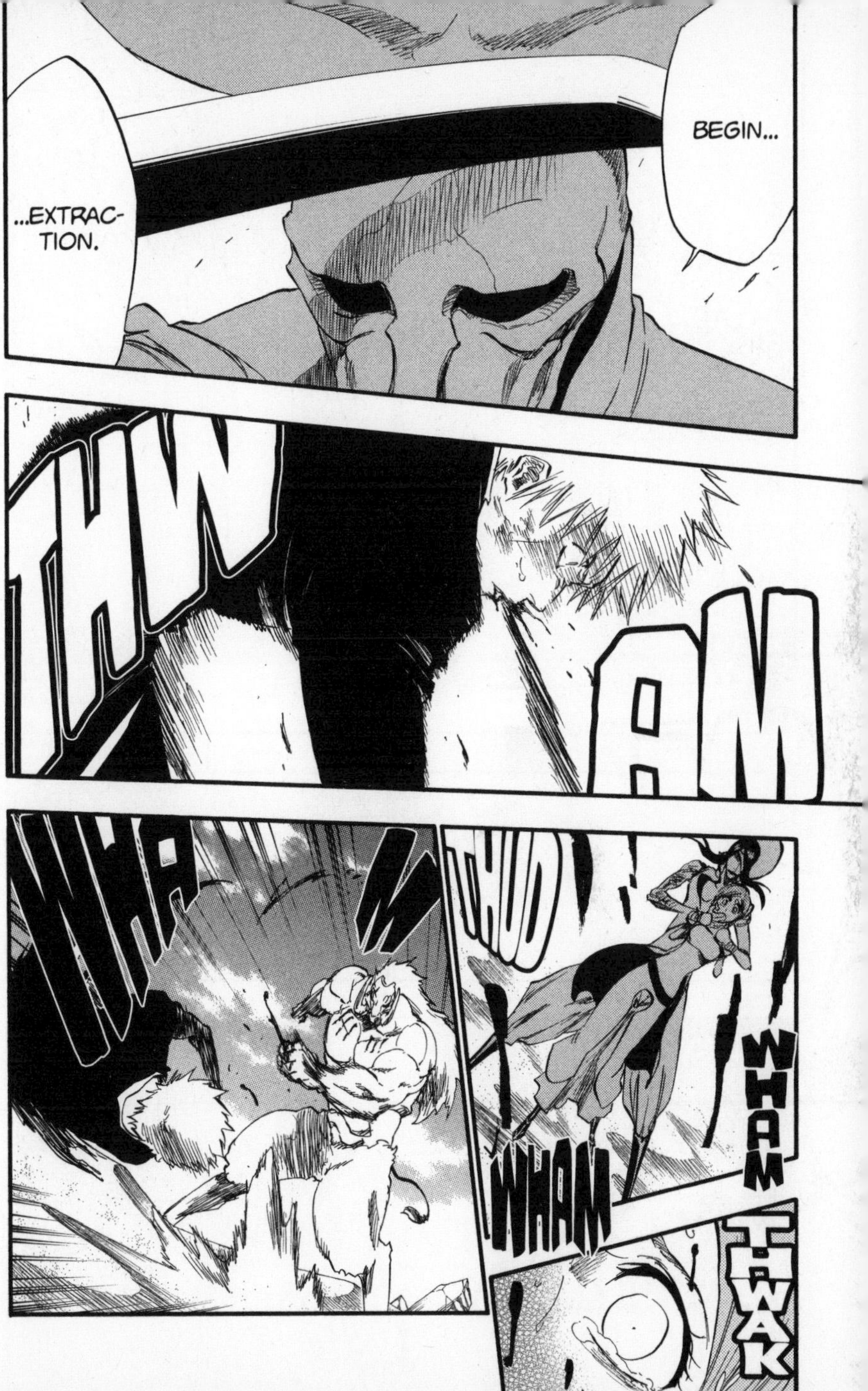
BEGIN...
...EXTRAC-
TION.
THWAM
THUD
WHAM
WHAM
THWAK
WHAM

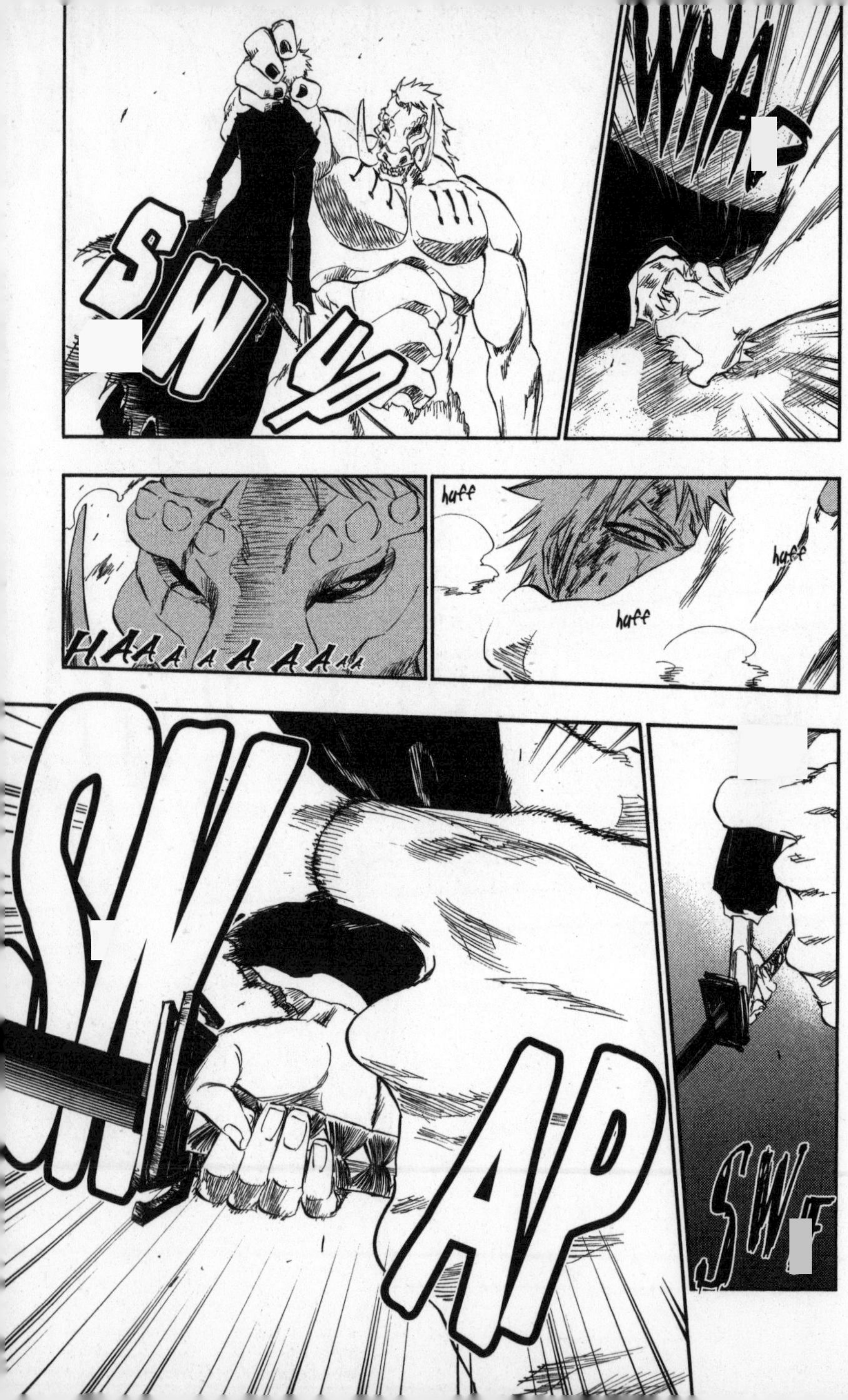
WHA
SW
sh
huff
huff
huff
HAAAAAAAAAA
SW
SNAP

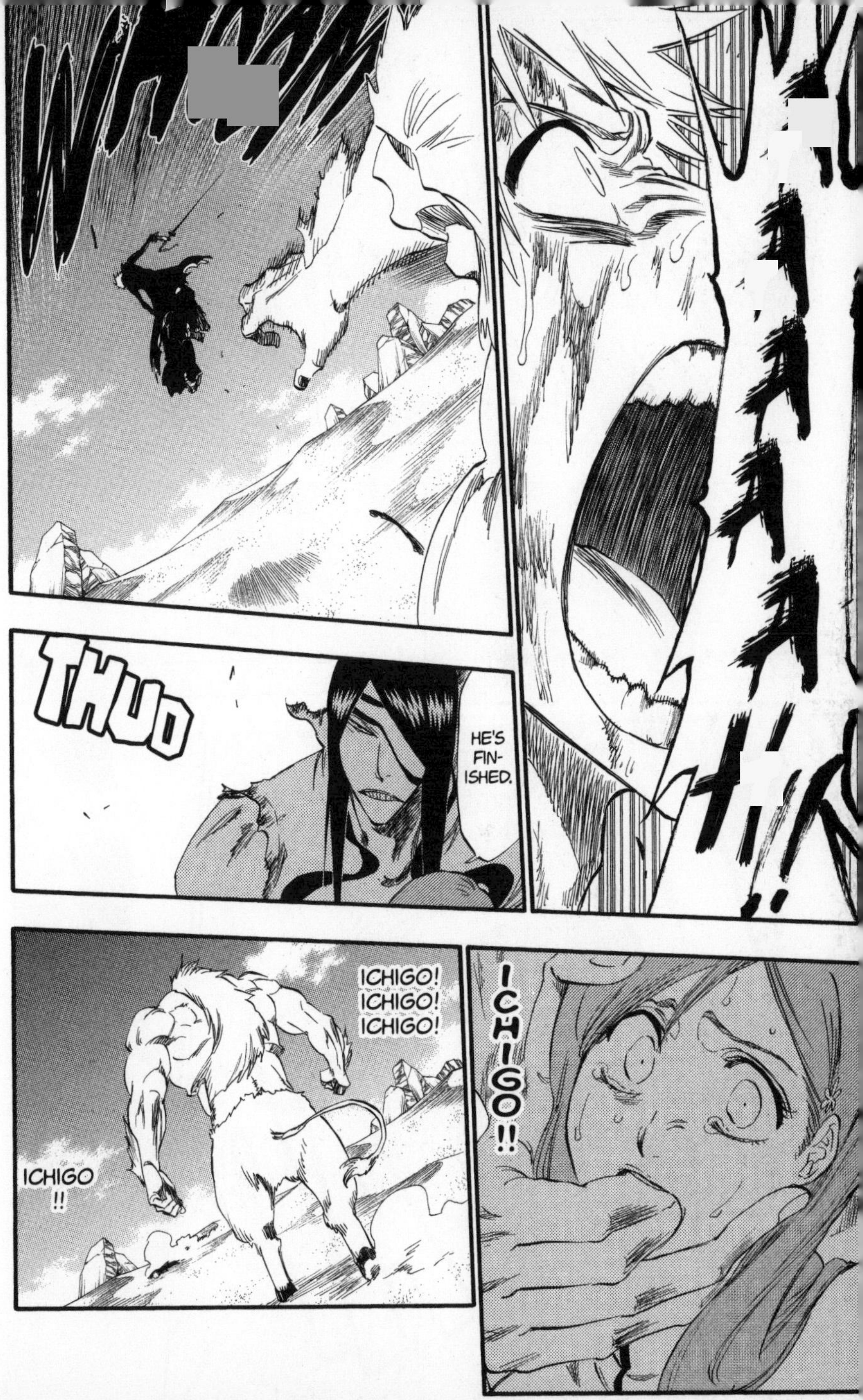
THUD
HE'S FIN-ISHED.
ICHIGO!!
ICHIGO! ICHIGO! ICHIGO!
ICHIGO!!

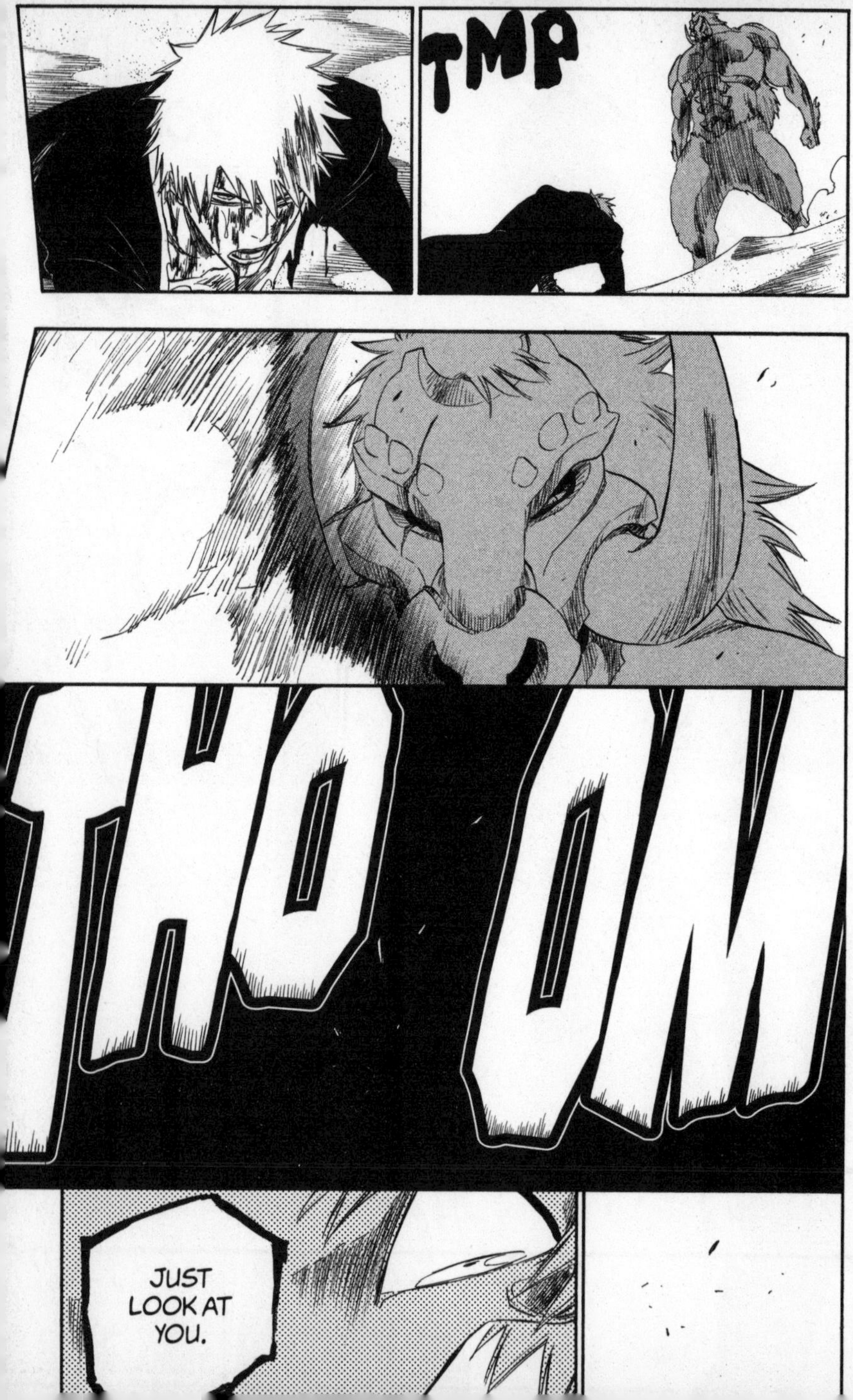
TMP
THOOM
JUST LOOK AT YOU.

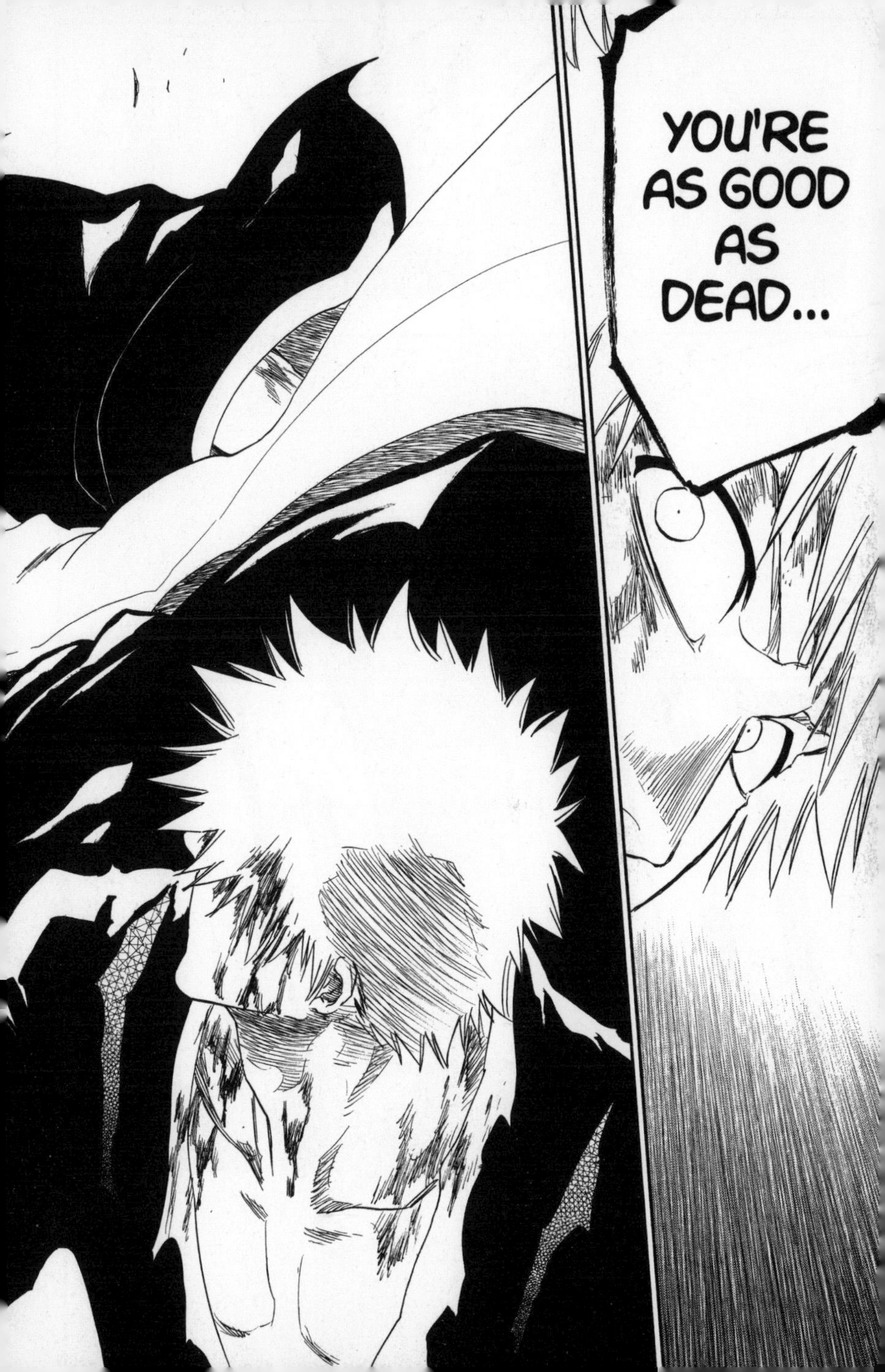
YOU'RE AS GOOD AS DEAD...

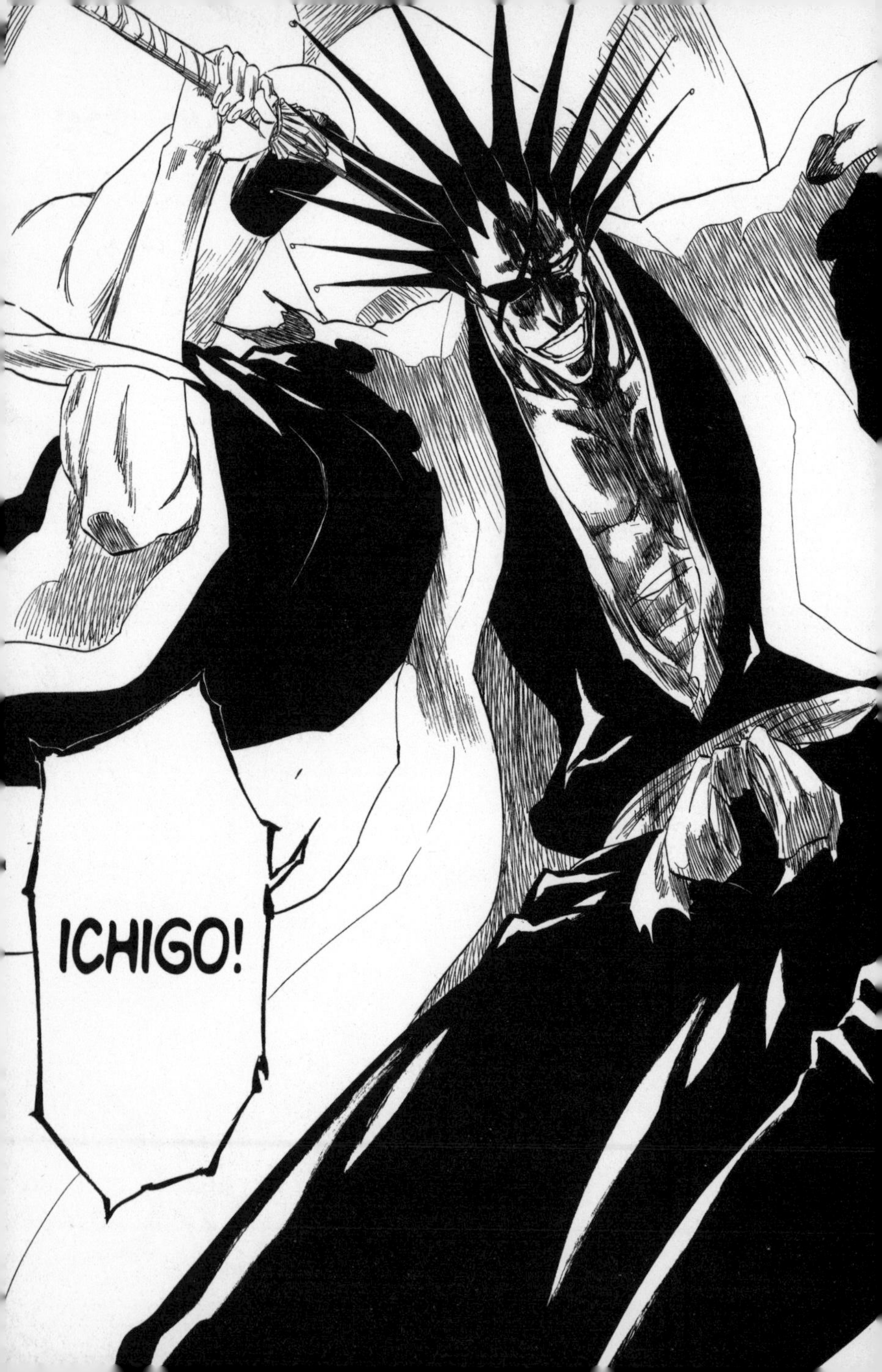
ICHIGO!

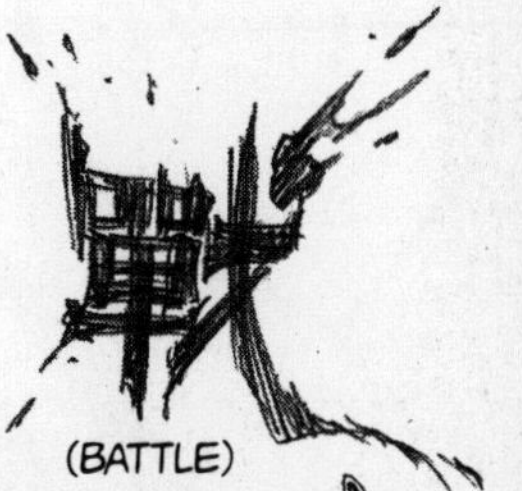
戰
(BATTLE)

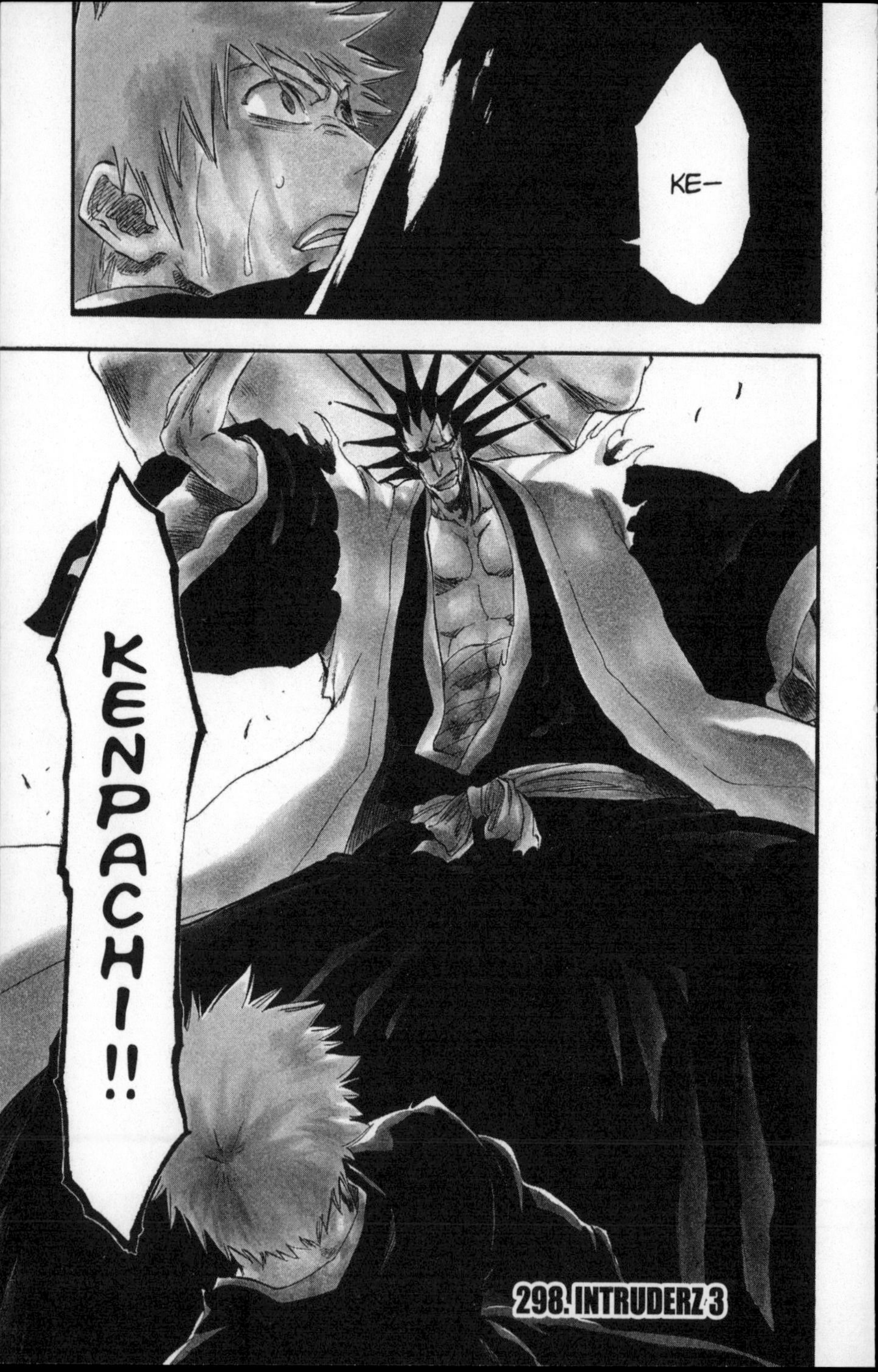
KE—
KENPACHI!!
298. INTRUDERZ 3

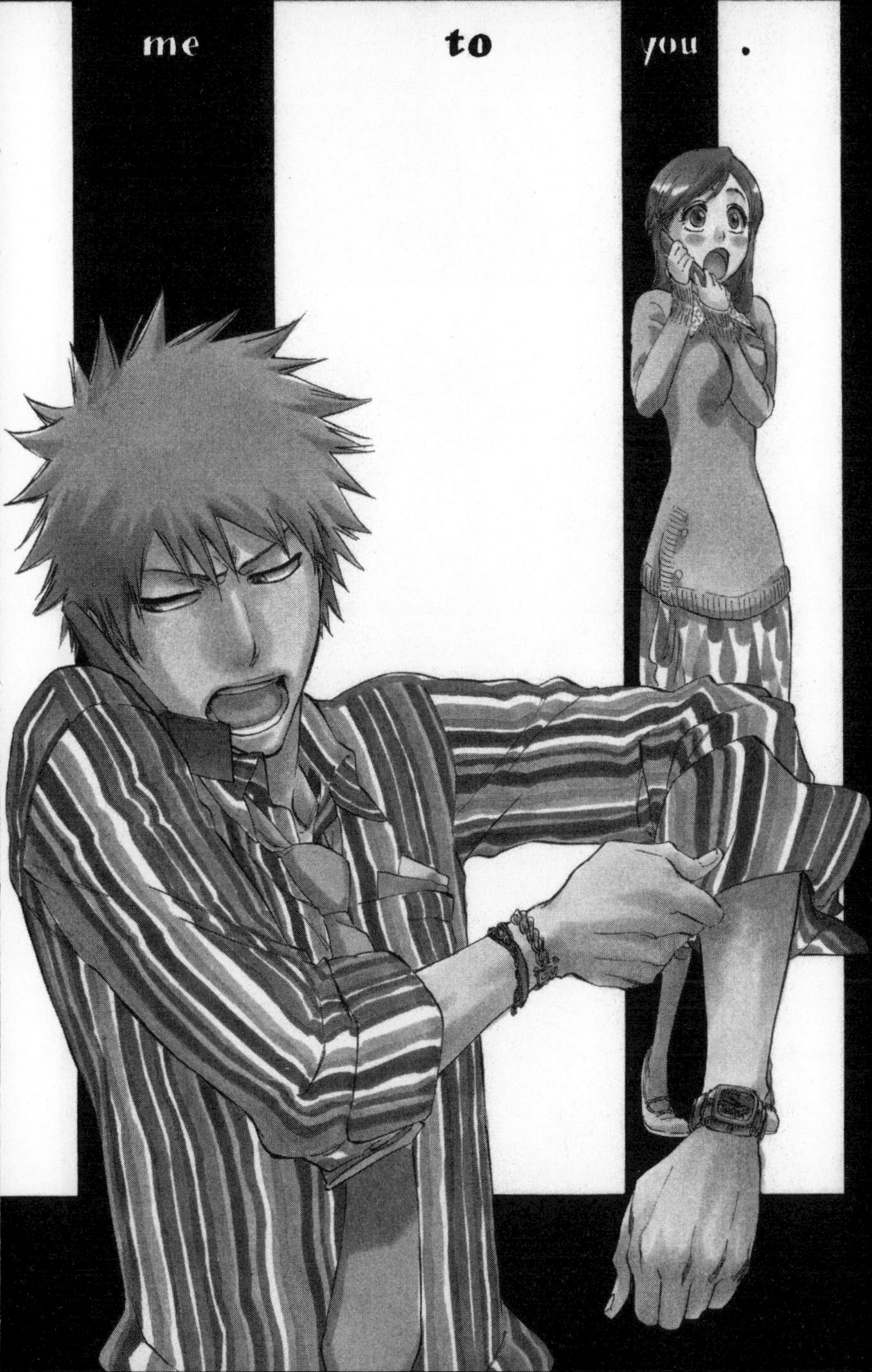
me
to
you
.

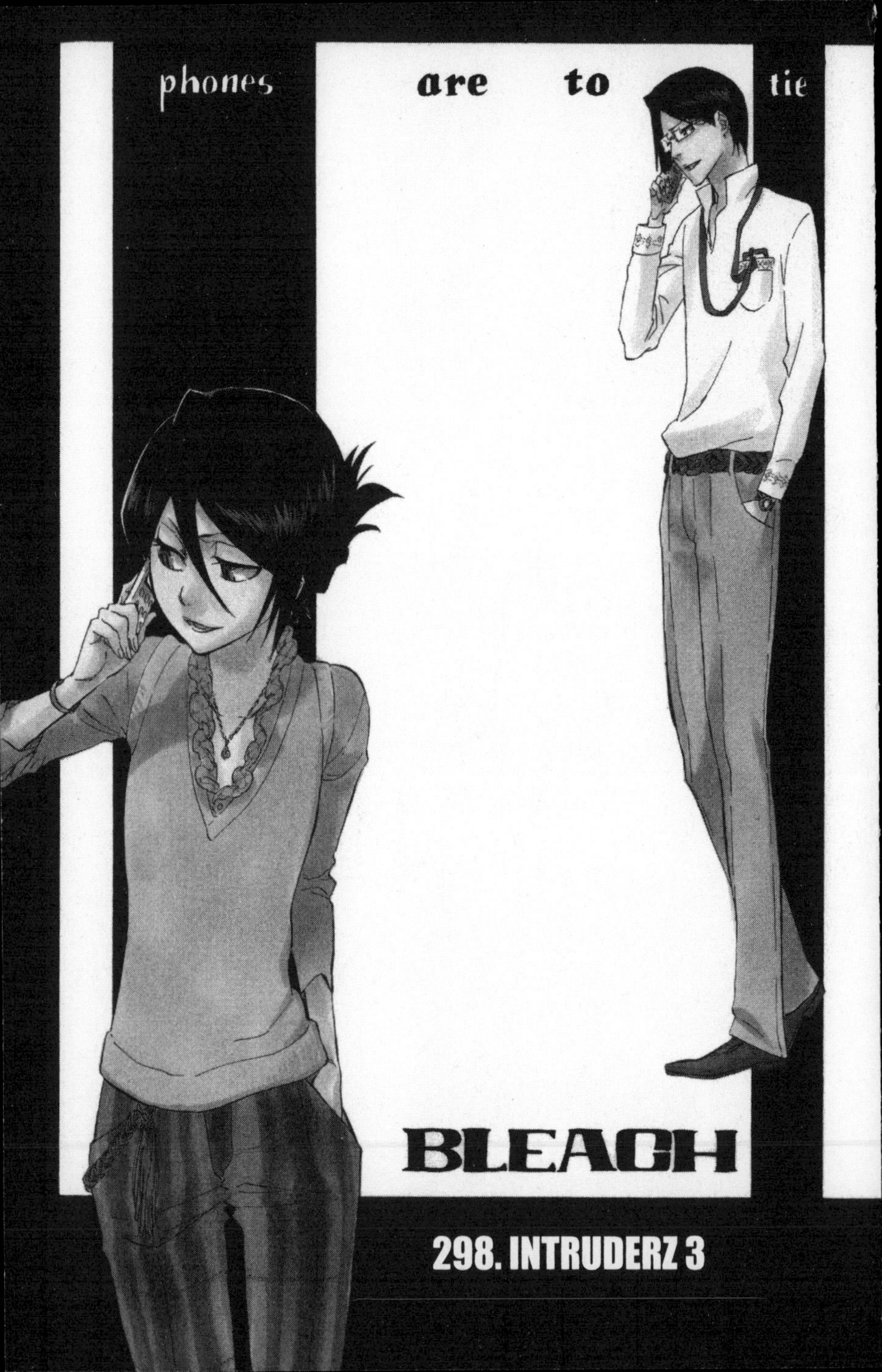
phones are to tie
BLEACH
298. INTRUDERZ 3

BLEACH

ブリーチ

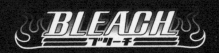

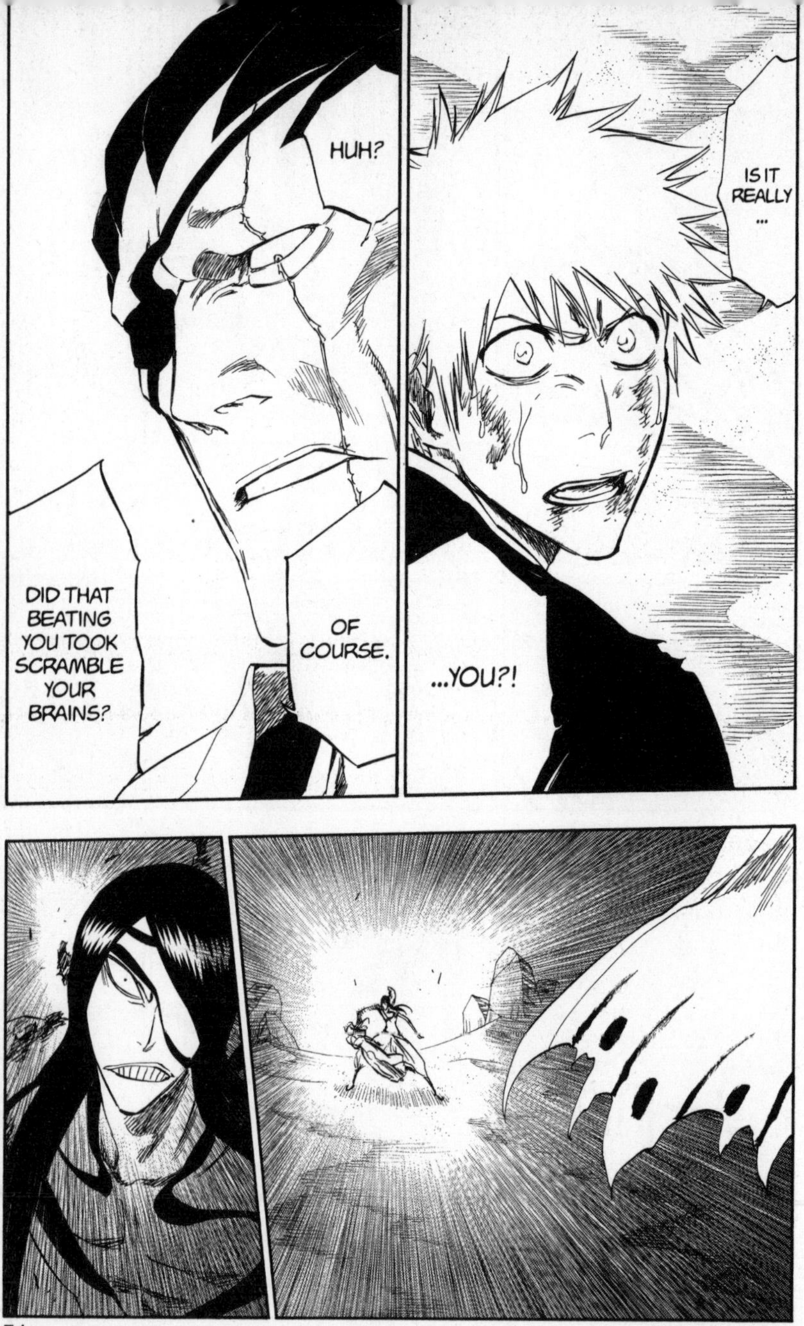
IS IT REALLY ...
...YOU?!
HUH?
OF COURSE.
DID THAT BEATING YOU TOOK SCRAMBLE YOUR BRAINS?

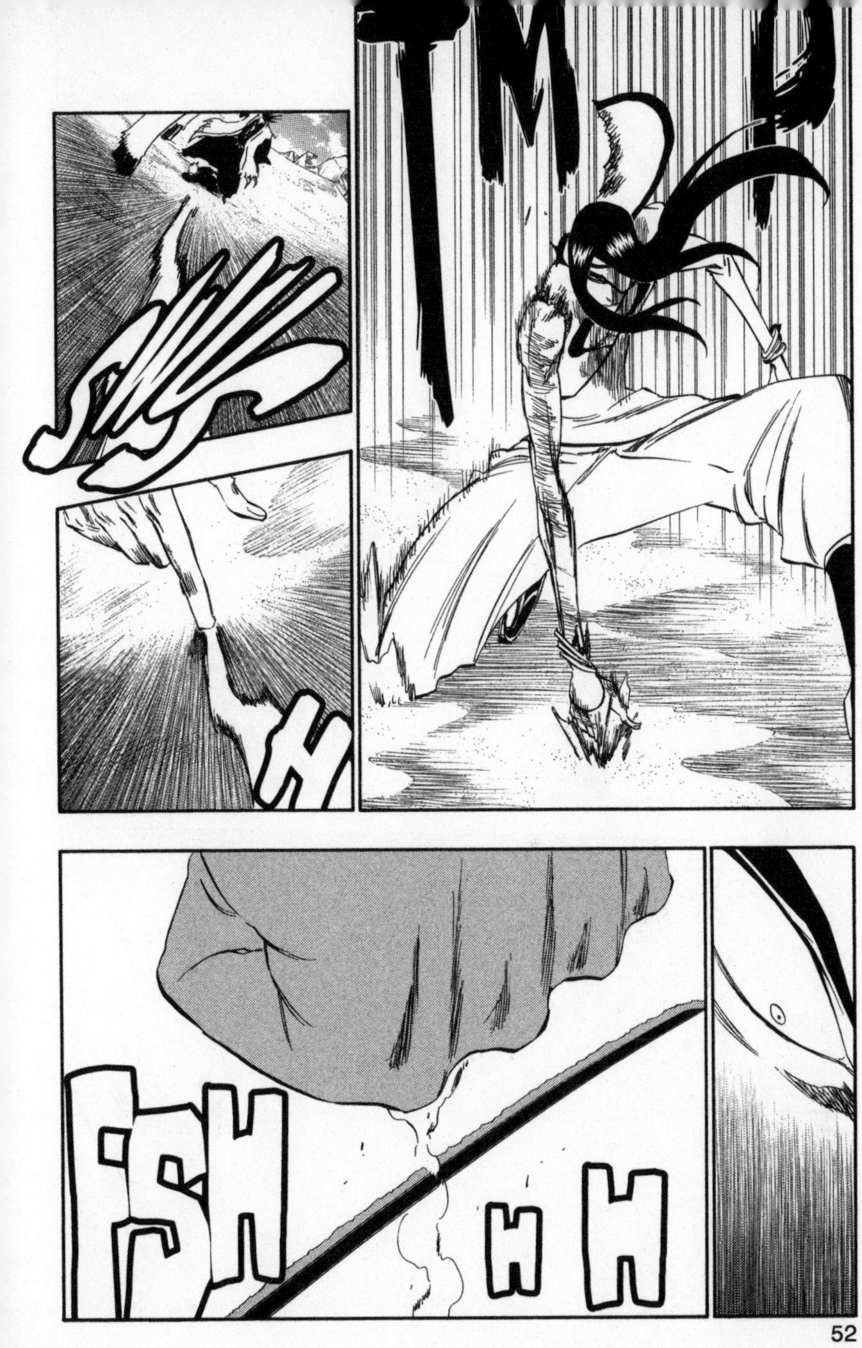
SHHH

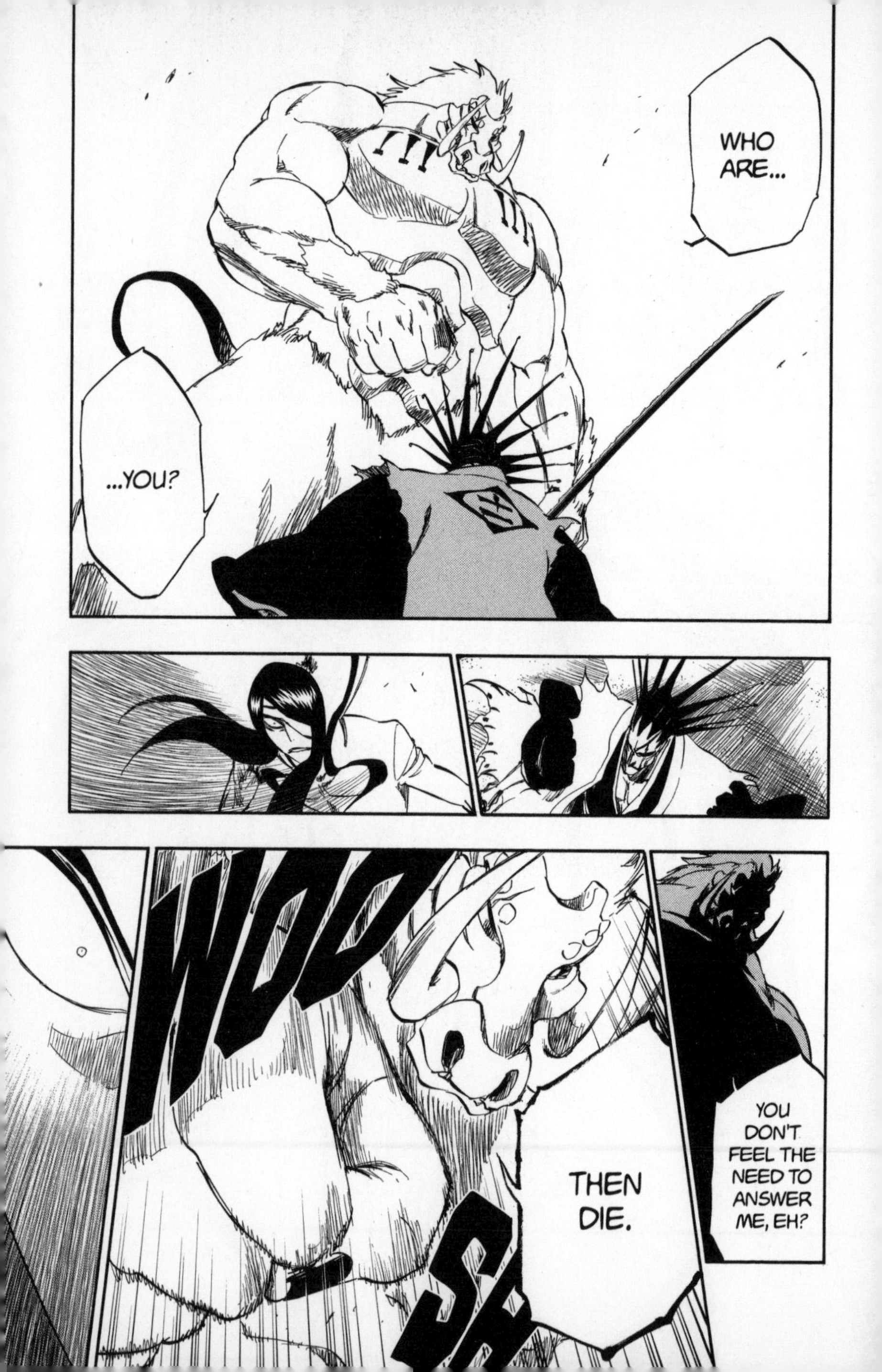
WHO ARE...
...YOU?
YOU DON'T FEEL THE NEED TO ANSWER ME, EH?
THEN DIE.

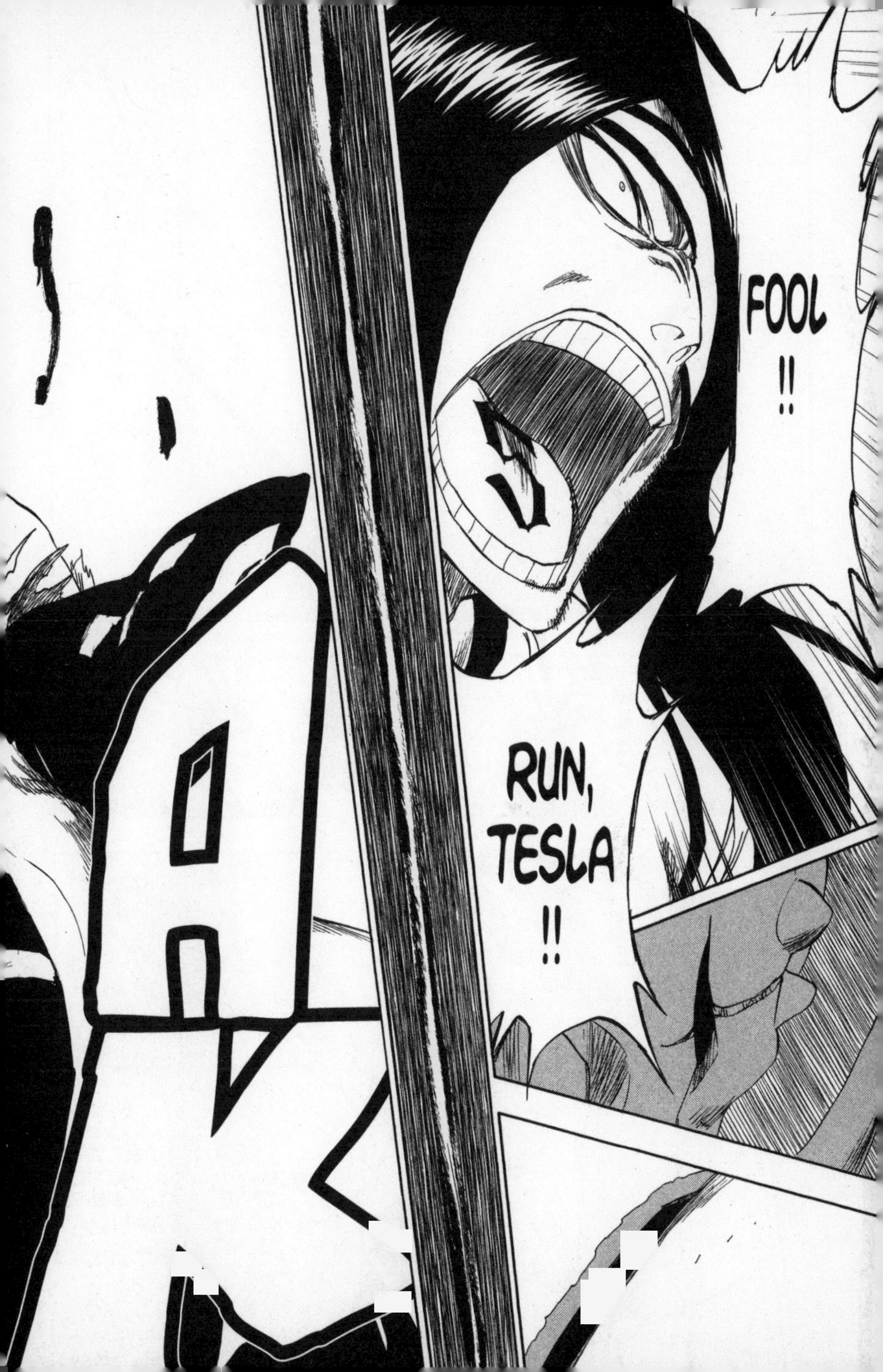
FOOL
!!
RUN, TESLA
!!

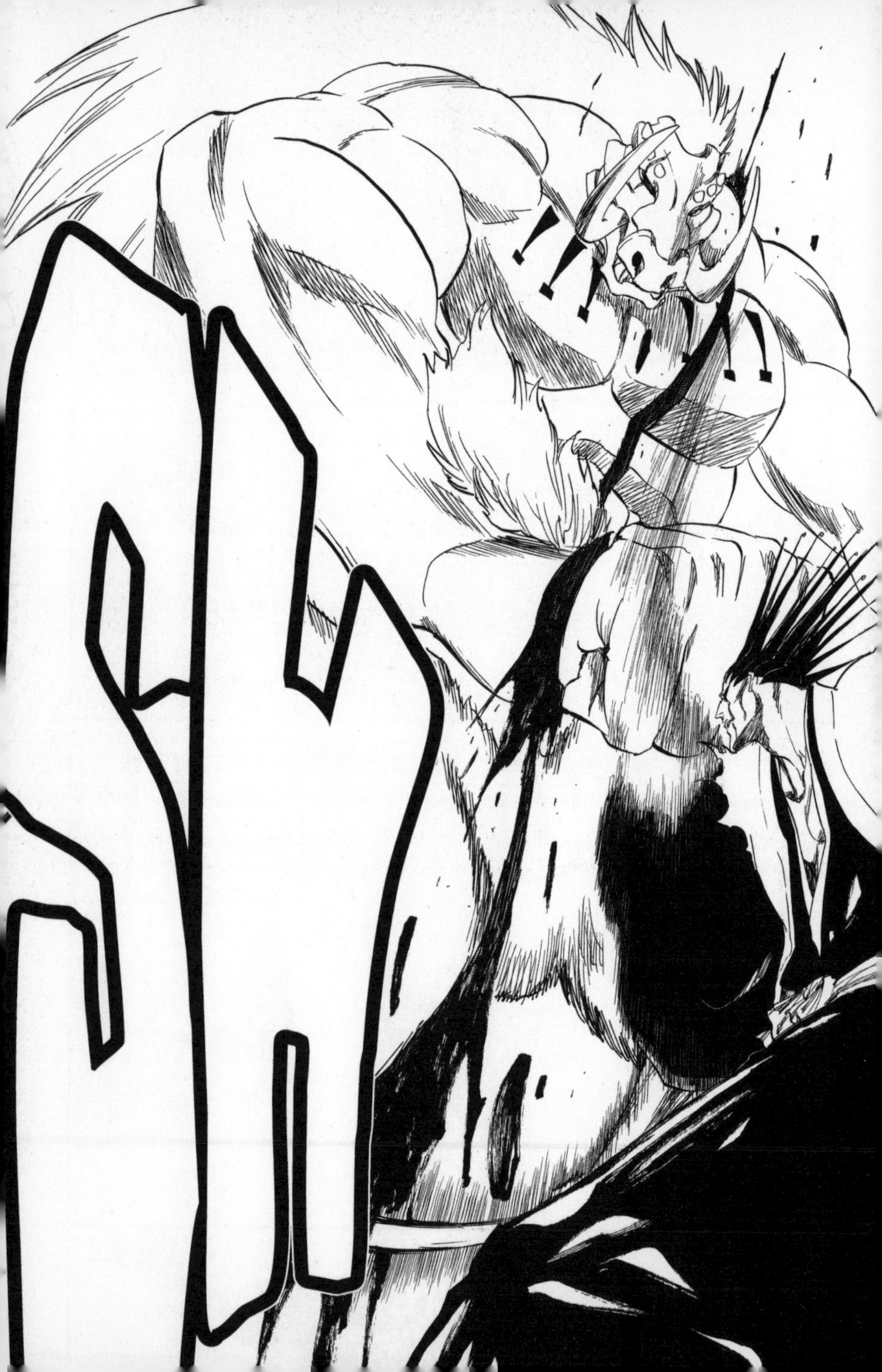

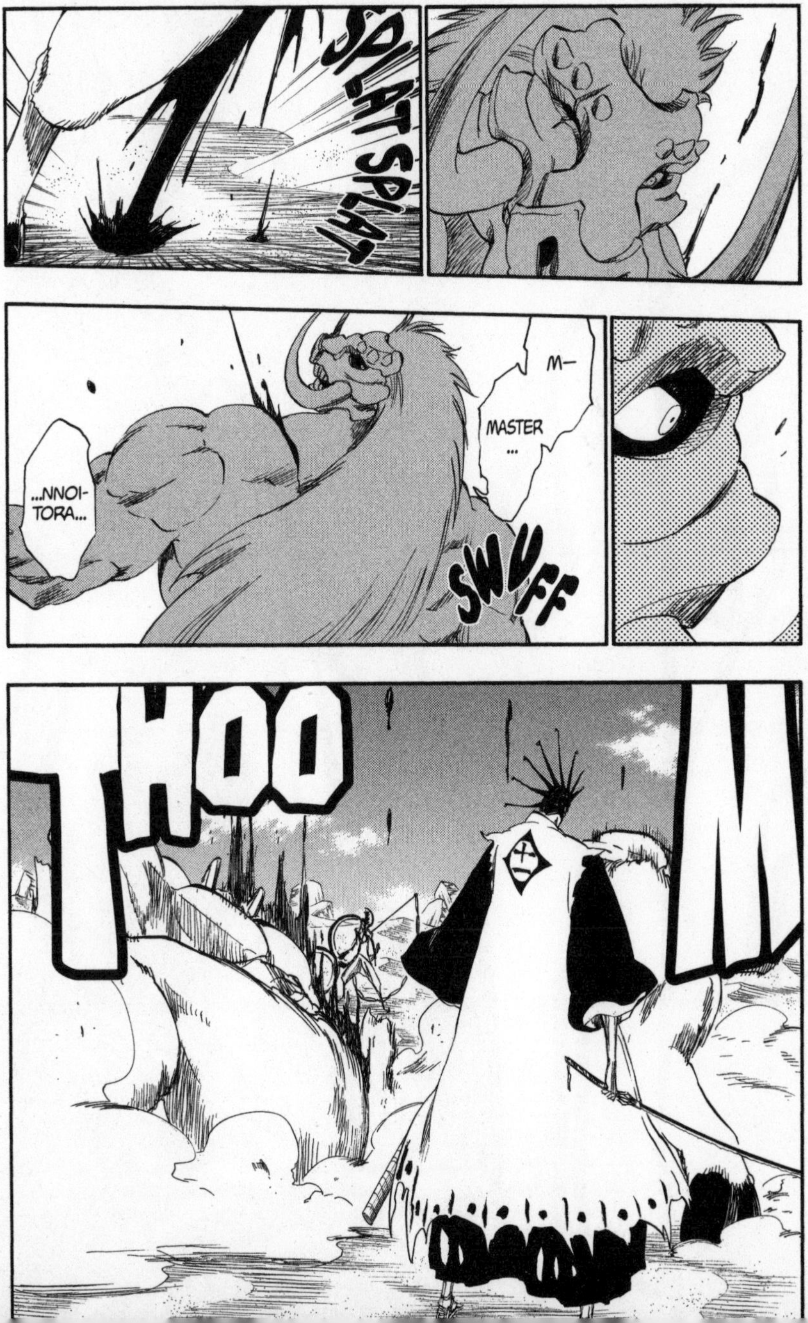
SPLAT SPLAT SPLAT
M— MASTER ...
...NNOI-TORA...
SWUFF
THOOM

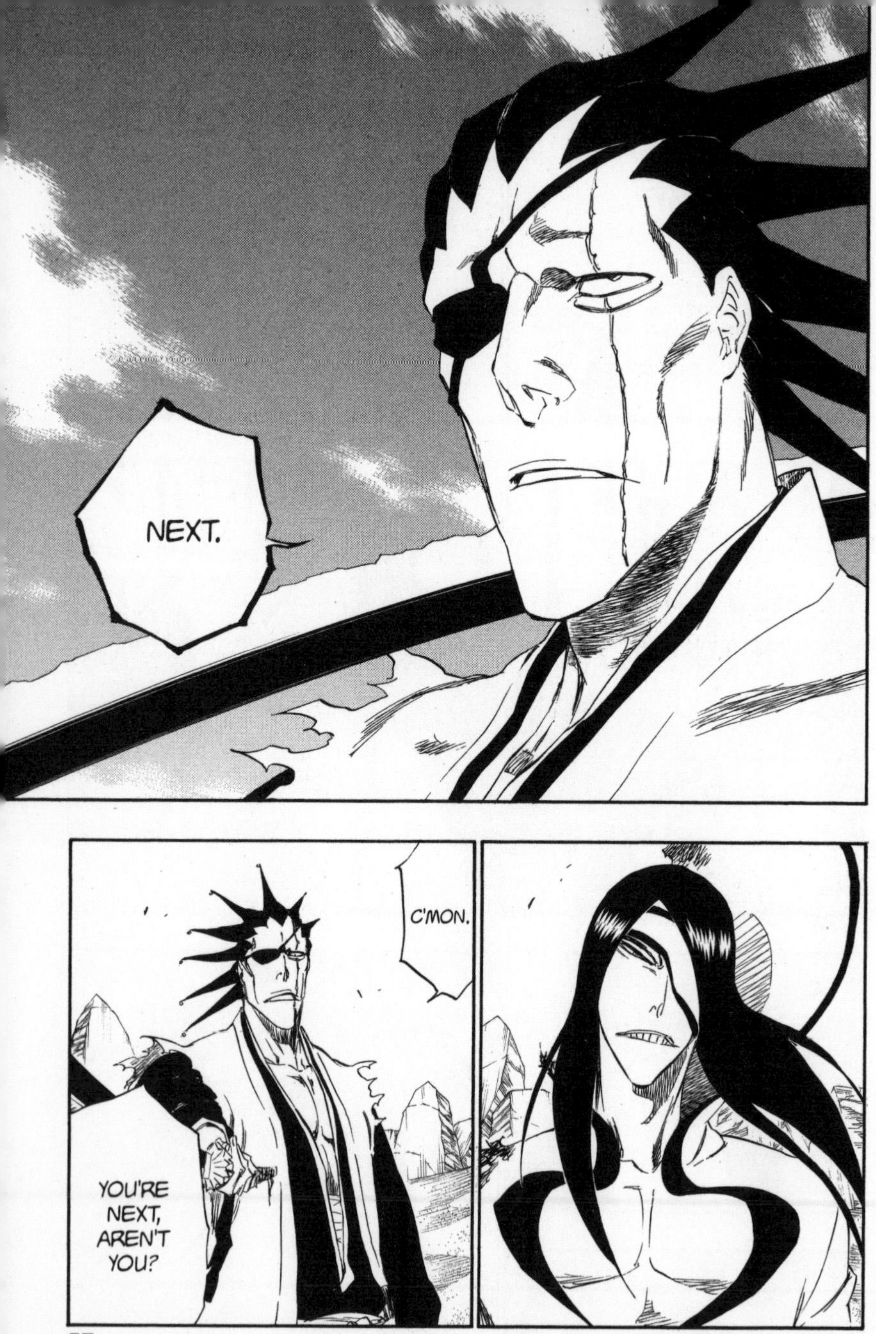
NEXT.
C'MON.
YOU'RE NEXT, AREN'T YOU?

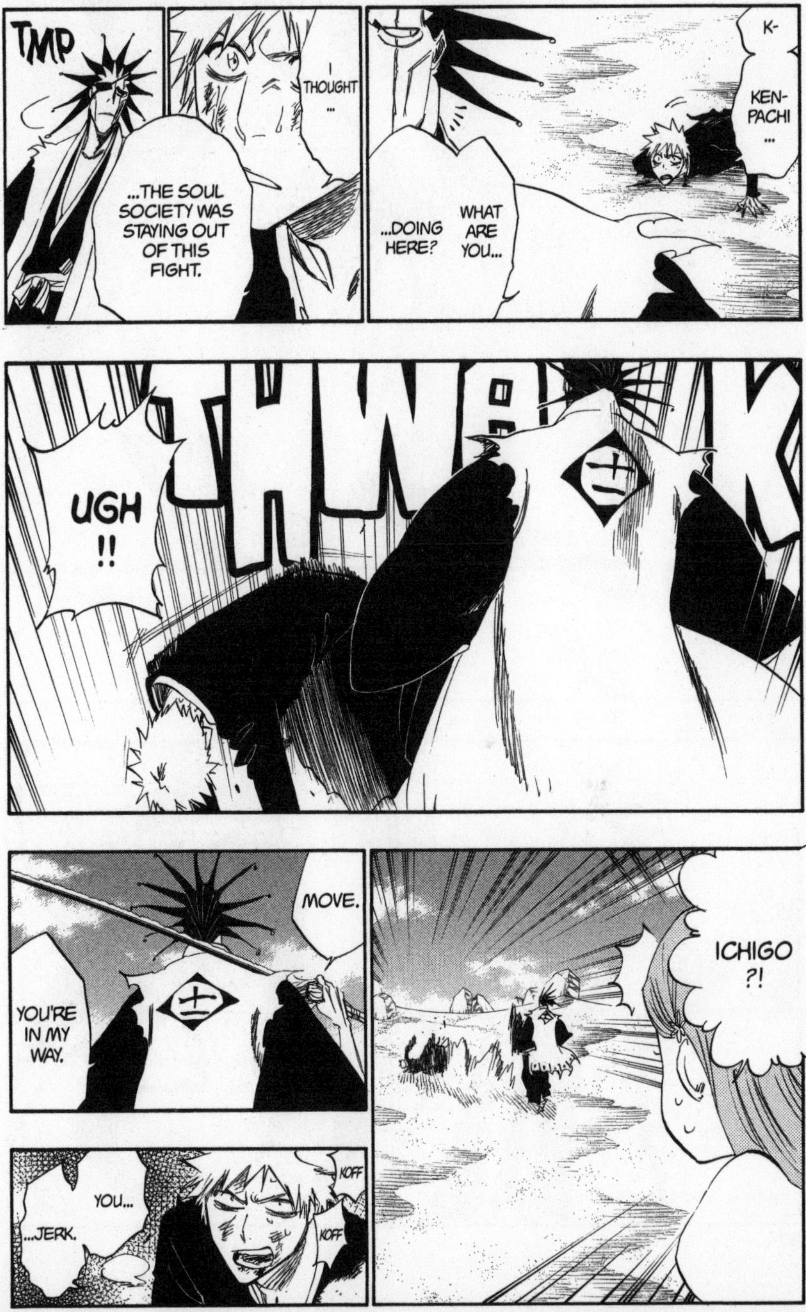
K-
KEN-PACHI ...
WHAT ARE YOU...
...DOING HERE?
I THOUGHT ...
...THE SOUL SOCIETY WAS STAYING OUT OF THIS FIGHT.
TMP
UGH !!
ICHIGO ?!
MOVE.
YOU'RE IN MY WAY.
KOFF
KOFF
YOU...
...JERK.

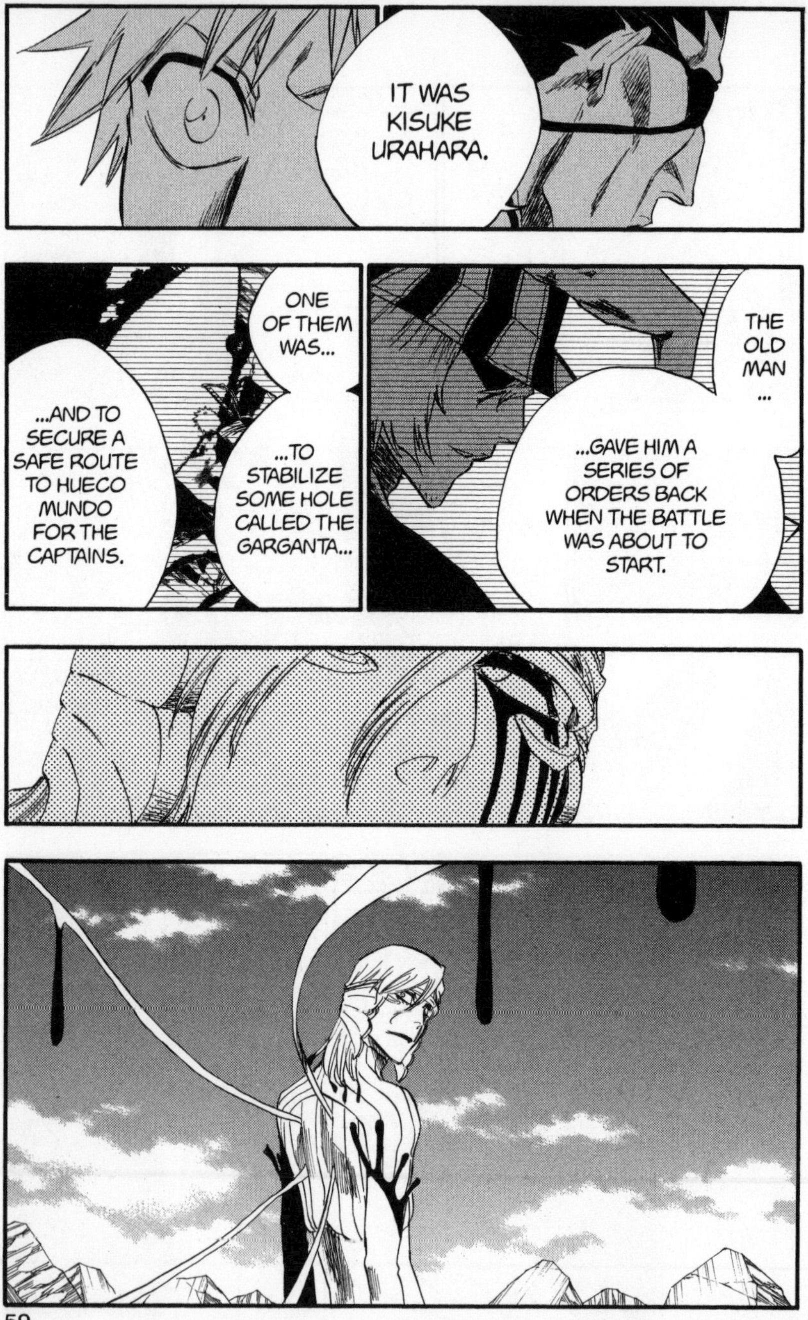
IT WAS KISUKE URAHARA.
THE OLD MAN ...
...GAVE HIM A SERIES OF ORDERS BACK WHEN THE BATTLE WAS ABOUT TO START.
ONE OF THEM WAS...
...TO STABILIZE SOME HOLE CALLED THE GARGANTA...
...AND TO SECURE A SAFE ROUTE TO HUECO MUNDO FOR THE CAPTAINS.

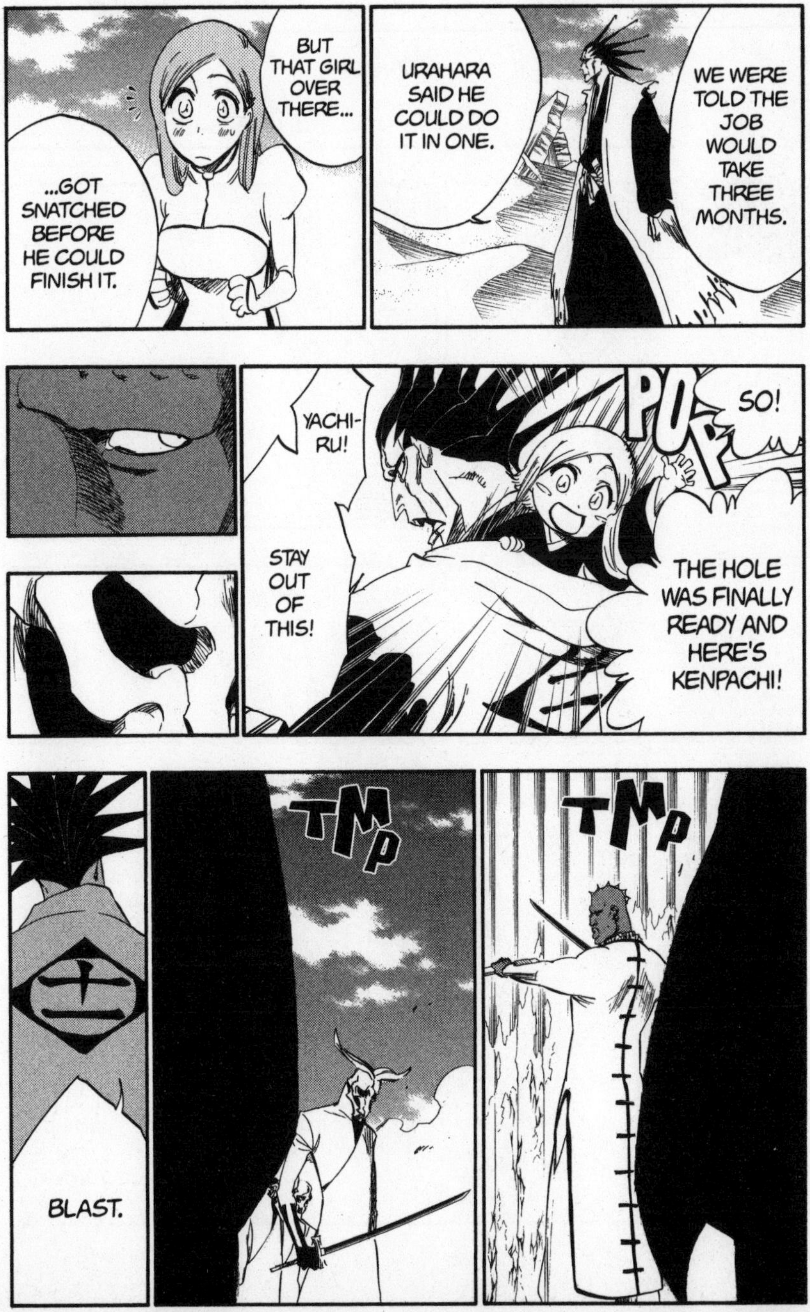
WE WERE TOLD THE JOB WOULD TAKE THREE MONTHS.
URAHARA SAID HE COULD DO IT IN ONE.
BUT THAT GIRL OVER THERE...
...GOT SNATCHED BEFORE HE COULD FINISH IT.
POP
SO!
THE HOLE WAS FINALLY READY AND HERE'S KENPACHI!
YACHI-RU!
STAY OUT OF THIS!
TMP
TMP
BLAST.

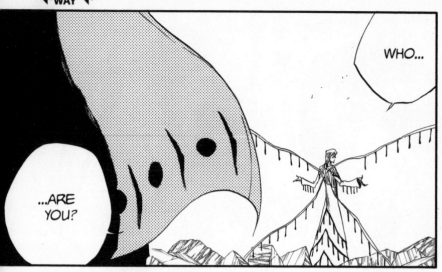

WHO...

...ARE
YOU?

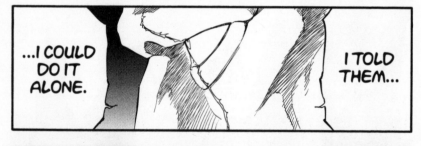

...I COULD
DO IT
ALONE.

I TOLD
THEM...

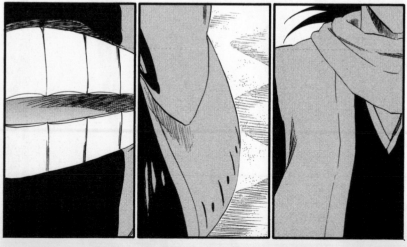

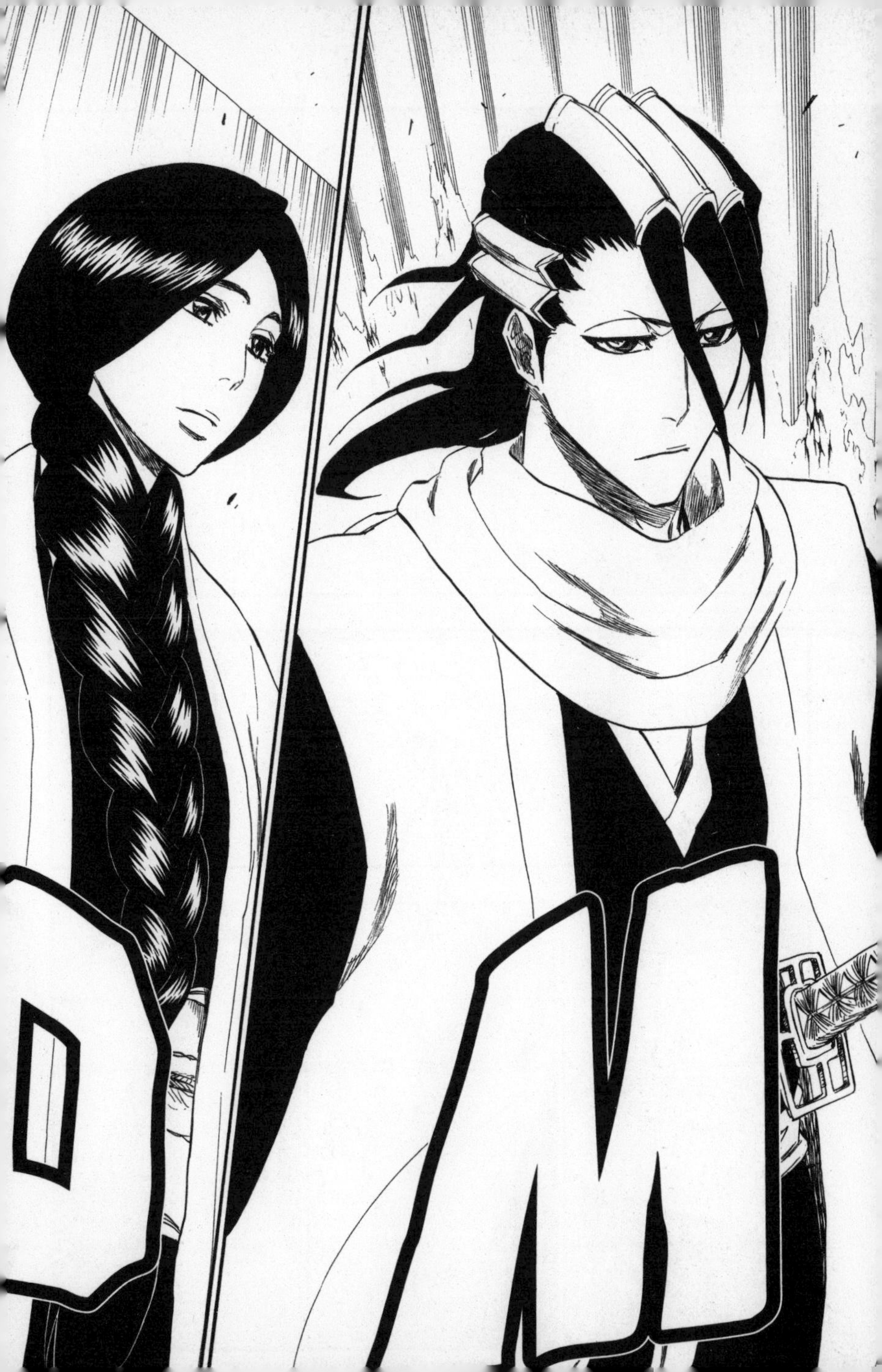

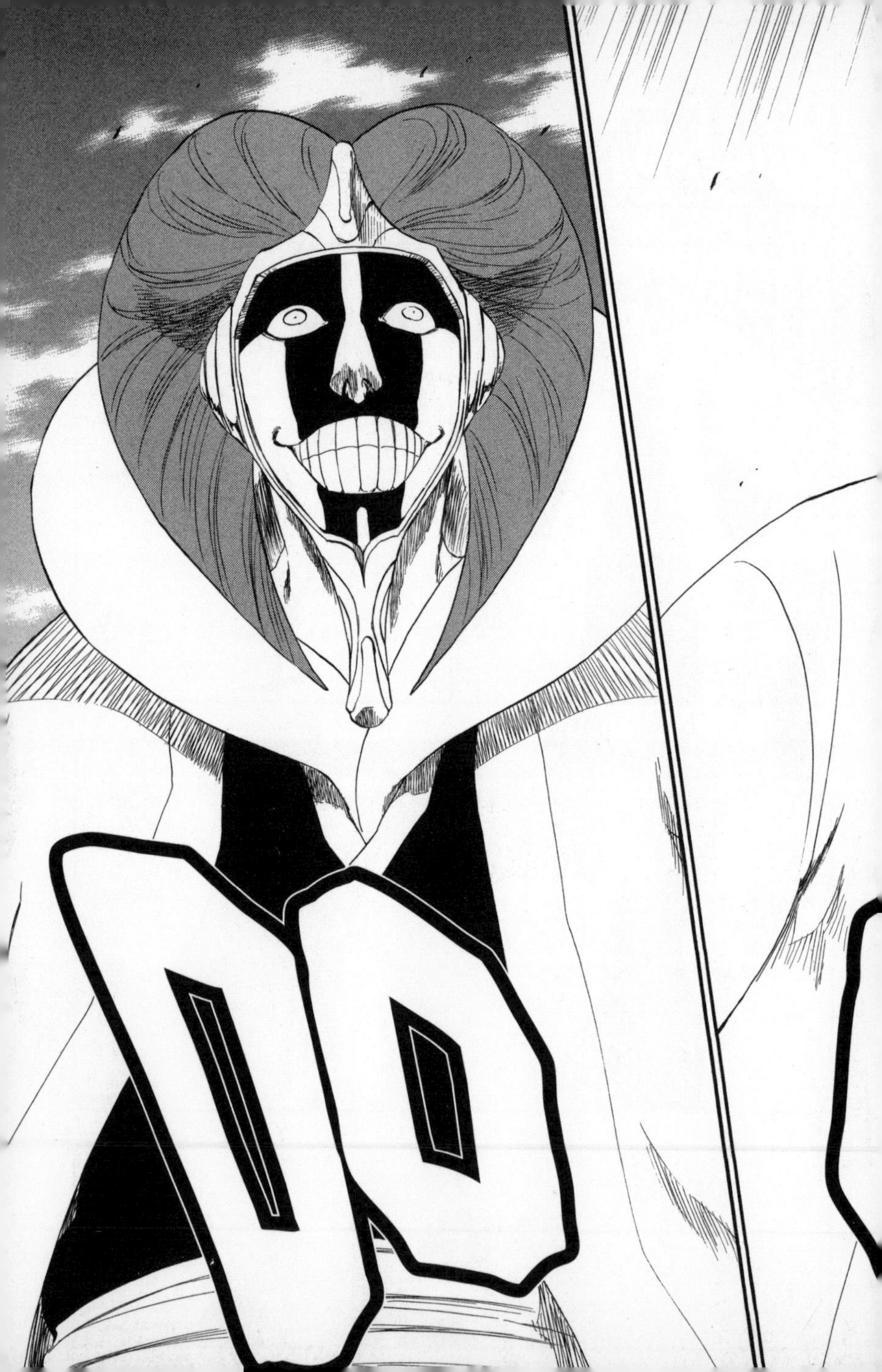

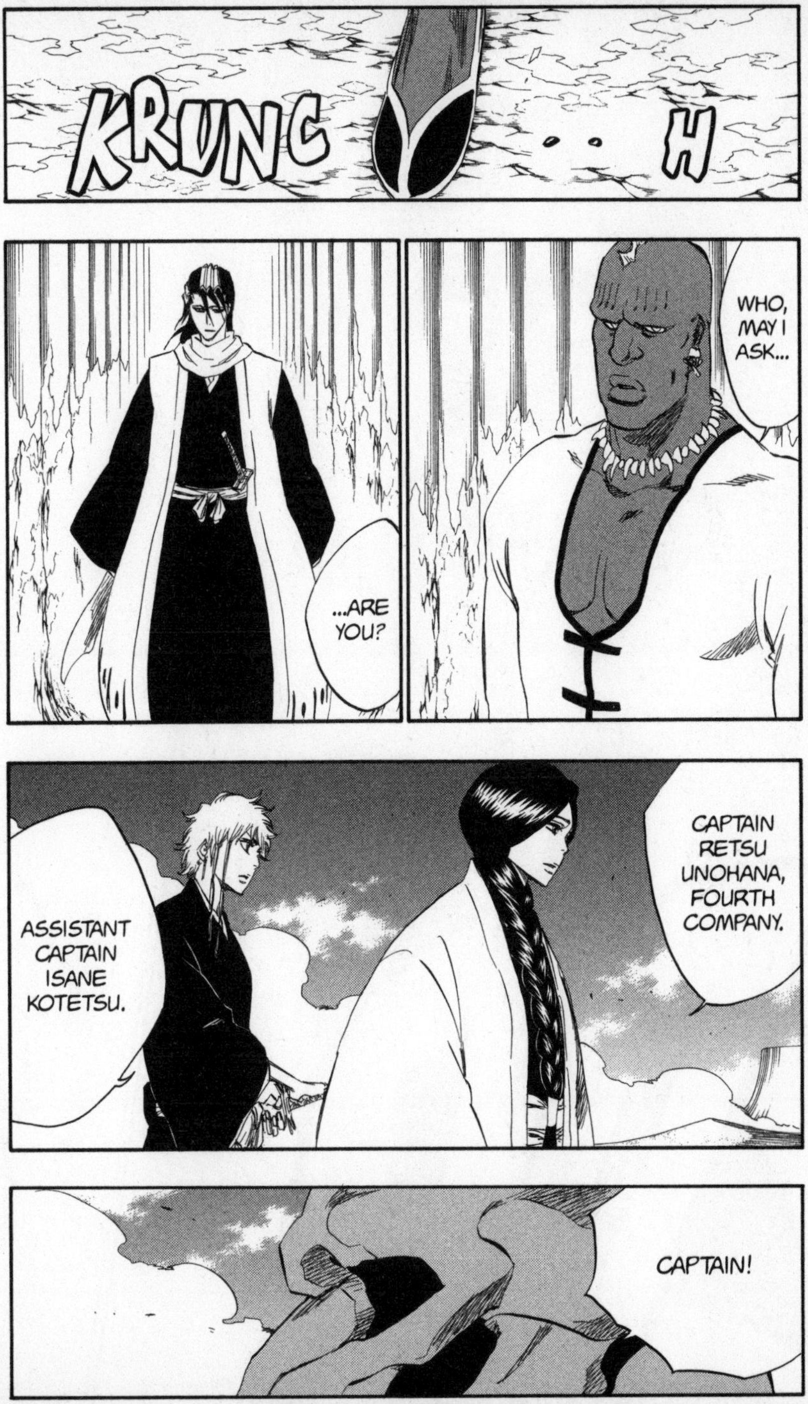
KRUNC . . H
WHO, MAY I ASK...
...ARE YOU?
CAPTAIN RETSU UNOHANA, FOURTH COMPANY.
ASSISTANT CAPTAIN ISANE KOTETSU.
CAPTAIN!

READ THIS WAY

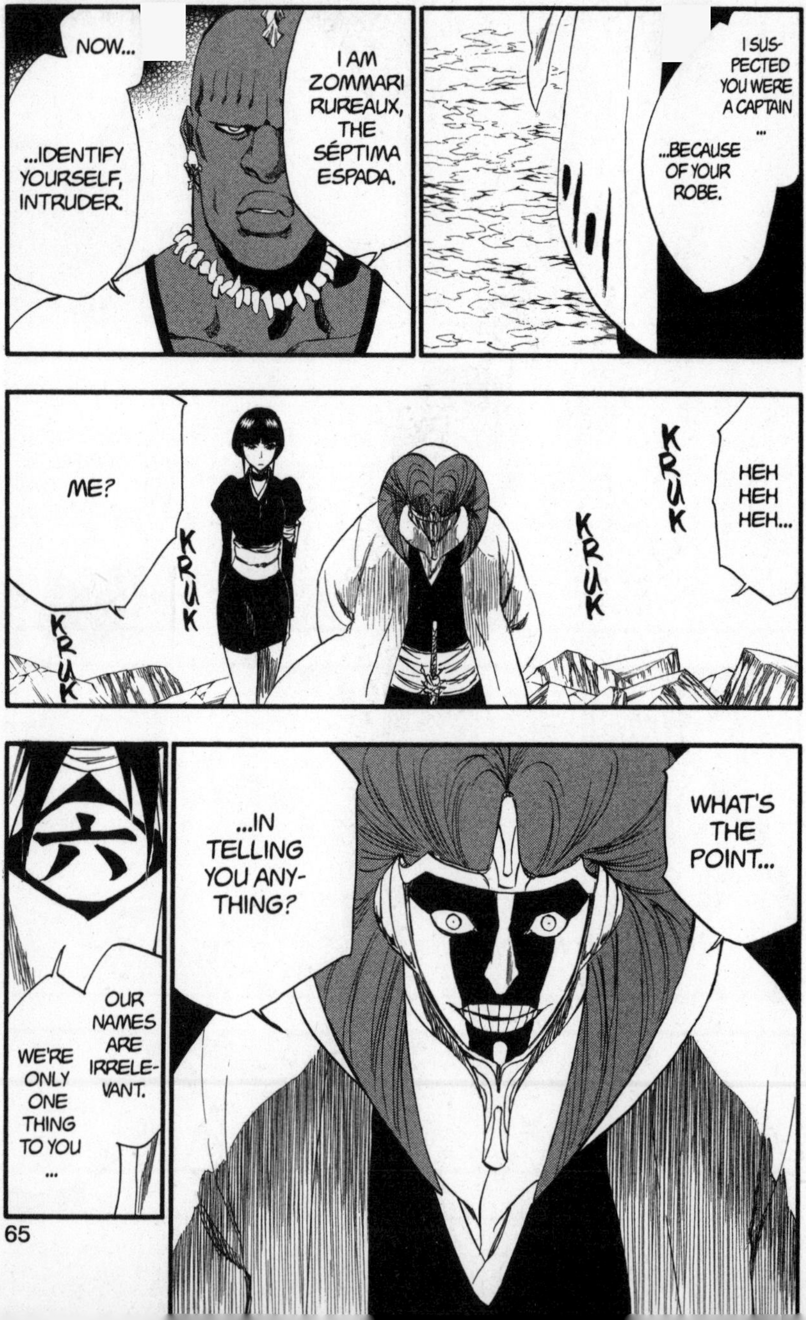
I SUSPECTED YOU WERE A CAPTAIN ...
...BECAUSE OF YOUR ROBE.
I AM ZOMMARI RUREAUX, THE SÉPTIMA ESPADA.
NOW...
...IDENTIFY YOURSELF, INTRUDER.
HEH HEH HEH...
KRUK
KRUK
ME?
KRUK
KRUK
WHAT'S THE POINT...
...IN TELLING YOU ANYTHING?
OUR NAMES ARE IRRELEVANT.
WE'RE ONLY ONE THING TO YOU ...

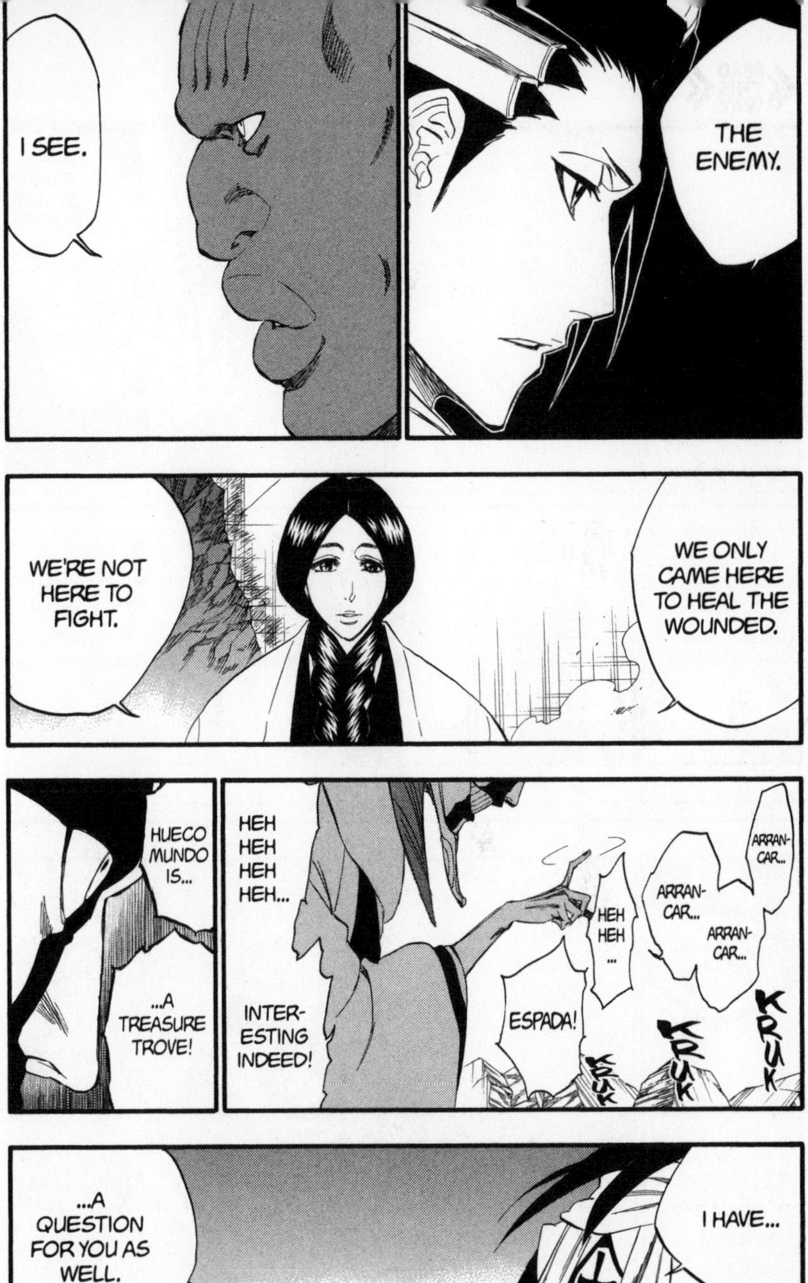
THE ENEMY.
I SEE.
WE ONLY CAME HERE TO HEAL THE WOUNDED.
WE'RE NOT HERE TO FIGHT.
ARRAN-CAR...
ARRAN-CAR...
ARRAN-CAR...
KRUK
KRUK
HEH HEH ...
HEH HEH HEH HEH...
ESPADA!
KRUK
INTER-ESTING INDEED!
HUECO MUNDO IS...
...A TREASURE TROVE!
I HAVE...
...A QUESTION FOR YOU AS WELL.

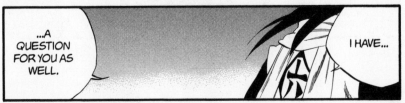

READ THIS WAY

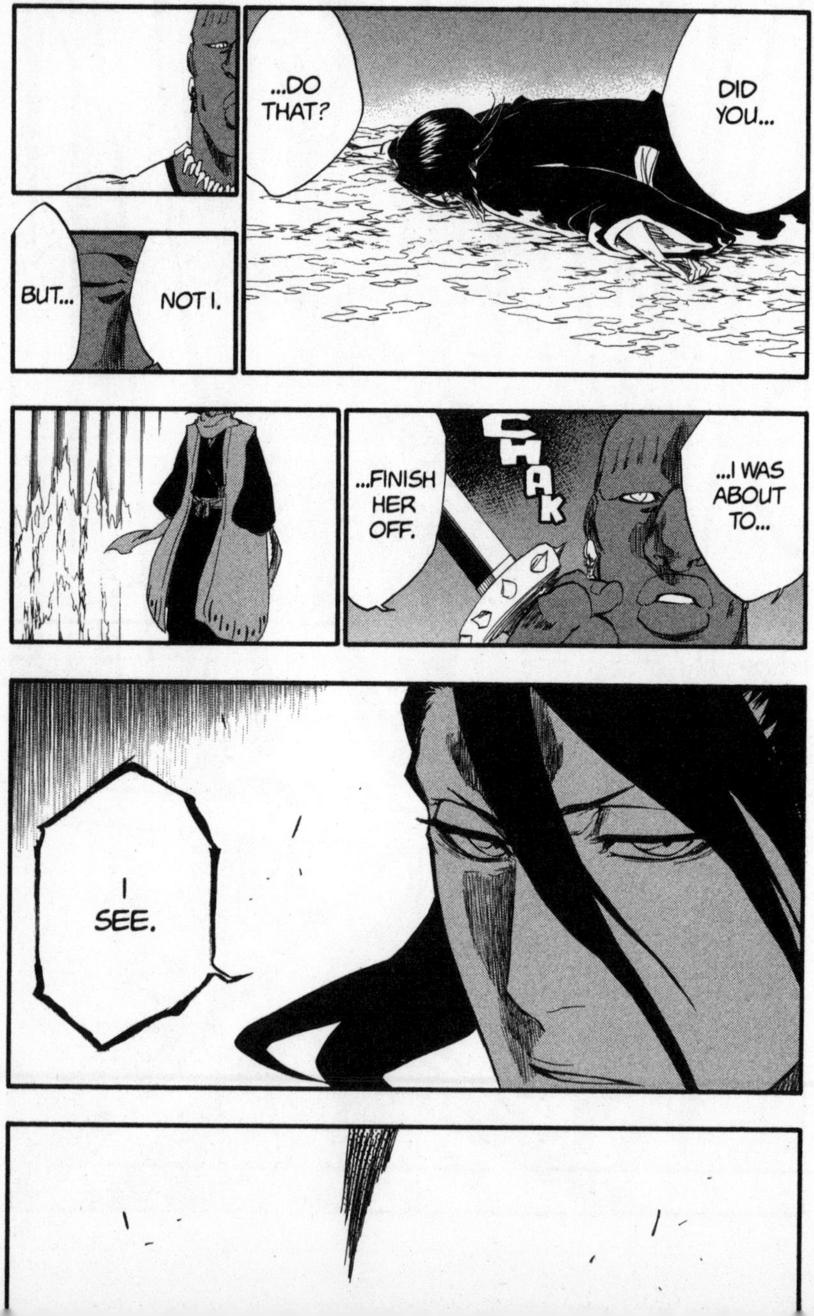

DID YOU...
...DO THAT?
NOT I.
BUT...
...I WAS ABOUT TO...
CHAK
...FINISH HER OFF.
I SEE.

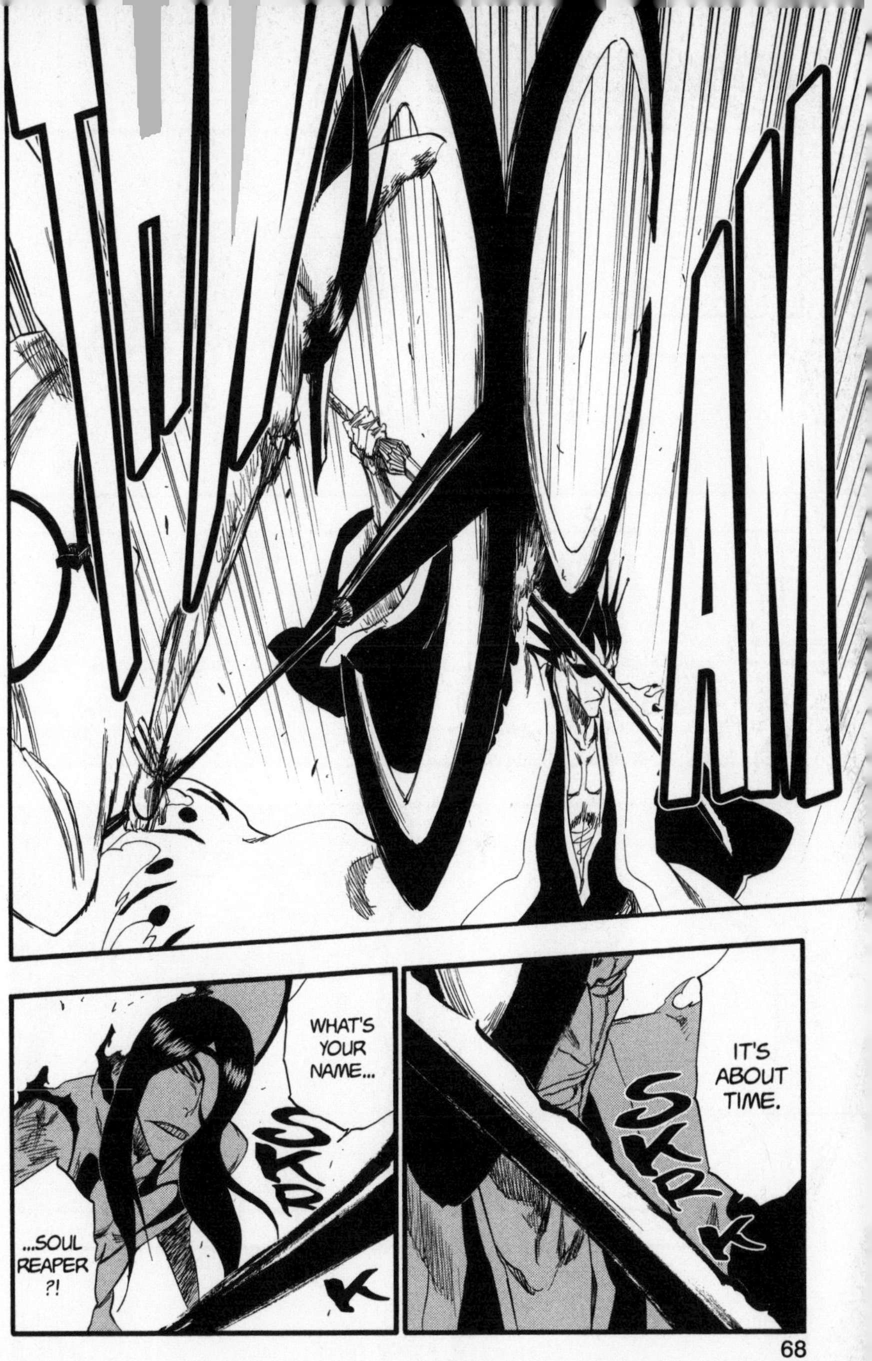
IT'S ABOUT TIME.
SKRK
WHAT'S YOUR NAME...
SKRK
...SOUL REAPER ?!

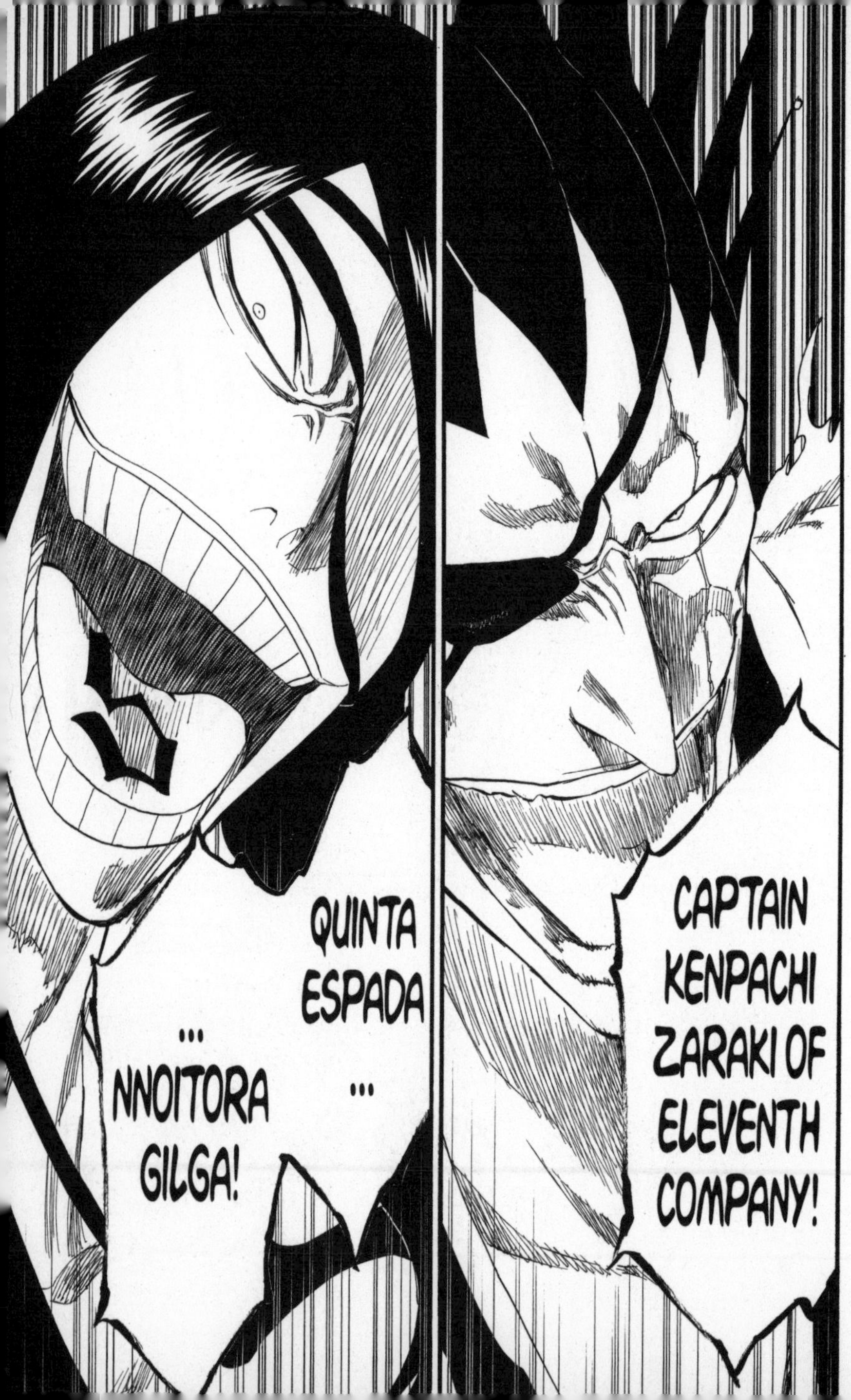
CAPTAIN KENPACHI ZARAKI OF ELEVENTH COMPANY!
QUINTA ESPADA ...
... NNOITORA GILGA!

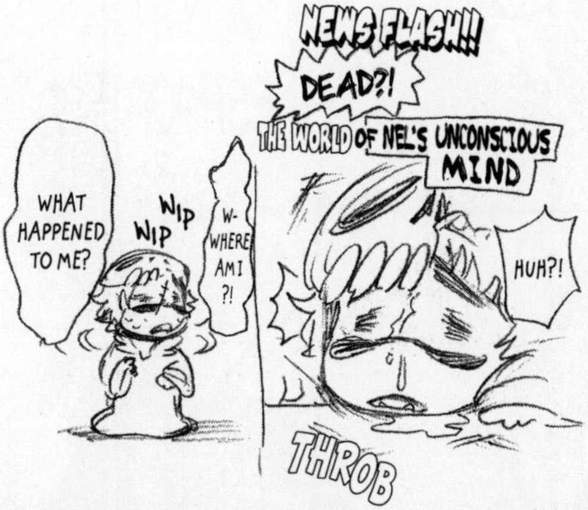
NEWS FLASH!!
DEAD?!
THE WORLD OF NEL'S UNCONSCIOUS MIND
HUH?!
THROB
W-WHERE AM I ?!
WIP WIP
WHAT HAPPENED TO ME?

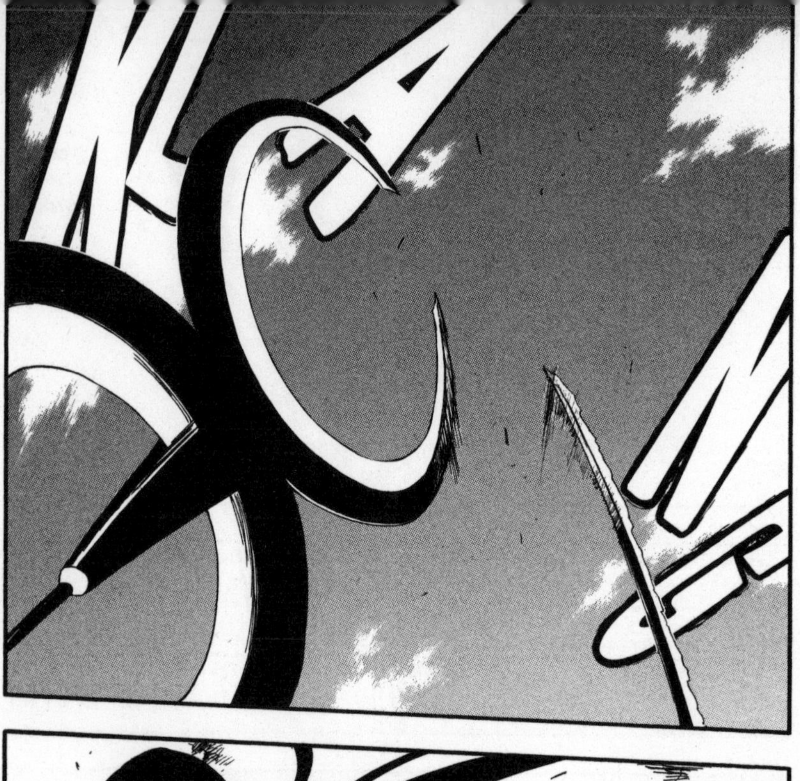
KLANG

299. The Verbal Warfare

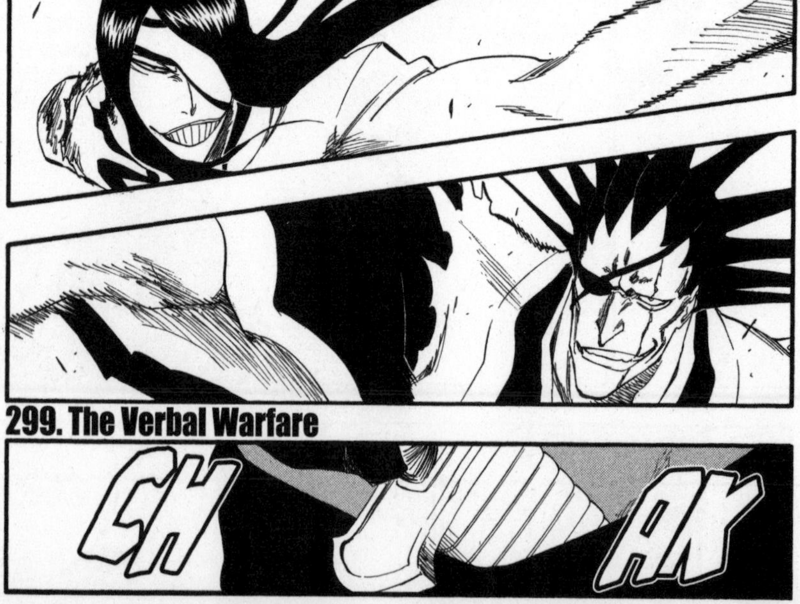
CHAK

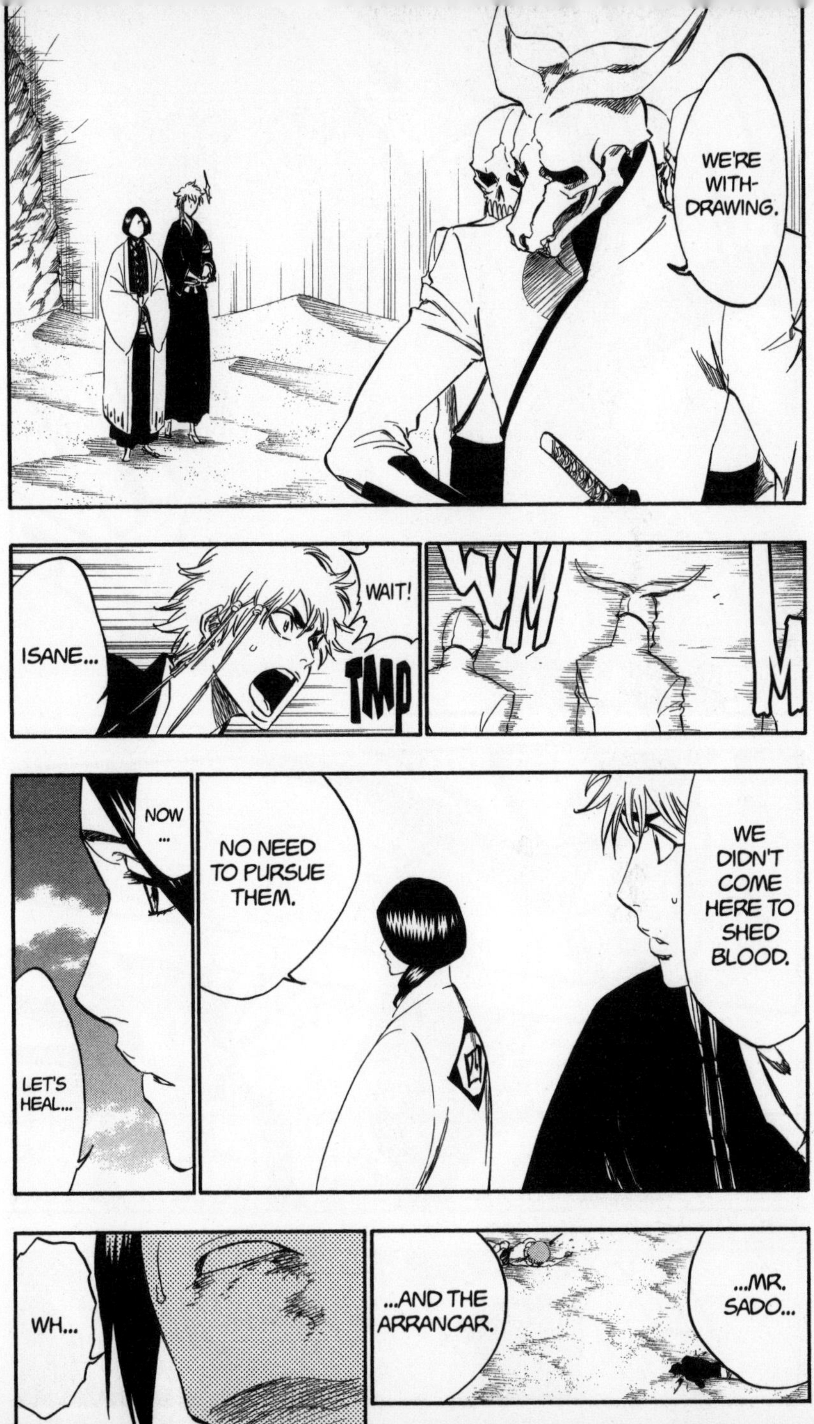
WE'RE WITH-DRAWING.
WAIT!
TMP
ISANE...
WE DIDN'T COME HERE TO SHED BLOOD.
NO NEED TO PURSUE THEM.
NOW ...
LET'S HEAL...
...MR. SADO...
...AND THE ARRANCAR.
WH...

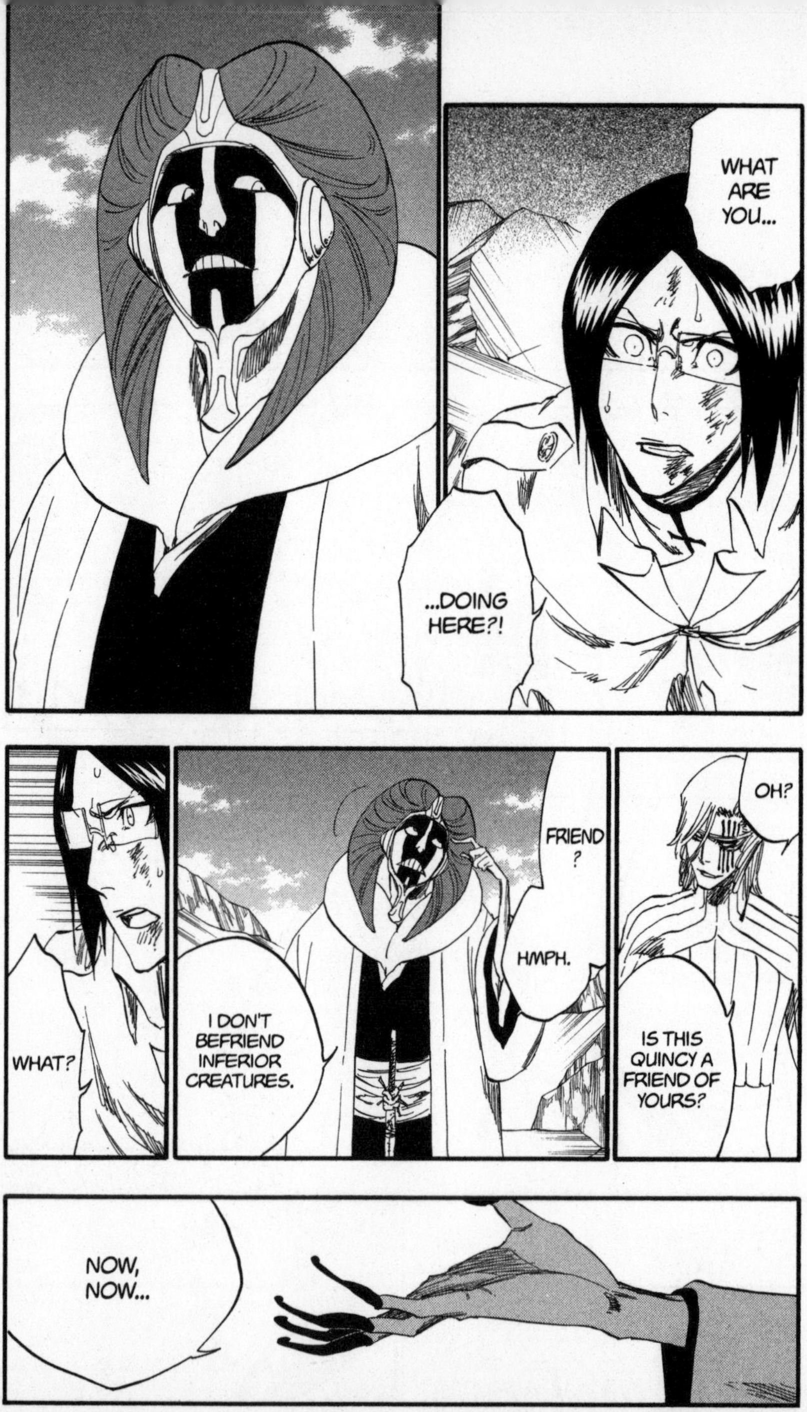
WHAT ARE YOU...
...DOING HERE?!
OH?
IS THIS QUINCY A FRIEND OF YOURS?
FRIEND?
HMPH.
I DON'T BEFRIEND INFERIOR CREATURES.
WHAT?
NOW, NOW...

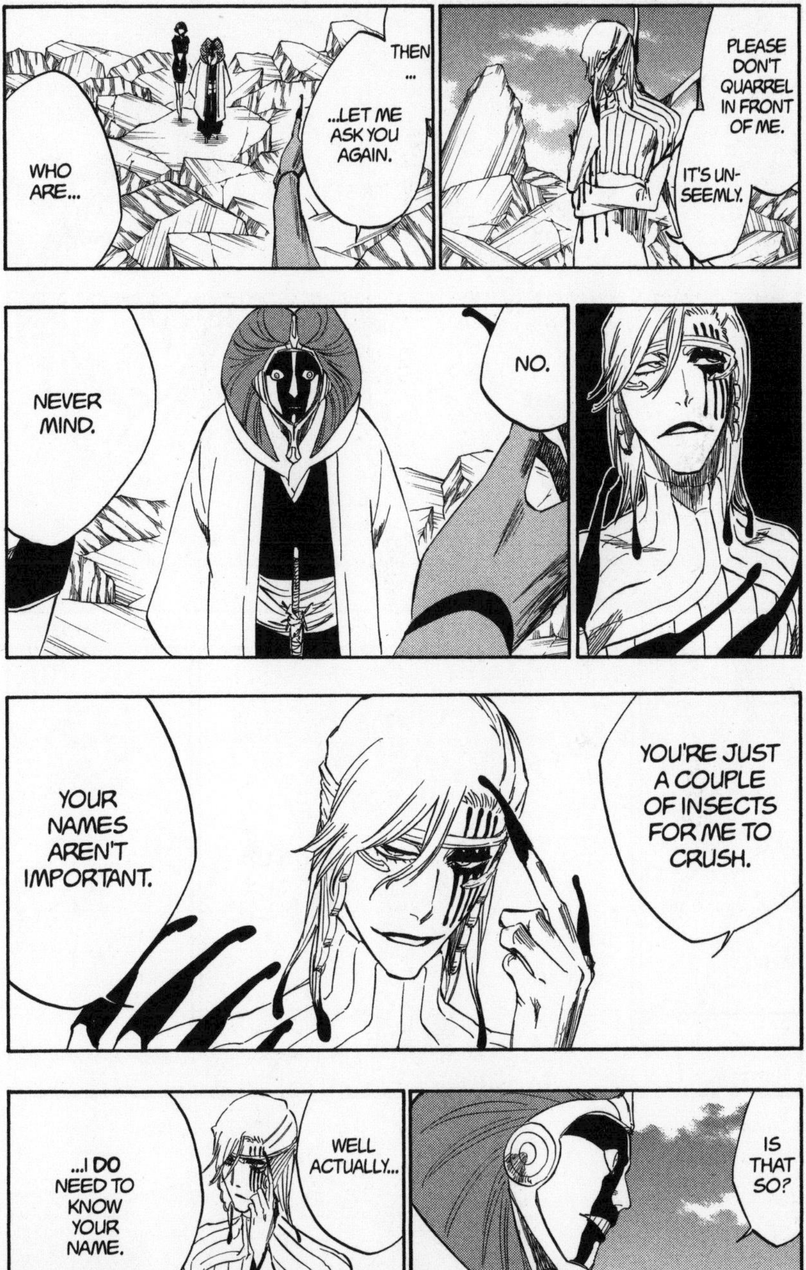
PLEASE DON'T QUARREL IN FRONT OF ME.
IT'S UN-SEEMLY.
THEN ...
...LET ME ASK YOU AGAIN.
WHO ARE...
NO.
NEVER MIND.
YOU'RE JUST A COUPLE OF INSECTS FOR ME TO CRUSH.
YOUR NAMES AREN'T IMPORTANT.
IS THAT SO?
WELL ACTUALLY...
...I DO NEED TO KNOW YOUR NAME.

READ THIS WAY

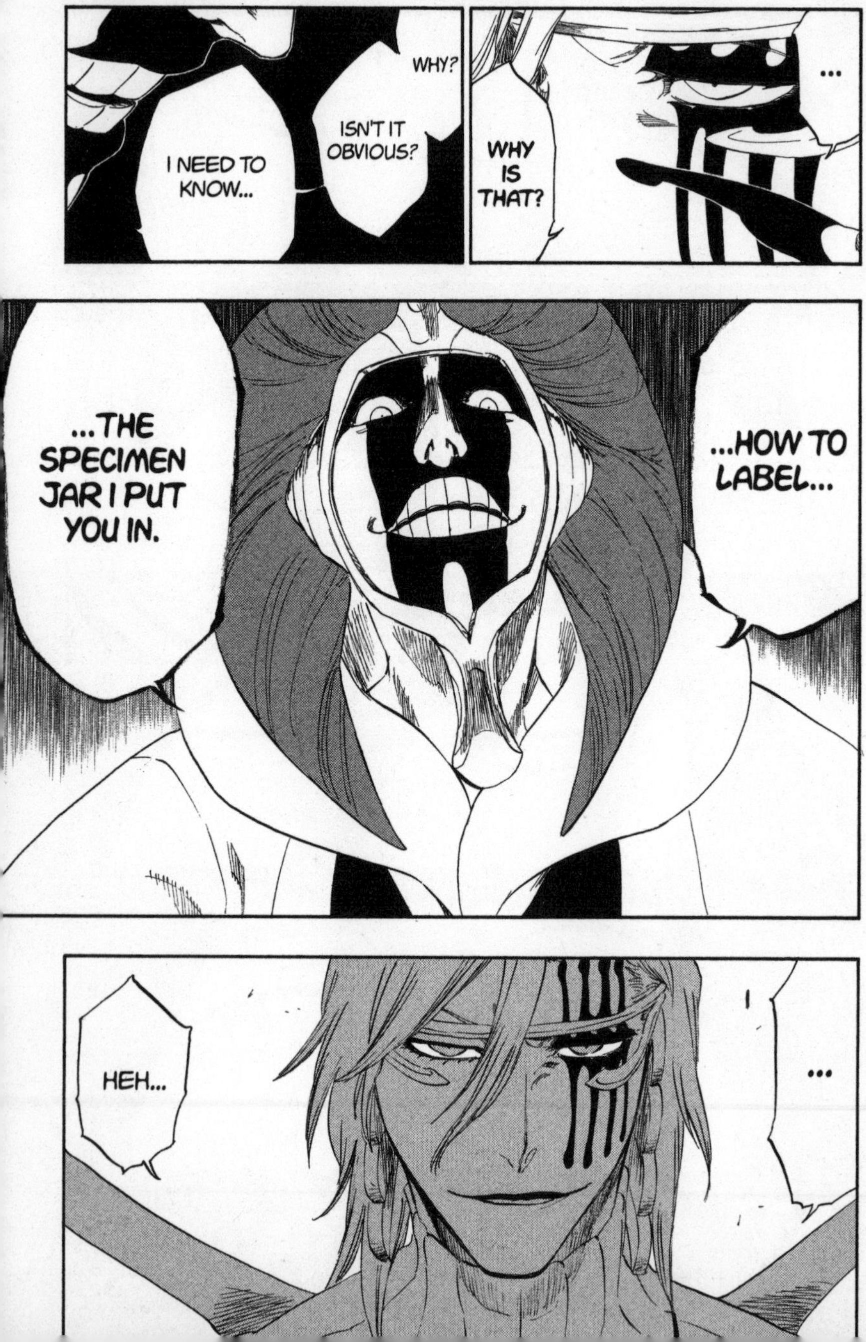
...
WHY IS THAT?
WHY?
ISN'T IT OBVIOUS?
I NEED TO KNOW...
...HOW TO LABEL...
...THE SPECIMEN JAR I PUT YOU IN.
...
HEH...

299. Warfare

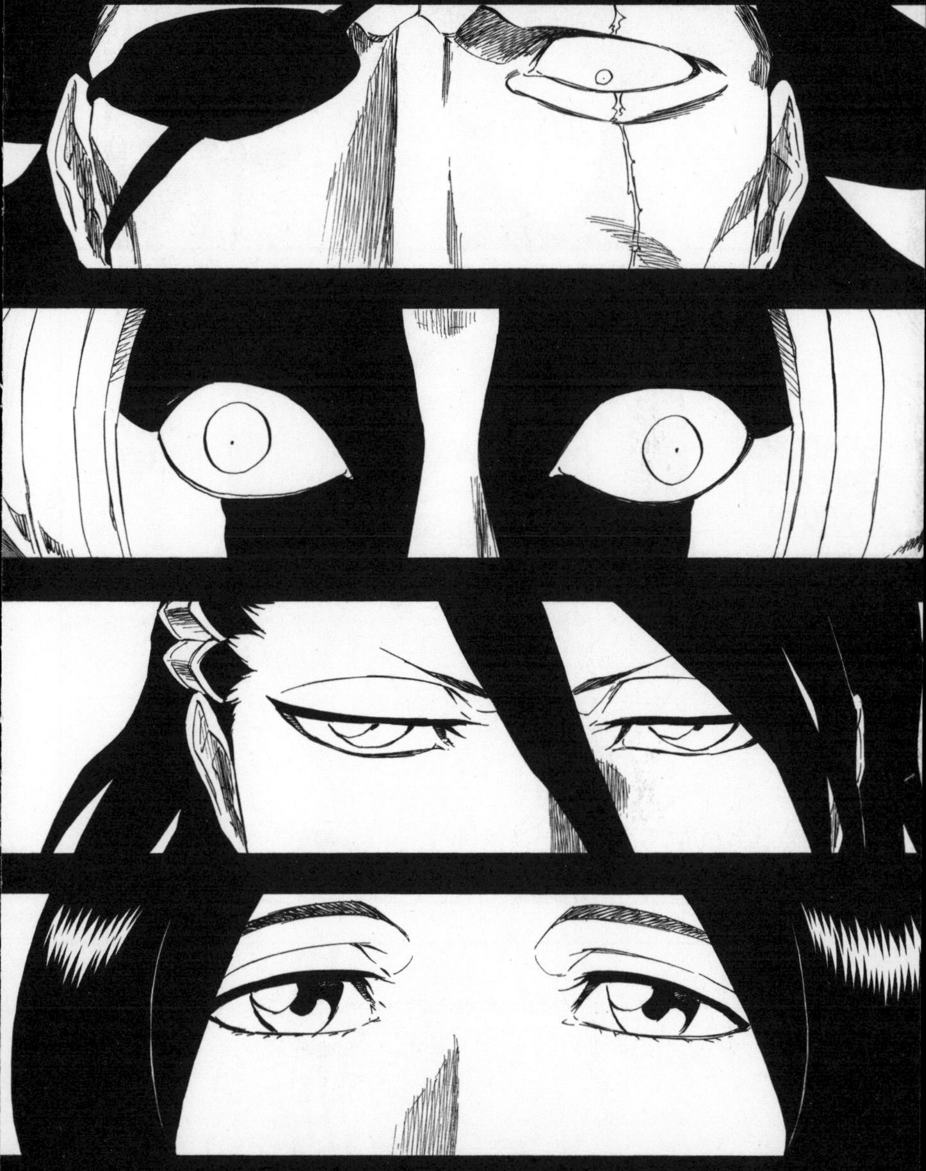

BLEACH

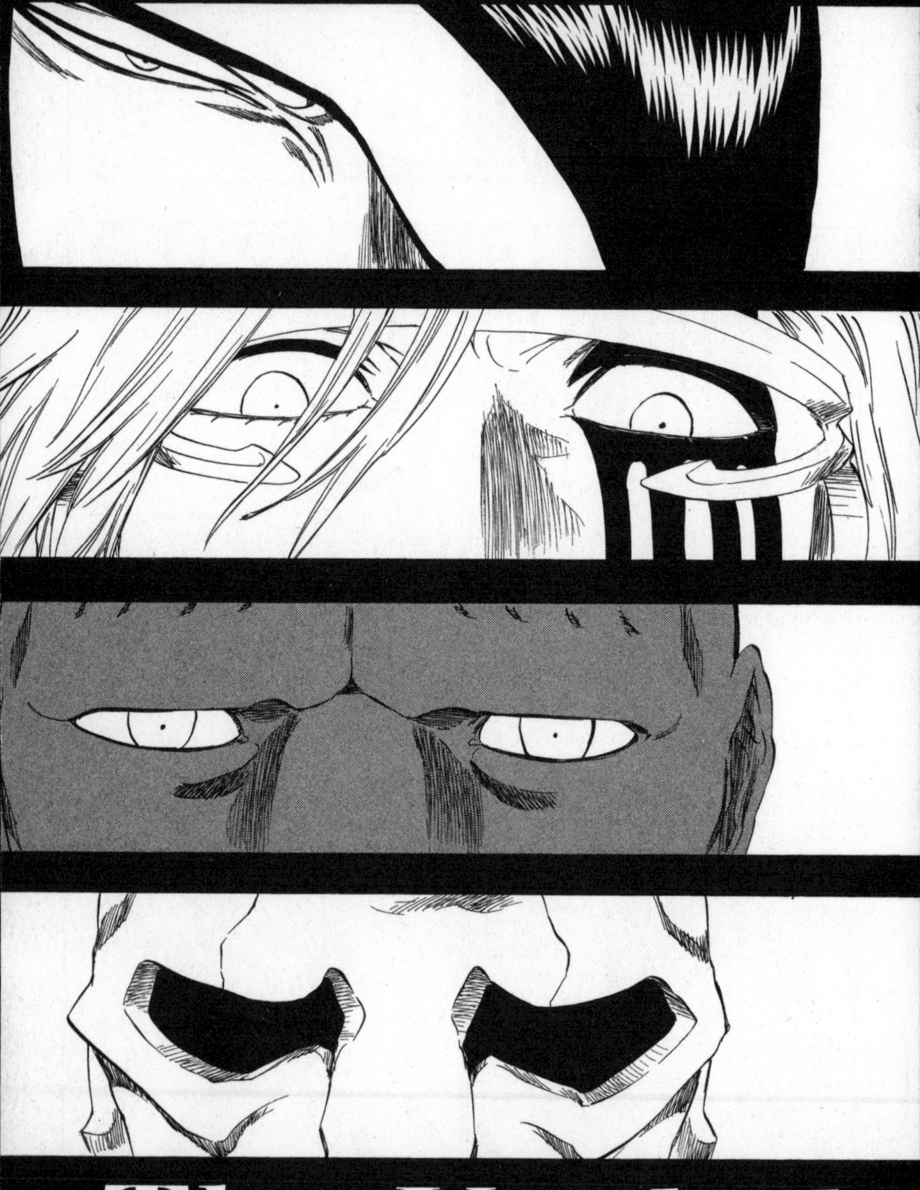

The Verbal

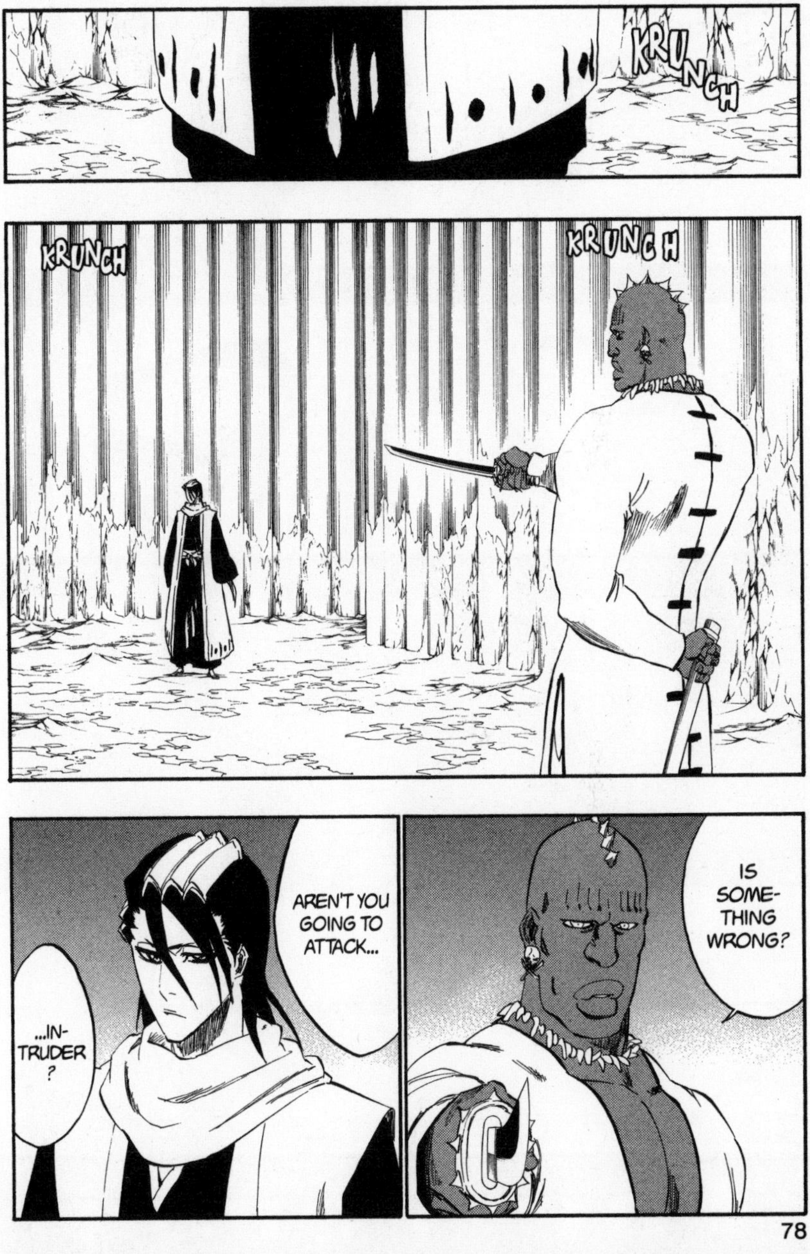
KRUNCH
KRUNCH
KRUNCH
IS SOME-THING WRONG?
AREN'T YOU GOING TO ATTACK...
...IN-TRUDER?

READ THIS WAY

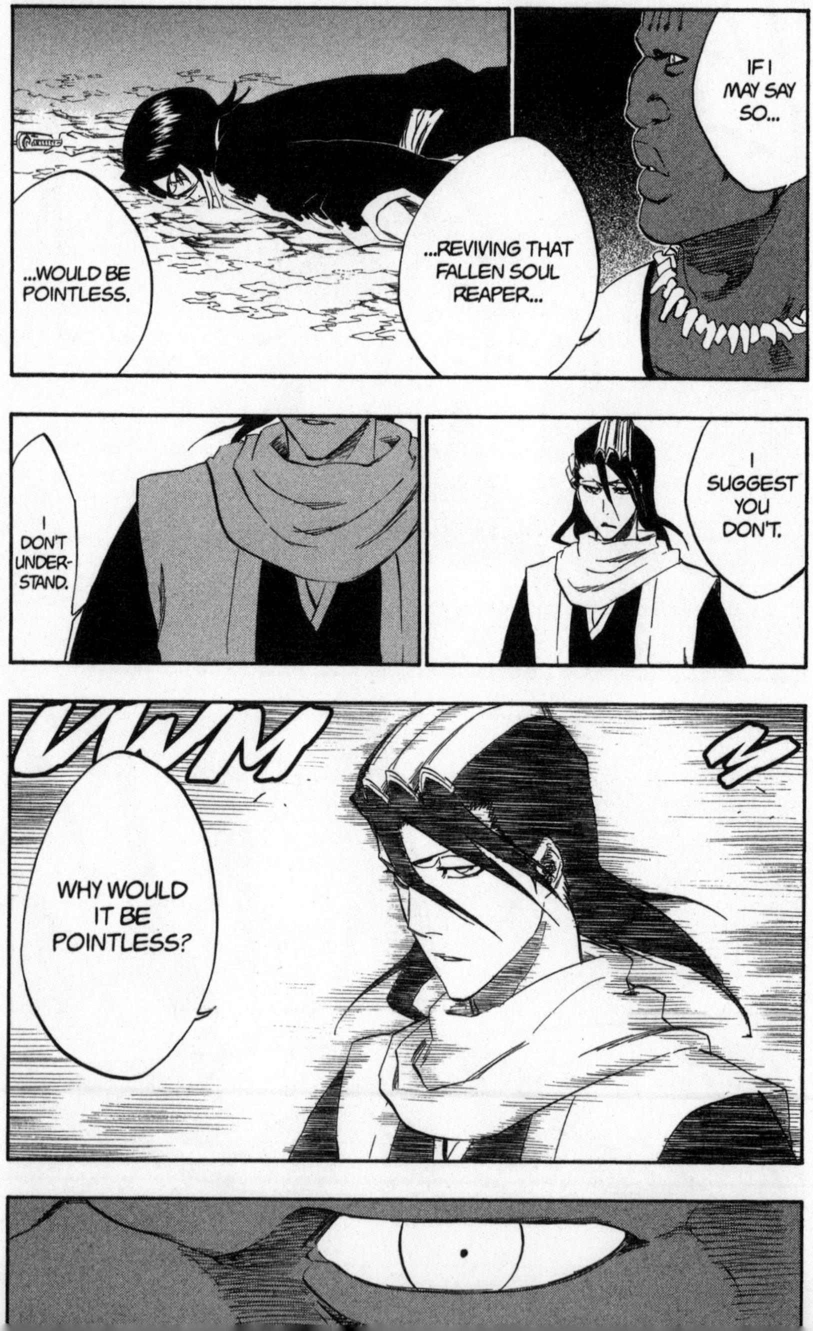
IF I MAY SAY SO...
...REVIVING THAT FALLEN SOUL REAPER...
...WOULD BE POINTLESS.
I SUGGEST YOU DON'T.
I DON'T UNDER-STAND.
UWM
M
WHY WOULD IT BE POINTLESS?

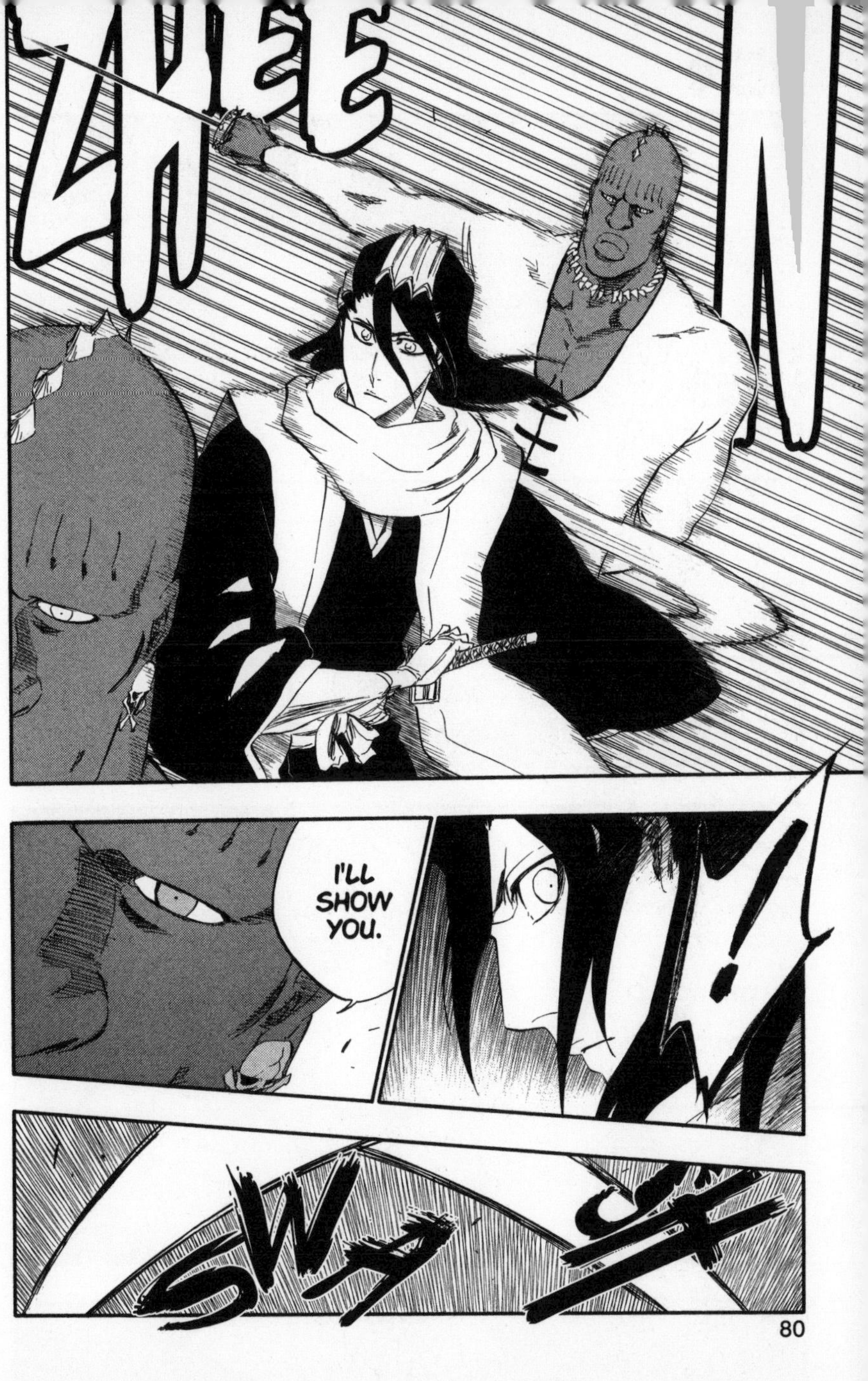
I'LL SHOW YOU.

READ THIS WAY

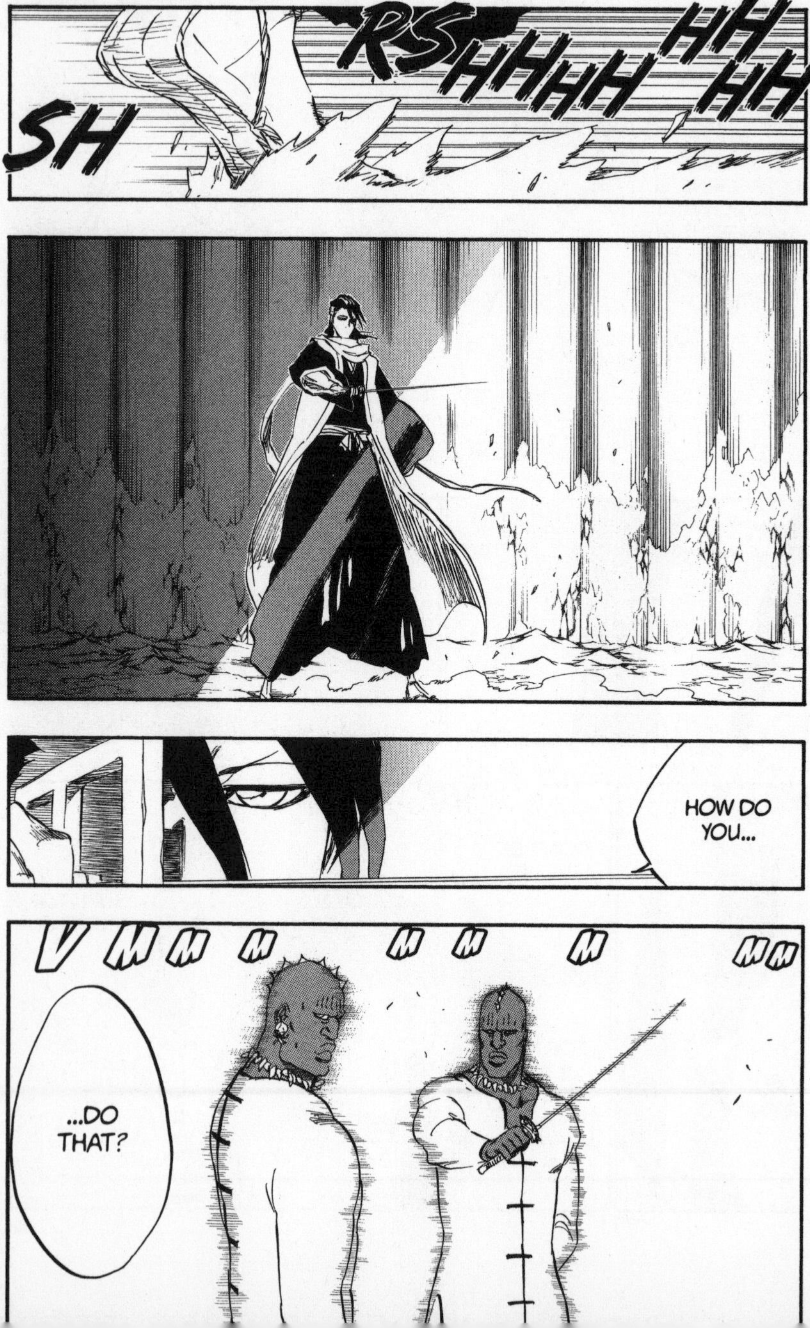
RSHHHHHHHHH
SH
HOW DO YOU...
VMMMMMMMMM
...DO THAT?

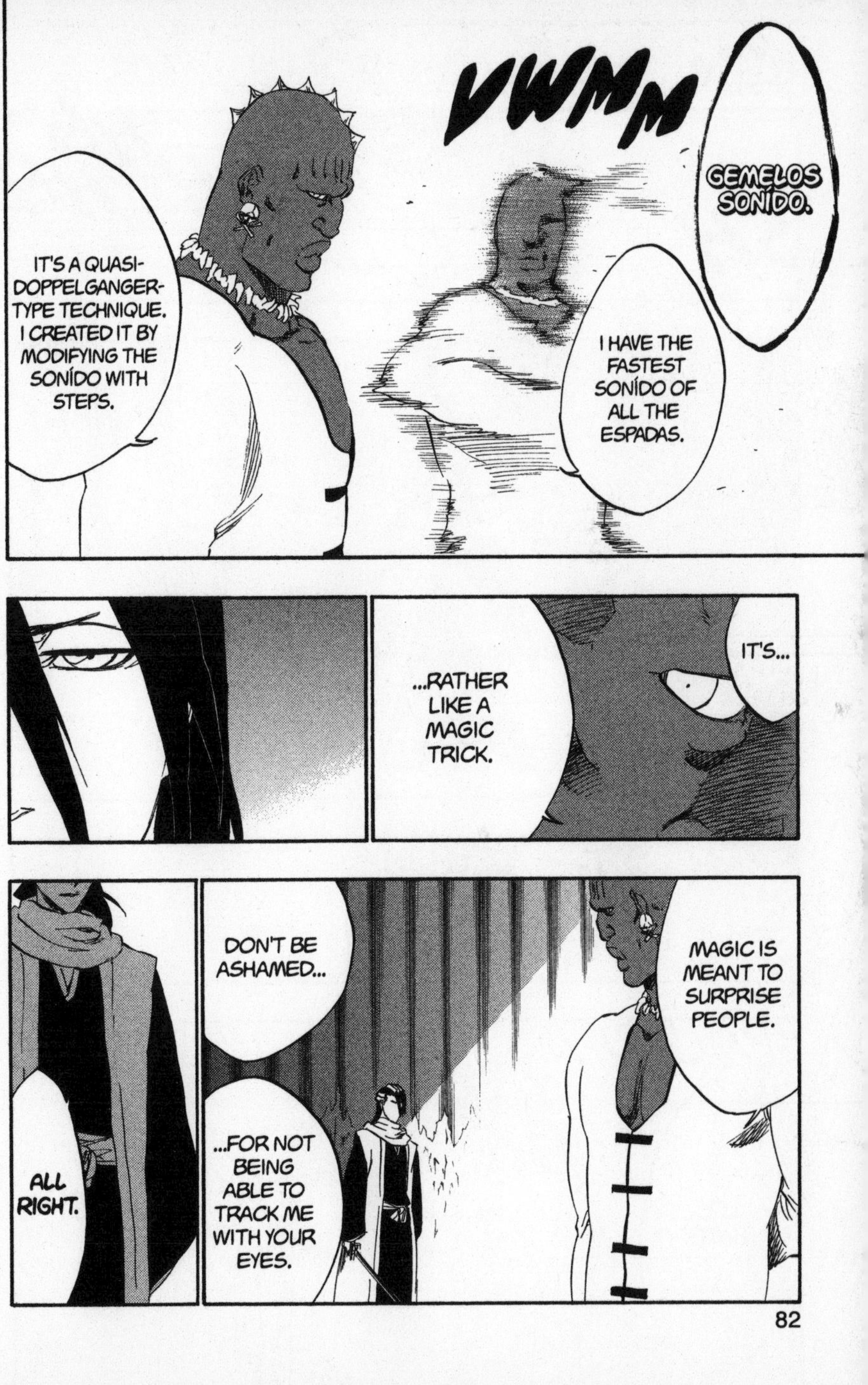
GEMELOS SONÍDO.
VWMM
I HAVE THE FASTEST SONÍDO OF ALL THE ESPADAS.
IT'S A QUASI-DOPPELGANGER-TYPE TECHNIQUE. I CREATED IT BY MODIFYING THE SONÍDO WITH STEPS.
IT'S...
...RATHER LIKE A MAGIC TRICK.
MAGIC IS MEANT TO SURPRISE PEOPLE.
DON'T BE ASHAMED...
...FOR NOT BEING ABLE TO TRACK ME WITH YOUR EYES.
ALL RIGHT.

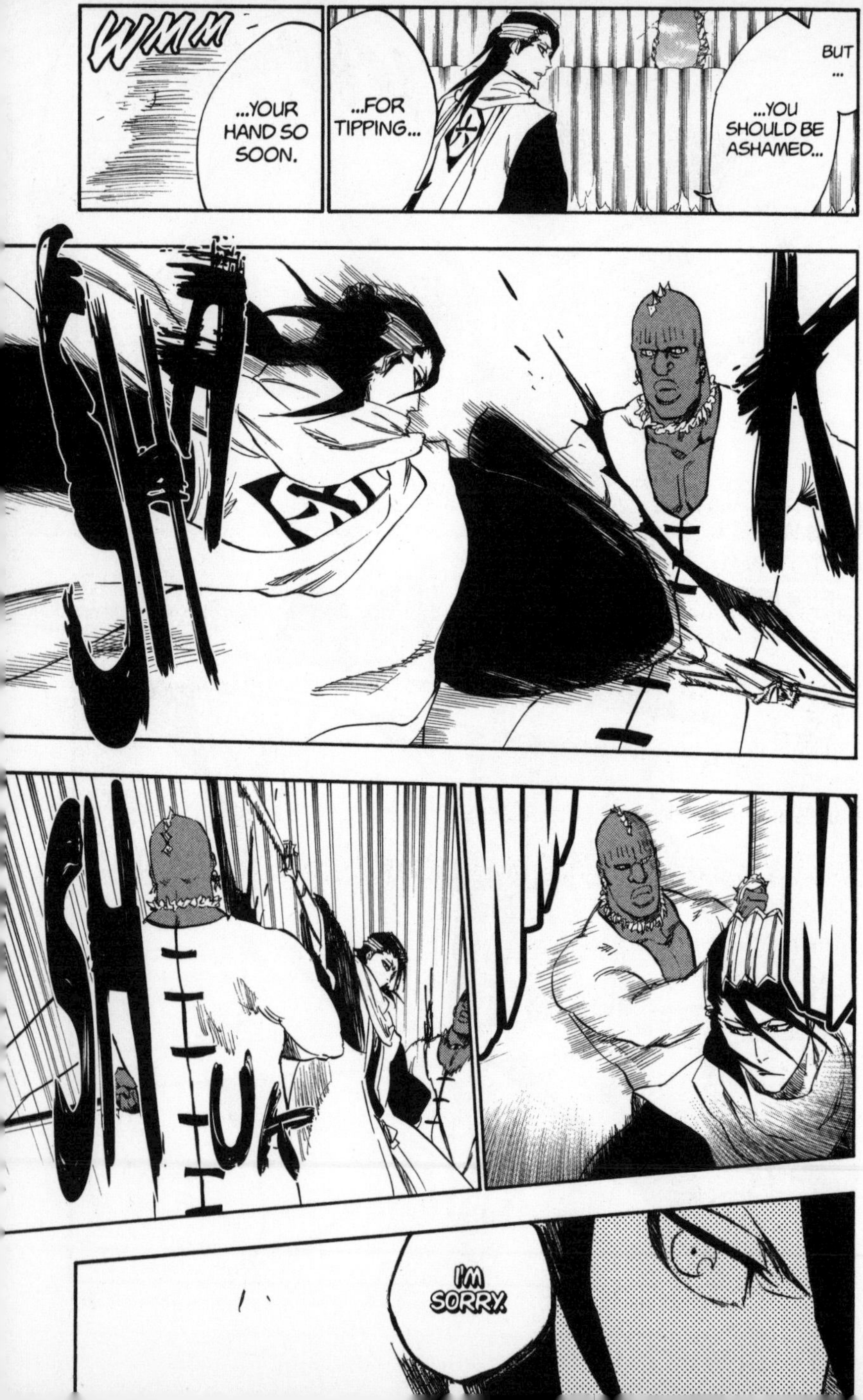
BUT ...
...YOU SHOULD BE ASHAMED...
...FOR TIPPING...
...YOUR HAND SO SOON.
WMM
I'M SORRY.

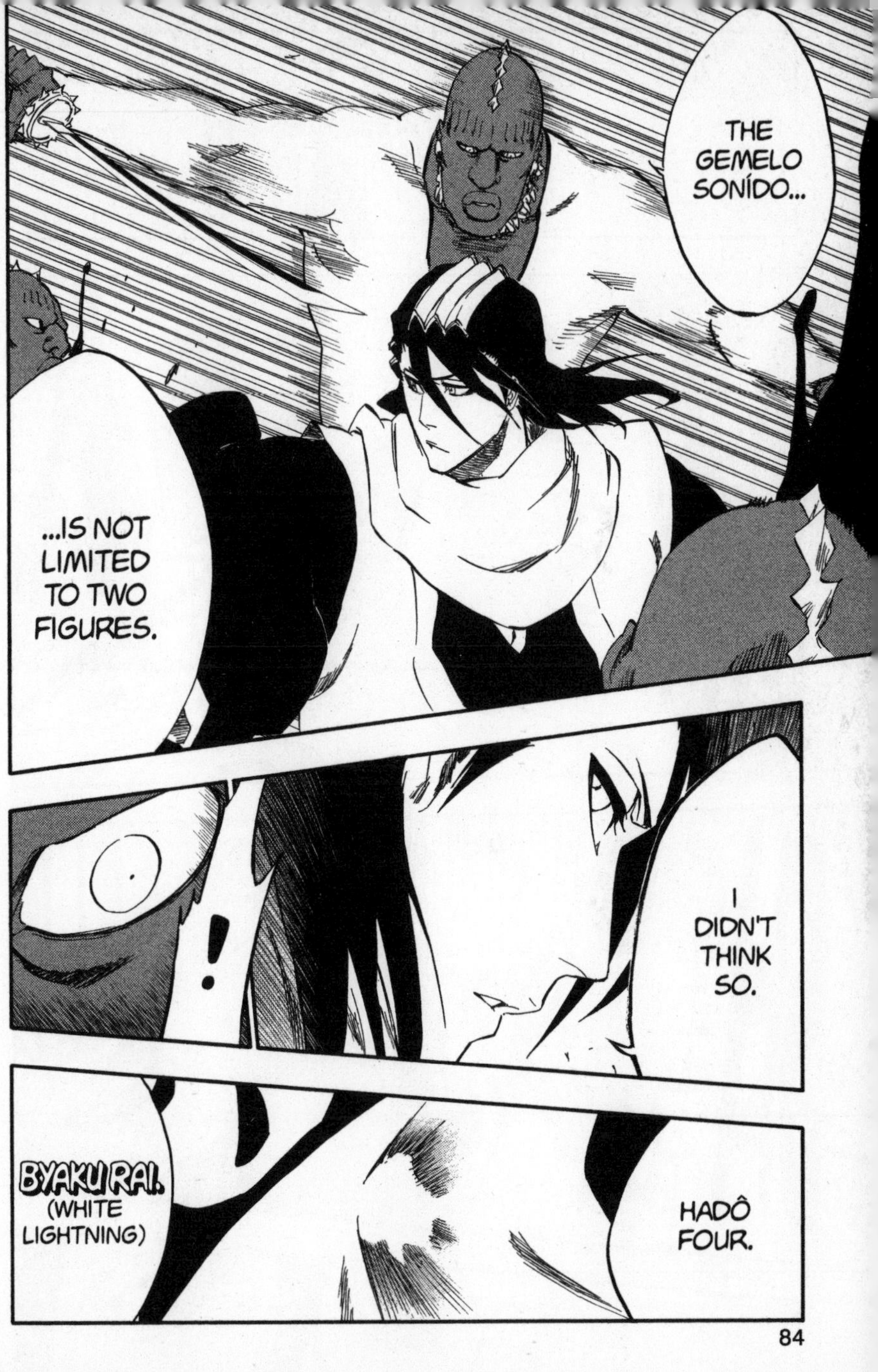
THE GEMELO SONÍDO...
...IS NOT LIMITED TO TWO FIGURES.
I DIDN'T THINK SO.
!
HADÔ FOUR.
BYAKU RAI.
(WHITE LIGHTNING)

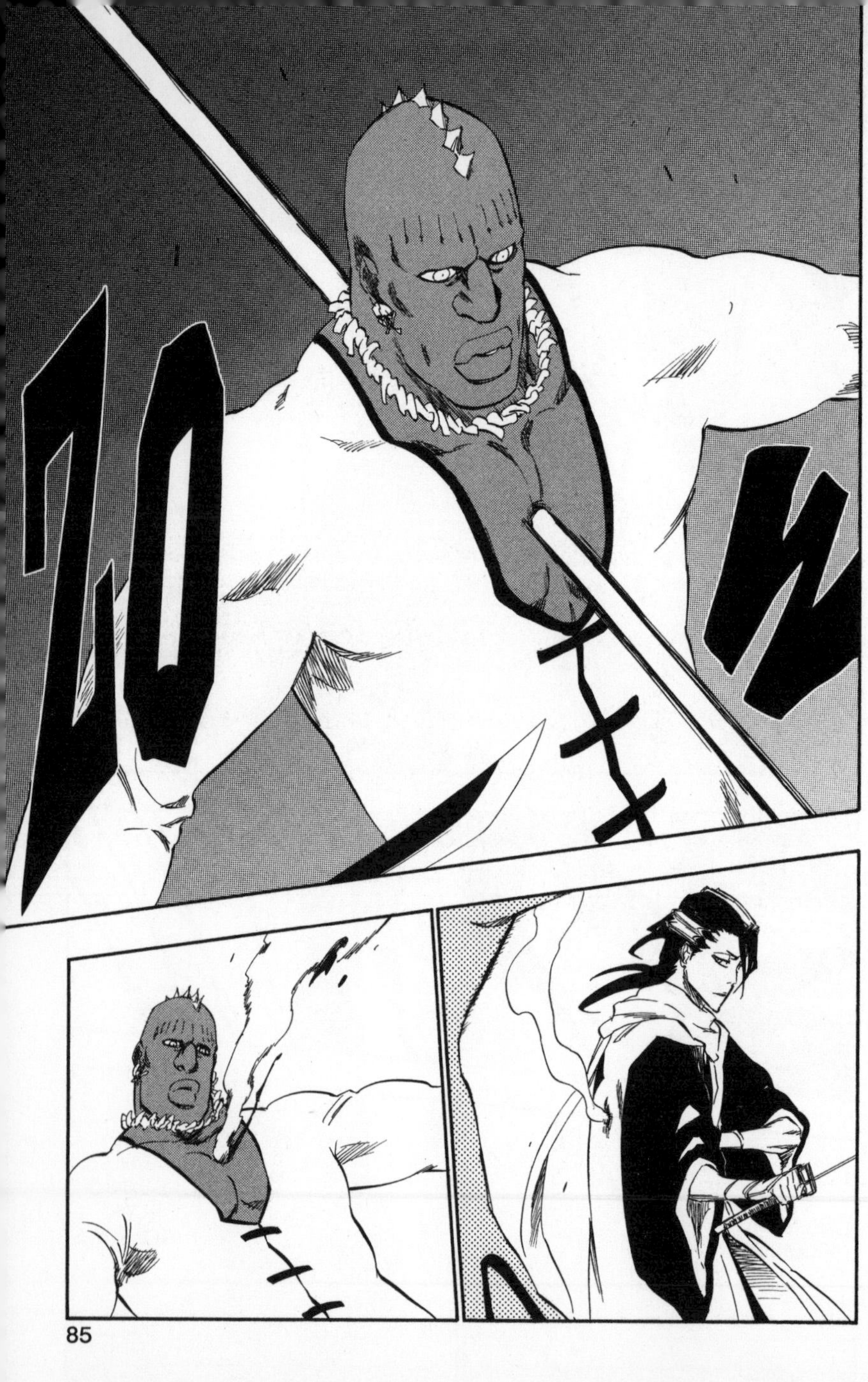

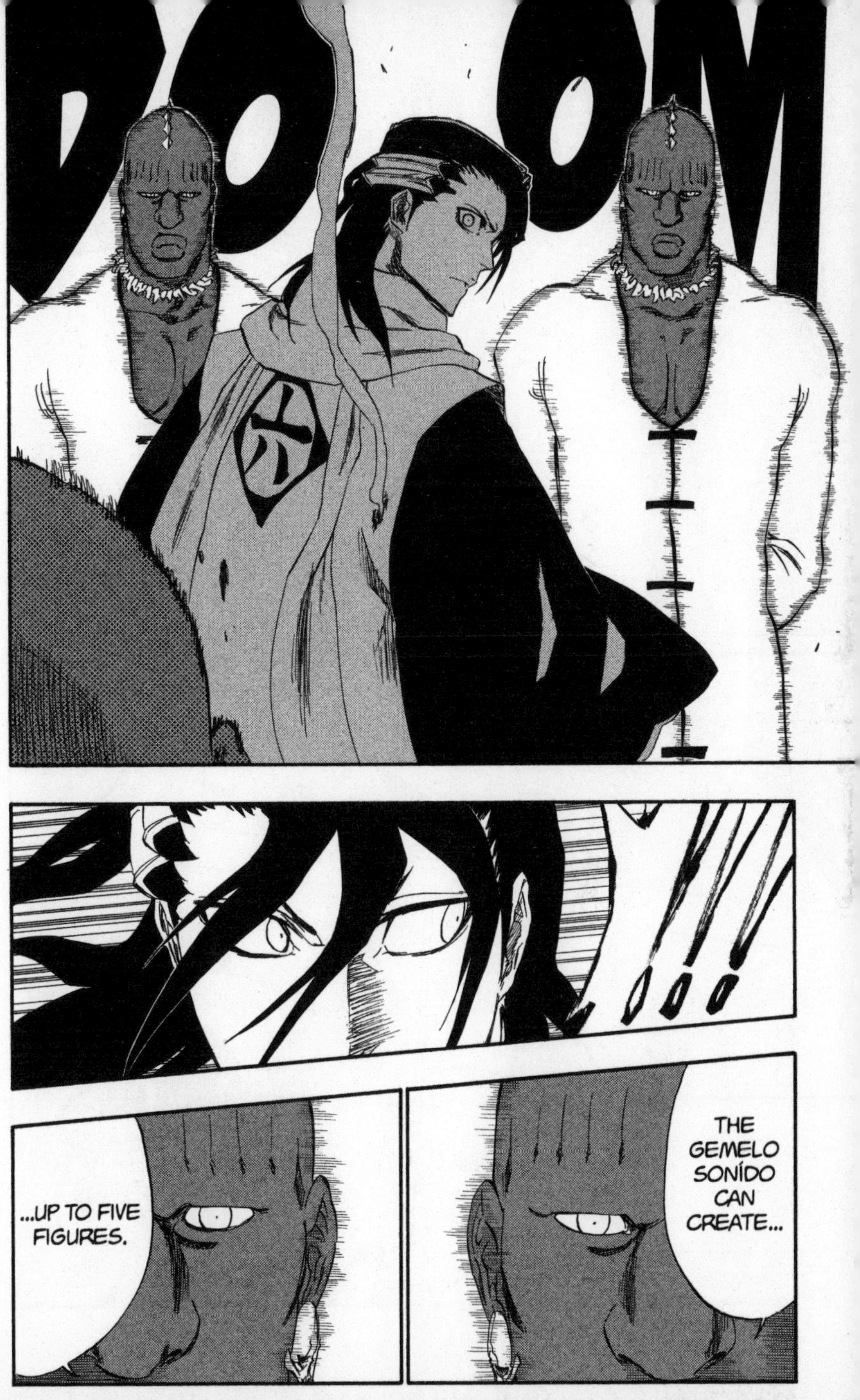
DOOM
THE GEMELO SONÍDO CAN CREATE...
...UP TO FIVE FIGURES.

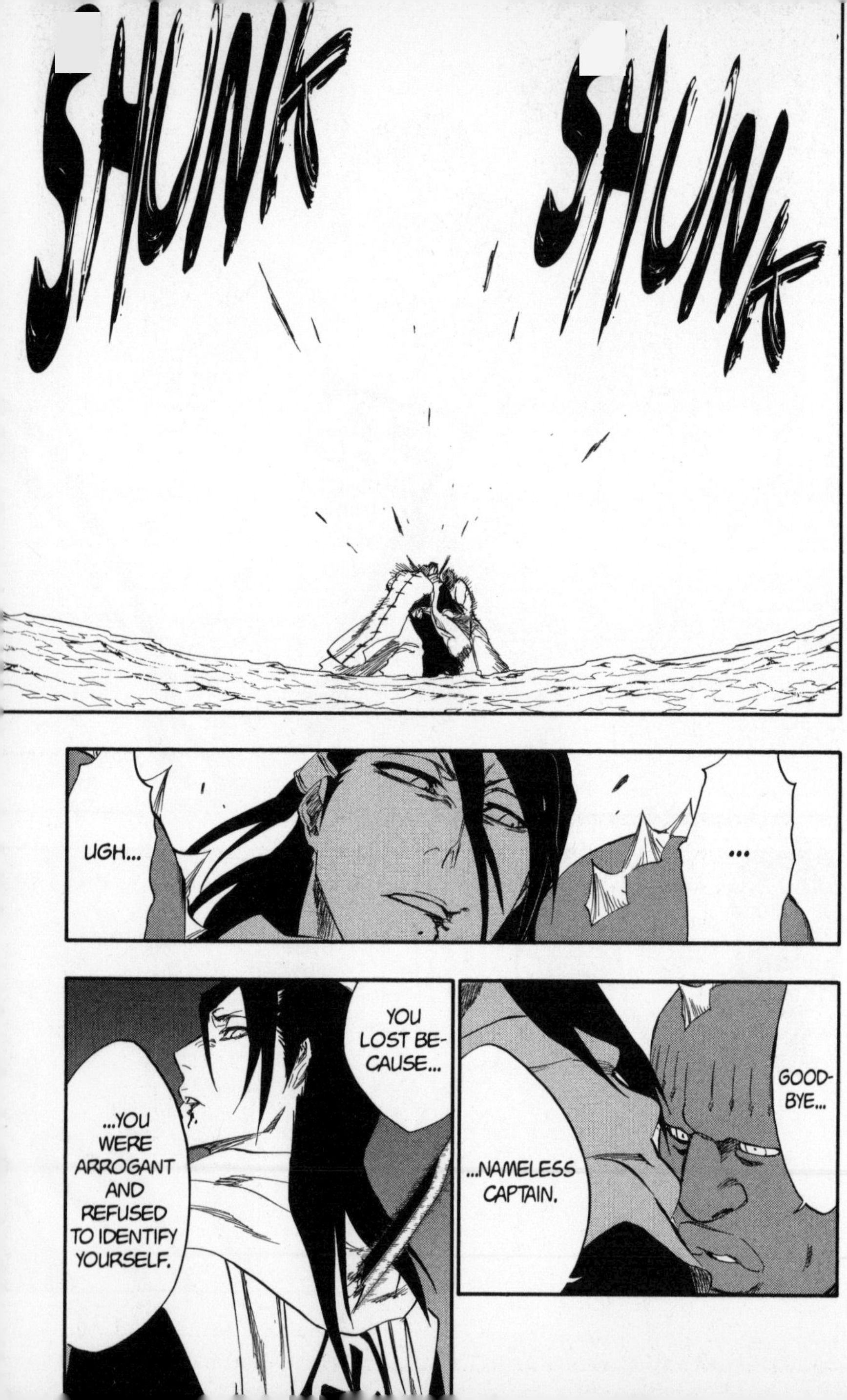
SHUNK
SHUNK
...
UGH...
GOOD-BYE...
...NAMELESS CAPTAIN.
YOU LOST BE-CAUSE...
...YOU WERE ARROGANT AND REFUSED TO IDENTIFY YOURSELF.

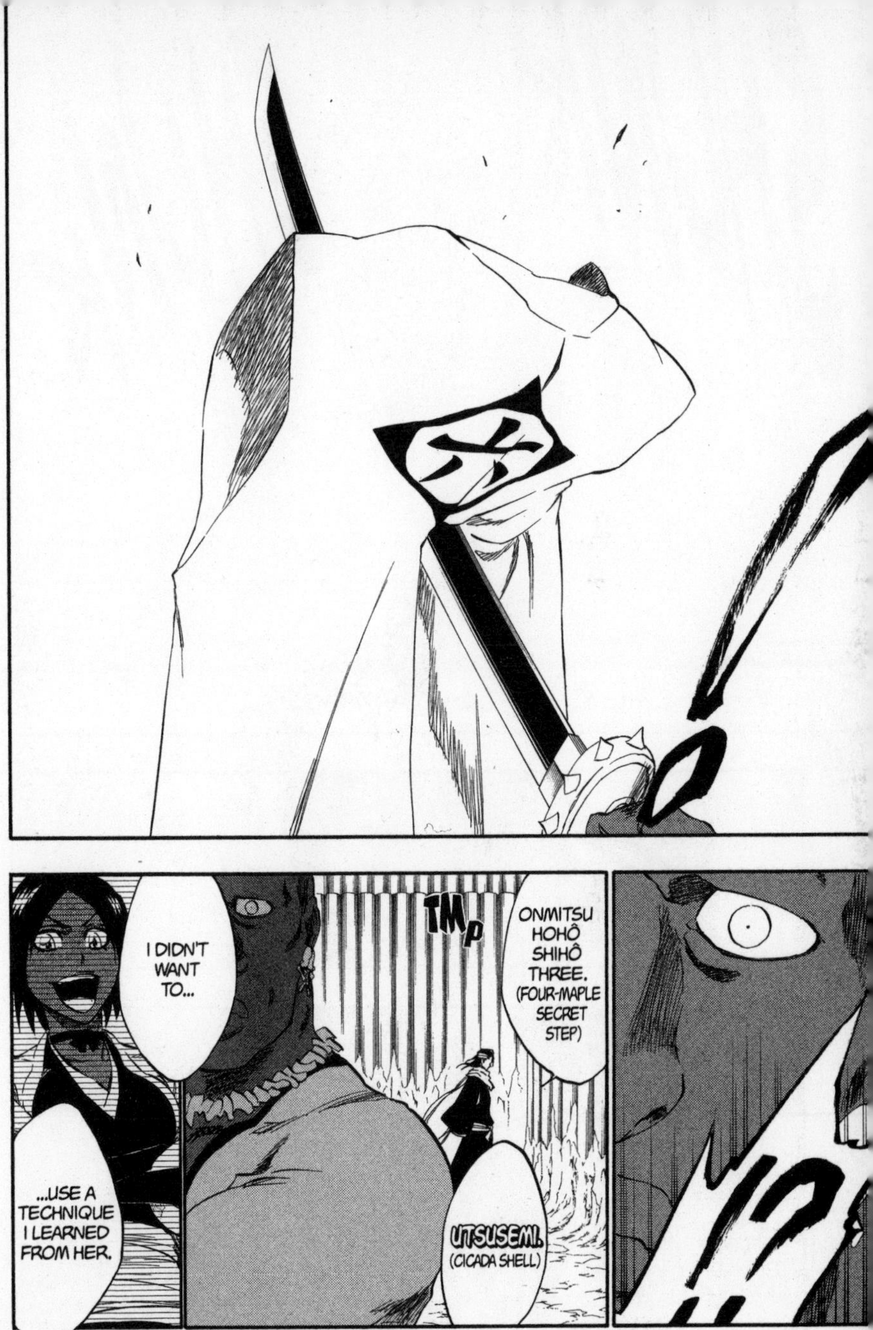

!?
ONMITSU HOHÔ SHIHÔ THREE.
(FOUR-MAPLE SECRET STEP)
TMP
I DIDN'T WANT TO...
UTSUSEMI.
(CICADA SHELL)
...USE A TECHNIQUE I LEARNED FROM HER.

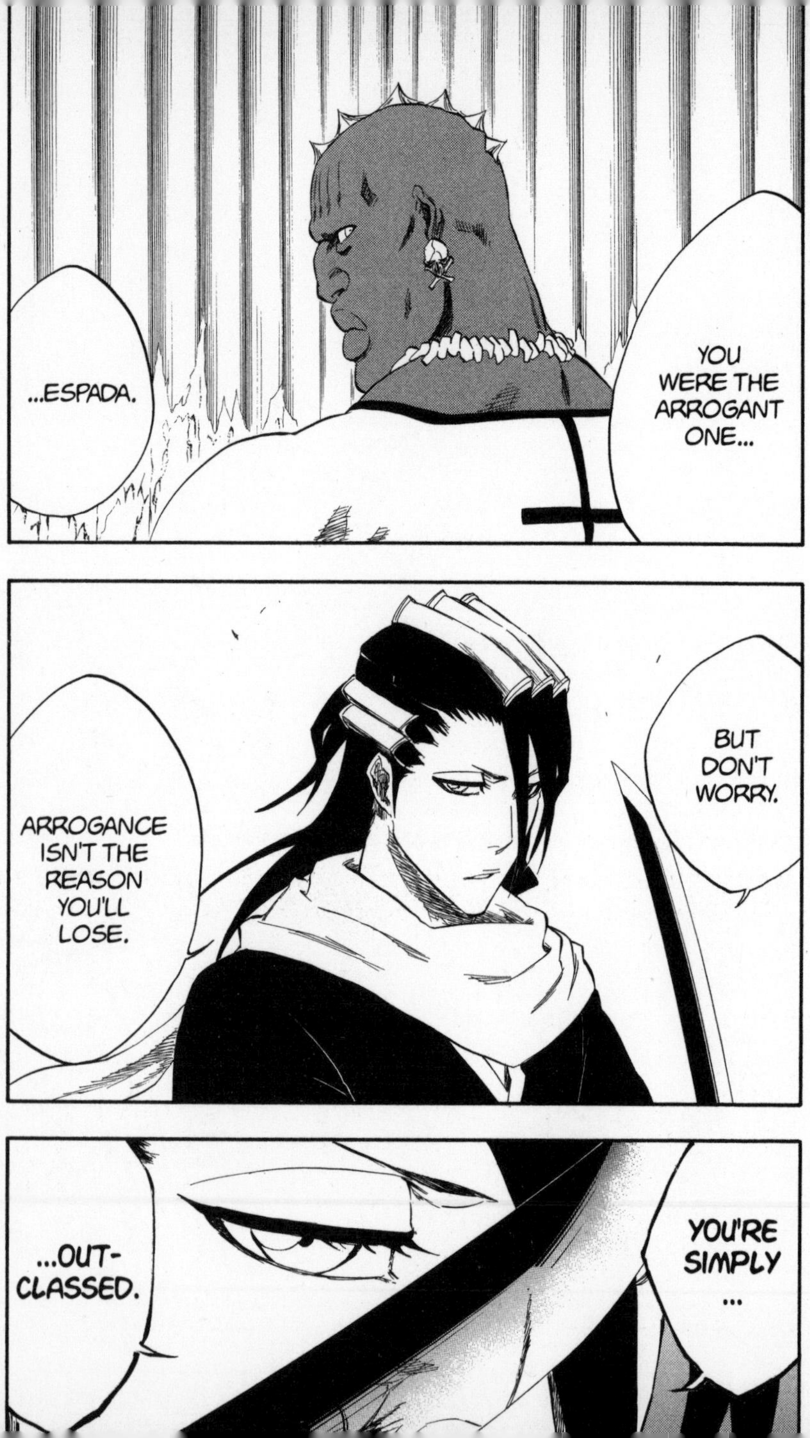
YOU WERE THE ARROGANT ONE...
...ESPADA.
BUT DON'T WORRY.
ARROGANCE ISN'T THE REASON YOU'LL LOSE.
YOU'RE SIMPLY ...
...OUT-CLASSED.

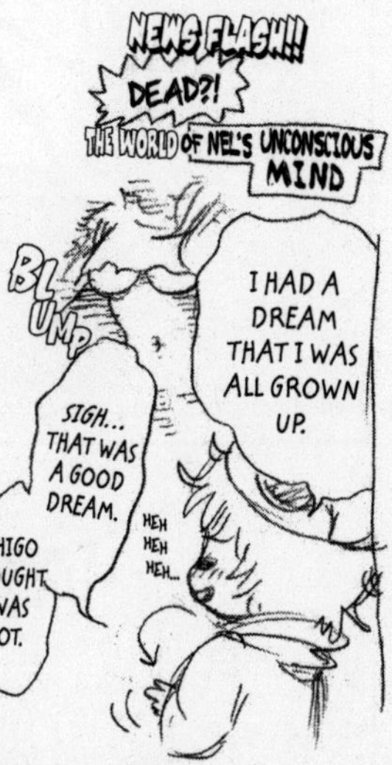
NEWS FLASH!!
DEAD?!
THE WORLD OF NEL'S UNCONSCIOUS MIND
I HAD A DREAM THAT I WAS ALL GROWN UP.
BLUMP
SIGH... THAT WAS A GOOD DREAM.
HEH HEH HEH...
ICHIGO THOUGHT I WAS HOT.

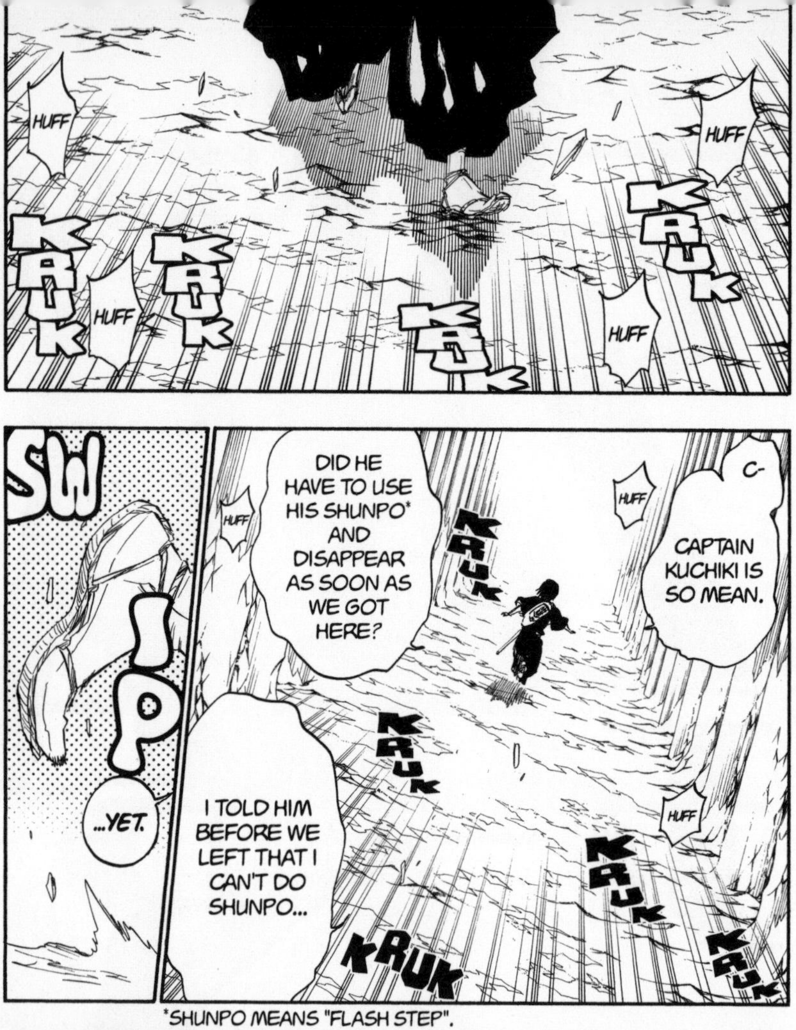
HUFF
KRUK
HUFF
KRUK
KRUK
KRUK
HUFF
KRUK
HUFF
C-
CAPTAIN KUCHIKI IS SO MEAN.
HUFF
HUFF
DID HE HAVE TO USE HIS SHUNPO* AND DISAPPEAR AS SOON AS WE GOT HERE?
HUFF
KRUK
KRUK
KRUK
KRUK
KRUK
I TOLD HIM BEFORE WE LEFT THAT I CAN'T DO SHUNPO...
SWIP
...YET.

*SHUNPO MEANS "FLASH STEP".

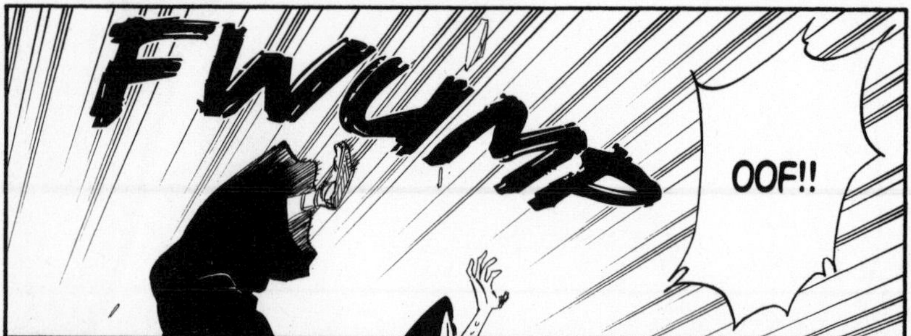
OOF!!
FWUMP

300. Curse Named Love

BLEACH. 300. Curse Named Love

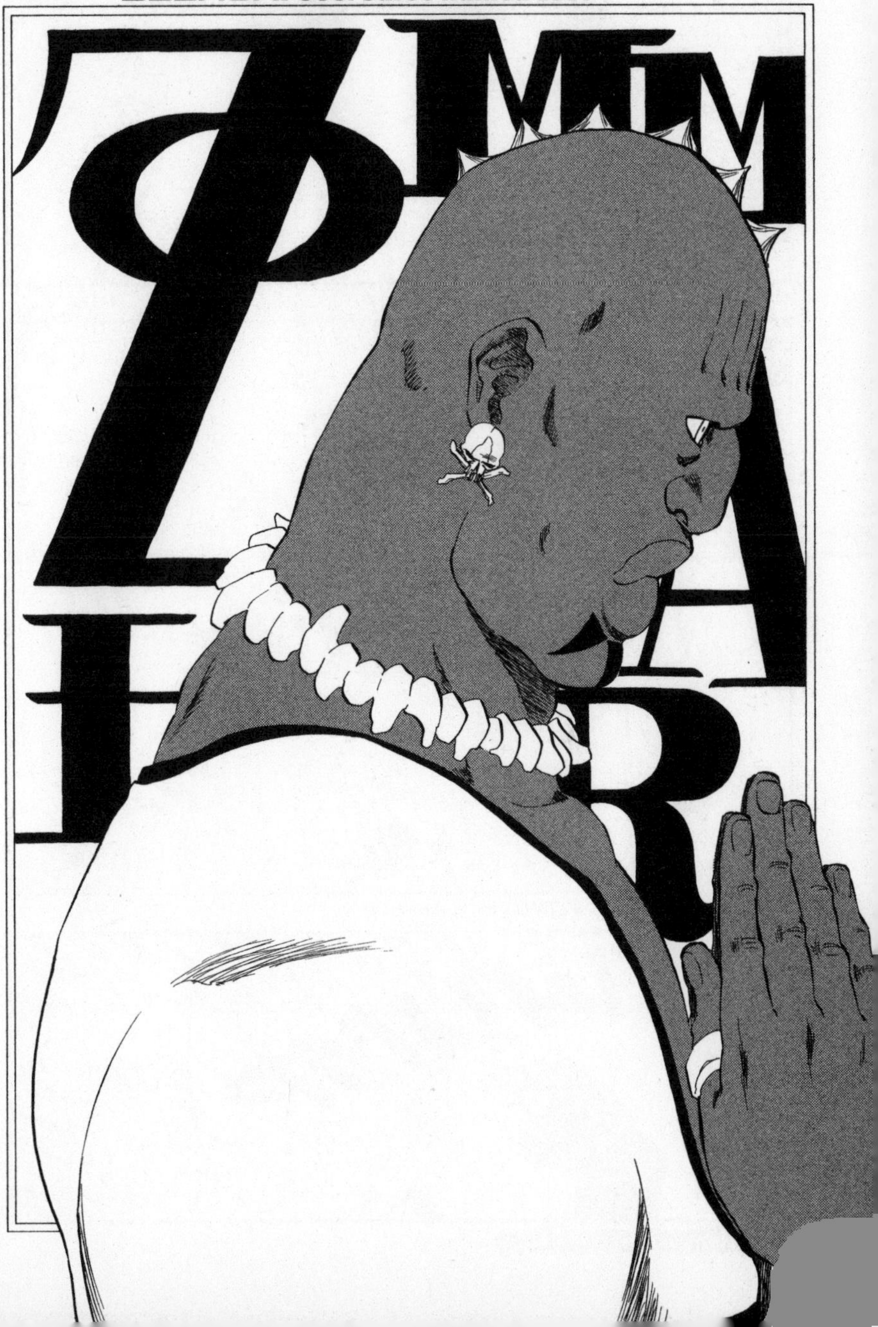

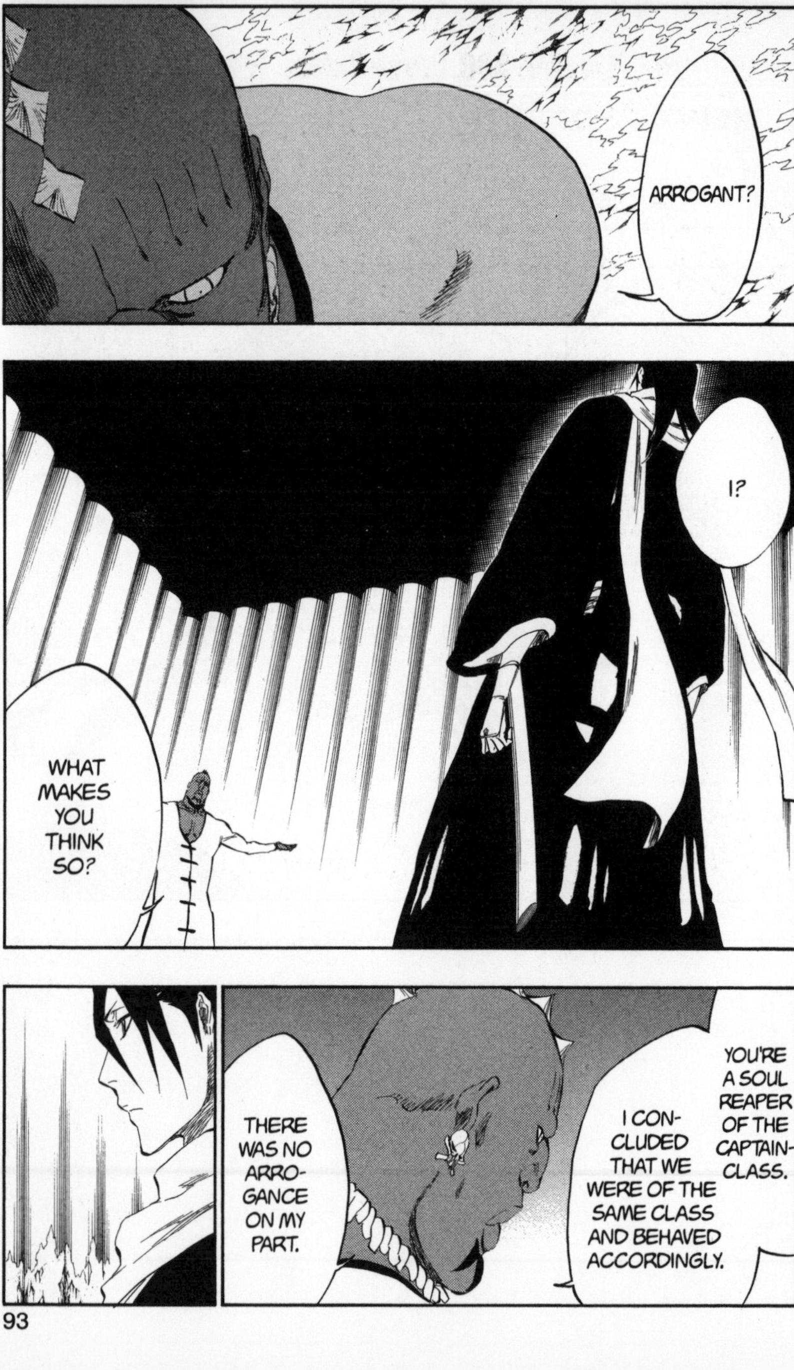
ARROGANT?
I?
WHAT MAKES YOU THINK SO?
YOU'RE A SOUL REAPER OF THE CAPTAIN-CLASS.
I CON-CLUDED THAT WE WERE OF THE SAME CLASS AND BEHAVED ACCORDINGLY.
THERE WAS NO ARRO-GANCE ON MY PART.

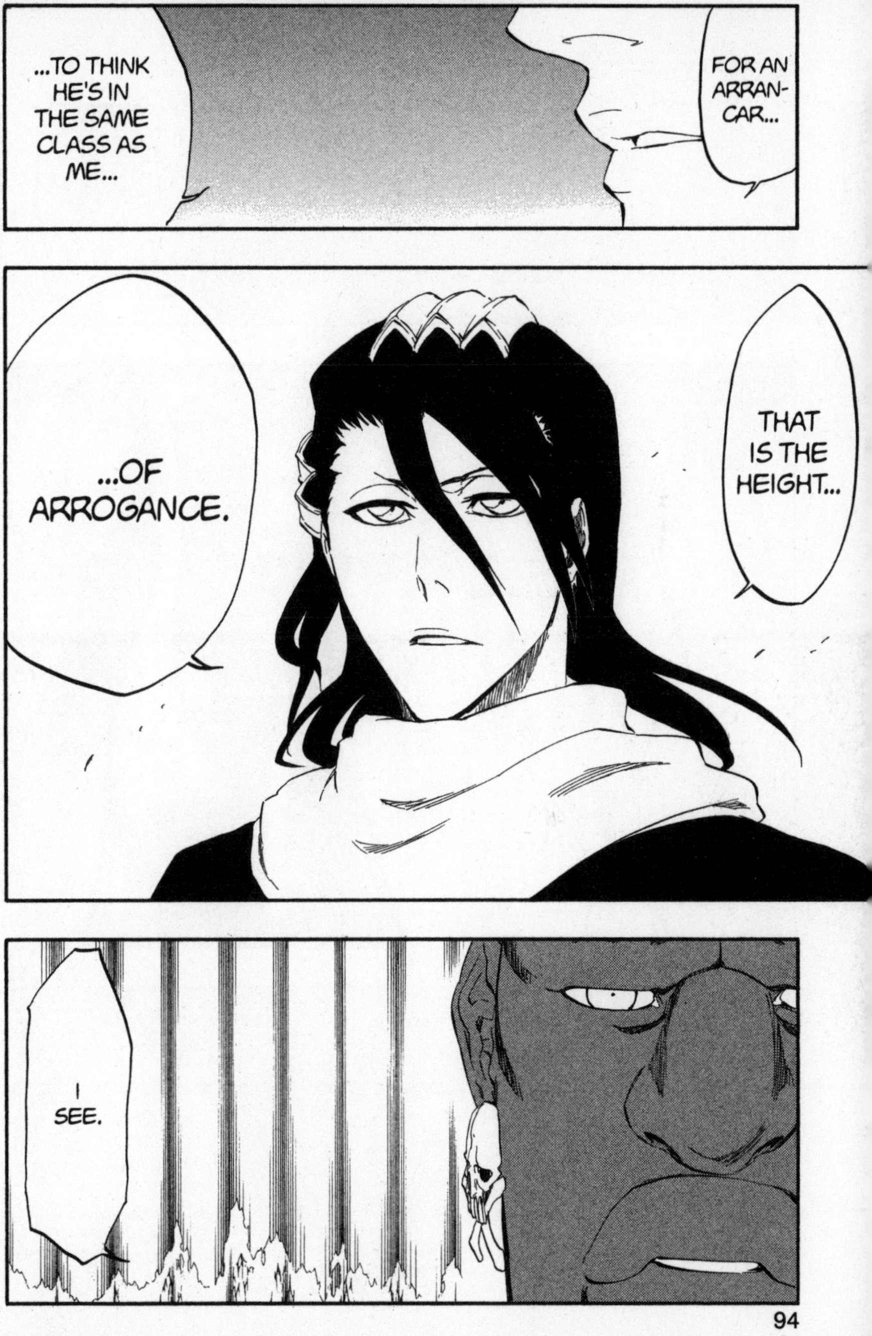
FOR AN ARRAN-CAR...
...TO THINK HE'S IN THE SAME CLASS AS ME...
THAT IS THE HEIGHT...
...OF ARROGANCE.
I SEE.

READ THIS WAY

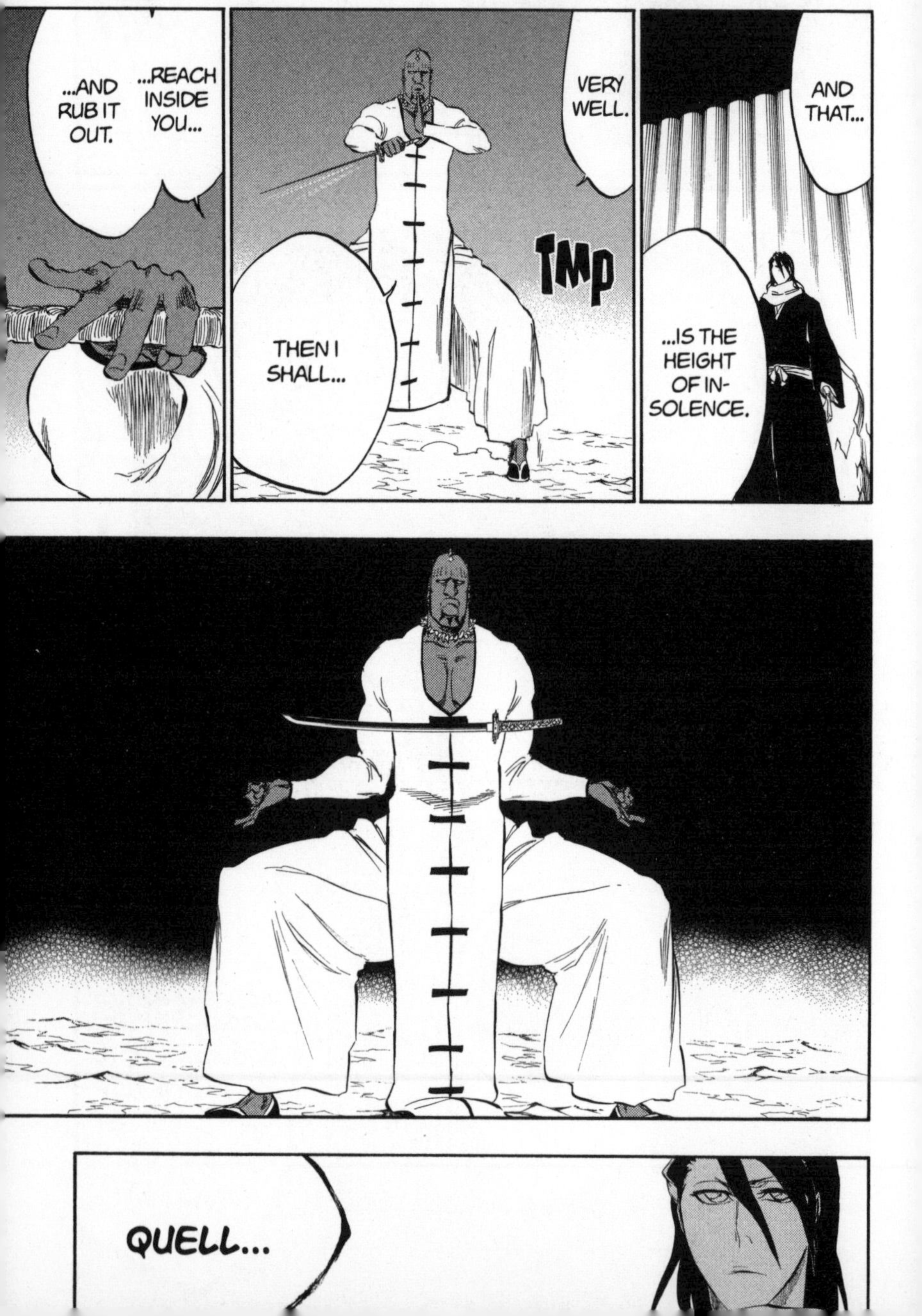
AND THAT...
...IS THE HEIGHT OF IN-SOLENCE.
VERY WELL.
THEN I SHALL...
TMP
...REACH INSIDE YOU...
...AND RUB IT OUT.
QUELL...

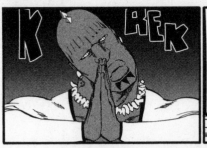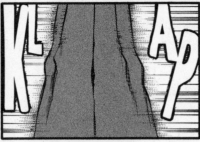

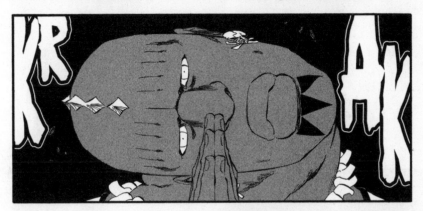

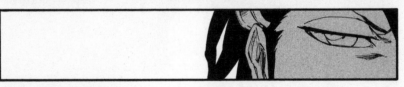

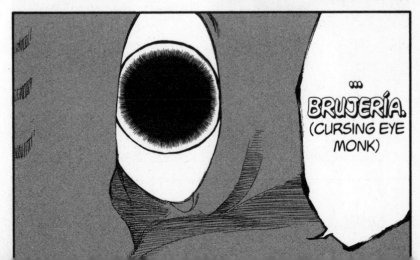

...
BRUJERÍA.
(CURSING EYE
MONK)

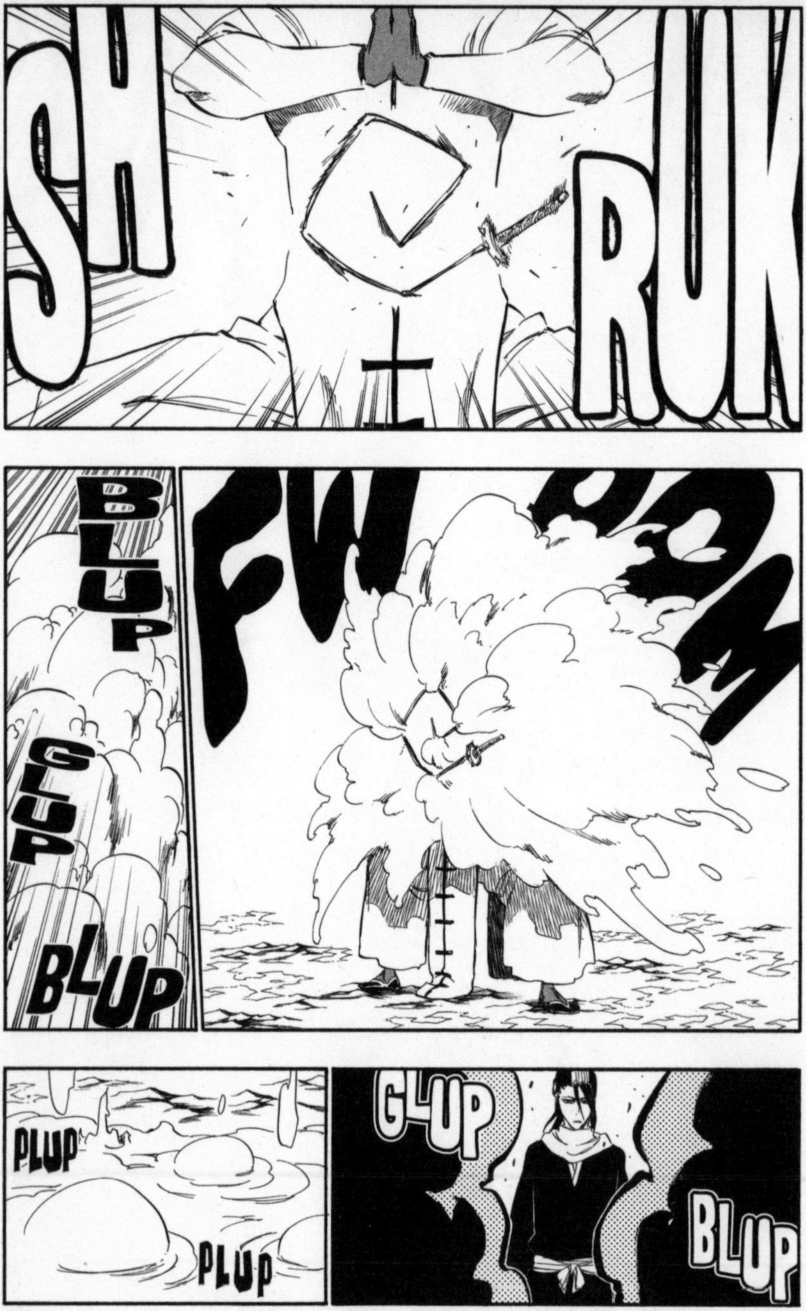
SHRUK
FWOOM
BLUP
GLUP
BLUP
GLUP
BLUP
PLUP
PLUP

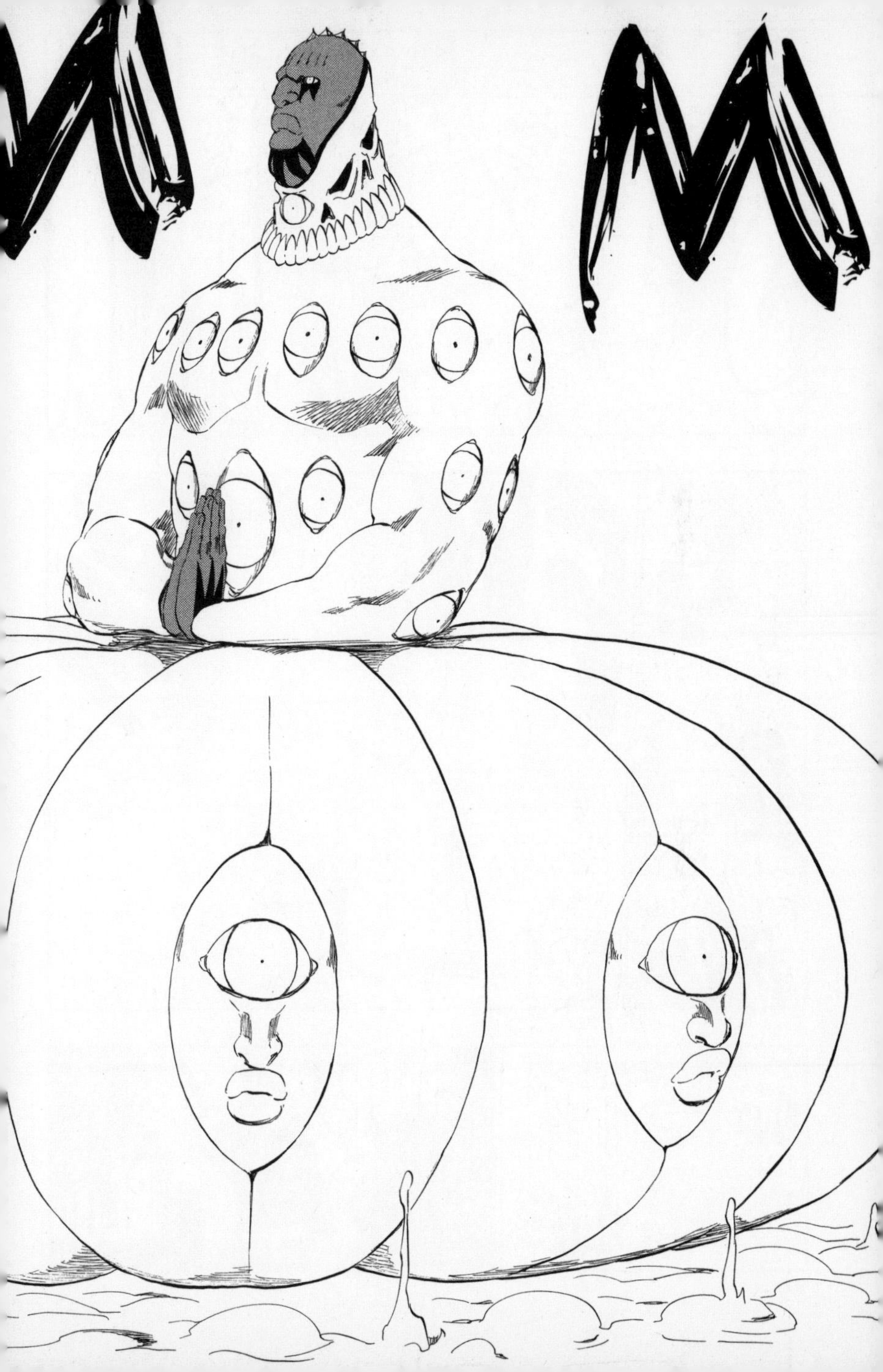
M
M

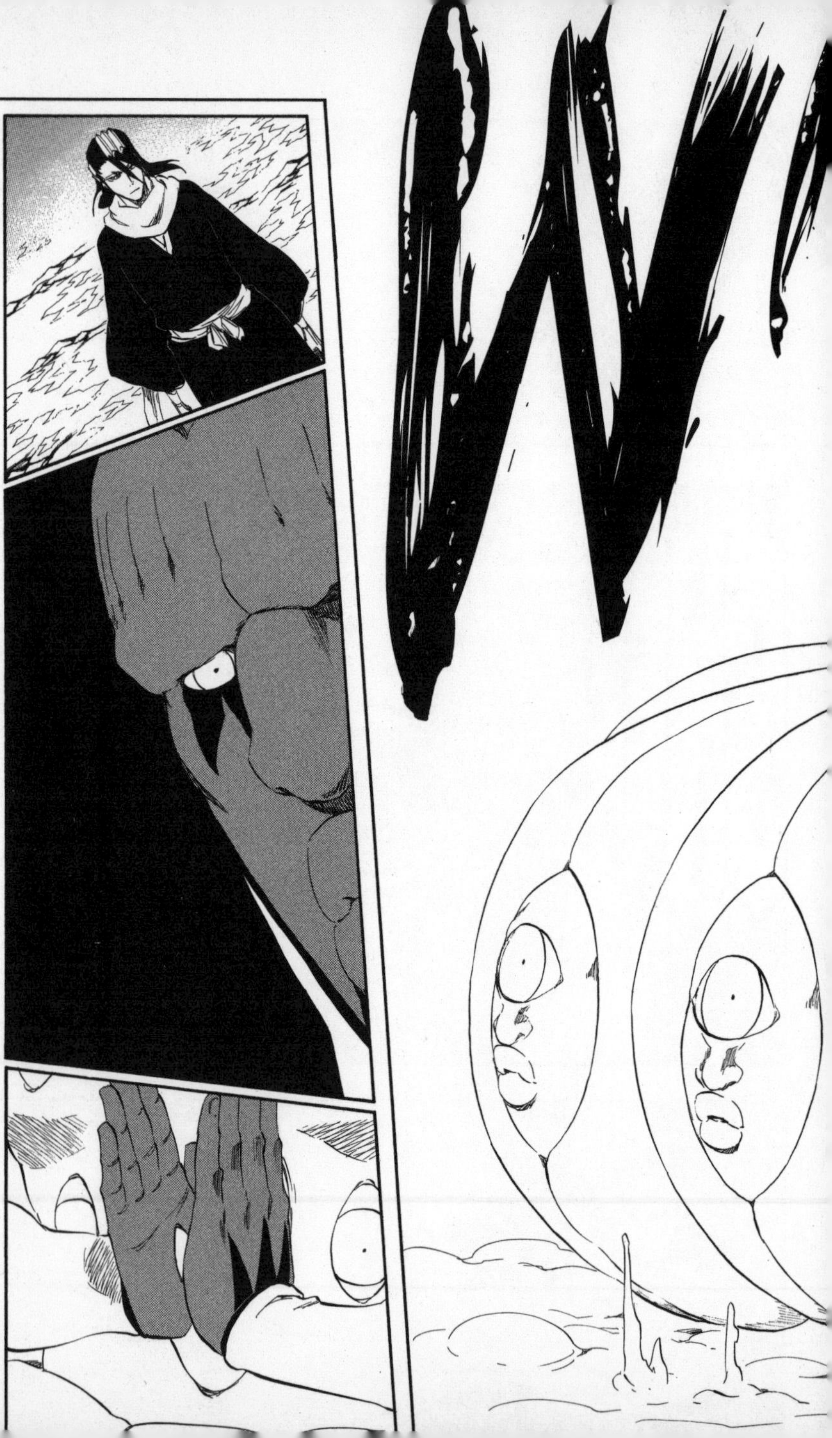

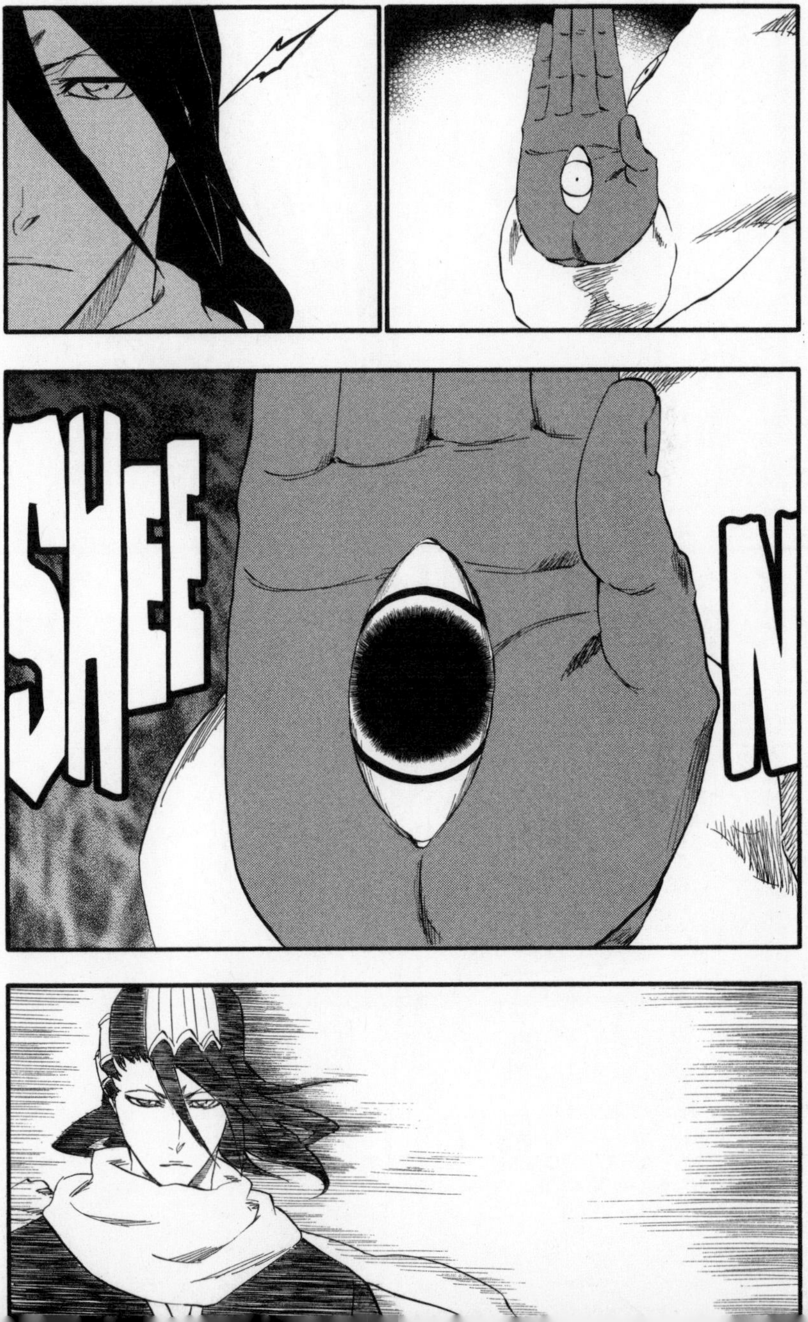
SHEE N

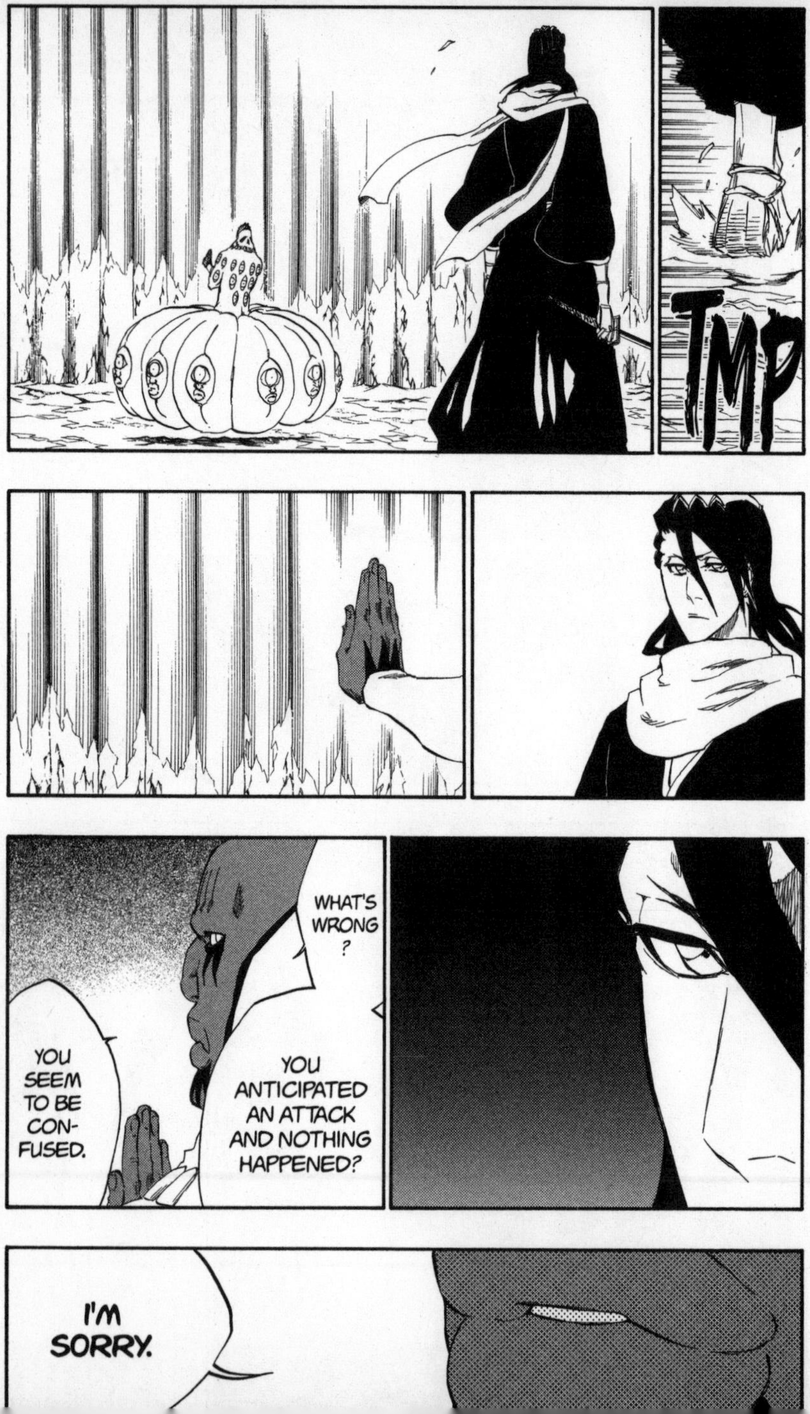
TMP
WHAT'S WRONG?
YOU ANTICIPATED AN ATTACK AND NOTHING HAPPENED?
YOU SEEM TO BE CON-FUSED.
I'M SORRY.

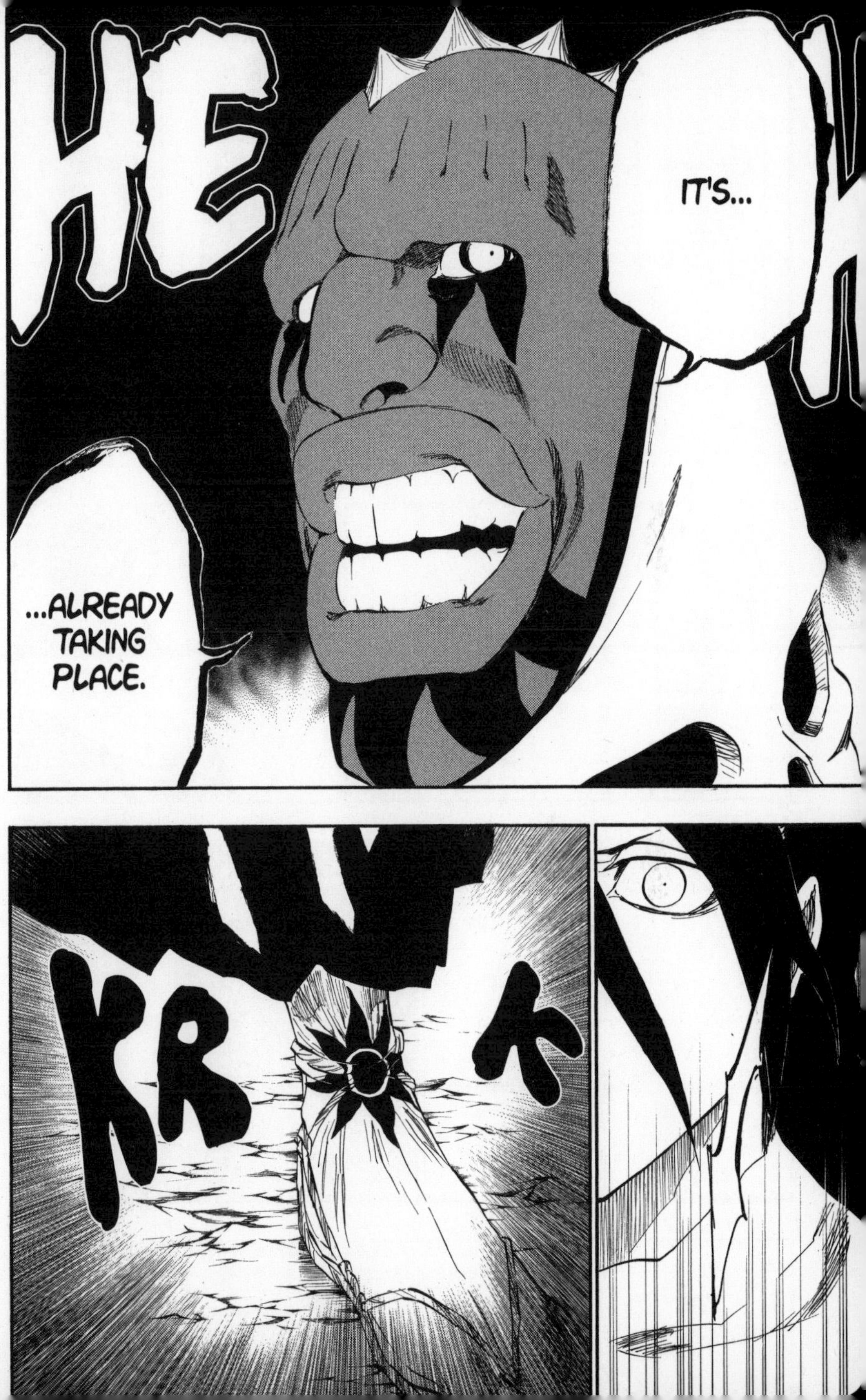
HE
IT'S...
...ALREADY TAKING PLACE.
KRK

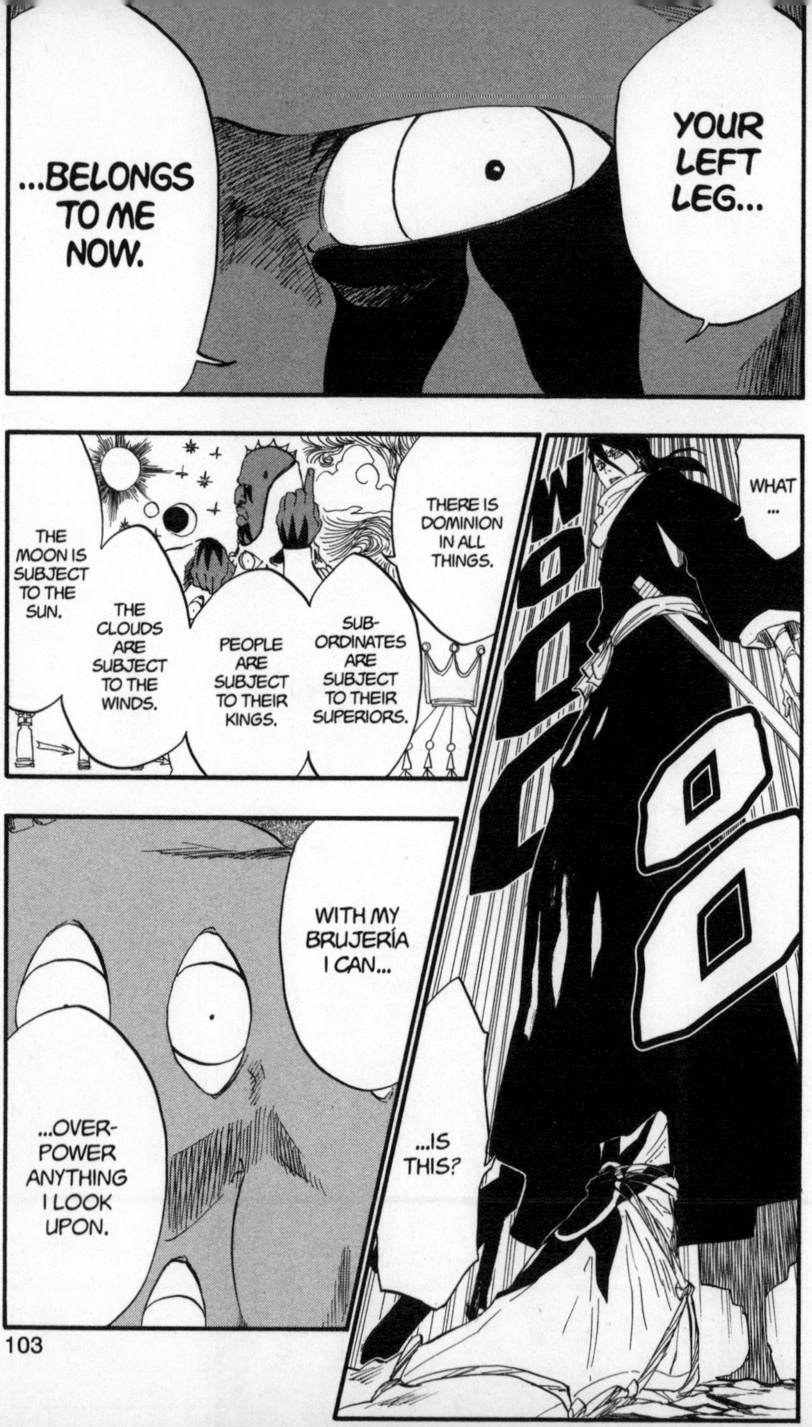

YOUR LEFT LEG...
...BELONGS TO ME NOW.
WHAT ...
...IS THIS?
THERE IS DOMINION IN ALL THINGS.
SUB-ORDINATES ARE SUBJECT TO THEIR SUPERIORS.
PEOPLE ARE SUBJECT TO THEIR KINGS.
THE CLOUDS ARE SUBJECT TO THE WINDS.
THE MOON IS SUBJECT TO THE SUN.
WITH MY BRUJERÍA I CAN...
...OVER-POWER ANYTHING I LOOK UPON.

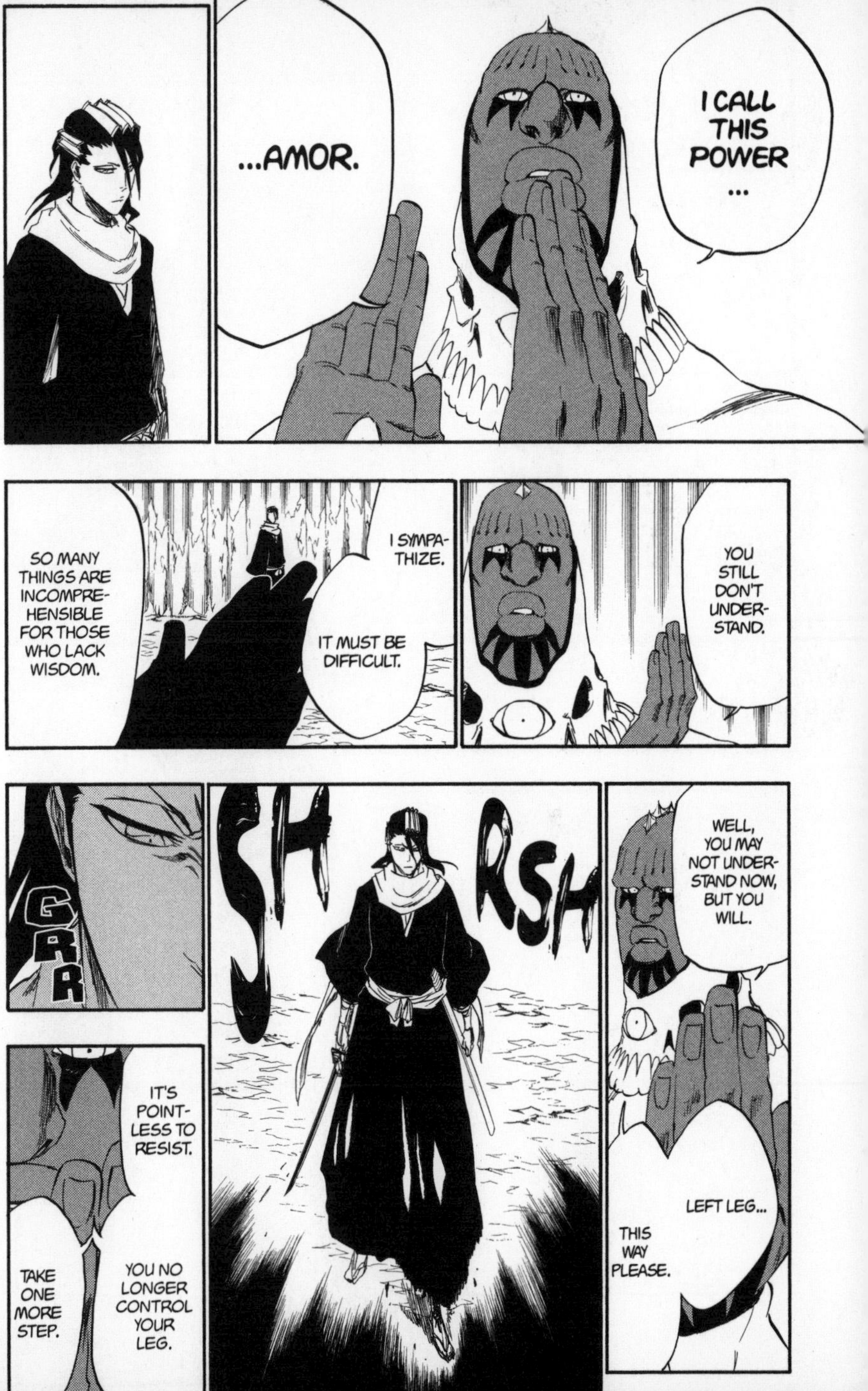
I CALL THIS POWER ...
...AMOR.
YOU STILL DON'T UNDER-STAND.
I SYMPA-THIZE.
IT MUST BE DIFFICULT.
SO MANY THINGS ARE INCOMPRE-HENSIBLE FOR THOSE WHO LACK WISDOM.
WELL, YOU MAY NOT UNDER-STAND NOW, BUT YOU WILL.
LEFT LEG...
THIS WAY PLEASE.
SH RSH
GRR
IT'S POINT-LESS TO RESIST.
YOU NO LONGER CONTROL YOUR LEG.
TAKE ONE MORE STEP.

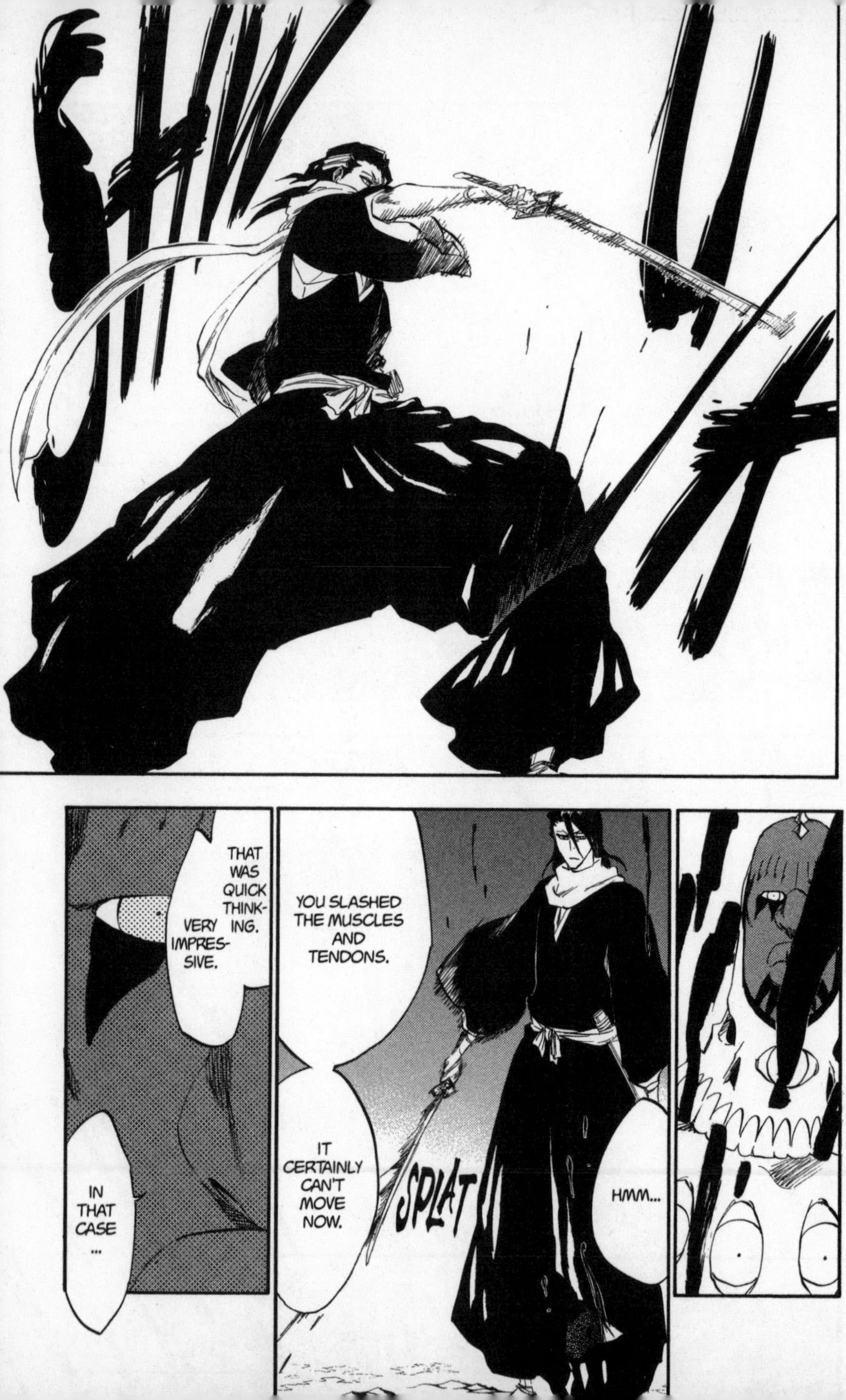
YOU SLASHED THE MUSCLES AND TENDONS.
IT CERTAINLY CAN'T MOVE NOW.
SPLAT
HMM...
THAT WAS QUICK THINKING.
VERY IMPRESSIVE.
IN THAT CASE...

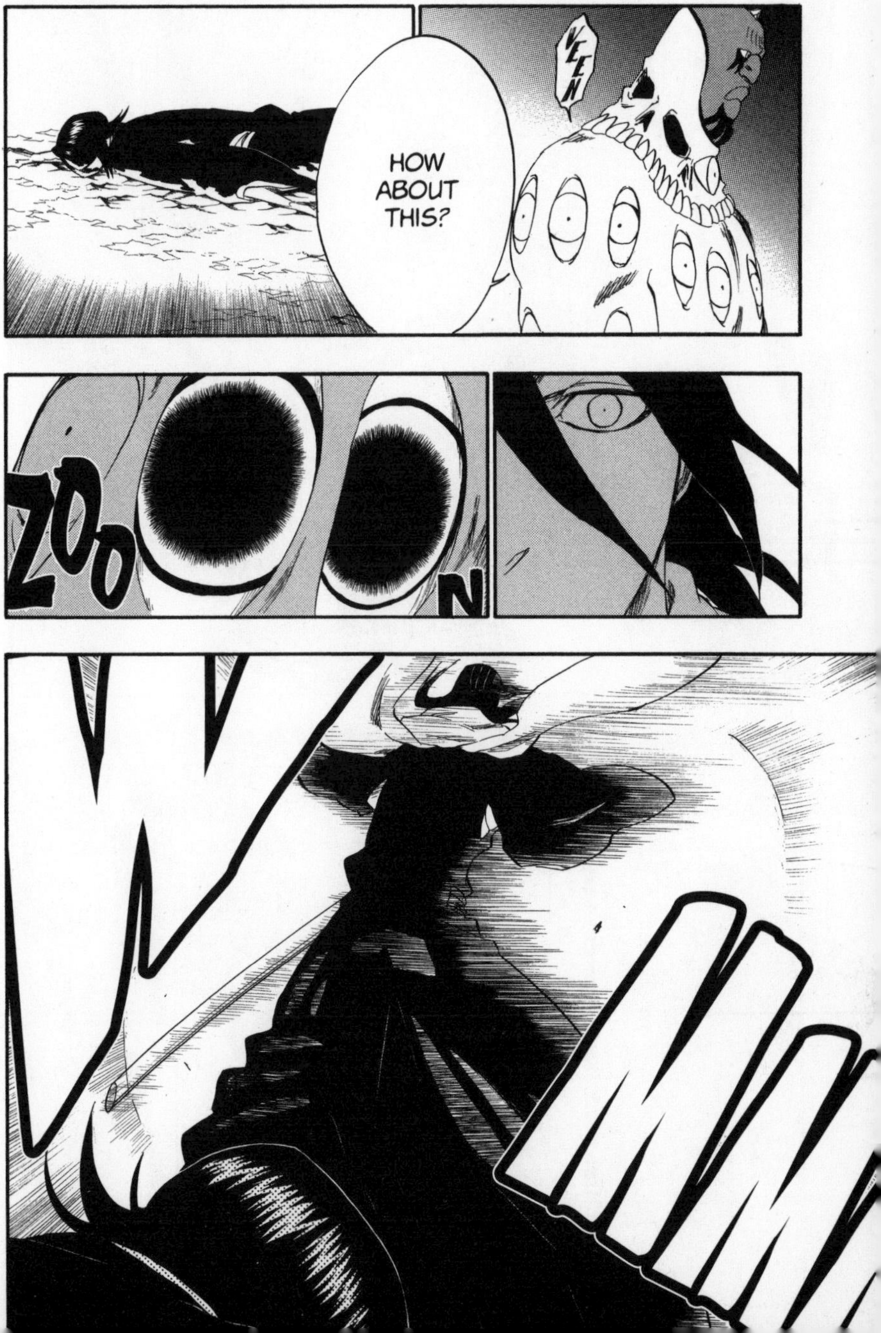
VEEN
HOW ABOUT THIS?
ZOOON

READ THIS WAY

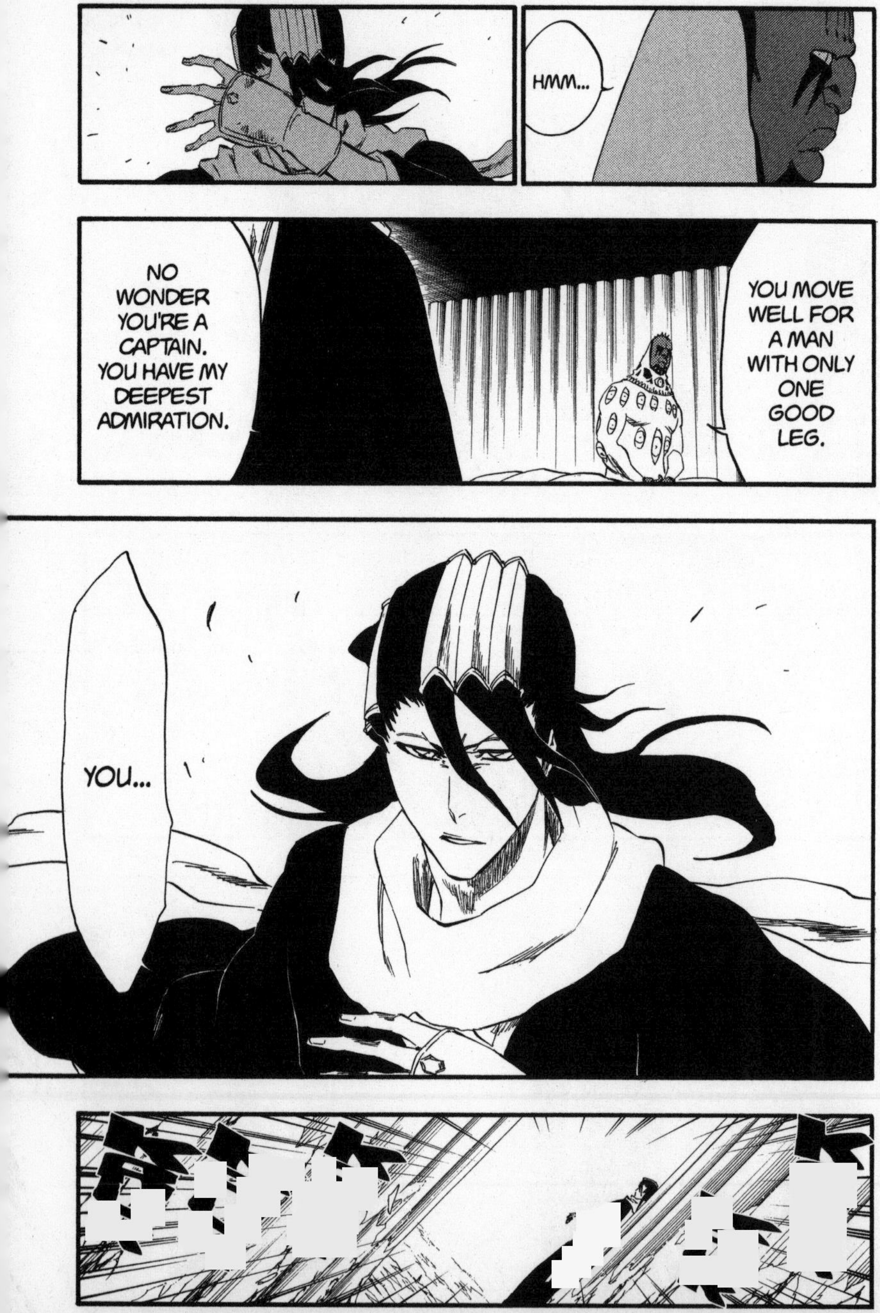
HMM...
YOU MOVE WELL FOR A MAN WITH ONLY ONE GOOD LEG.
NO WONDER YOU'RE A CAPTAIN. YOU HAVE MY DEEPEST ADMIRATION.
YOU...

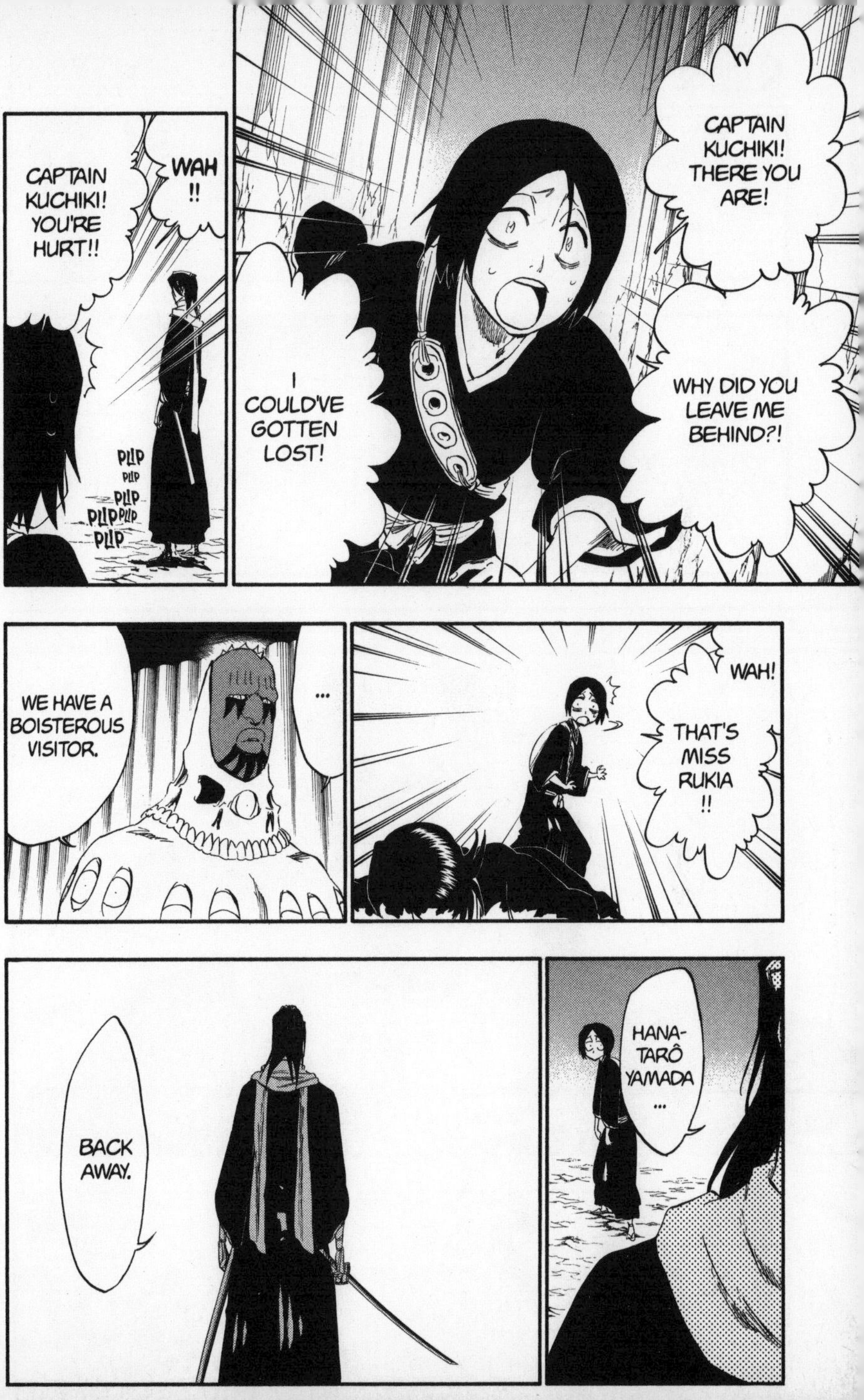
CAPTAIN KUCHIKI! THERE YOU ARE!
WHY DID YOU LEAVE ME BEHIND?!
I COULD'VE GOTTEN LOST!
WAH !!
CAPTAIN KUCHIKI! YOU'RE HURT!!
PLIP PLIP PLIP PLIP PLIP PLIP
WAH!
THAT'S MISS RUKIA !!
...
WE HAVE A BOISTEROUS VISITOR.
HANA-TARÔ YAMADA ...
BACK AWAY.

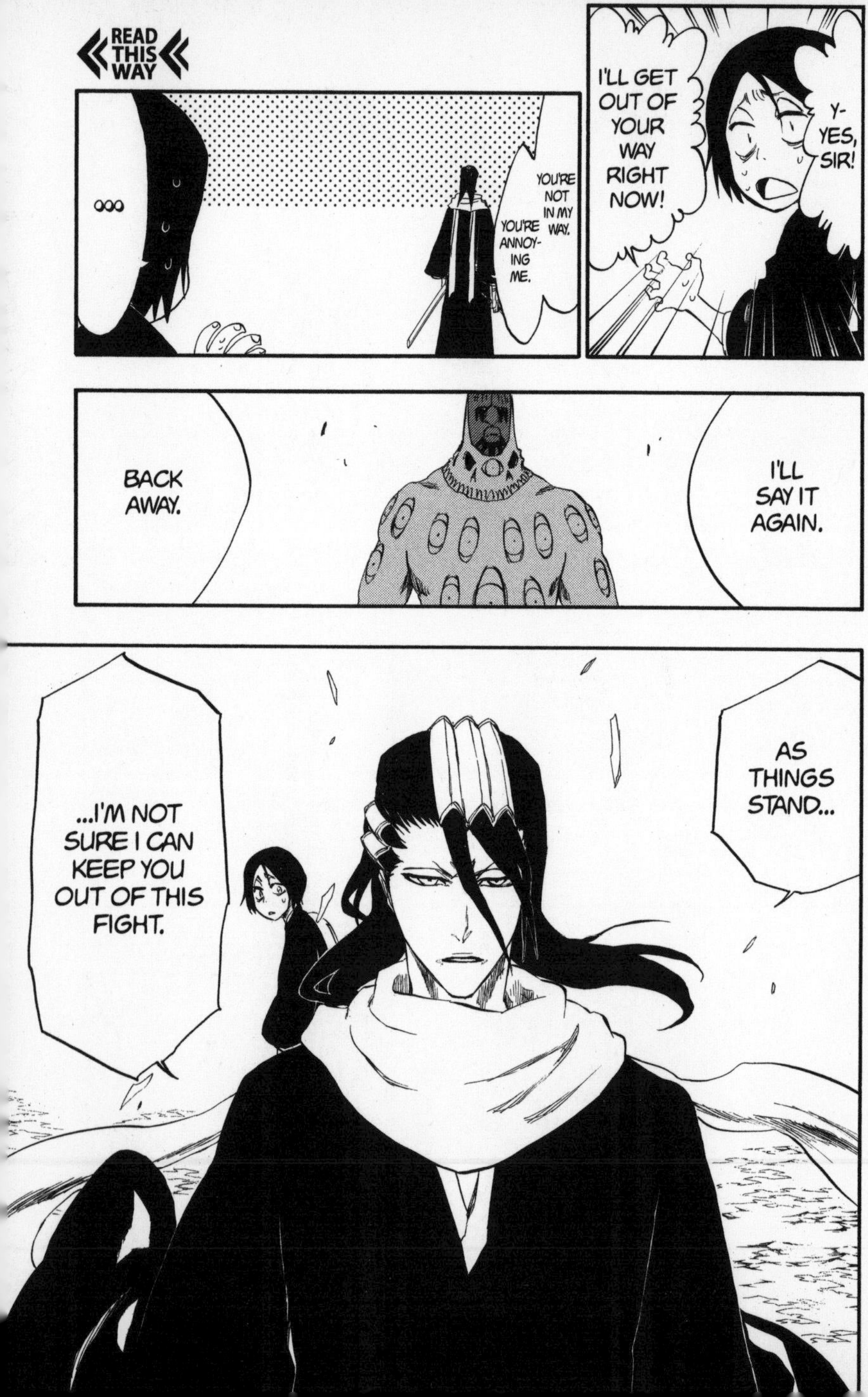
READ THIS WAY
Y-YES, SIR!
I'LL GET OUT OF YOUR WAY RIGHT NOW!
YOU'RE NOT IN MY WAY.
YOU'RE ANNOY-ING ME.
I'LL SAY IT AGAIN.
BACK AWAY.
AS THINGS STAND...
...I'M NOT SURE I CAN KEEP YOU OUT OF THIS FIGHT.

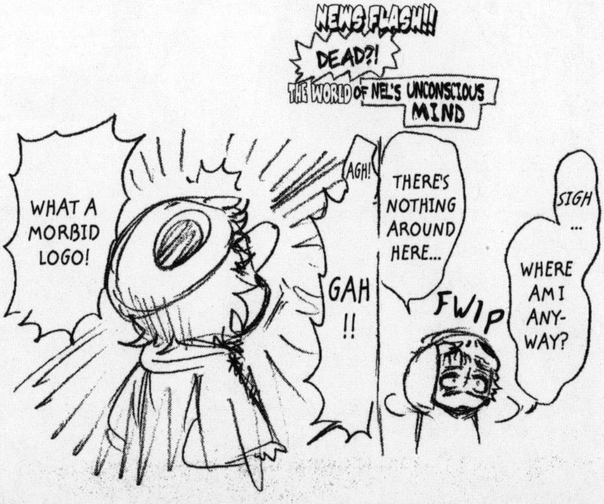
NEWS FLASH!!
DEAD?!
THE WORLD OF NEL'S UNCONSCIOUS MIND
THERE'S NOTHING AROUND HERE...
SIGH...
WHERE AM I ANY-WAY?
FWIP
AGH!
GAH !!
WHAT A MORBID LOGO!

301. Nothing Like Equal

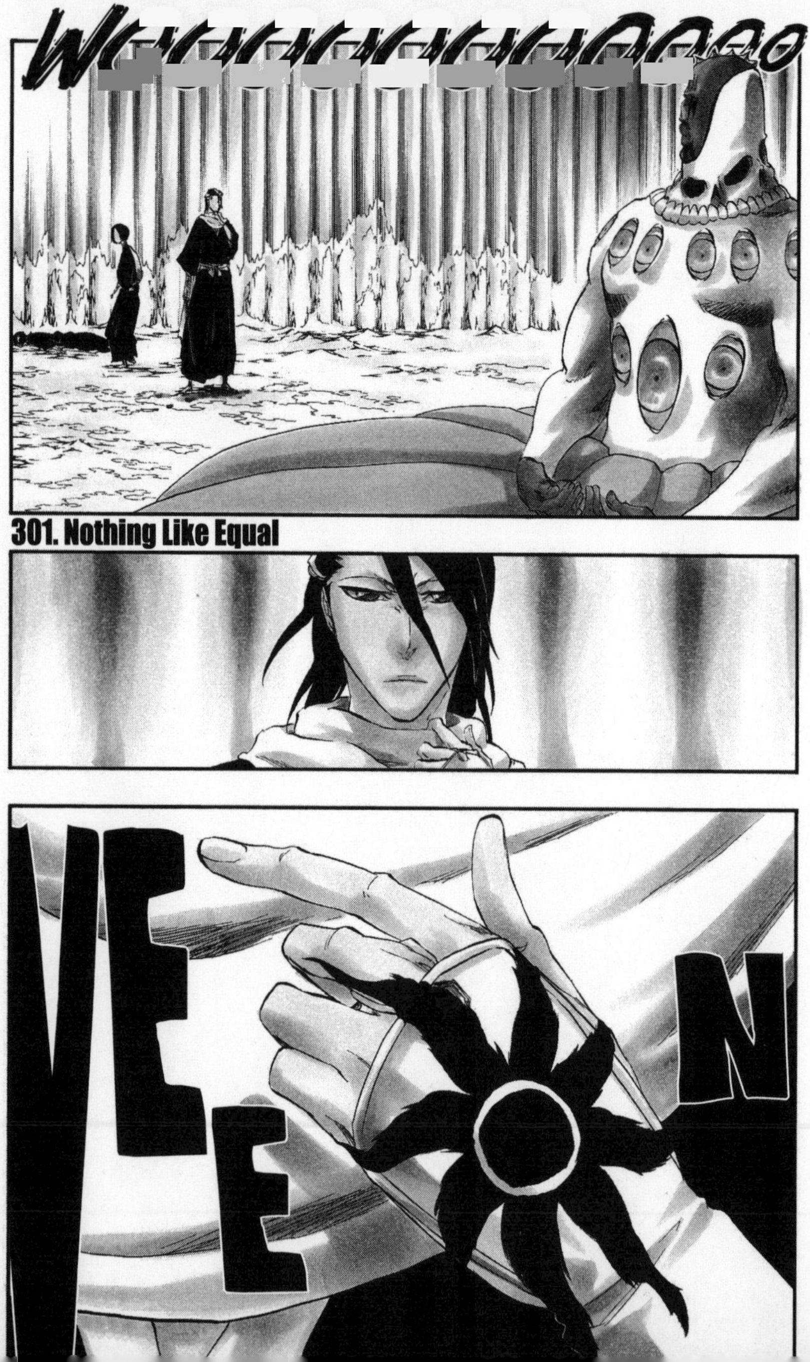

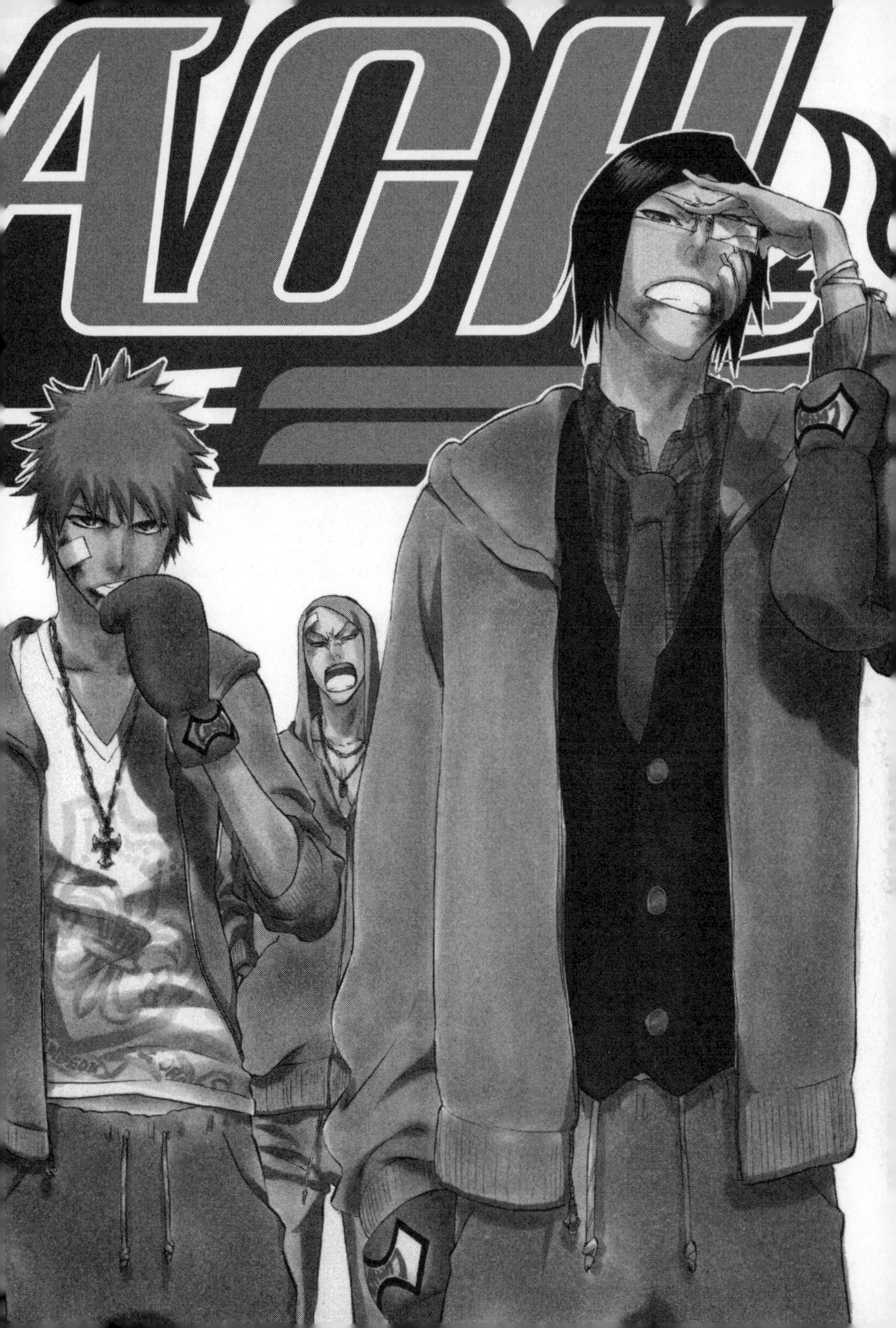

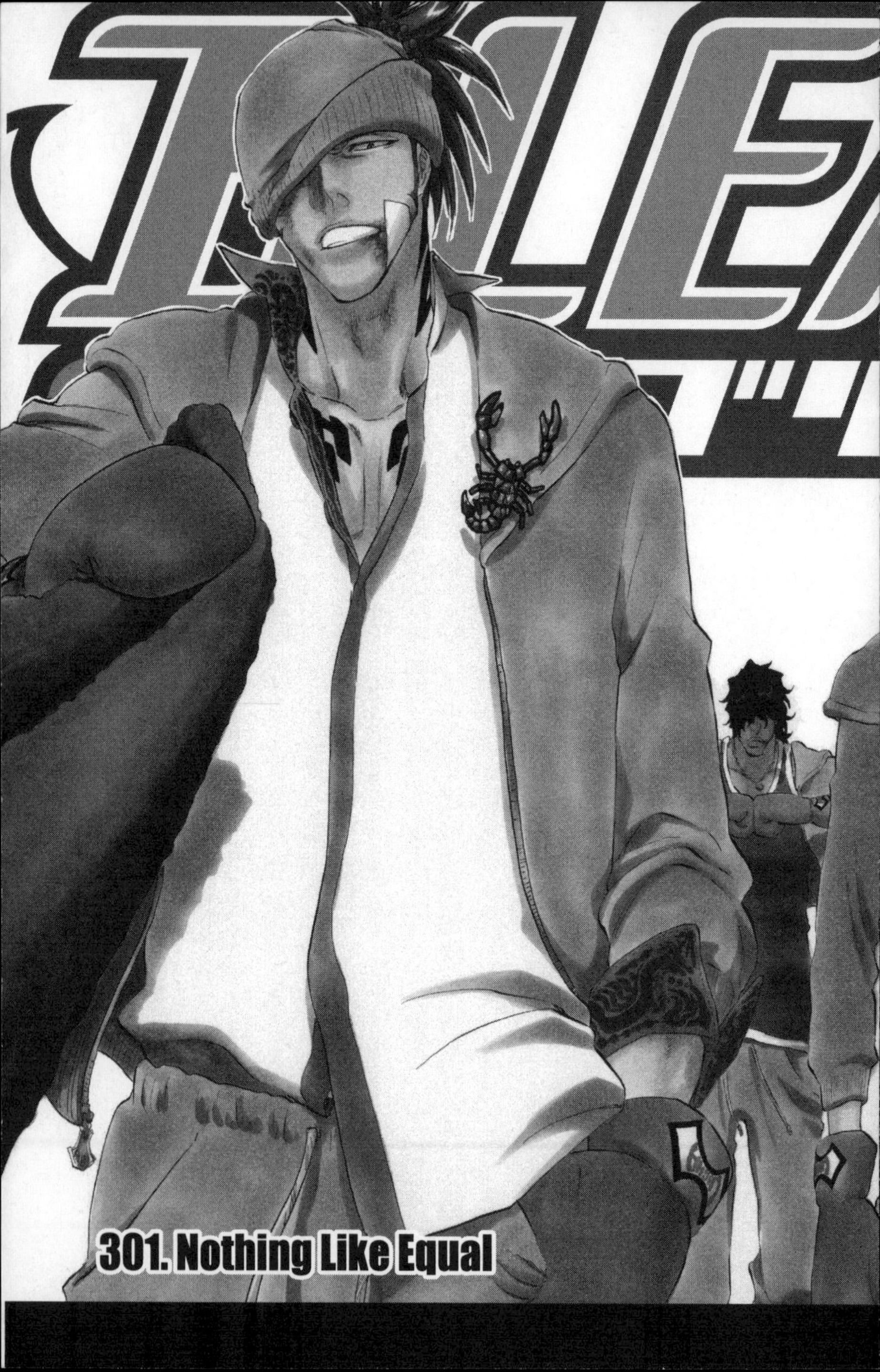
301. Nothing Like Equal

BLEACH
ブリーチ

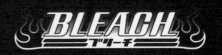

READ THIS WAY

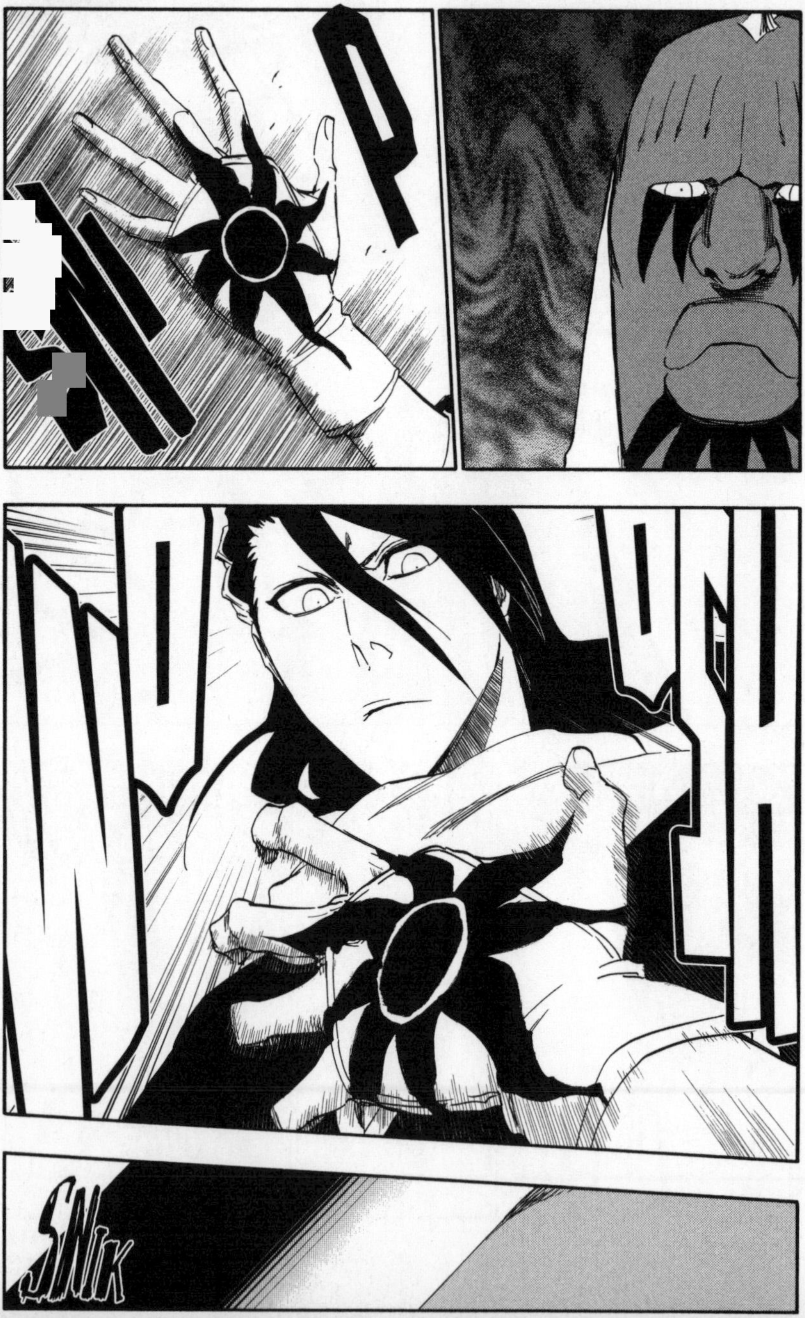
SNIP
SNIK

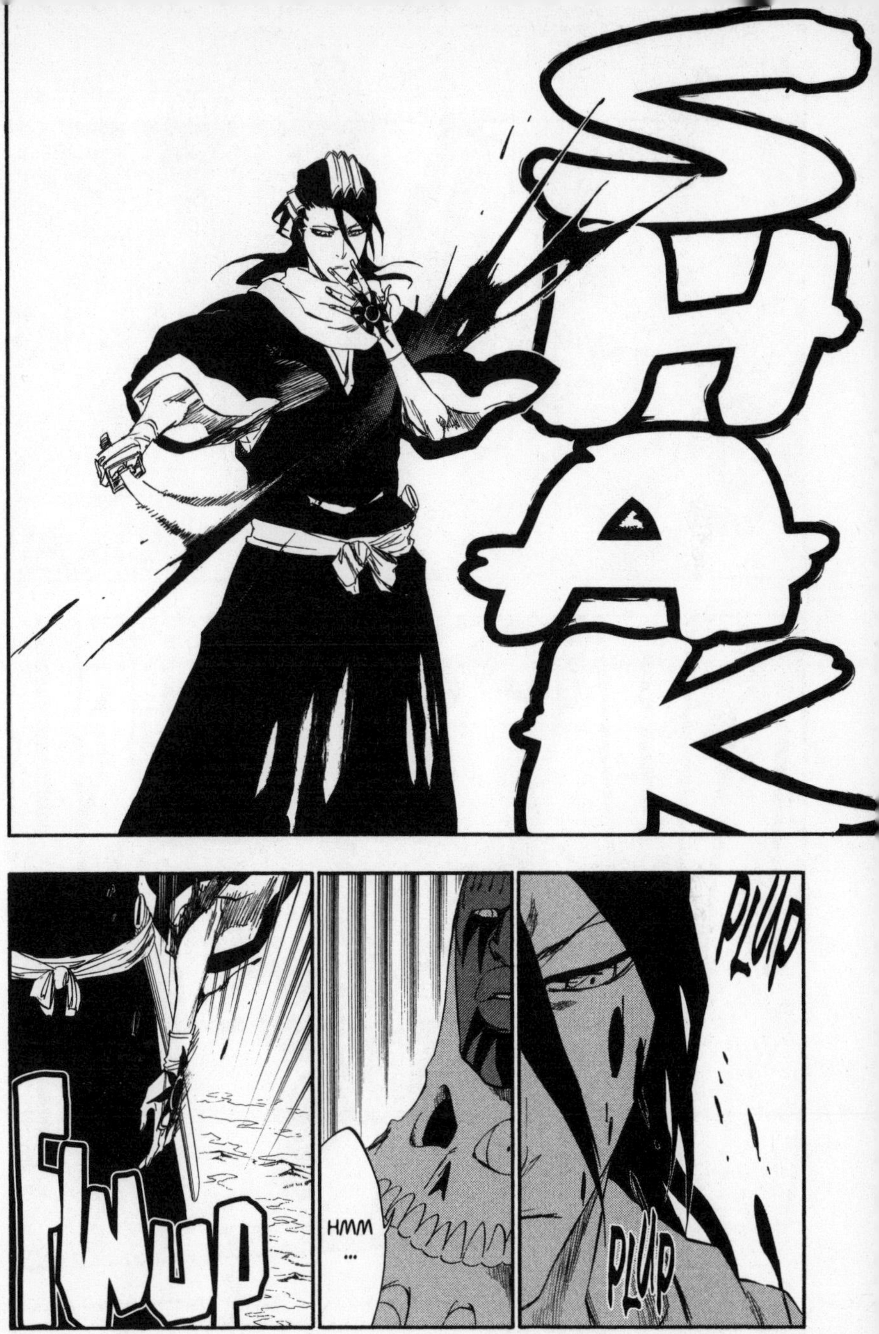
SHAK
PLUP
PLUP
HMM
...
FWUP

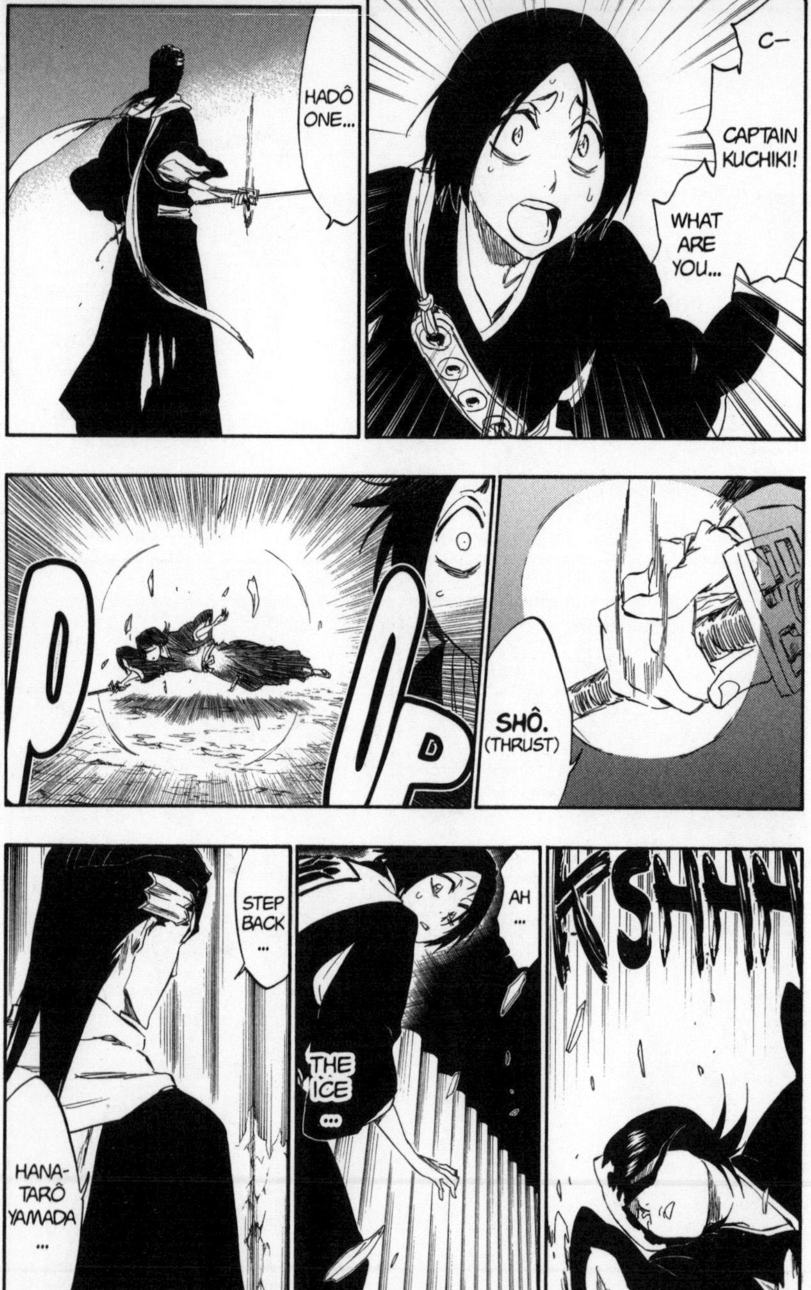
C—
CAPTAIN KUCHIKI!
WHAT ARE YOU...
HADÔ ONE...
SHÔ. (THRUST)
POP
KSHHH
AH ...
THE ICE ...
STEP BACK ...
HANA-TARÔ YAMADA ...

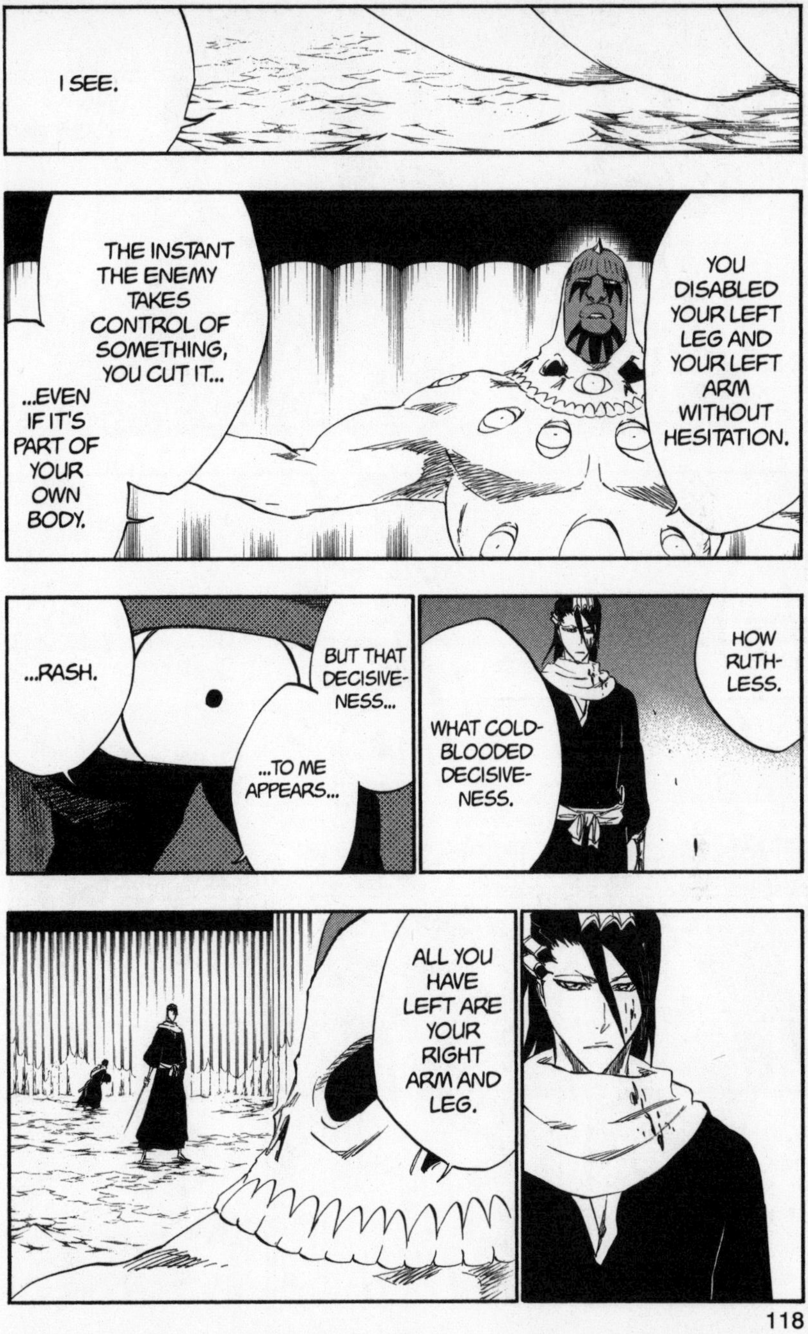
I SEE.
YOU DISABLED YOUR LEFT LEG AND YOUR LEFT ARM WITHOUT HESITATION.
THE INSTANT THE ENEMY TAKES CONTROL OF SOMETHING, YOU CUT IT...
...EVEN IF IT'S PART OF YOUR OWN BODY.
HOW RUTH-LESS.
WHAT COLD-BLOODED DECISIVE-NESS.
BUT THAT DECISIVE-NESS...
...TO ME APPEARS...
...RASH.
ALL YOU HAVE LEFT ARE YOUR RIGHT ARM AND LEG.

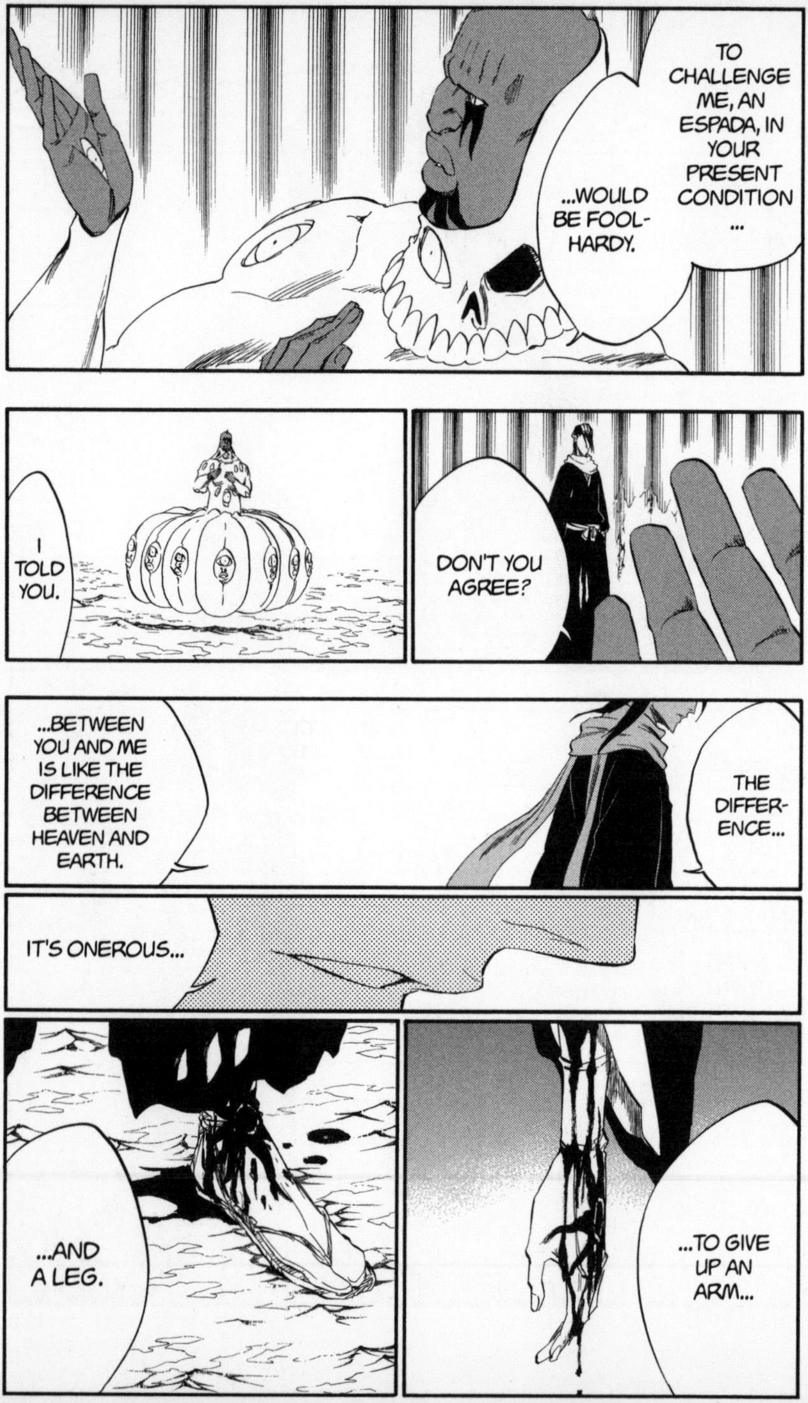
TO CHALLENGE ME, AN ESPADA, IN YOUR PRESENT CONDITION ...
...WOULD BE FOOL-HARDY.
DON'T YOU AGREE?
I TOLD YOU.
THE DIFFER-ENCE...
...BETWEEN YOU AND ME IS LIKE THE DIFFERENCE BETWEEN HEAVEN AND EARTH.
IT'S ONEROUS...
...TO GIVE UP AN ARM...
...AND A LEG.

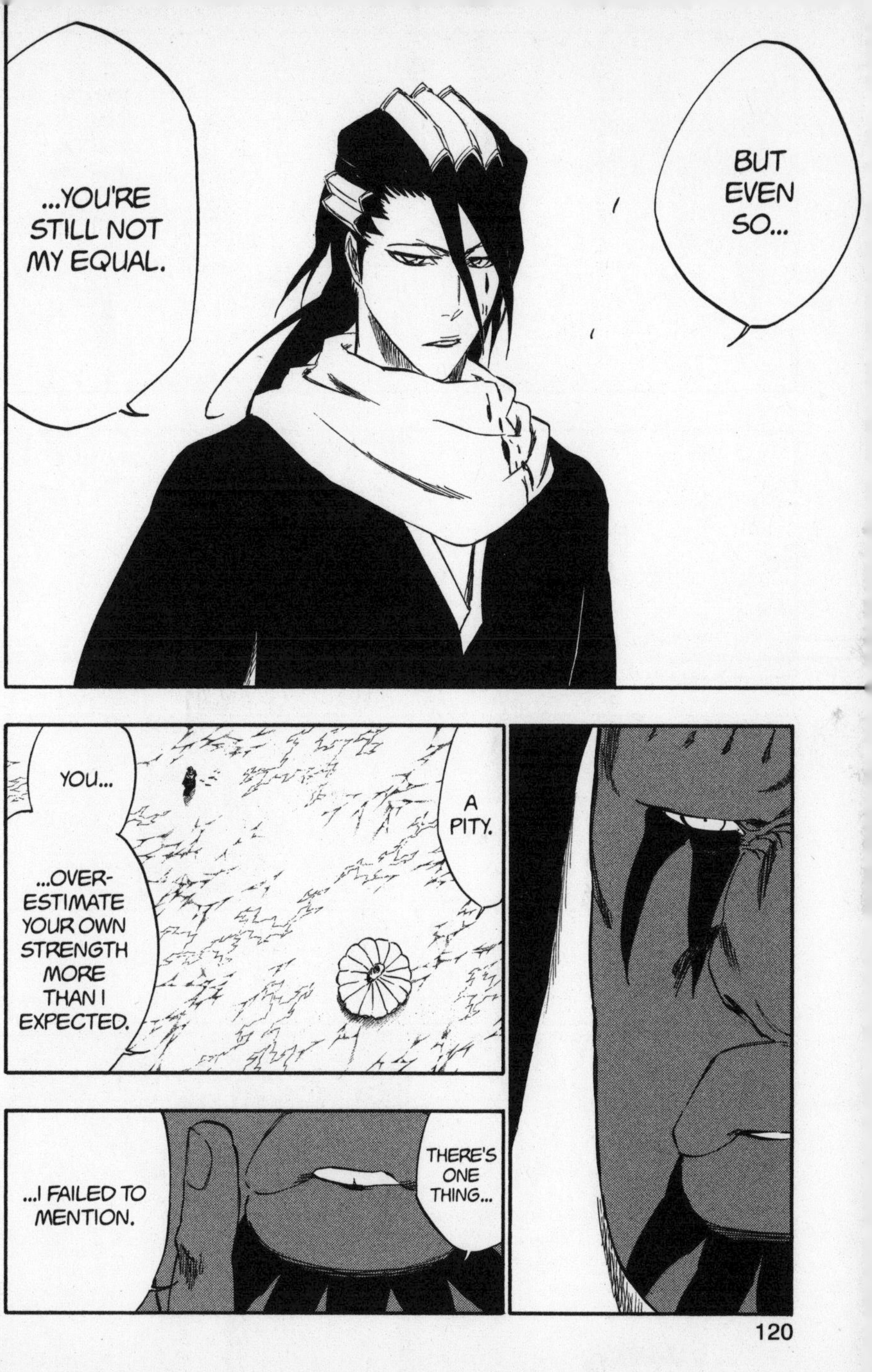
BUT EVEN SO...
...YOU'RE STILL NOT MY EQUAL.
A PITY.
YOU...
...OVER-ESTIMATE YOUR OWN STRENGTH MORE THAN I EXPECTED.
THERE'S ONE THING...
...I FAILED TO MENTION.

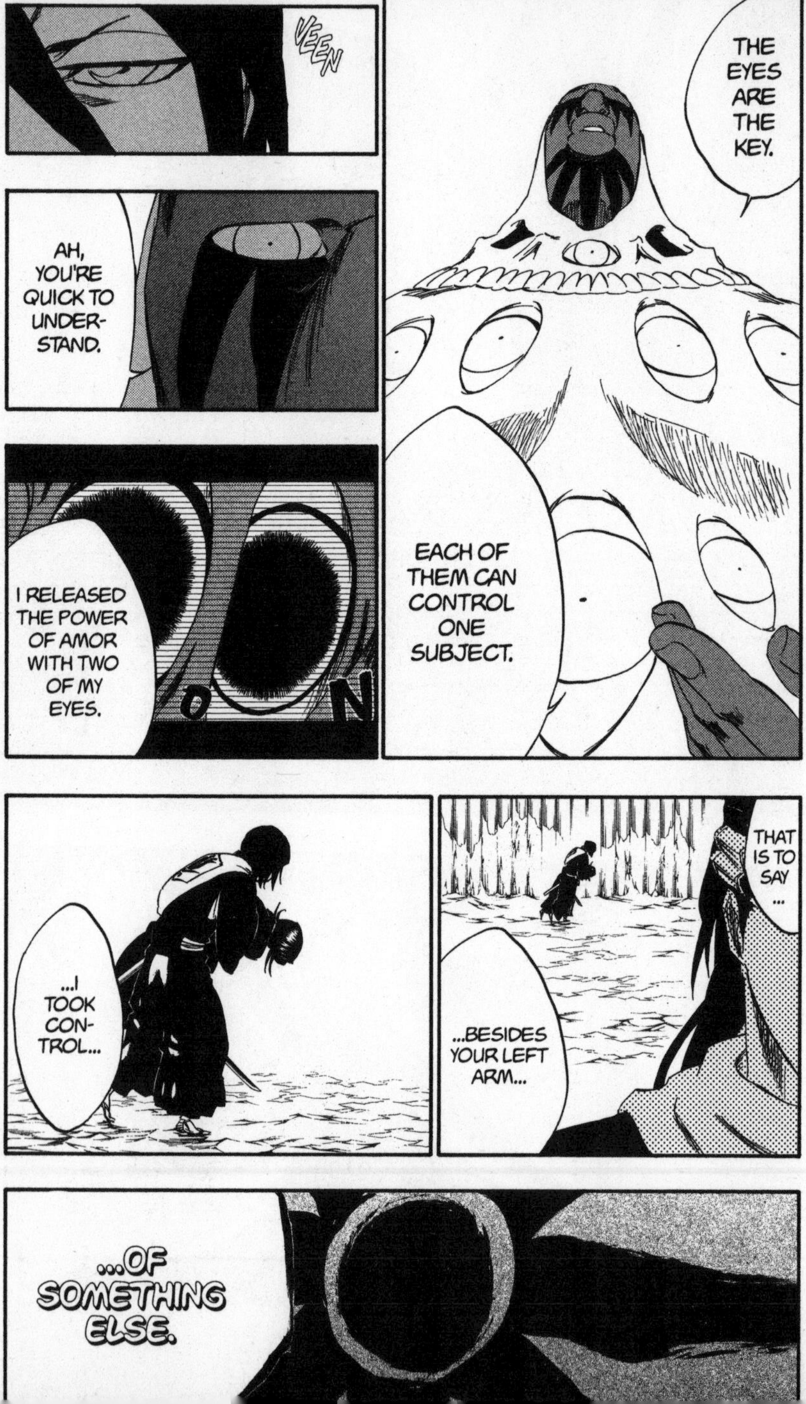
THE EYES ARE THE KEY.
EACH OF THEM CAN CONTROL ONE SUBJECT.
VEEN
AH, YOU'RE QUICK TO UNDER-STAND.
I RELEASED THE POWER OF AMOR WITH TWO OF MY EYES.
ON
THAT IS TO SAY ...
...BESIDES YOUR LEFT ARM...
...I TOOK CON-TROL...
...OF SOMETHING ELSE.

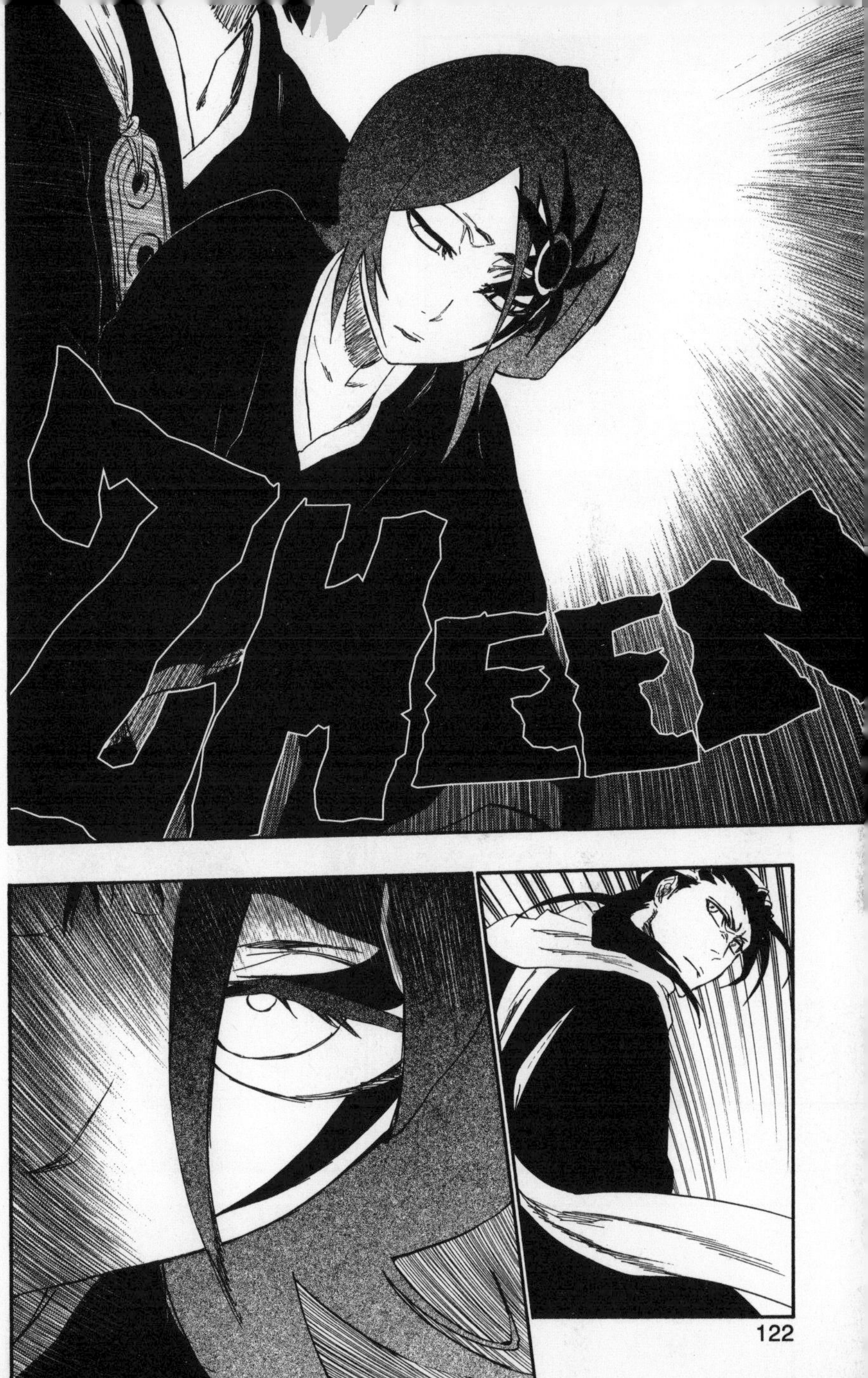

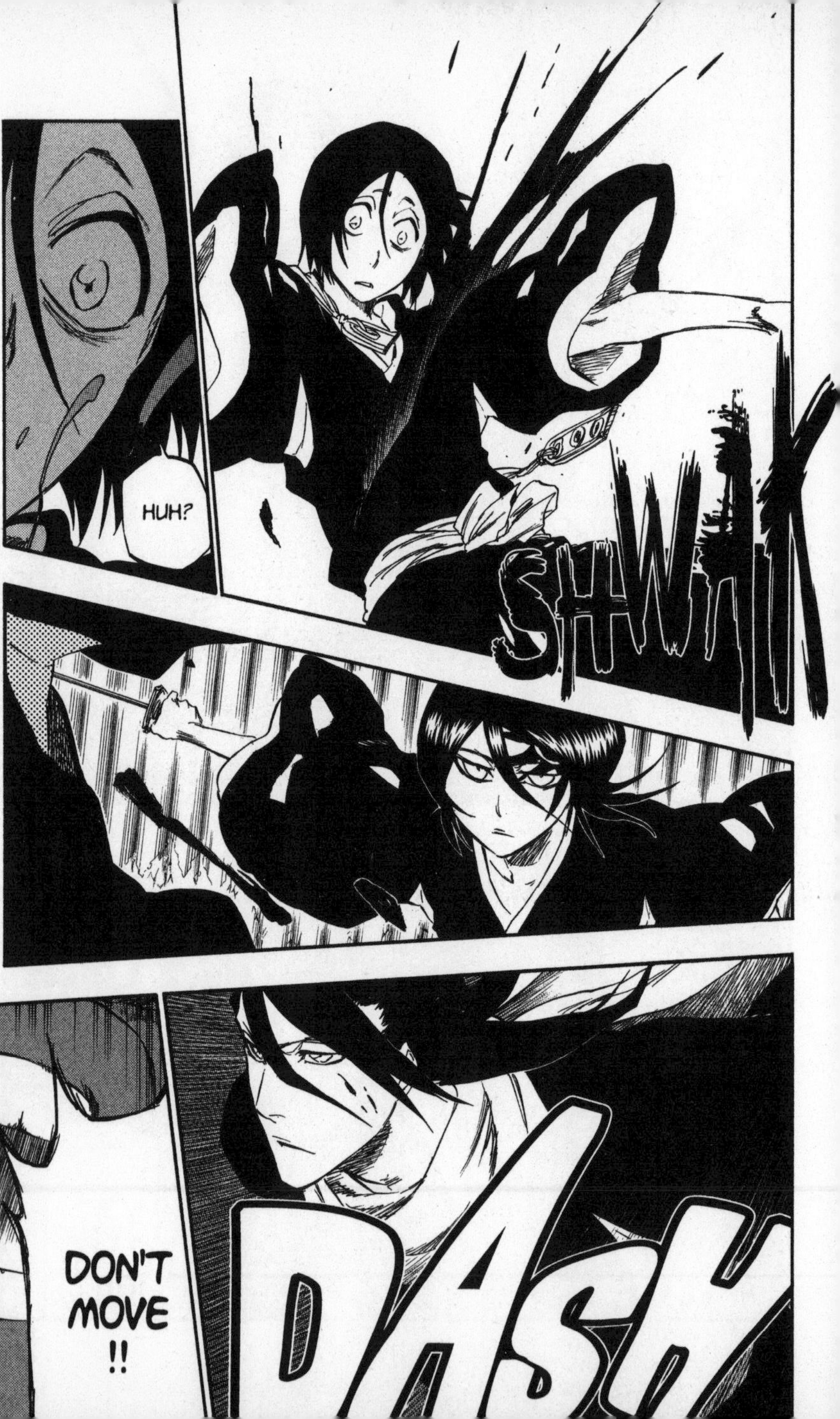
SHWAK
HUH?
DASH
DON'T MOVE !!

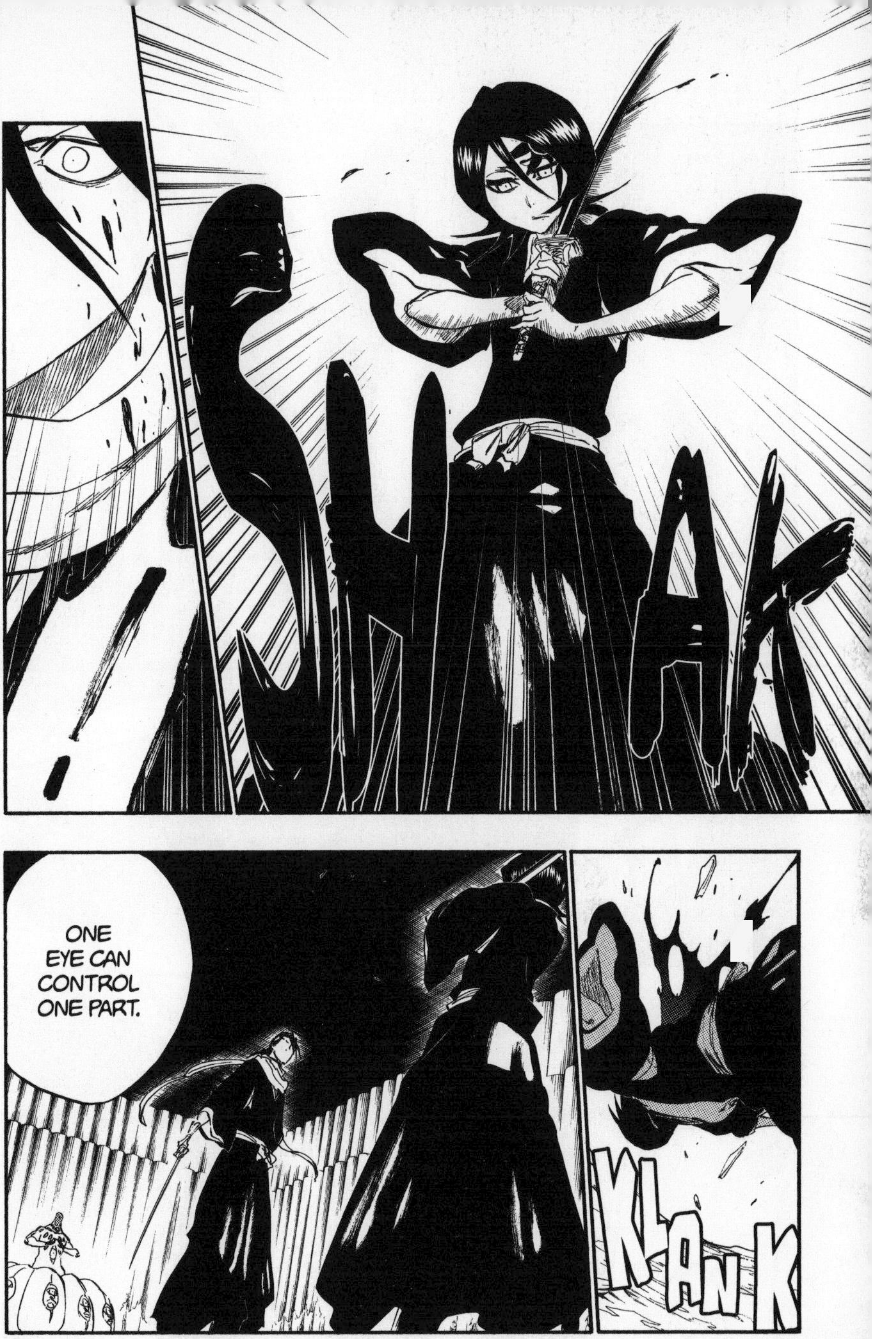
SHAK
KLANK
ONE EYE CAN CONTROL ONE PART.

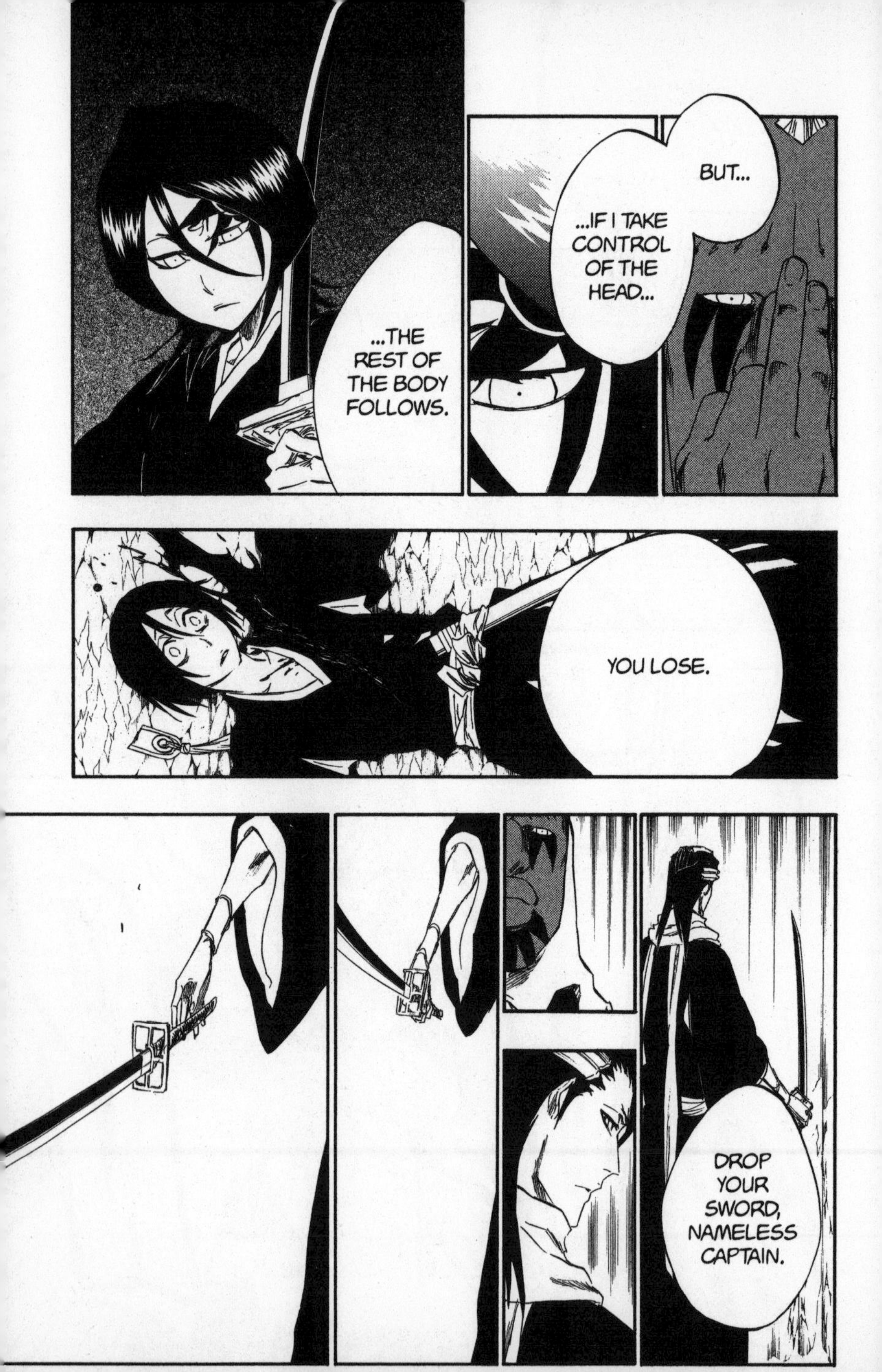
BUT...
...IF I TAKE CONTROL OF THE HEAD...
...THE REST OF THE BODY FOLLOWS.
YOU LOSE.
DROP YOUR SWORD, NAMELESS CAPTAIN.

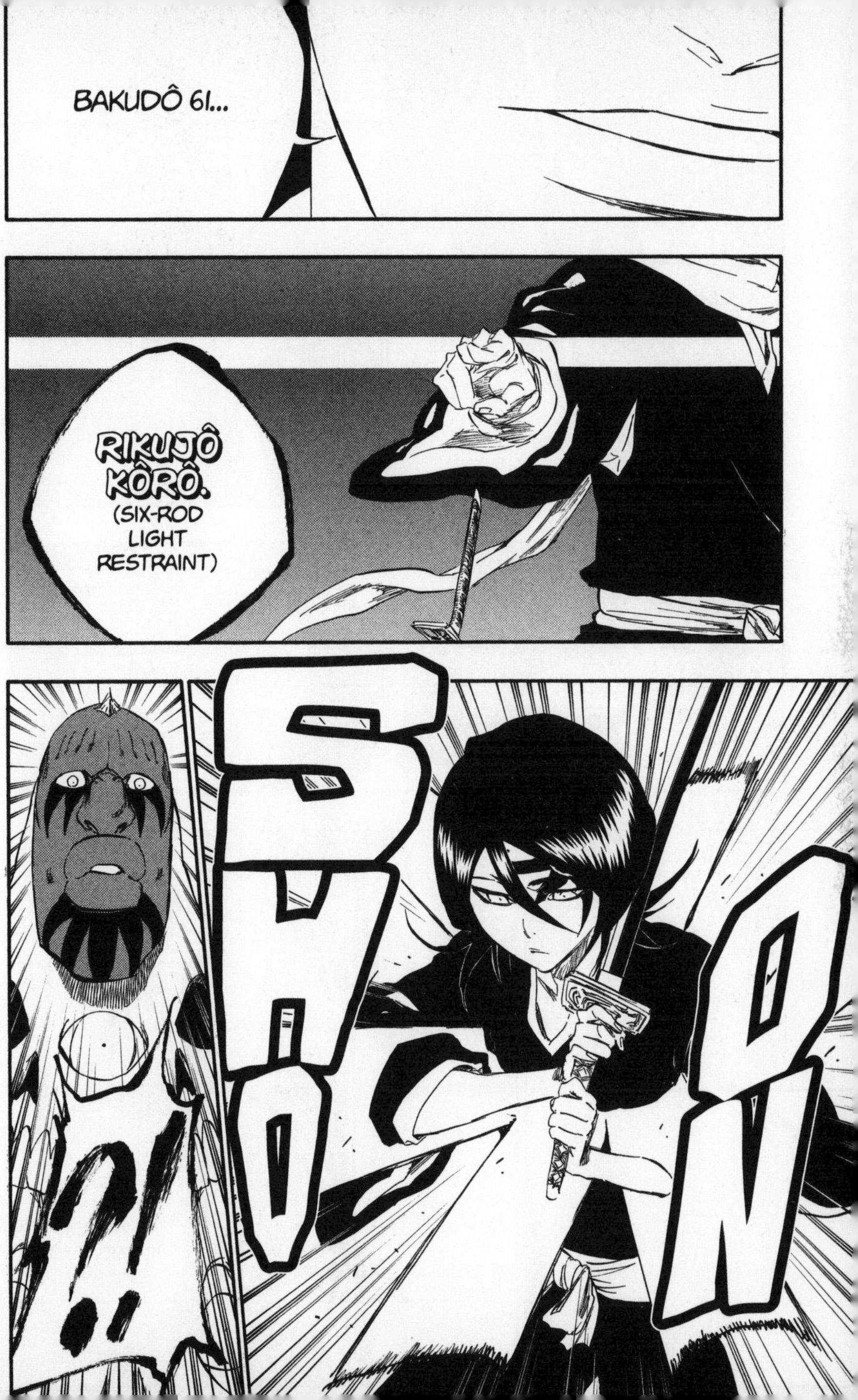
BAKUDÔ 61...
RIKUJÔ KÔRÔ. (SIX-ROD LIGHT RESTRAINT)
SHOOON
?!

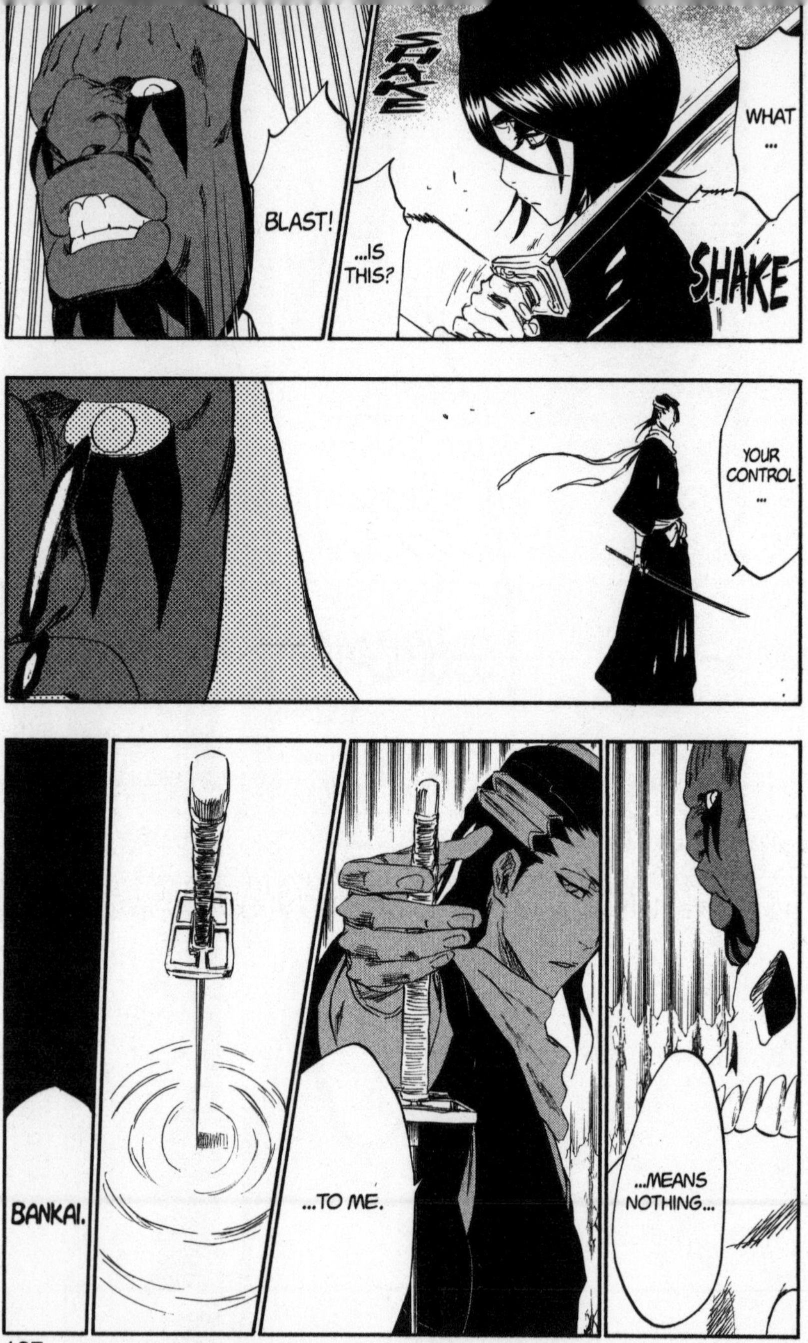
SHAKE
WHAT ...
SHAKE
...IS THIS?
BLAST!
YOUR CONTROL ...
...MEANS NOTHING...
...TO ME.
BANKAI.

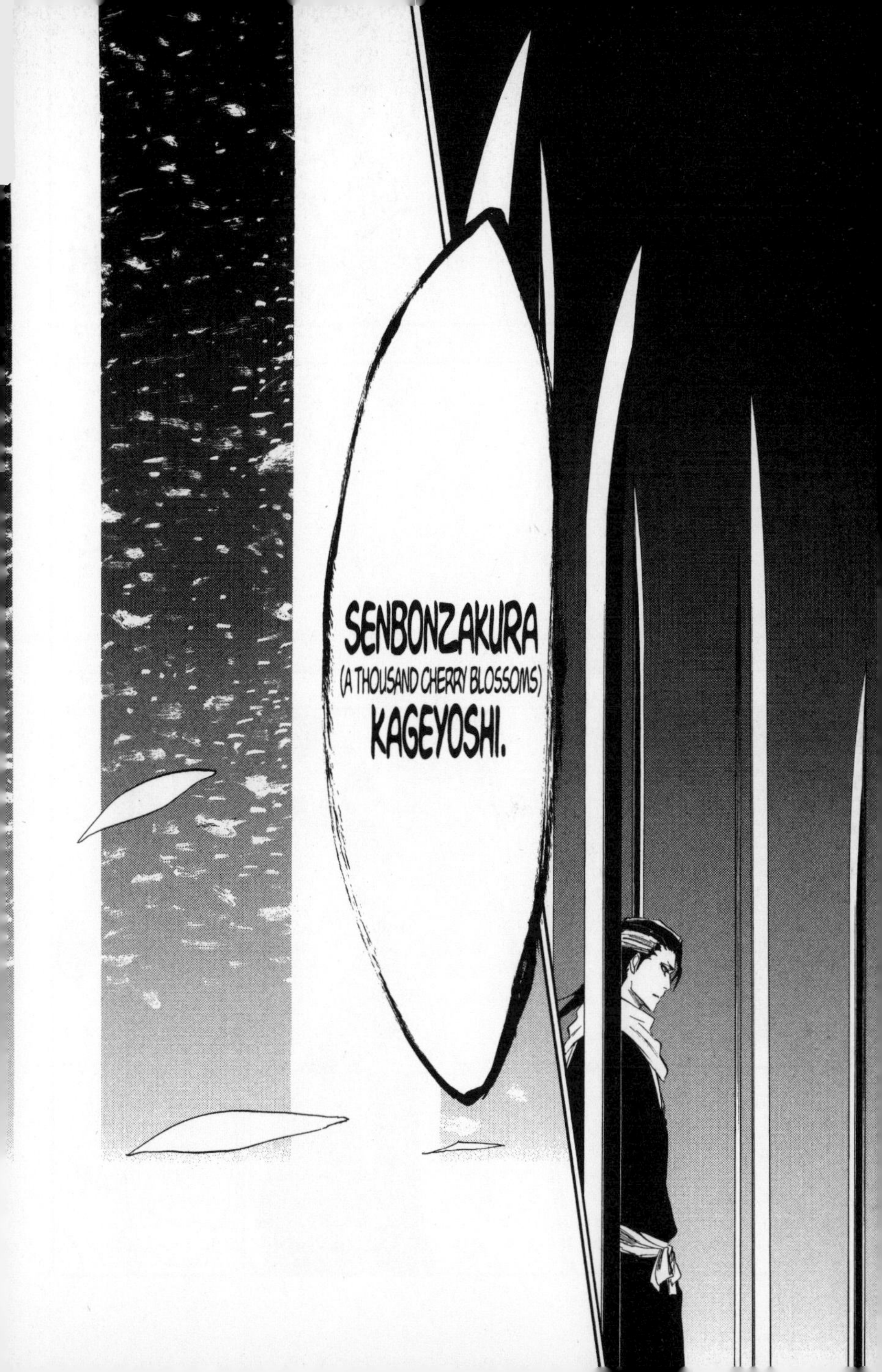
SENBONZAKURA (A THOUSAND CHERRY BLOSSOMS) KAGEYOSHI.

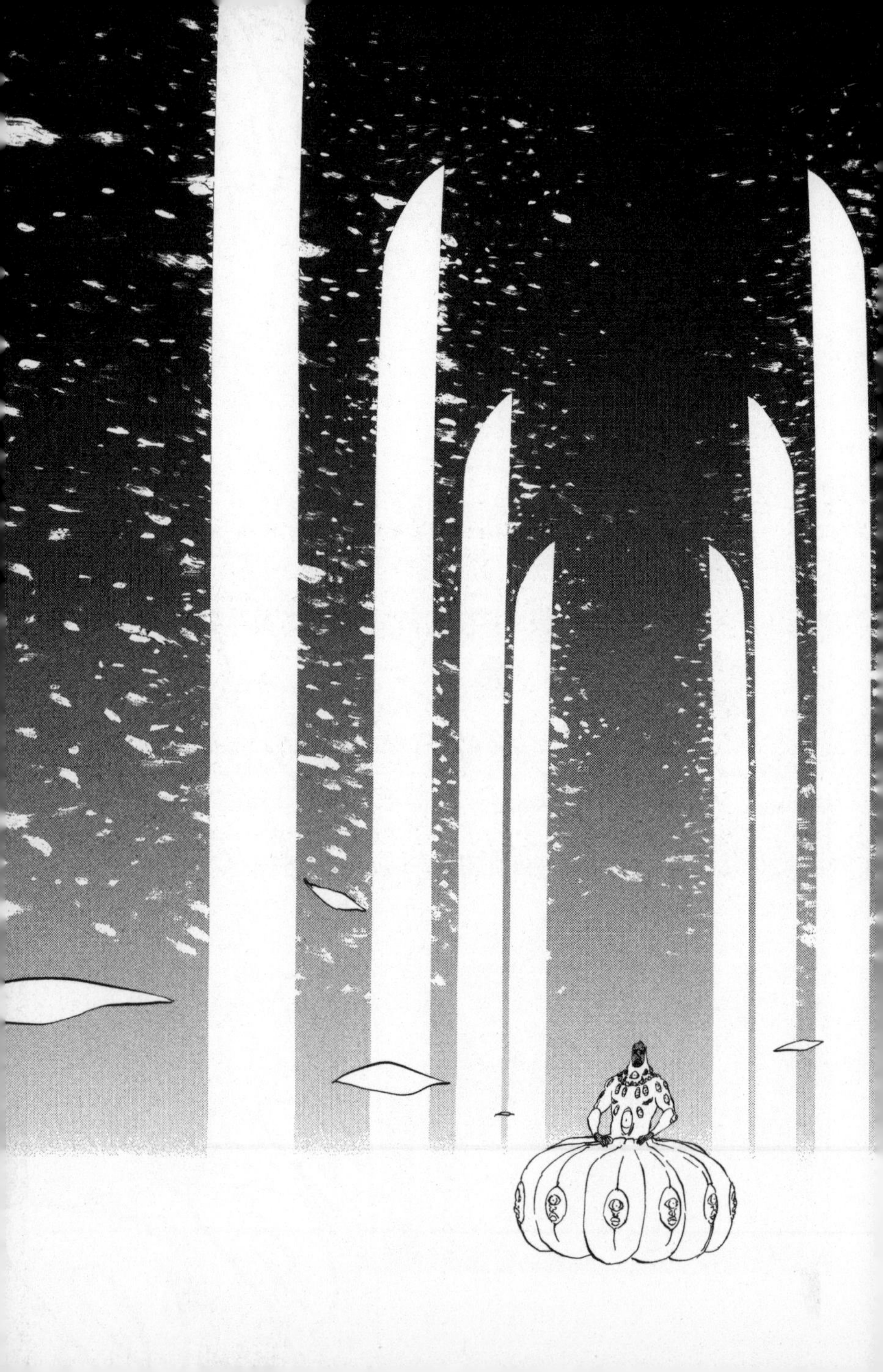

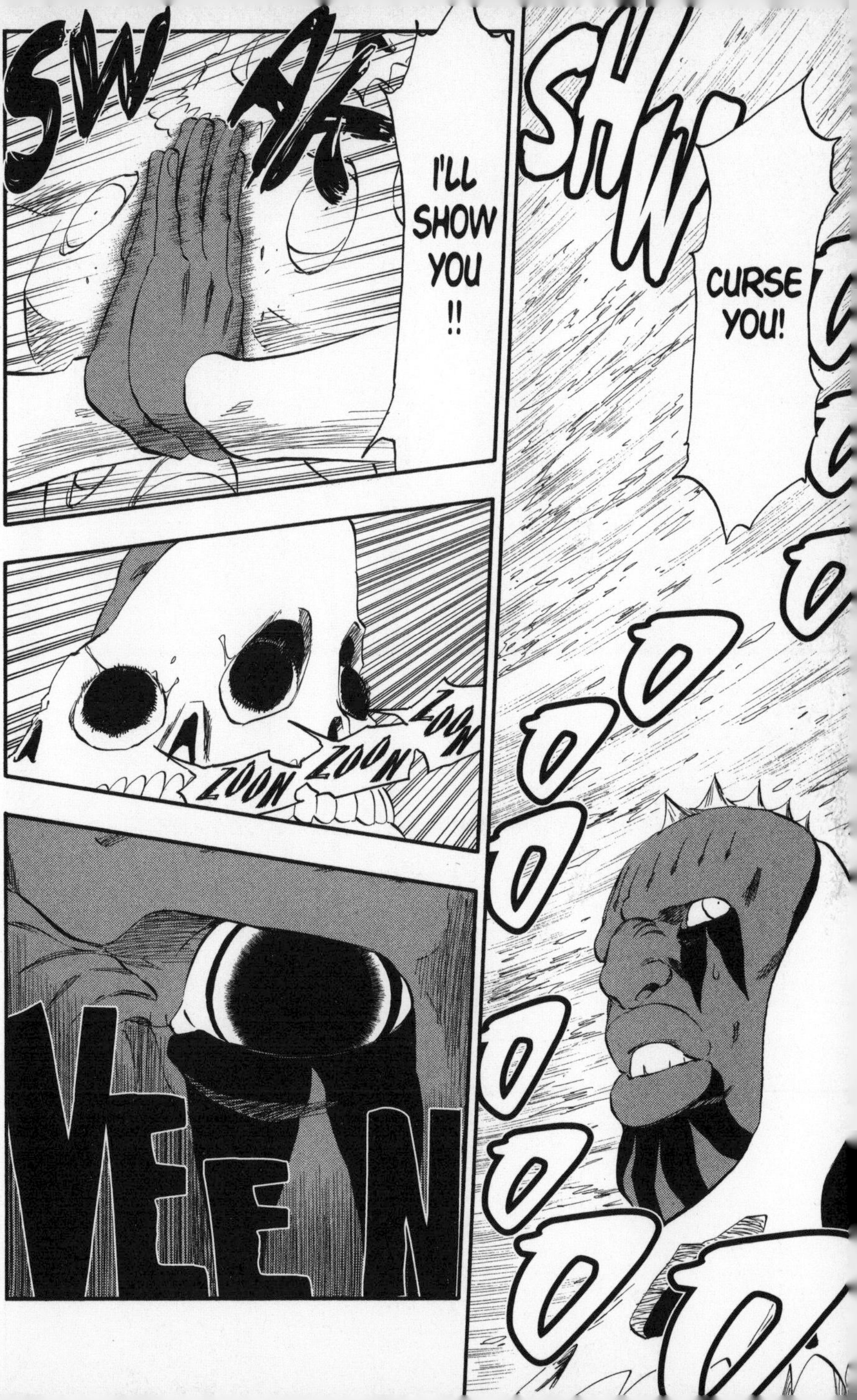
SHW
CURSE YOU!
OOOOOOOOOOOOOOOOOO
SWAK
I'LL SHOW YOU!!
ZOON ZOON ZOON
WEEN

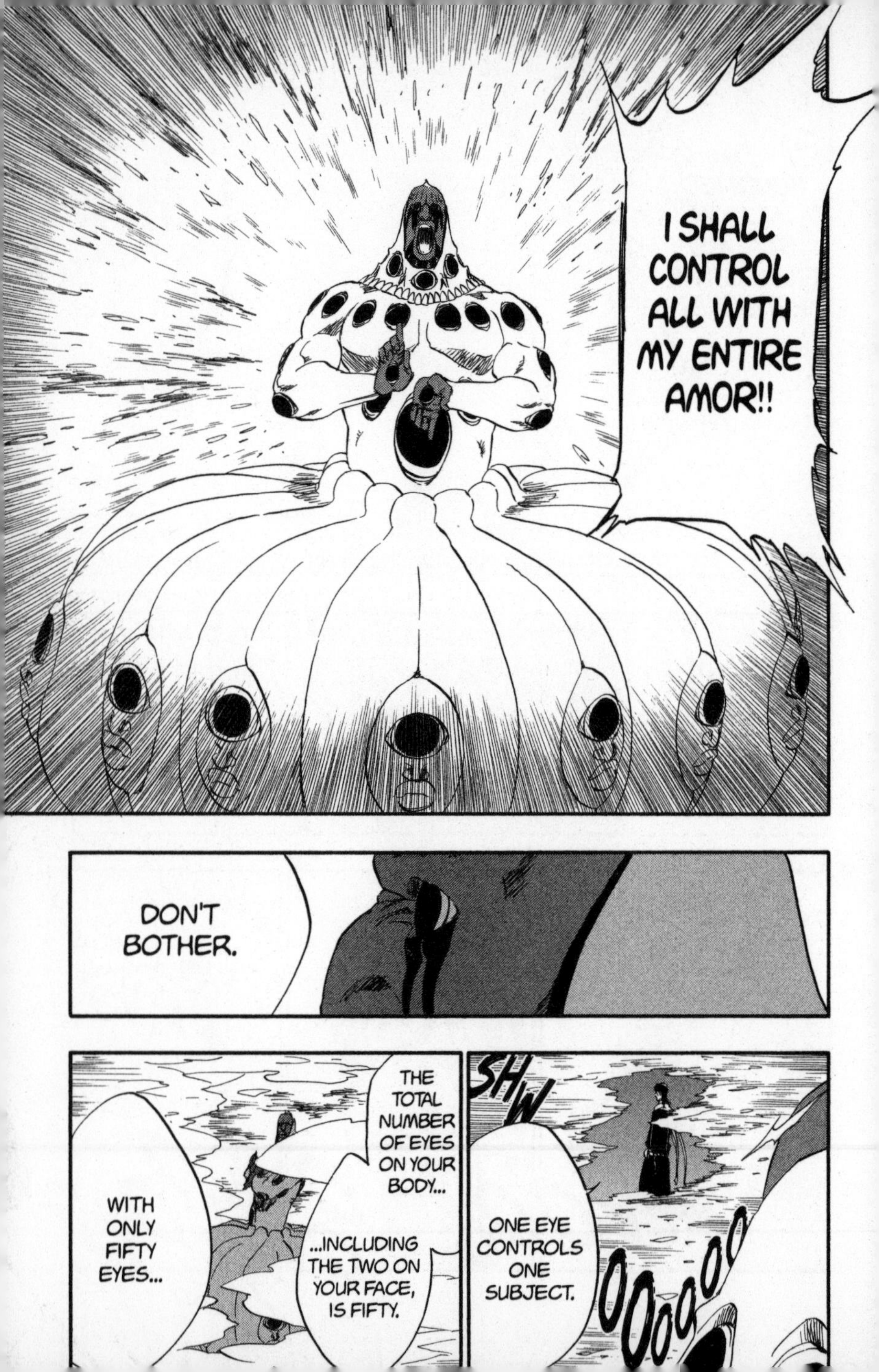
I SHALL CONTROL ALL WITH MY ENTIRE AMOR!!
DON'T BOTHER.
SHW
ONE EYE CONTROLS ONE SUBJECT.
OOOOOOO
THE TOTAL NUMBER OF EYES ON YOUR BODY...
...INCLUDING THE TWO ON YOUR FACE, IS FIFTY.
WITH ONLY FIFTY EYES...

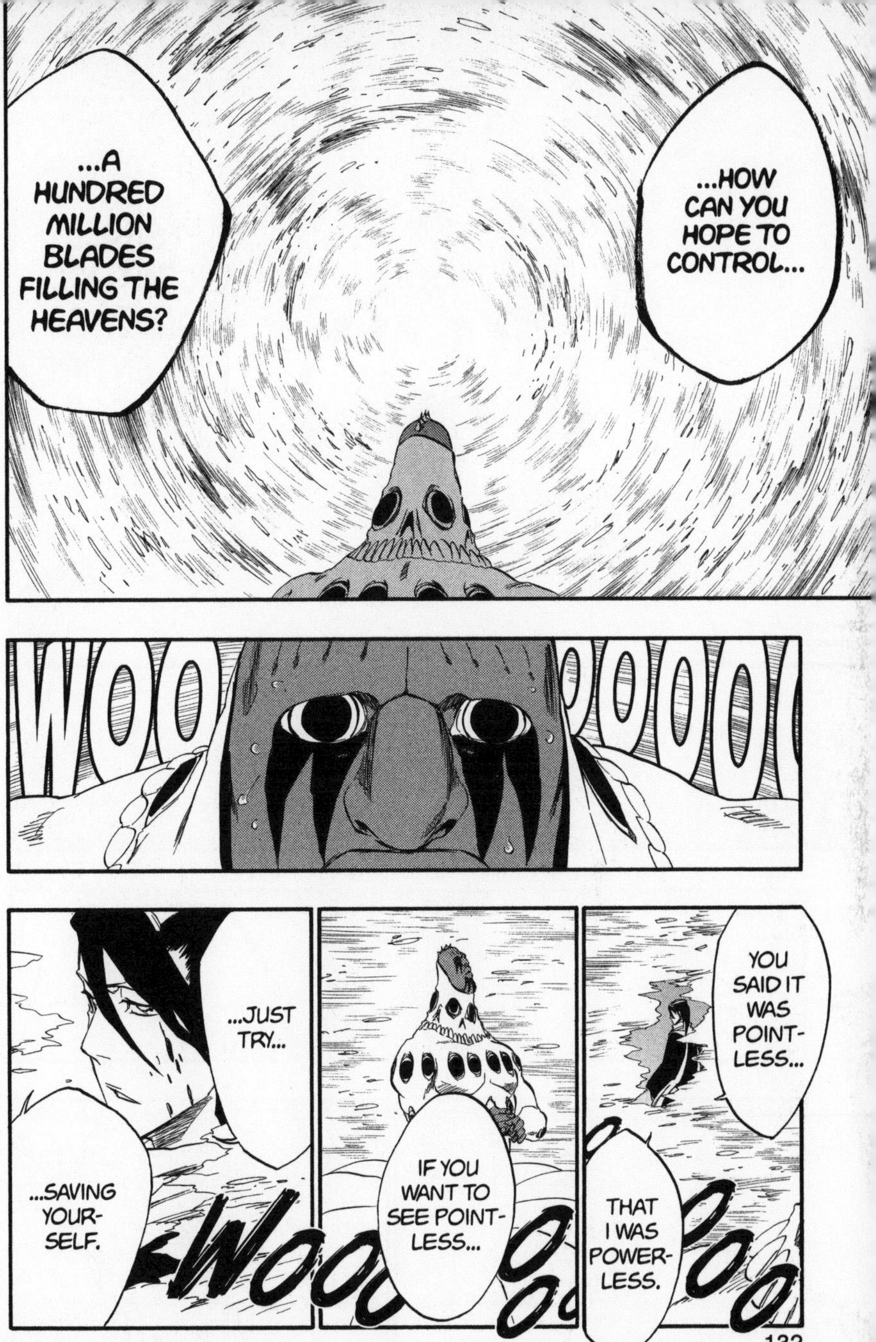
...HOW CAN YOU HOPE TO CONTROL...
...A HUNDRED MILLION BLADES FILLING THE HEAVENS?
WOOOOOOOO
YOU SAID IT WAS POINT-LESS...
THAT I WAS POWER-LESS.
IF YOU WANT TO SEE POINT-LESS...
...JUST TRY...
...SAVING YOUR-SELF.
WOOOOOOO

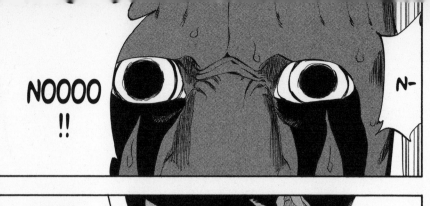

NOOOO
!!

N-

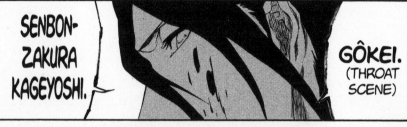

SENBON-
ZAKURA
KAGEYOSHI.

GÔKEI.
(THROAT
SCENE)

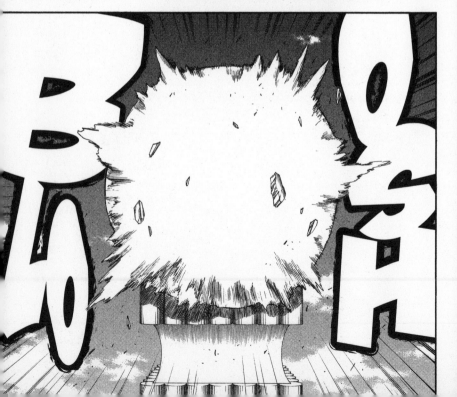

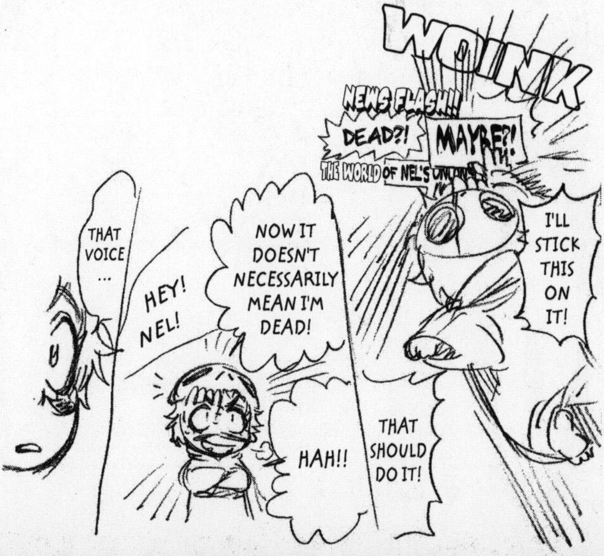
WOINK
NEWS FLASH!!
MAYBE?!
DEAD?!
THE WORLD OF NEL'S
I'LL STICK THIS ON IT!
THAT SHOULD DO IT!
NOW IT DOESN'T NECESSARILY MEAN I'M DEAD!
HEY! NEL!
HAH!!
THAT VOICE...

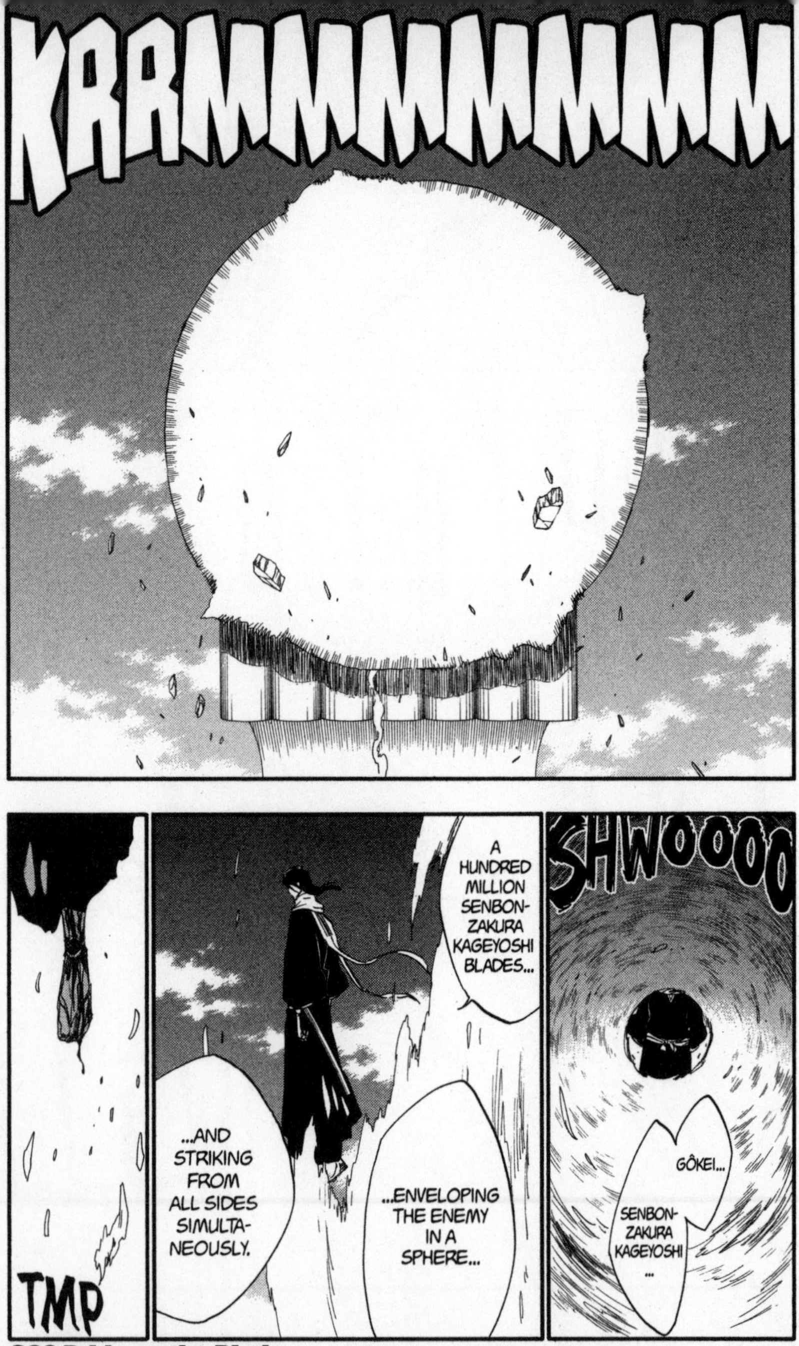
KRMMMMMMMMM
SHWOOOO
GÔKEI...
SENBON-ZAKURA KAGEYOSHI ...
A HUNDRED MILLION SENBON-ZAKURA KAGEYOSHI BLADES...
...ENVELOPING THE ENEMY IN A SPHERE...
...AND STRIKING FROM ALL SIDES SIMULTA-NEOUSLY.
TMP

302.Pride on the Blade

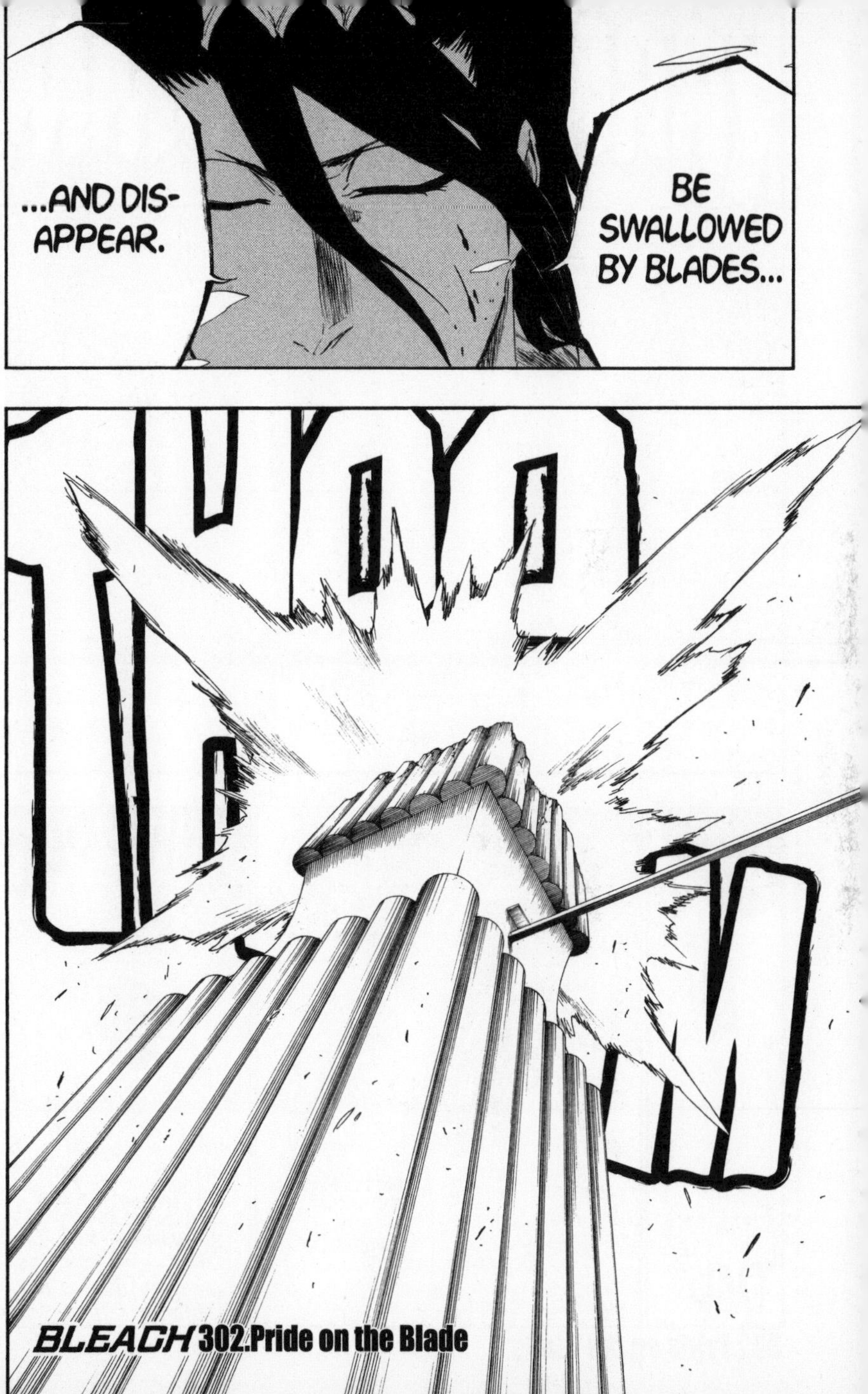
BE SWALLOWED BY BLADES...
...AND DIS-APPEAR.

BLEACH 302.Pride on the Blade

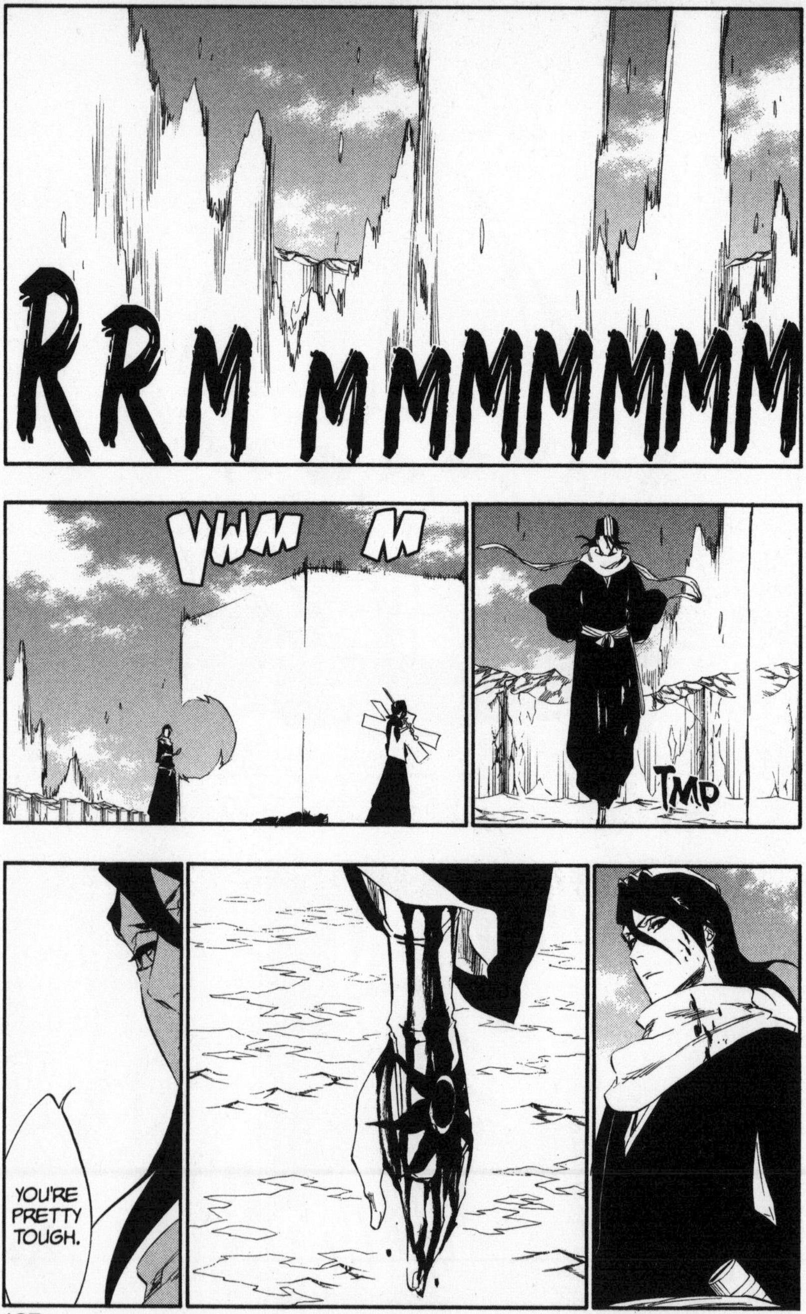
RRM MMMMMMM
TMP
VWM M
YOU'RE PRETTY TOUGH.

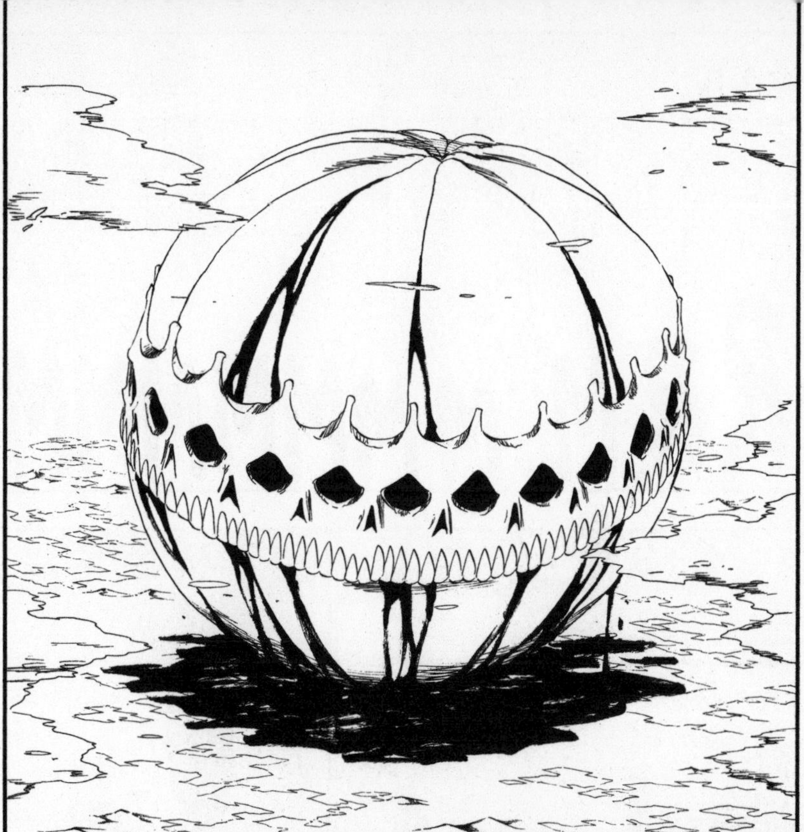

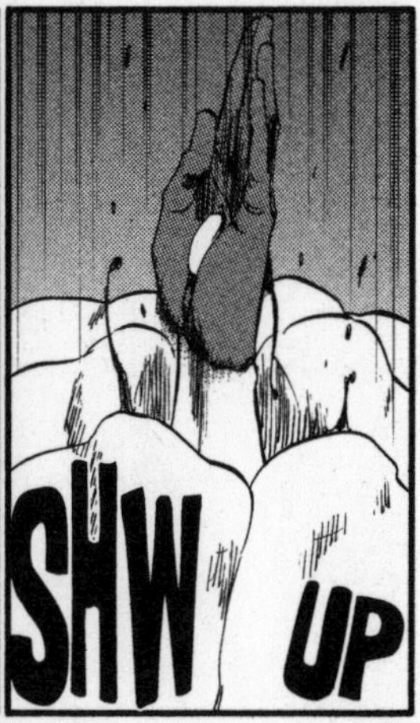
SHW
UP

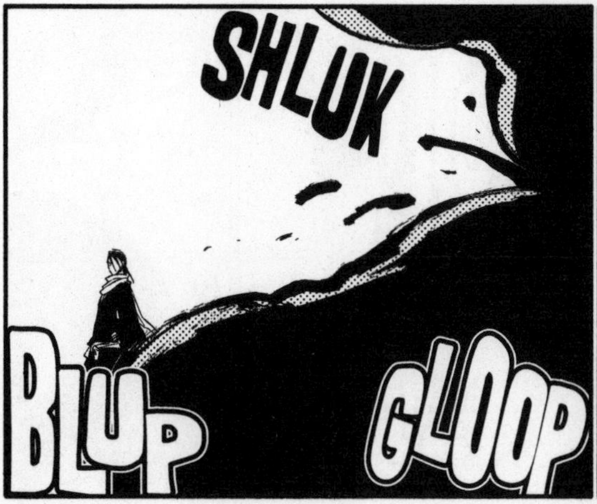
SHLUK
GLOOP
BLUP

READ THIS WAY

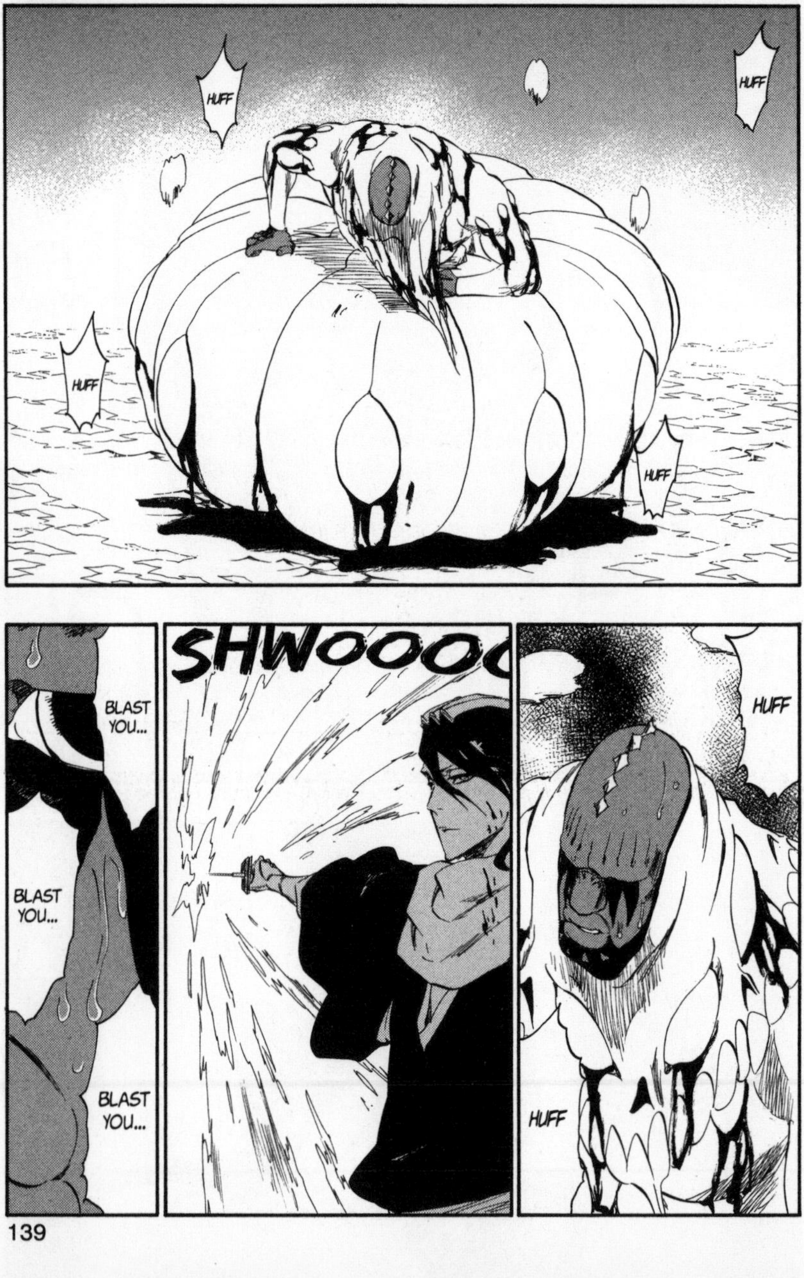
HUFF
HUFF
HUFF
HUFF
HUFF
HUFF
SHWOOOO
BLAST YOU...
BLAST YOU...
BLAST YOU...

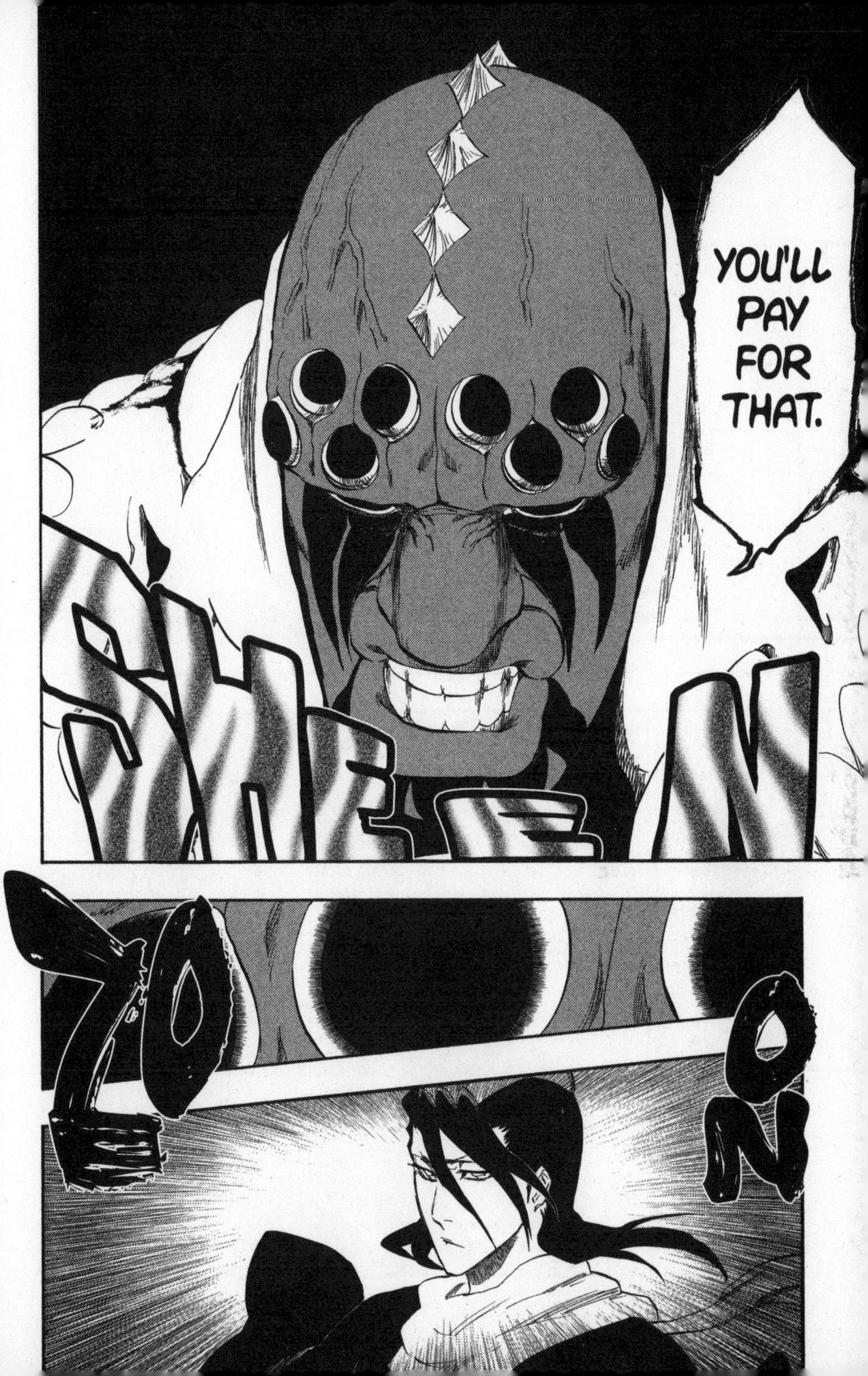
YOU'LL PAY FOR THAT.

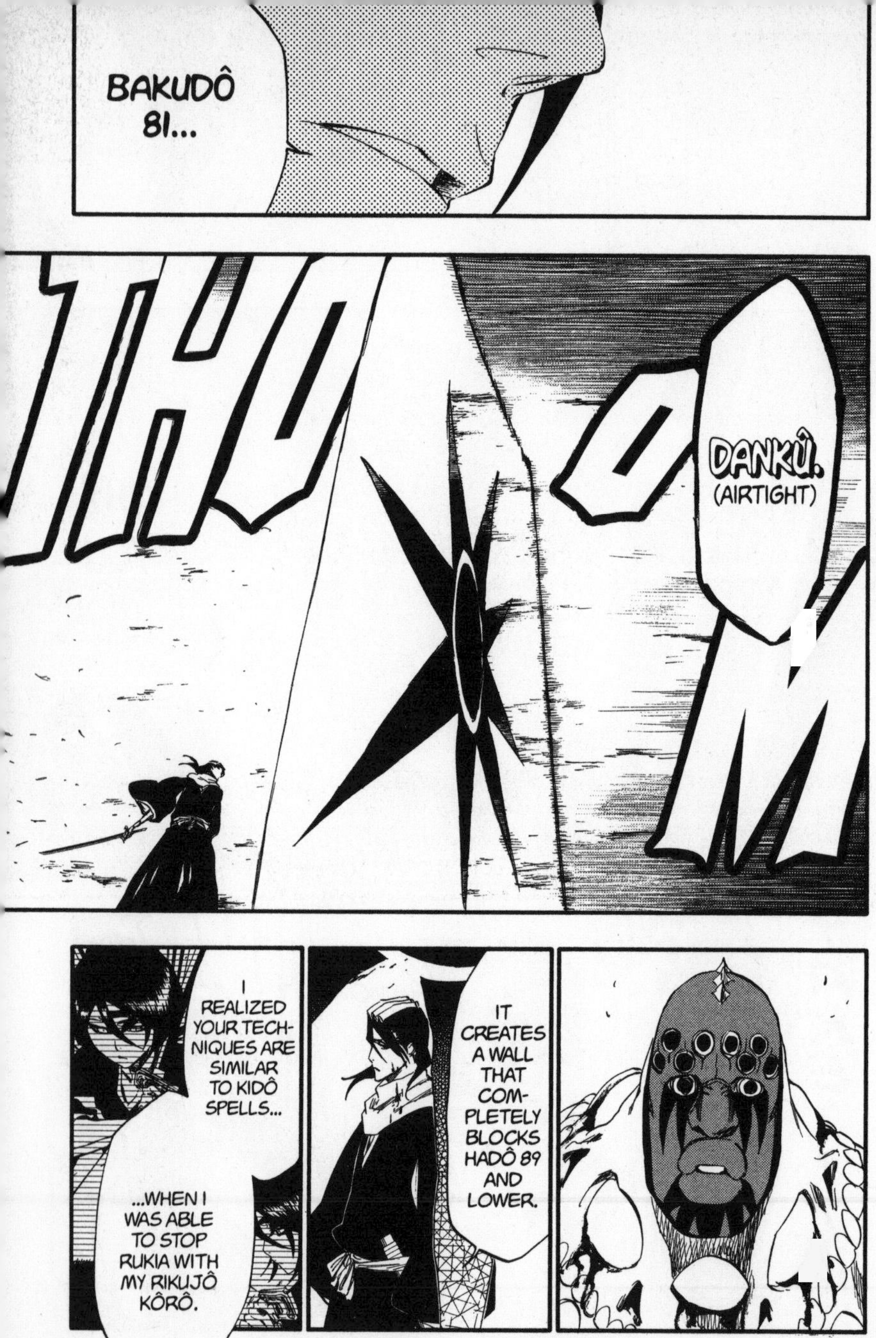
BAKUDÔ 81...
DANKÛ.
(AIRTIGHT)
THOOM
IT CREATES A WALL THAT COMPLETELY BLOCKS HADÔ 89 AND LOWER.
I REALIZED YOUR TECHNIQUES ARE SIMILAR TO KIDÔ SPELLS...
...WHEN I WAS ABLE TO STOP RUKIA WITH MY RIKUJÔ KÔRÔ.

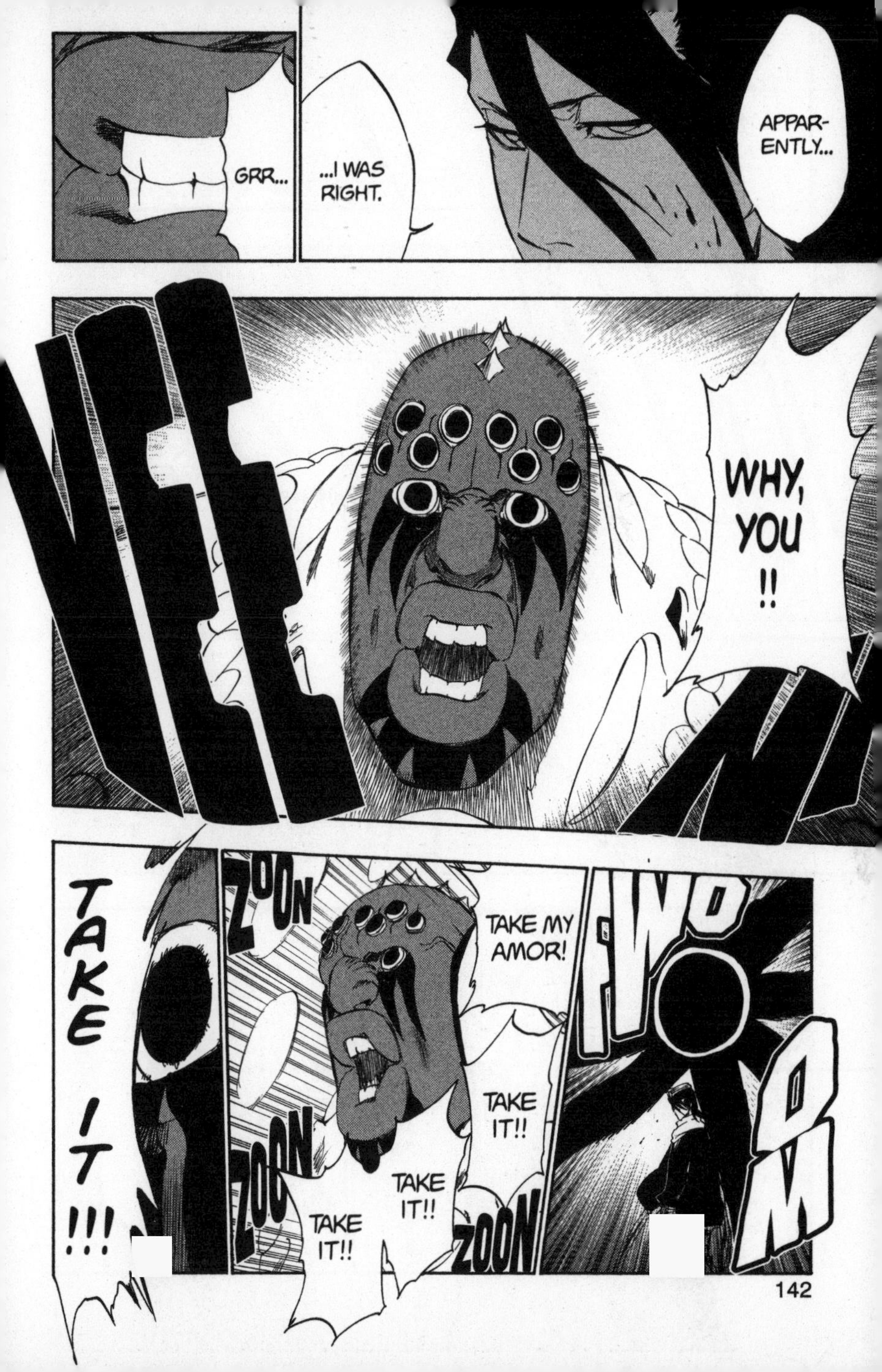
APPAR-
ENTLY...
...I WAS
RIGHT.
GRR...
WHY,
YOU
!!
TAKE MY
AMOR!
ZOON
TAKE
IT!!
ZOON
ZOON
TAKE
IT!!
ZOON
TAKE
IT!!
TAKE
IT
!!!

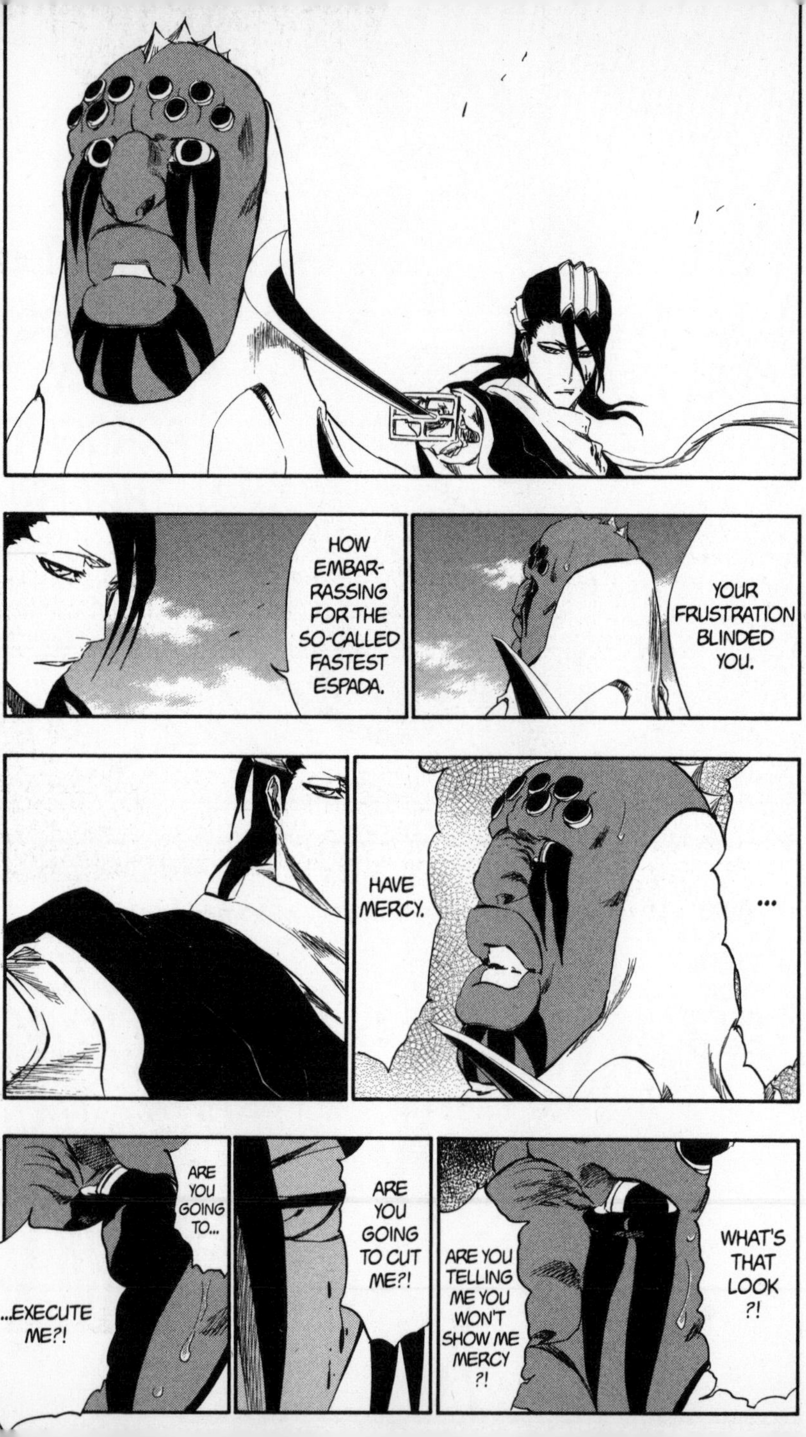
YOUR FRUSTRATION BLINDED YOU.
HOW EMBARRASSING FOR THE SO-CALLED FASTEST ESPADA.
...
HAVE MERCY.
WHAT'S THAT LOOK ?!
ARE YOU TELLING ME YOU WON'T SHOW ME MERCY ?!
ARE YOU GOING TO CUT ME?!
ARE YOU GOING TO...
...EXECUTE ME?!

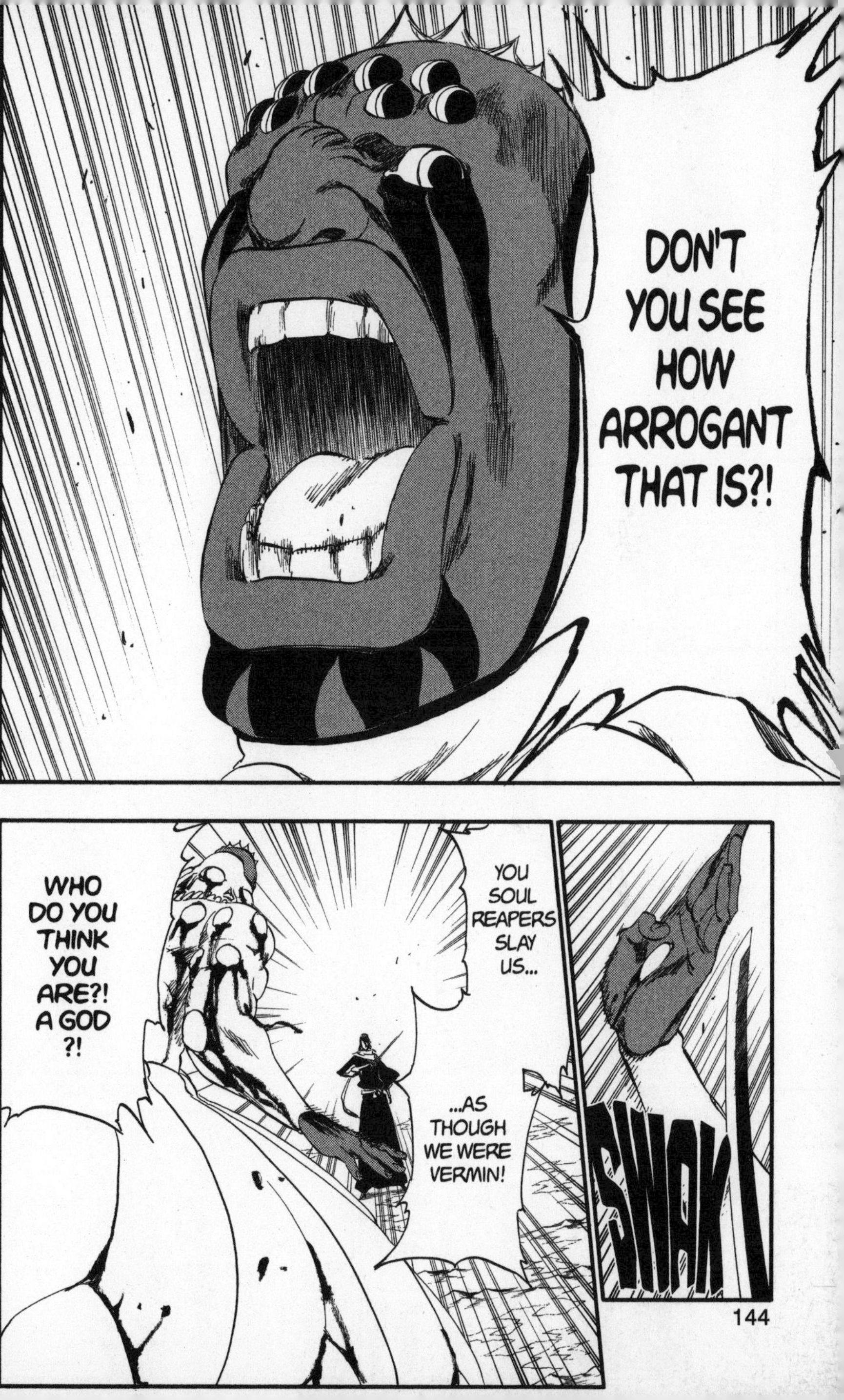
DON'T YOU SEE HOW ARROGANT THAT IS?!
SWAK
YOU SOUL REAPERS SLAY US...
...AS THOUGH WE WERE VERMIN!
WHO DO YOU THINK YOU ARE?! A GOD ?!

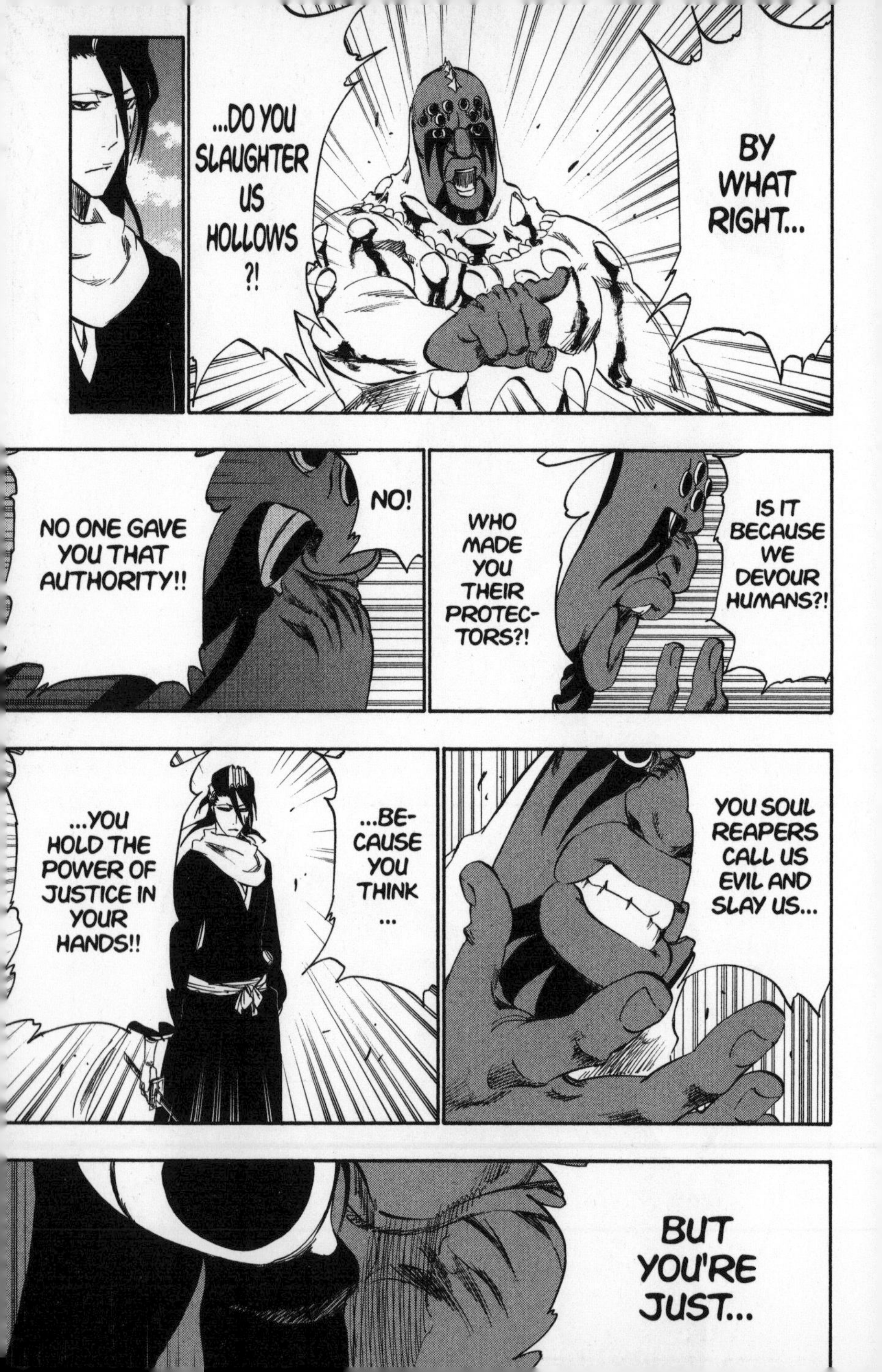
BY WHAT RIGHT...
...DO YOU SLAUGHTER US HOLLOWS ?!
IS IT BECAUSE WE DEVOUR HUMANS?!
WHO MADE YOU THEIR PROTECTORS?!
NO!
NO ONE GAVE YOU THAT AUTHORITY!!
YOU SOUL REAPERS CALL US EVIL AND SLAY US...
...BE-CAUSE YOU THINK ...
...YOU HOLD THE POWER OF JUSTICE IN YOUR HANDS!!
BUT YOU'RE JUST...

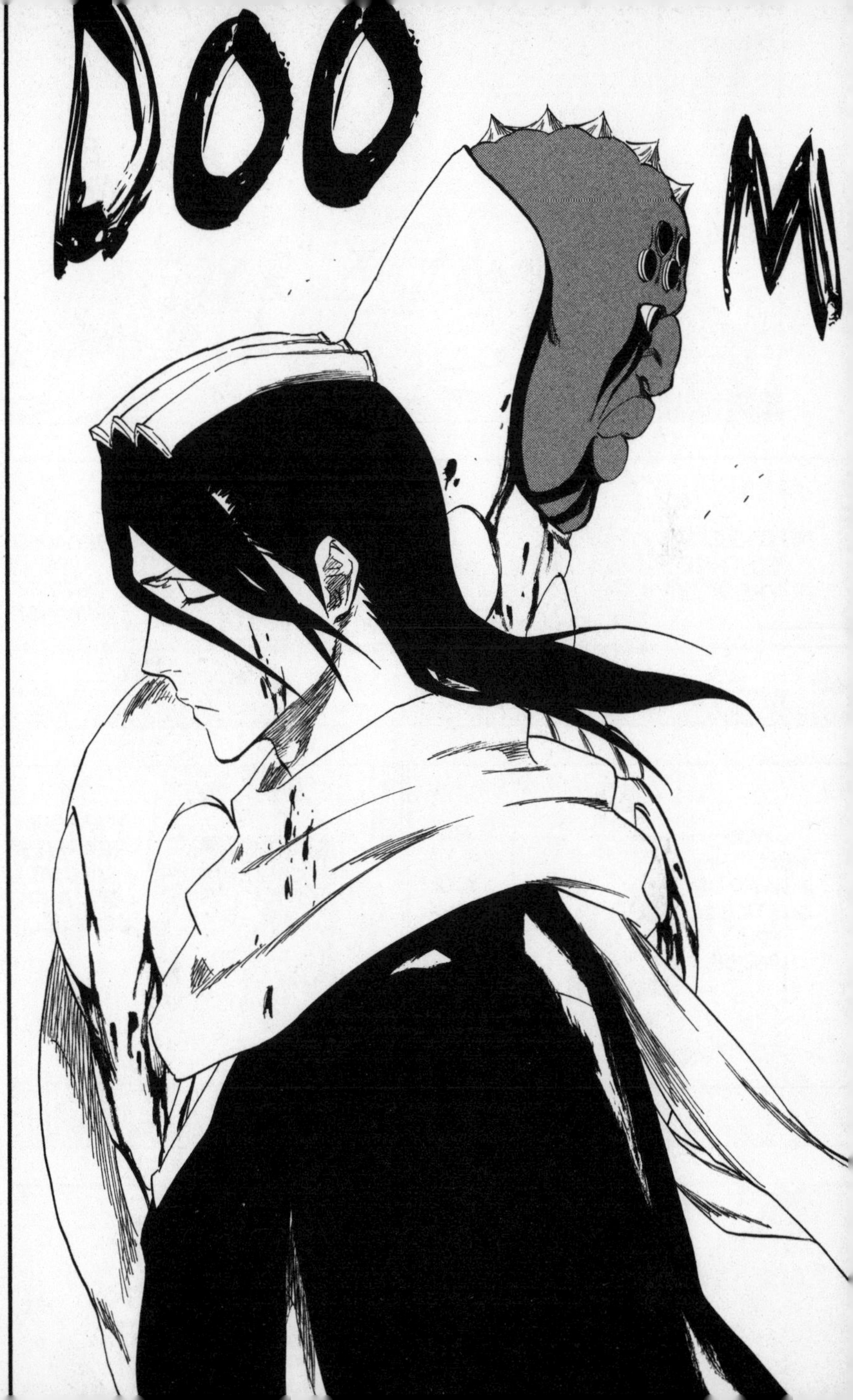
DOOM

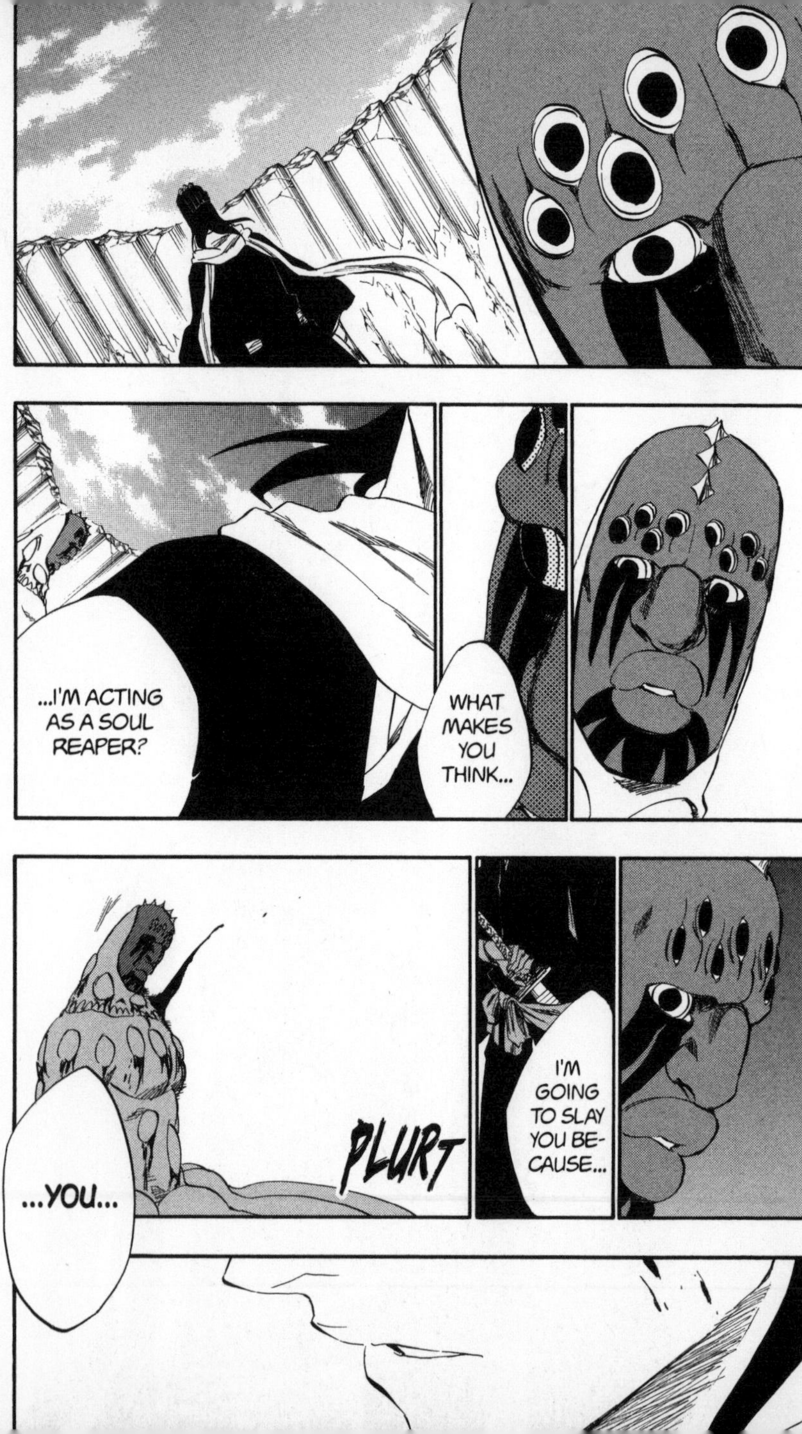
WHAT MAKES YOU THINK...
...I'M ACTING AS A SOUL REAPER?
I'M GOING TO SLAY YOU BECAUSE...
PLURT
...YOU...

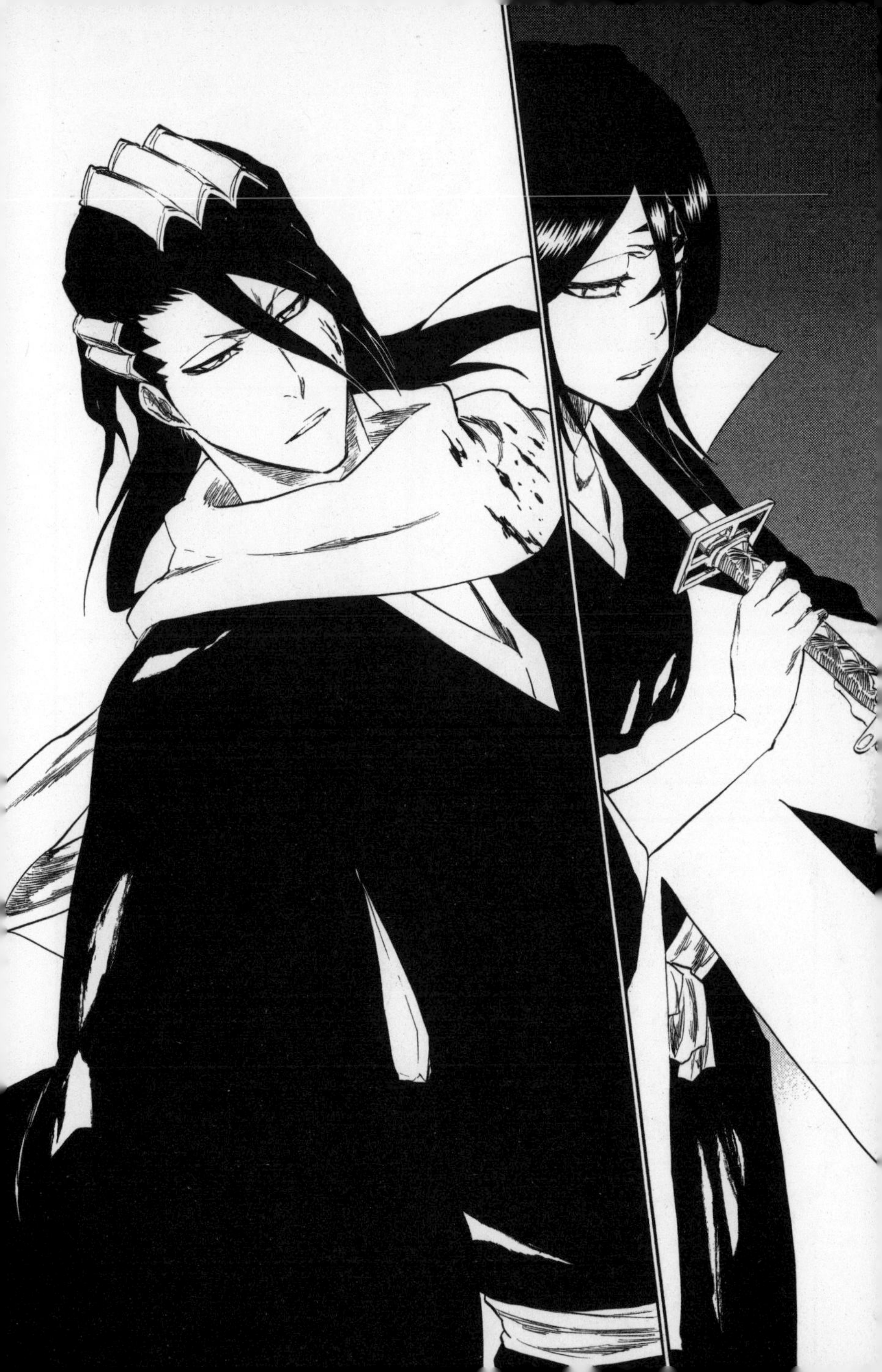

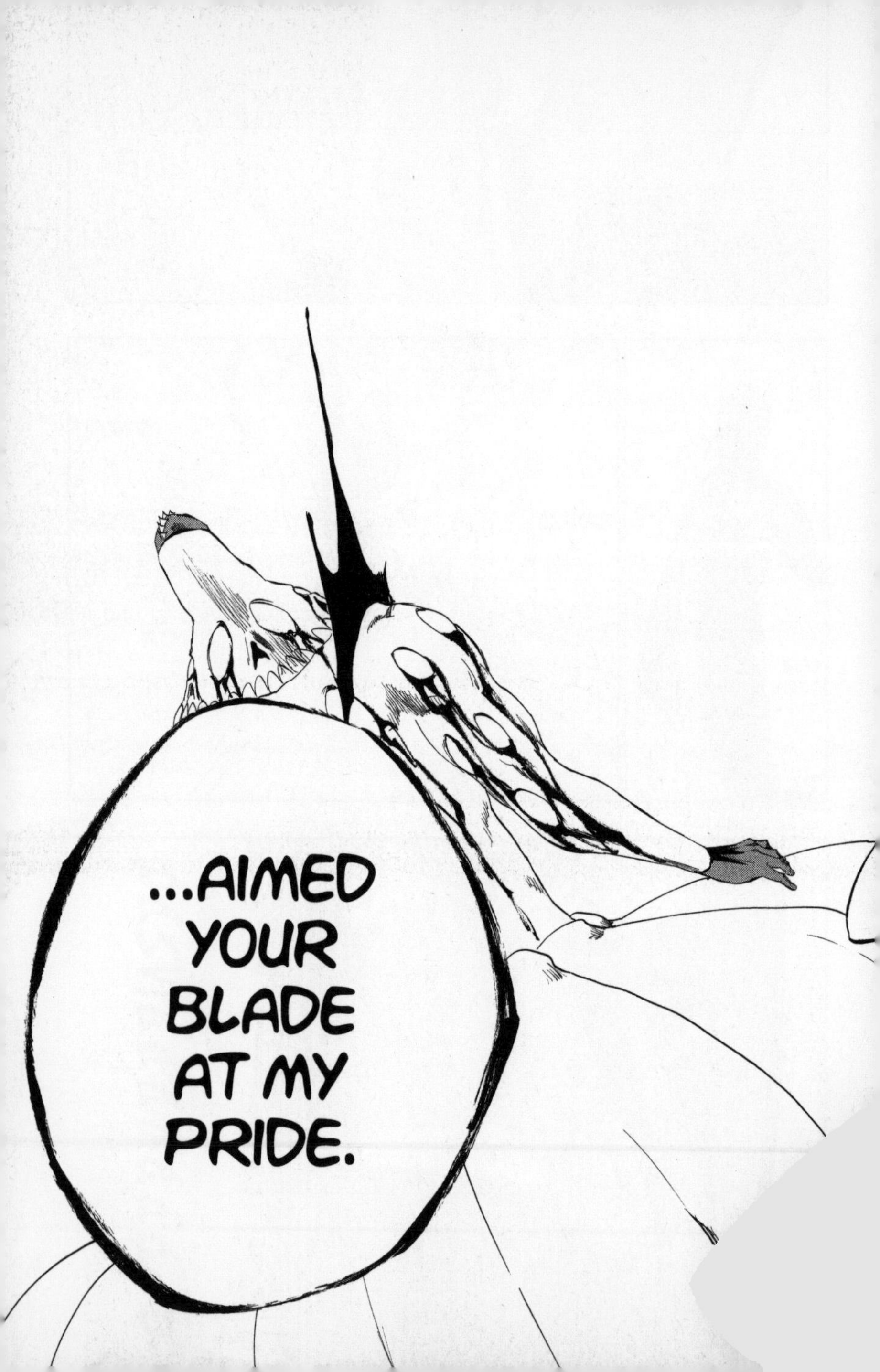
...AIMED YOUR BLADE AT MY PRIDE.

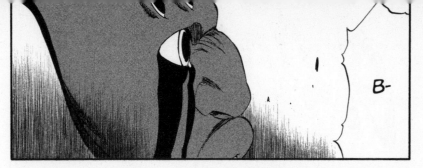

B-

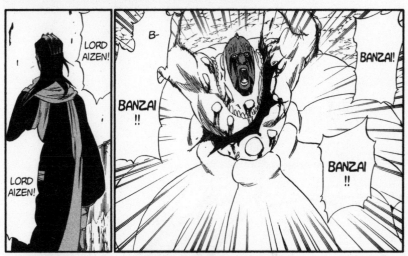

LORD
AIZEN!

LORD
AIZEN!

B-

BANZAI
!!

BANZAI!

BANZAI
!!

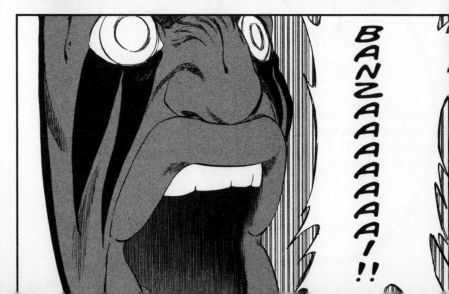

BANZAAAAAAAI!!

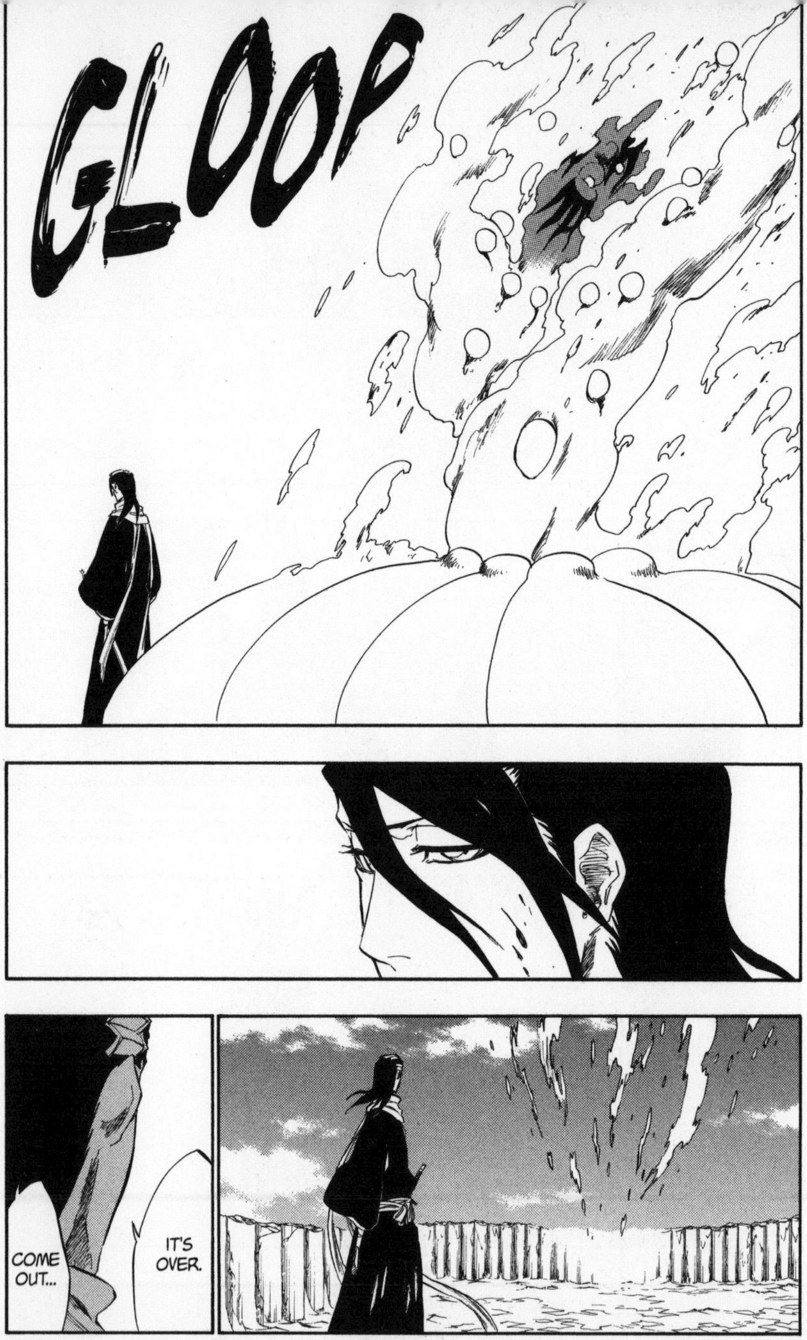
GLOOP
IT'S OVER.
COME OUT...

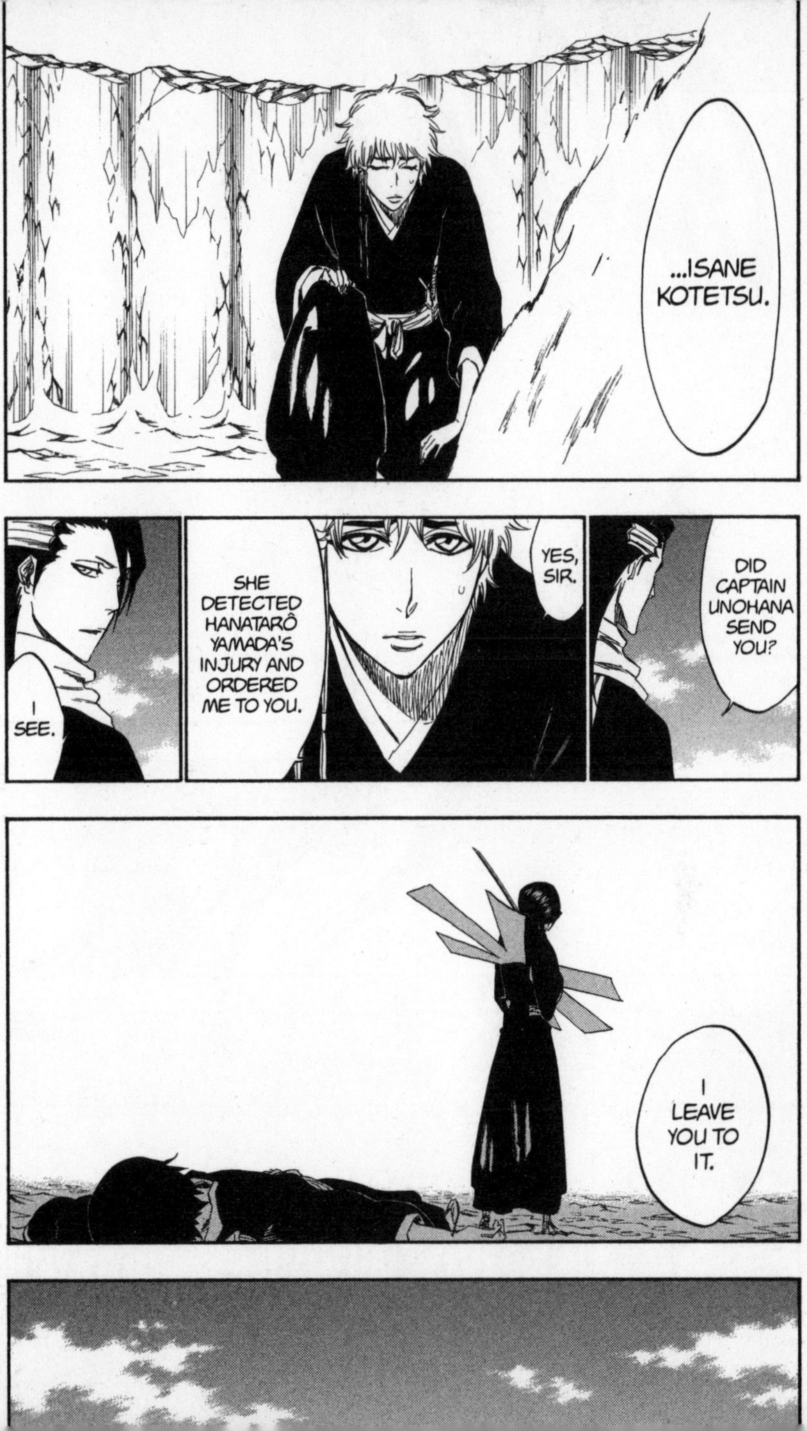
...ISANE KOTETSU.
DID CAPTAIN UNOHANA SEND YOU?
YES, SIR.
SHE DETECTED HANATARÔ YAMADA'S INJURY AND ORDERED ME TO YOU.
I SEE.
I LEAVE YOU TO IT.

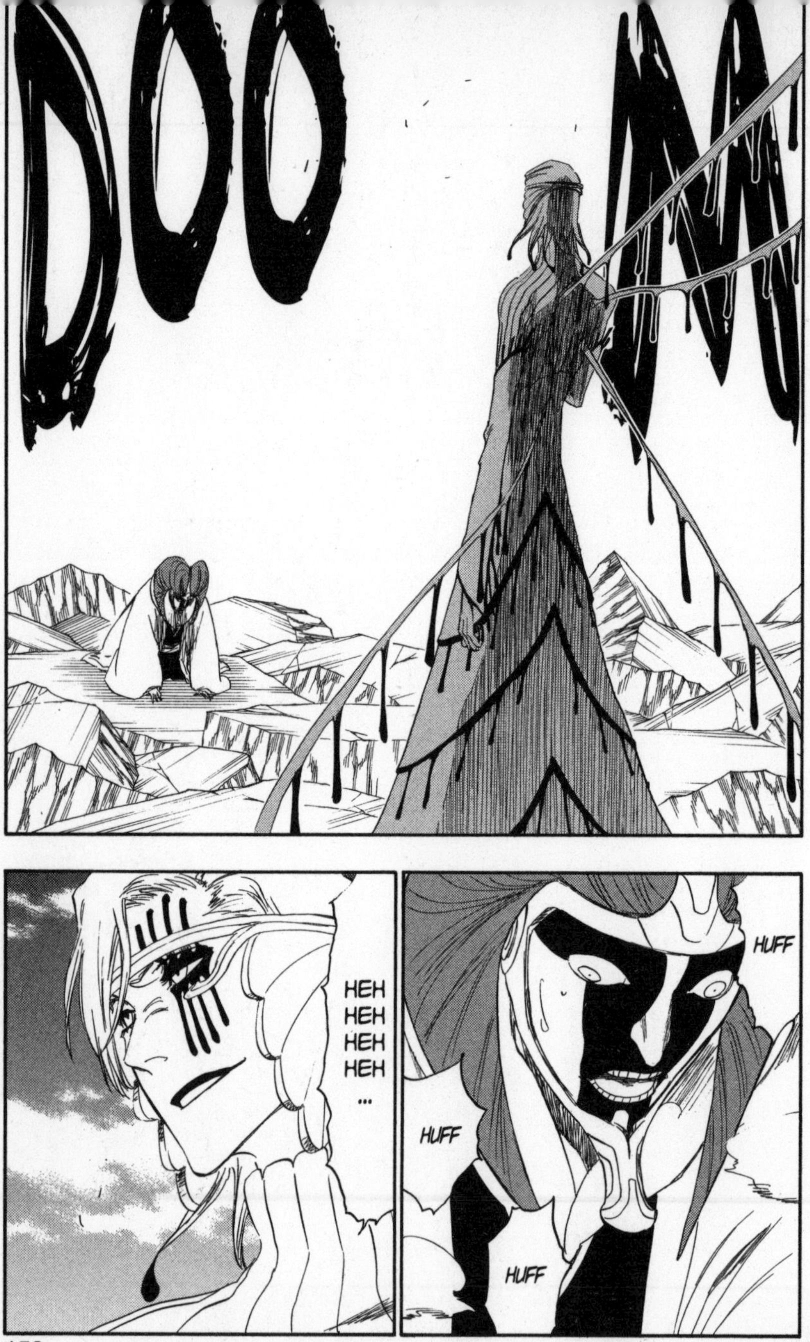
DOOM
HUFF
HUFF
HUFF
HEH HEH HEH HEH ...

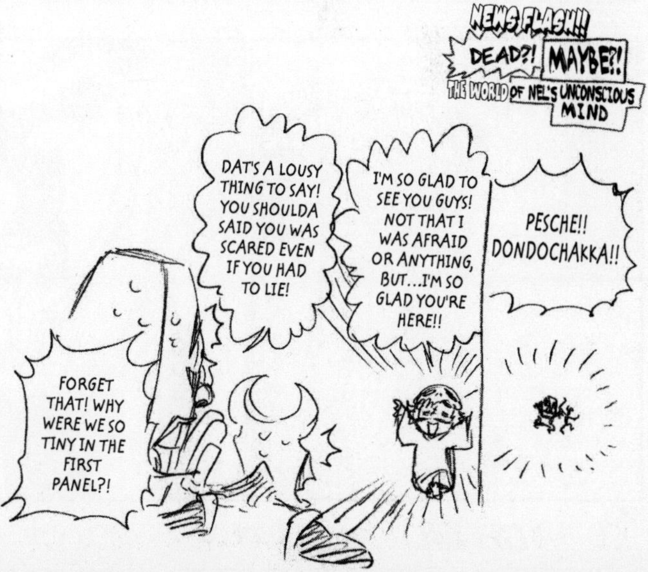
NEWS FLASH!!
DEAD?! MAYBE?!
THE WORLD OF NEL'S UNCONSCIOUS MIND
PESCHE!! DONDOCHAKKA!!
I'M SO GLAD TO SEE YOU GUYS! NOT THAT I WAS AFRAID OR ANYTHING, BUT...I'M SO GLAD YOU'RE HERE!!
DAT'S A LOUSY THING TO SAY! YOU SHOULDA SAID YOU WAS SCARED EVEN IF YOU HAD TO LIE!
FORGET THAT! WHY WERE WE SO TINY IN THE FIRST PANEL?!

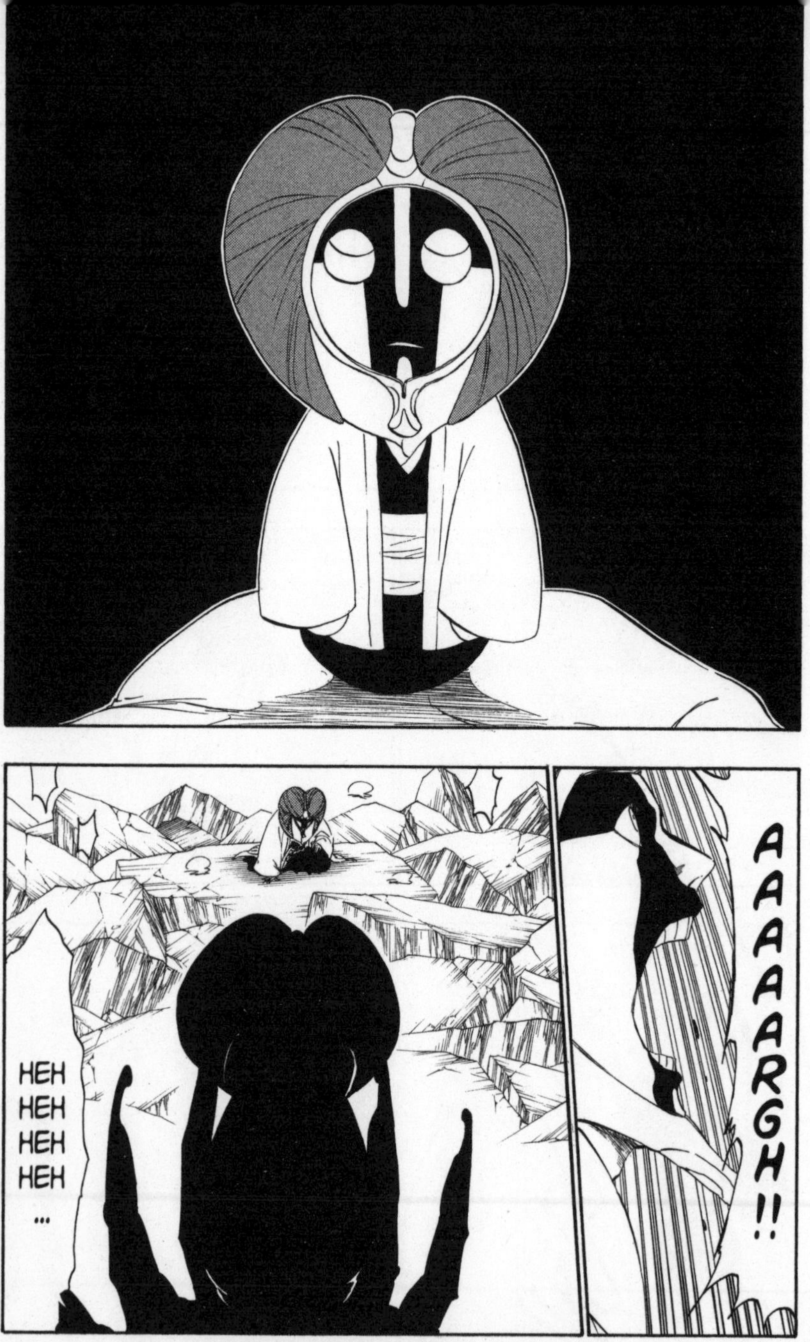
AAAAAARGH!!
HEH HEH HEH HEH ...

BLEACH 303. Dumdum-Dummy-Dumbstruck

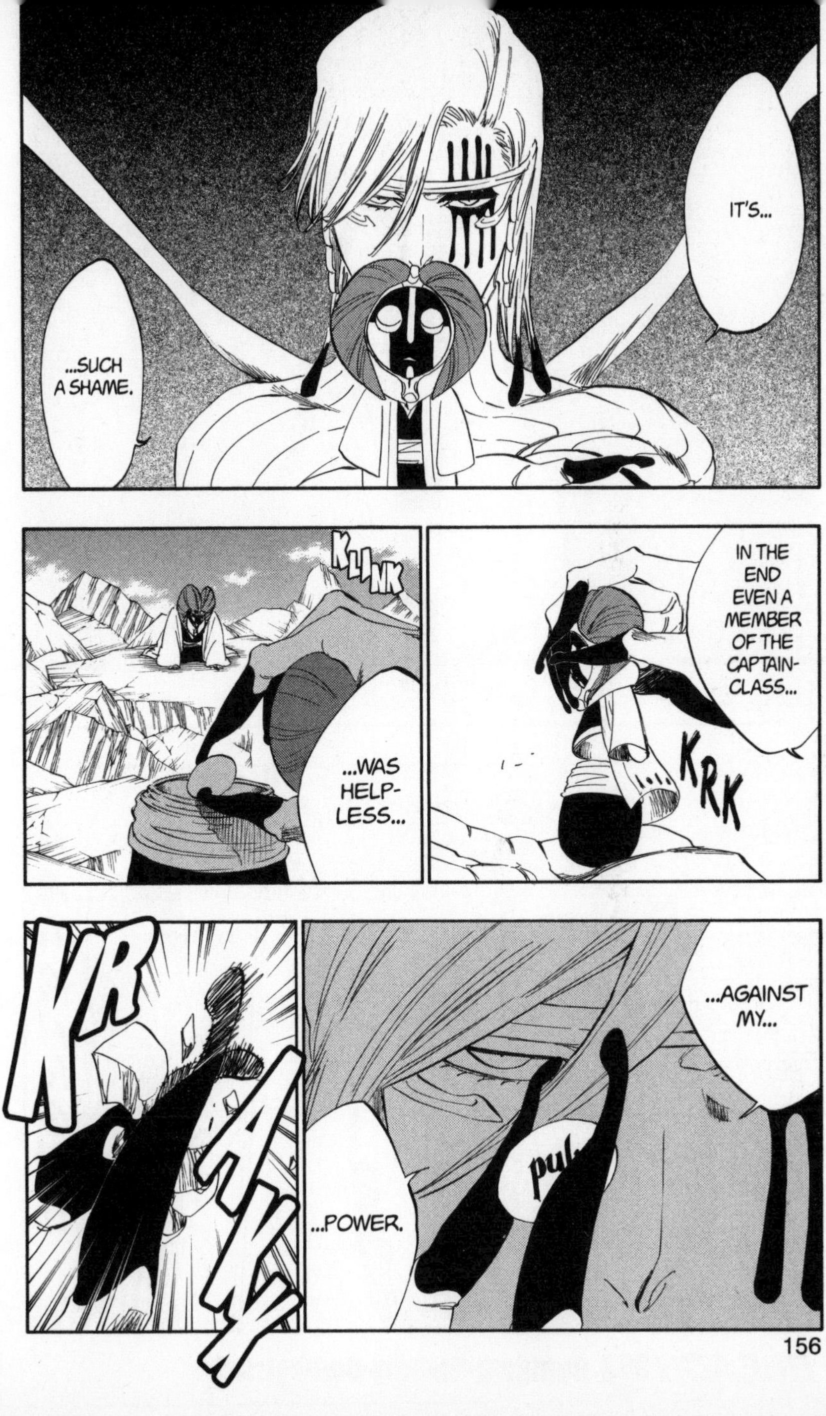
IT'S...
...SUCH A SHAME.
IN THE END EVEN A MEMBER OF THE CAPTAIN-CLASS...
KRK
KLINK
...WAS HELPLESS...
...AGAINST MY...
...POWER.

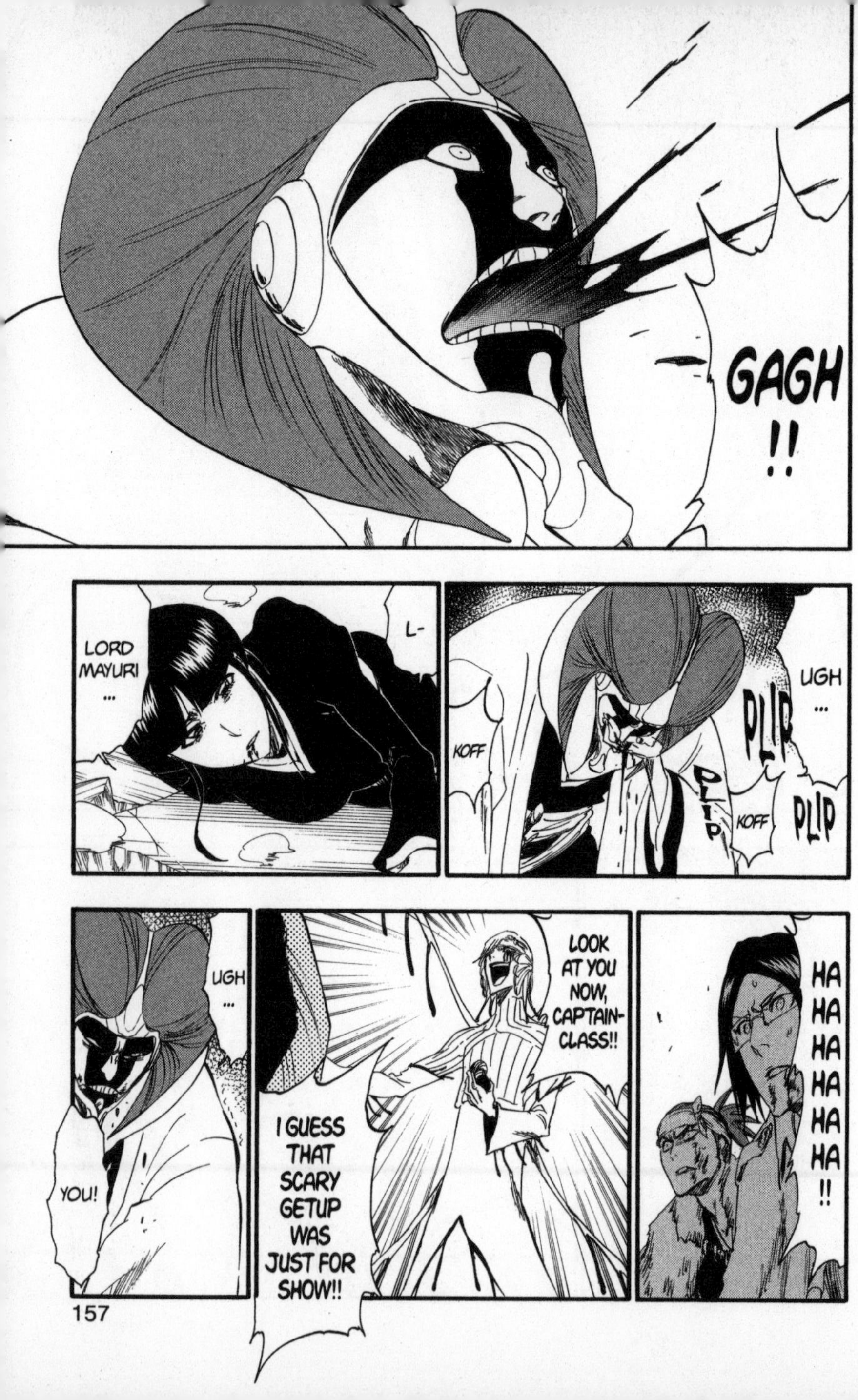
GAGH!!
UGH...
PLIP
KOFF
PLIP
KOFF
PLIP
L-
LORD MAYURI...
HA HA HA HA HA HA!!
LOOK AT YOU NOW, CAPTAIN-CLASS!!
I GUESS THAT SCARY GETUP WAS JUST FOR SHOW!!
UGH...
YOU!

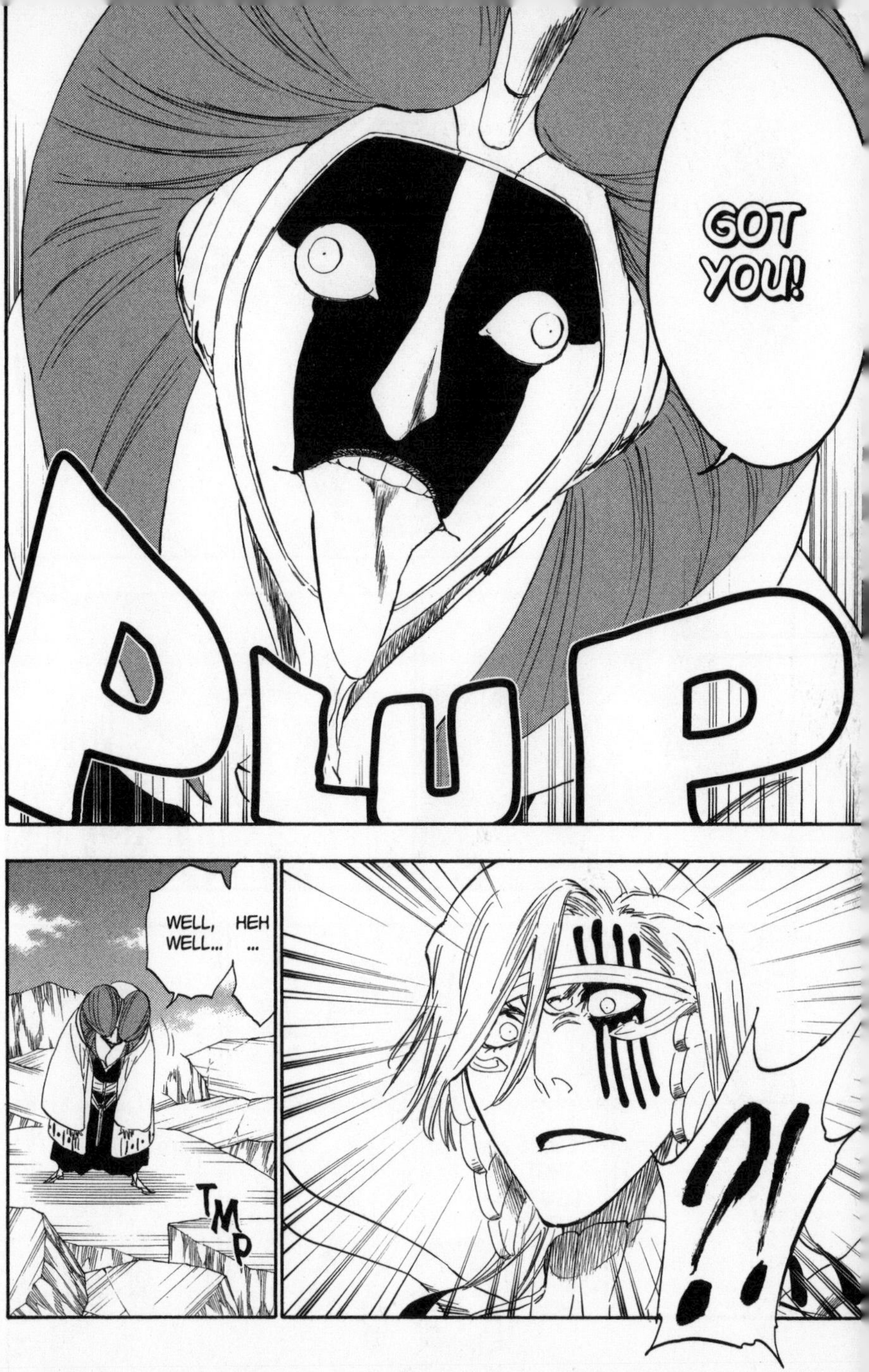
GOT YOU!
PLUP
?!
WELL, WELL... HEH ...
TMP

READ THIS WAY

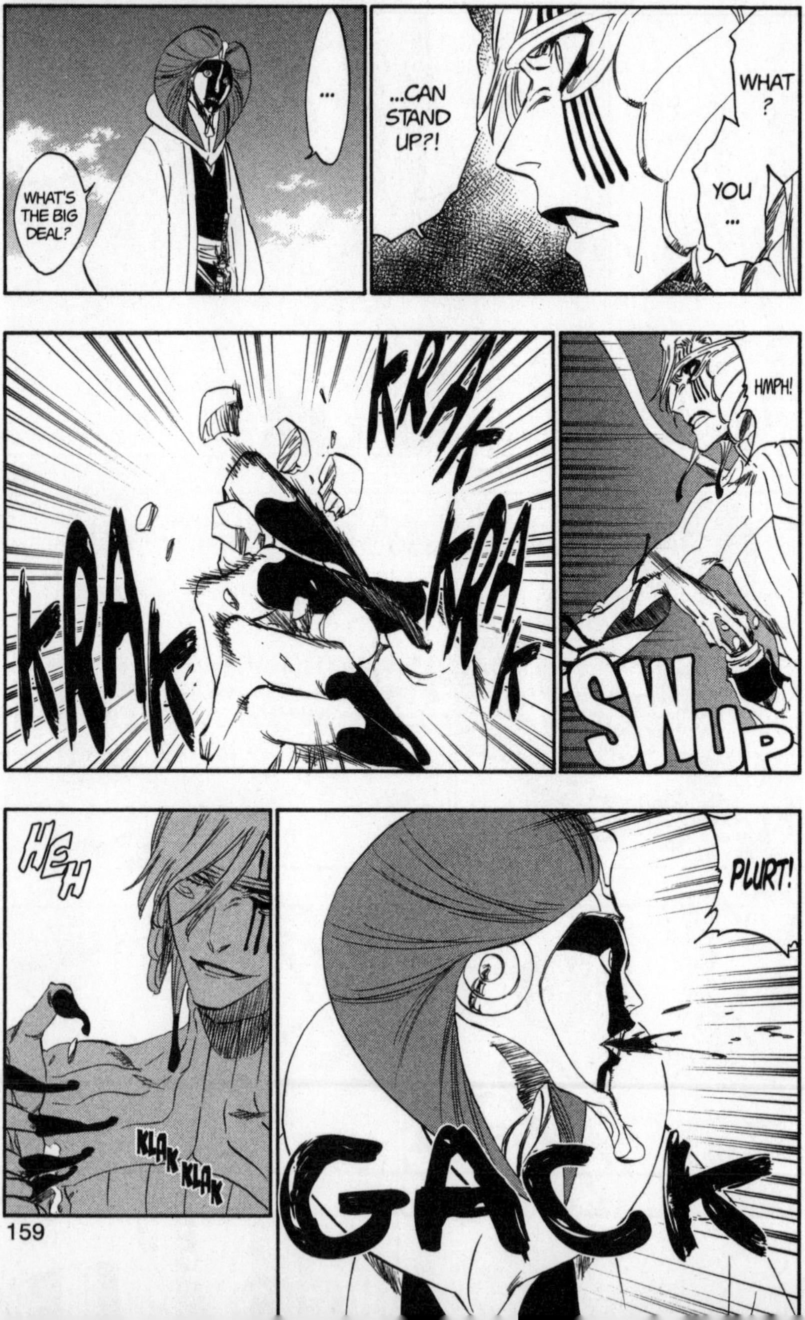

WHAT? YOU...
...CAN STAND UP?!
...
WHAT'S THE BIG DEAL?
HMPH!
SWUP
KRAK
KRAK
KRAK
PLURT!
GACK
HEH
KLAK KLAK

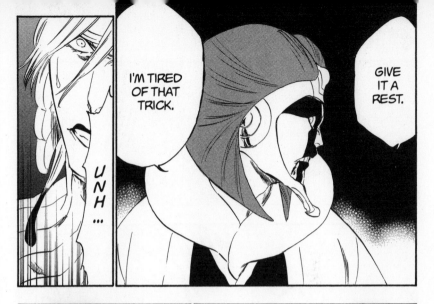

I'M TIRED OF THAT TRICK.

GIVE IT A REST.

UNH...

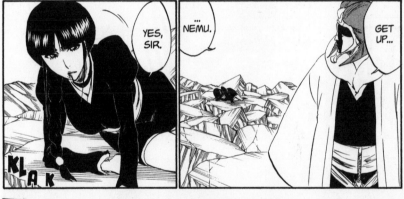

YES, SIR.

...NEMU.

GET UP...

KLAK

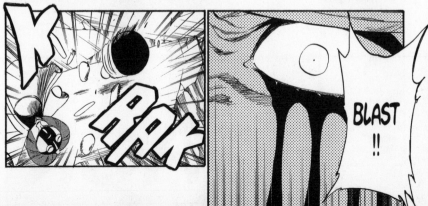

K RAK

BLAST!!

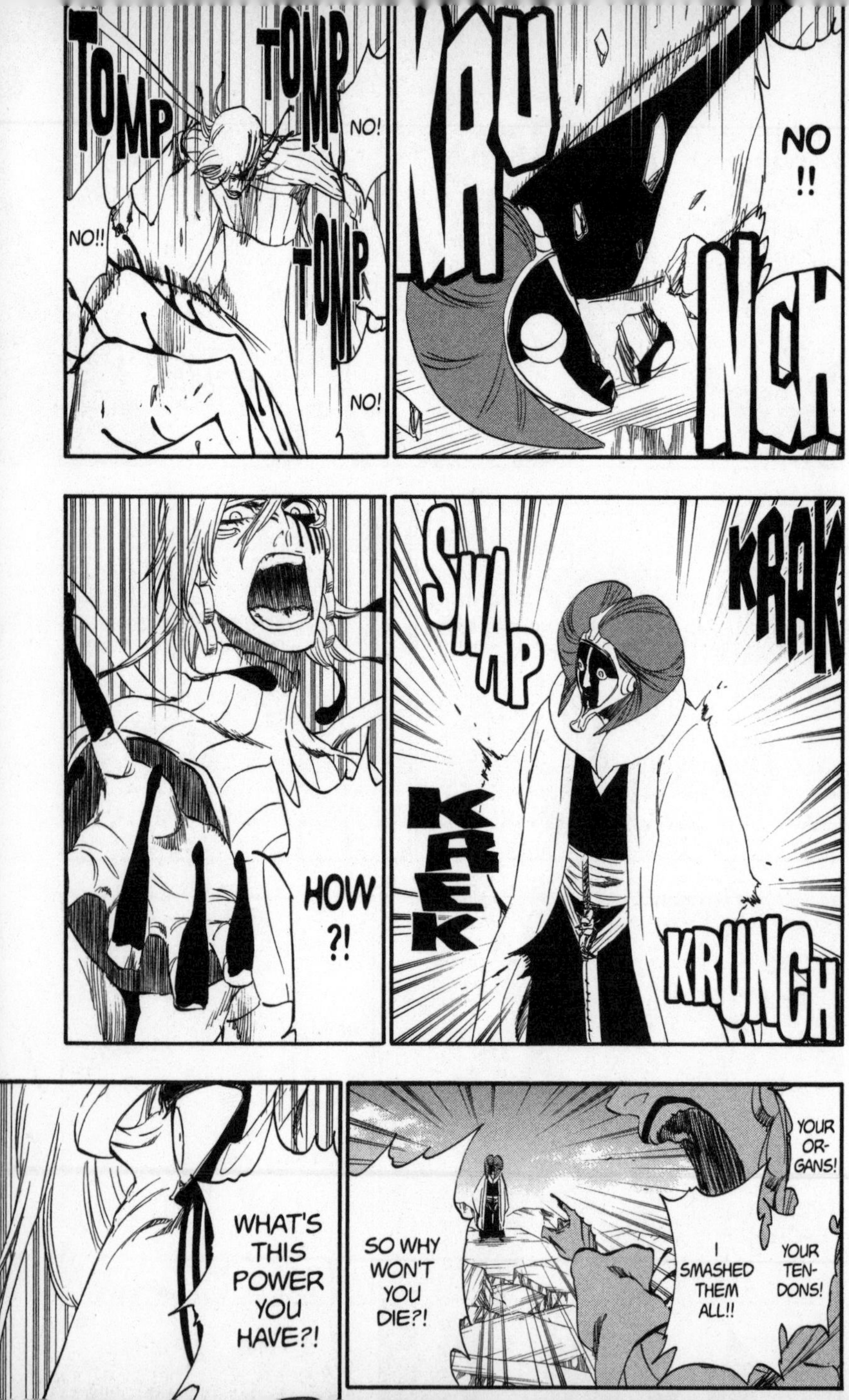
KRA
NO !!
NCH
TOMP
NO!
TOMP
NO!!
TOMP
NO!
KRAK
SNAP
KREK
KRUNCH
HOW ?!
YOUR OR-GANS!
YOUR TEN-DONS!
I SMASHED THEM ALL!!
SO WHY WON'T YOU DIE?!
WHAT'S THIS POWER YOU HAVE?!

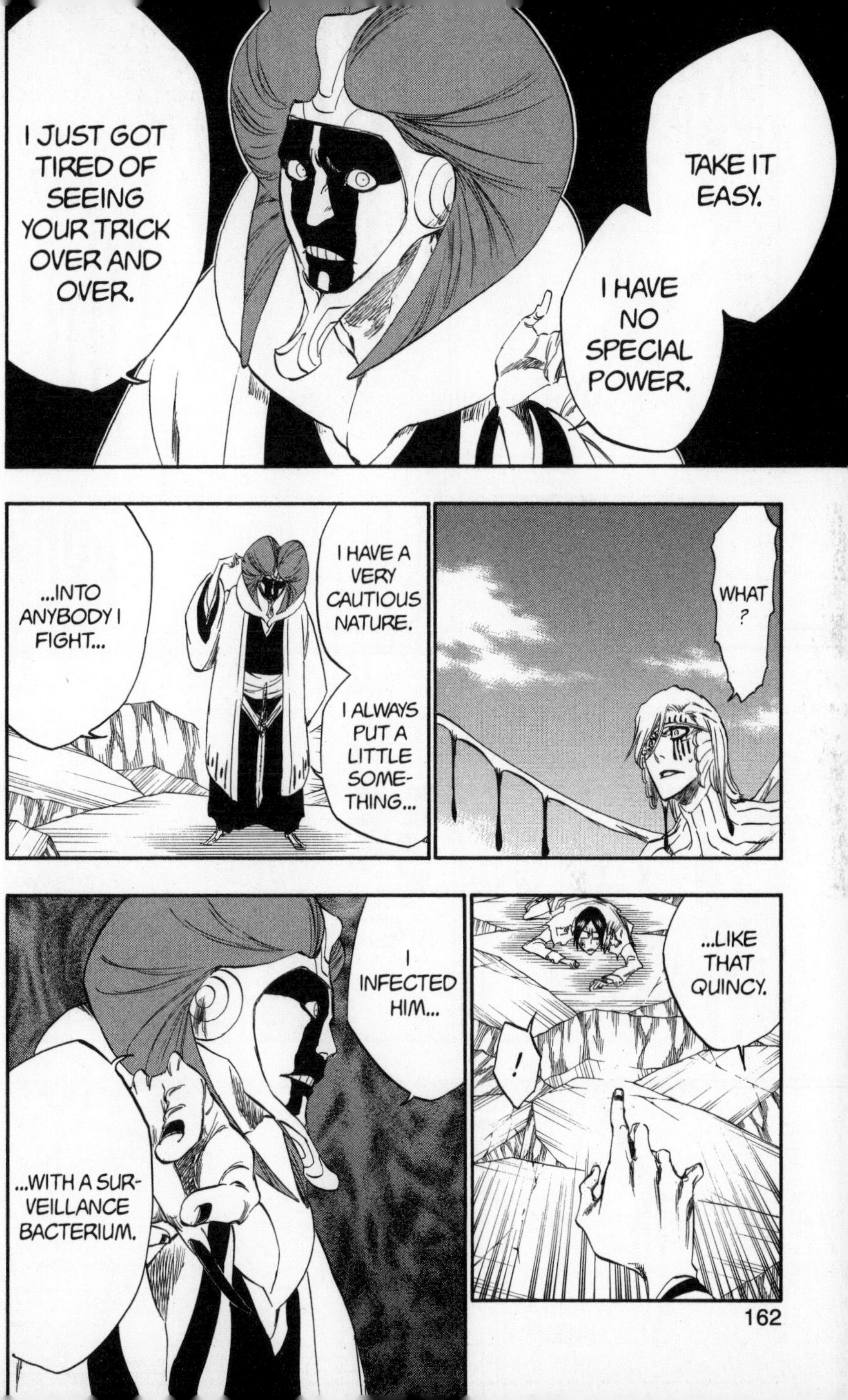
TAKE IT EASY.
I HAVE NO SPECIAL POWER.
I JUST GOT TIRED OF SEEING YOUR TRICK OVER AND OVER.
WHAT?
I HAVE A VERY CAUTIOUS NATURE.
I ALWAYS PUT A LITTLE SOME-THING...
...INTO ANYBODY I FIGHT...
...LIKE THAT QUINCY.
!
I INFECTED HIM...
...WITH A SUR-VEILLANCE BACTERIUM.

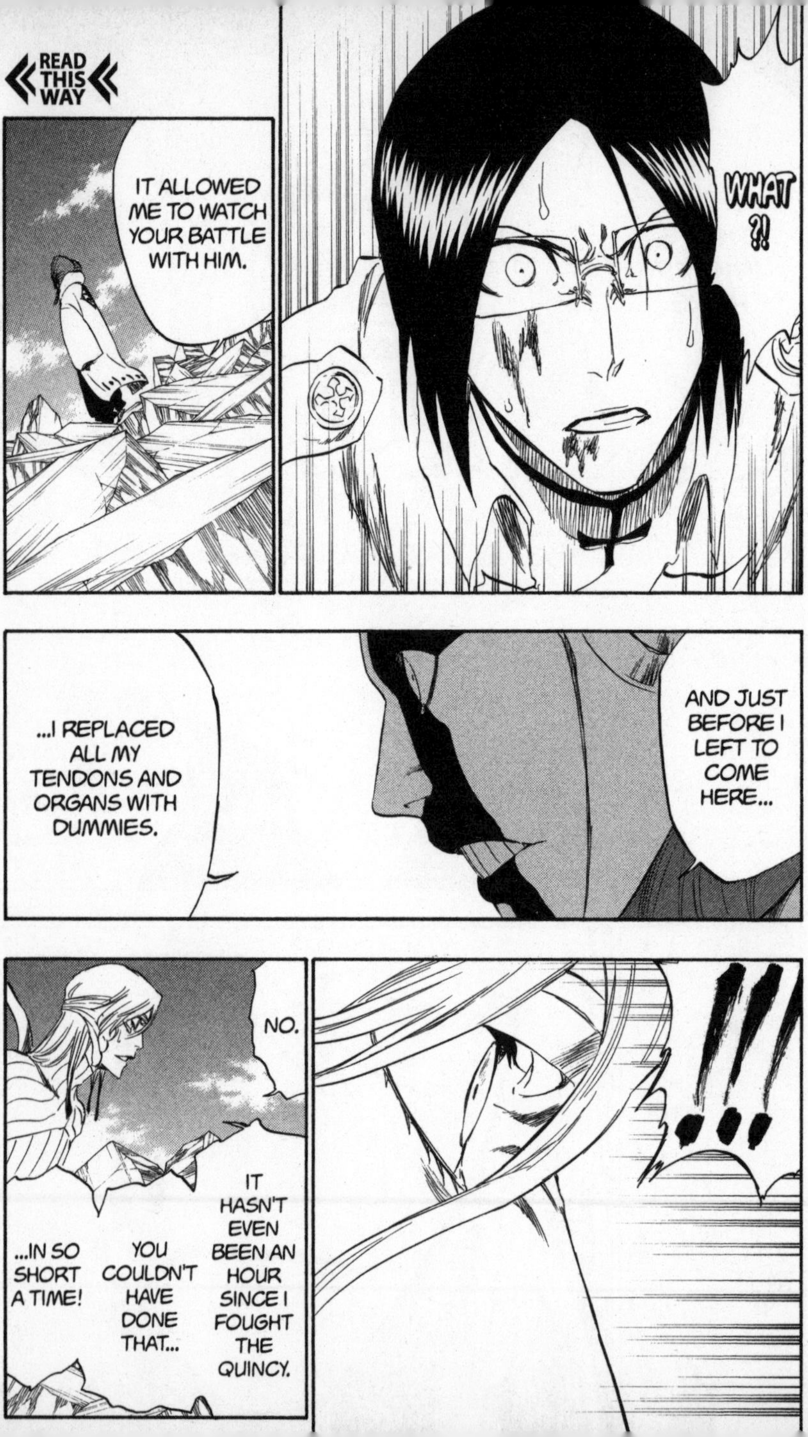
READ THIS WAY
WHAT ?!
IT ALLOWED ME TO WATCH YOUR BATTLE WITH HIM.
AND JUST BEFORE I LEFT TO COME HERE...
...I REPLACED ALL MY TENDONS AND ORGANS WITH DUMMIES.
!!!
NO.
IT HASN'T EVEN BEEN AN HOUR SINCE I FOUGHT THE QUINCY.
YOU COULDN'T HAVE DONE THAT...
...IN SO SHORT A TIME!

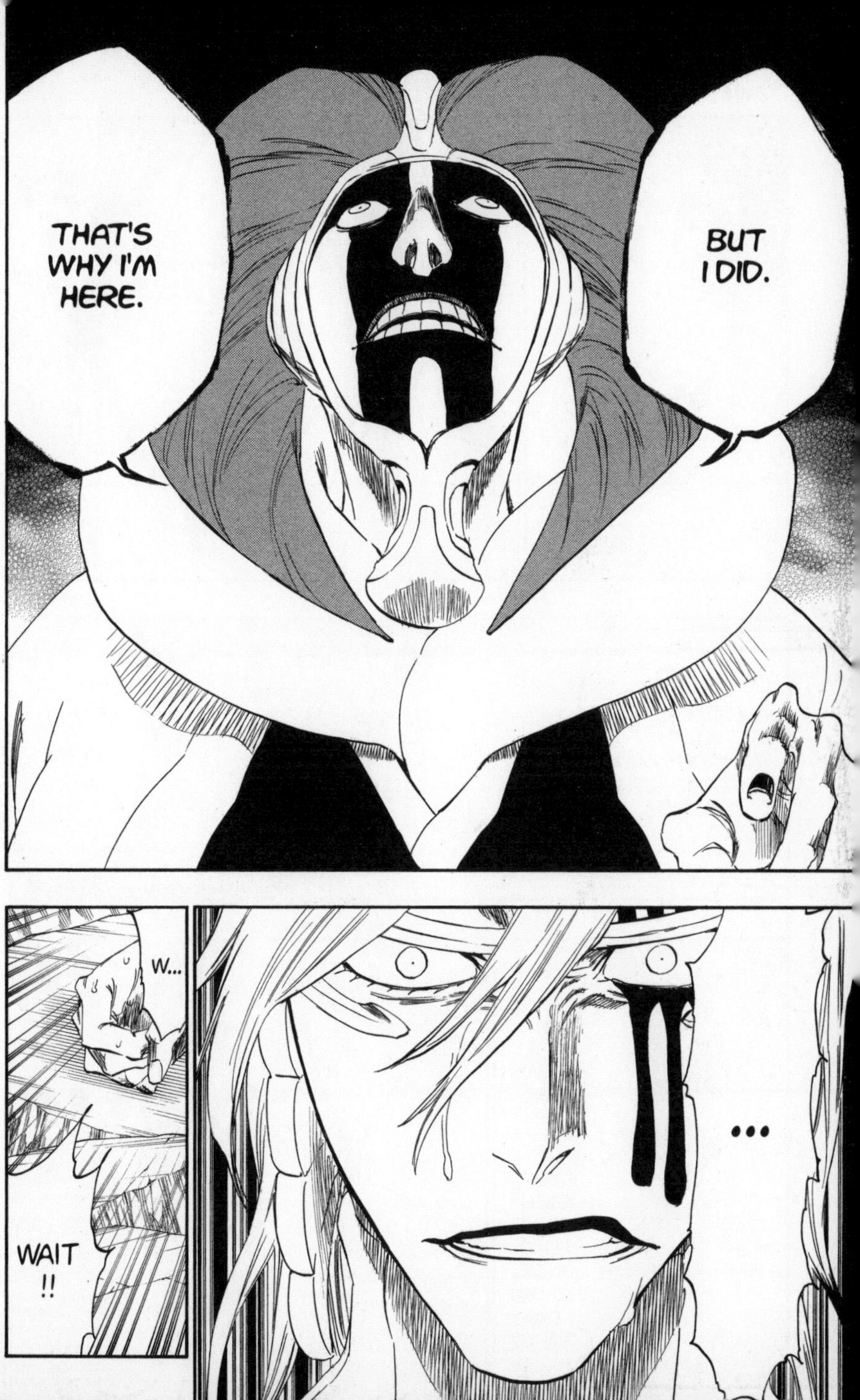
BUT I DID.
THAT'S WHY I'M HERE.
...
W...
WAIT !!

READ THIS WAY

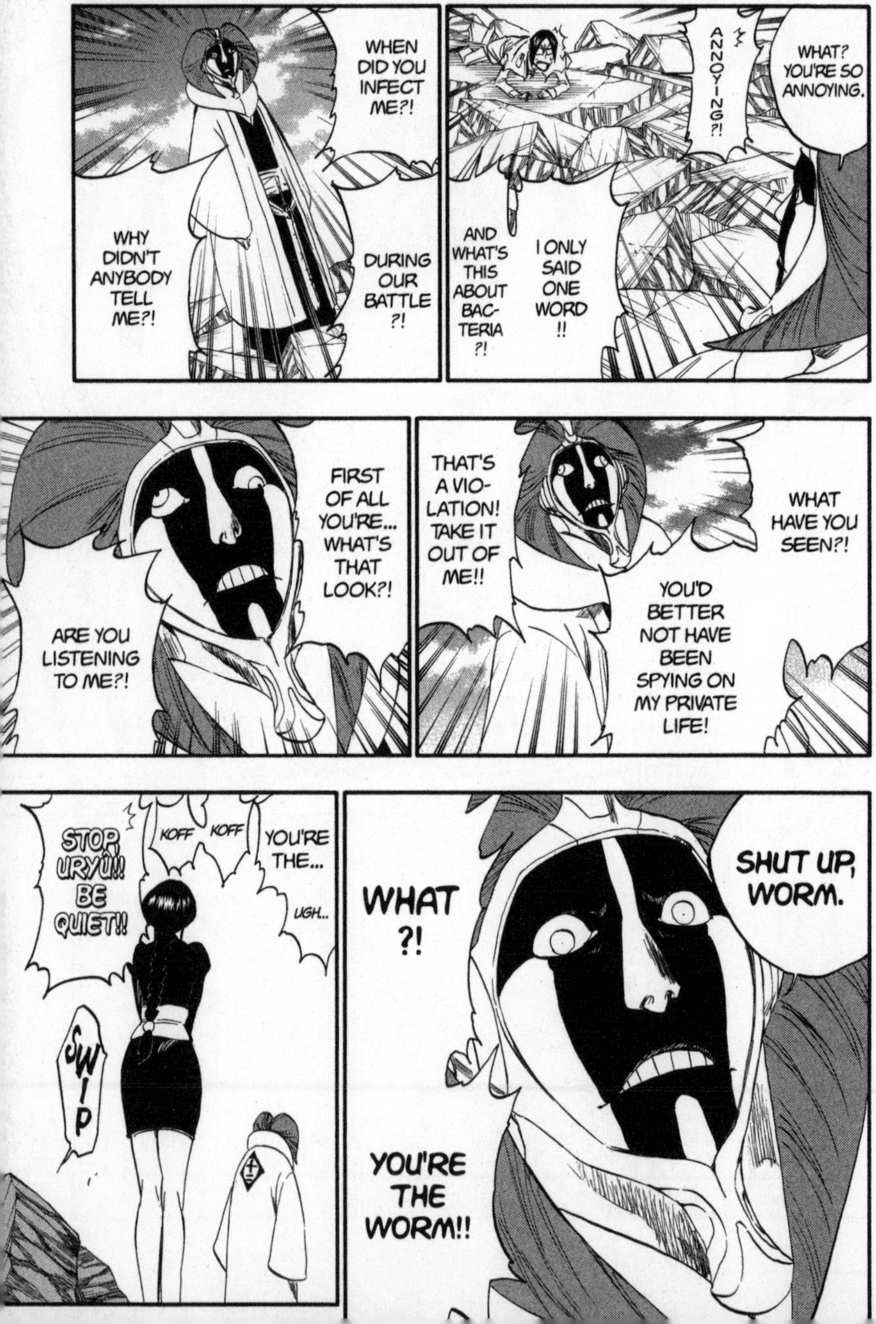
WHAT? YOU'RE SO ANNOYING.
ANNOYING?!
I ONLY SAID ONE WORD!!
AND WHAT'S THIS ABOUT BACTERIA?!
WHEN DID YOU INFECT ME?!
DURING OUR BATTLE?!
WHY DIDN'T ANYBODY TELL ME?!
WHAT HAVE YOU SEEN?!
YOU'D BETTER NOT HAVE BEEN SPYING ON MY PRIVATE LIFE!
THAT'S A VIOLATION! TAKE IT OUT OF ME!!
FIRST OF ALL YOU'RE... WHAT'S THAT LOOK?!
ARE YOU LISTENING TO ME?!
SHUT UP, WORM.
WHAT?!
YOU'RE THE WORM!!
YOU'RE THE...
UGH..
KOFF
KOFF
STOP, URYŪ!! BE QUIET!!
SWIP

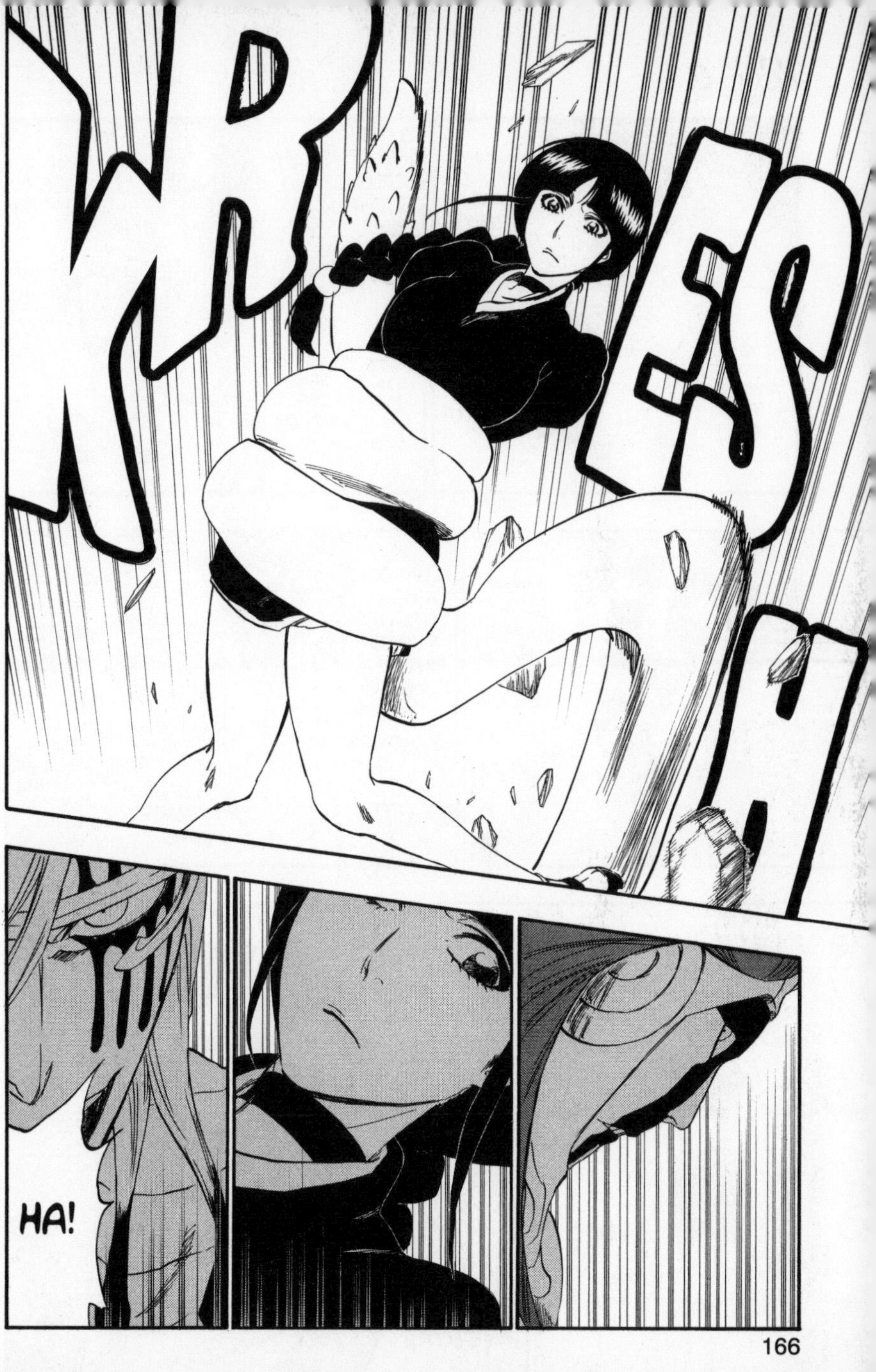
KRESH
HA!

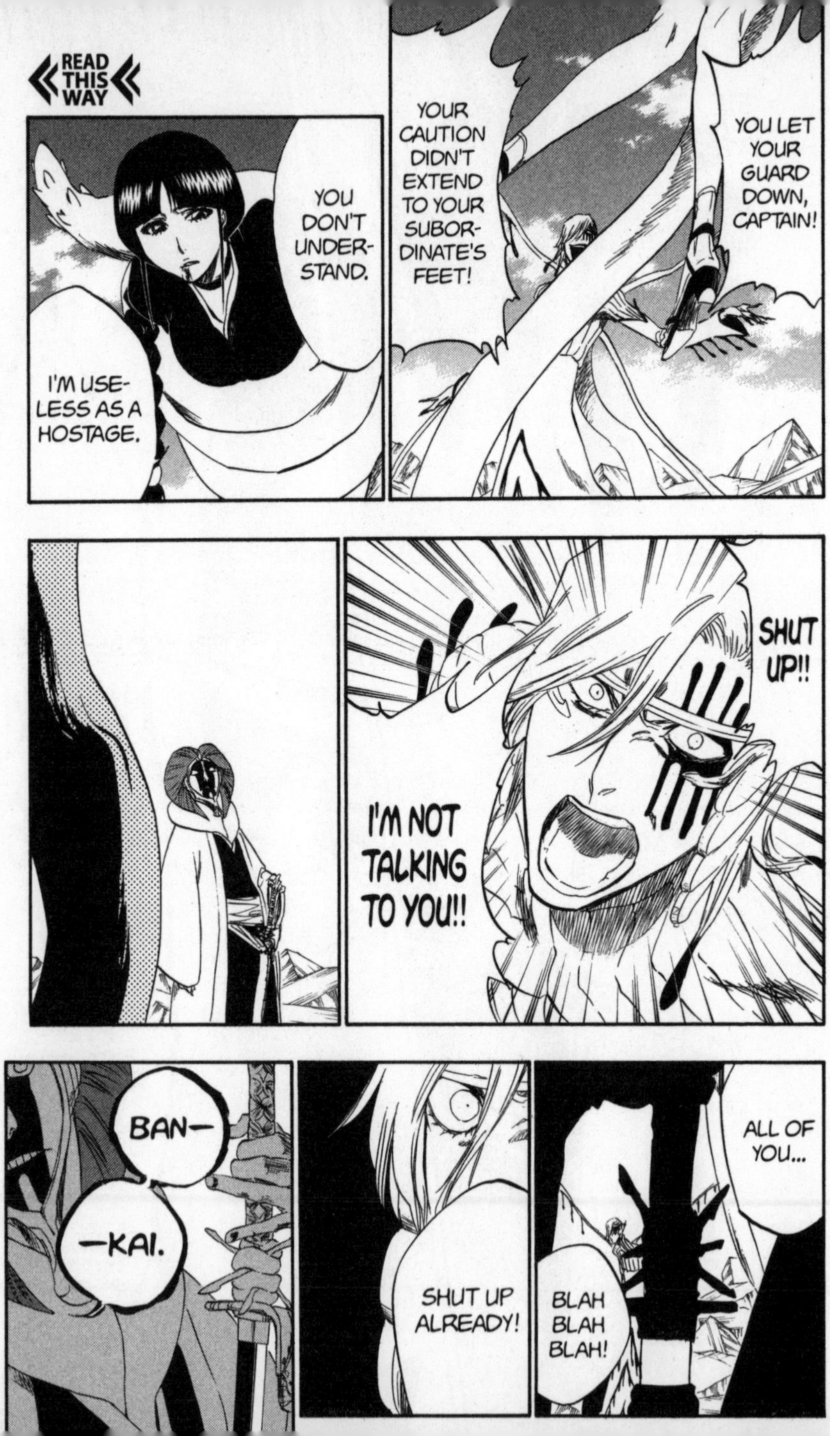
READ THIS WAY
YOU LET YOUR GUARD DOWN, CAPTAIN!
YOUR CAUTION DIDN'T EXTEND TO YOUR SUBOR-DINATE'S FEET!
YOU DON'T UNDER-STAND.
I'M USE-LESS AS A HOSTAGE.
SHUT UP!!
I'M NOT TALKING TO YOU!!
ALL OF YOU...
BLAH BLAH BLAH!
SHUT UP ALREADY!
BAN—
—KAI.

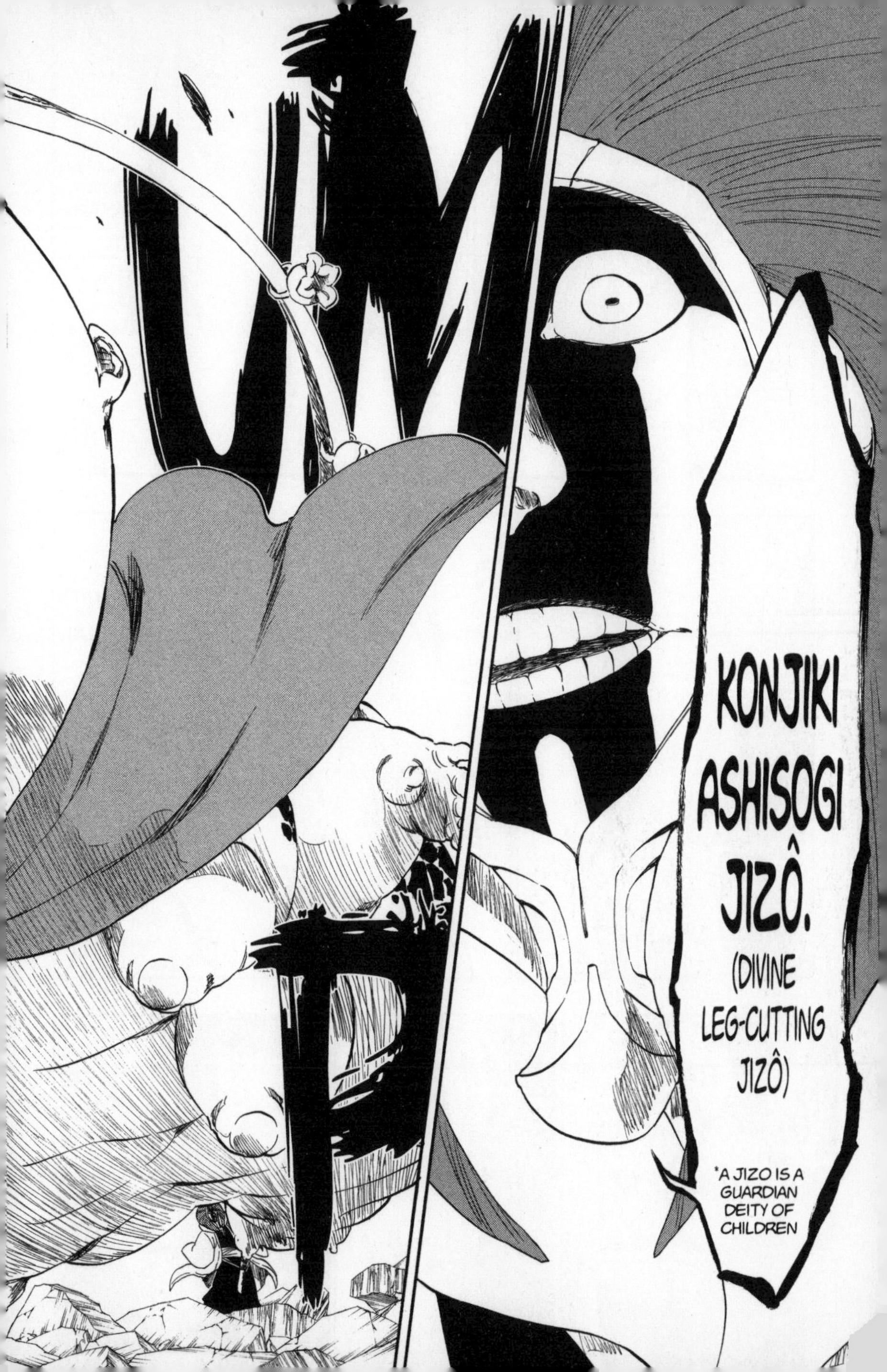
KONJIKI ASHISOGI JIZÔ.
(DIVINE LEG-CUTTING JIZÔ)
*A JIZO IS A GUARDIAN DEITY OF CHILDREN

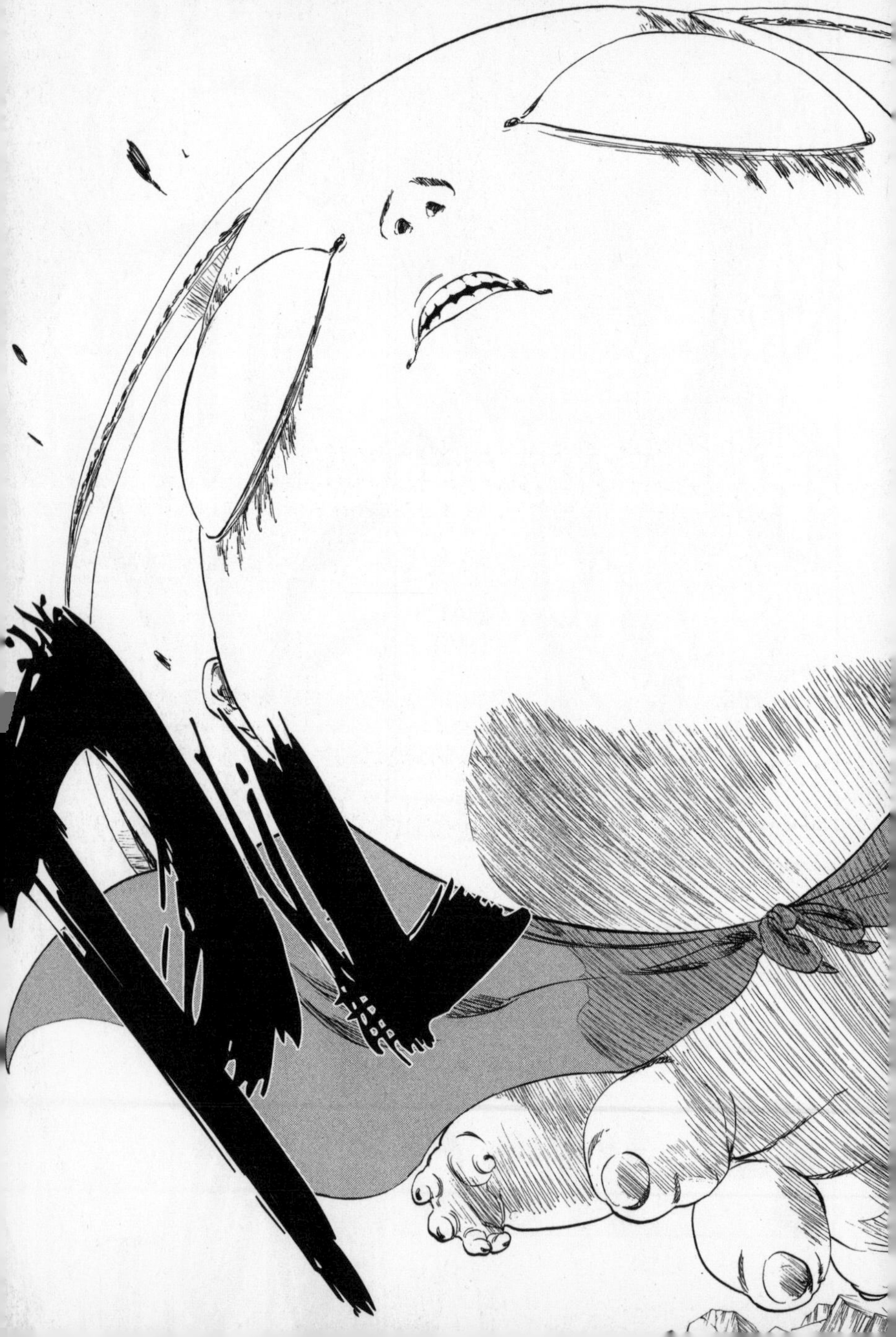

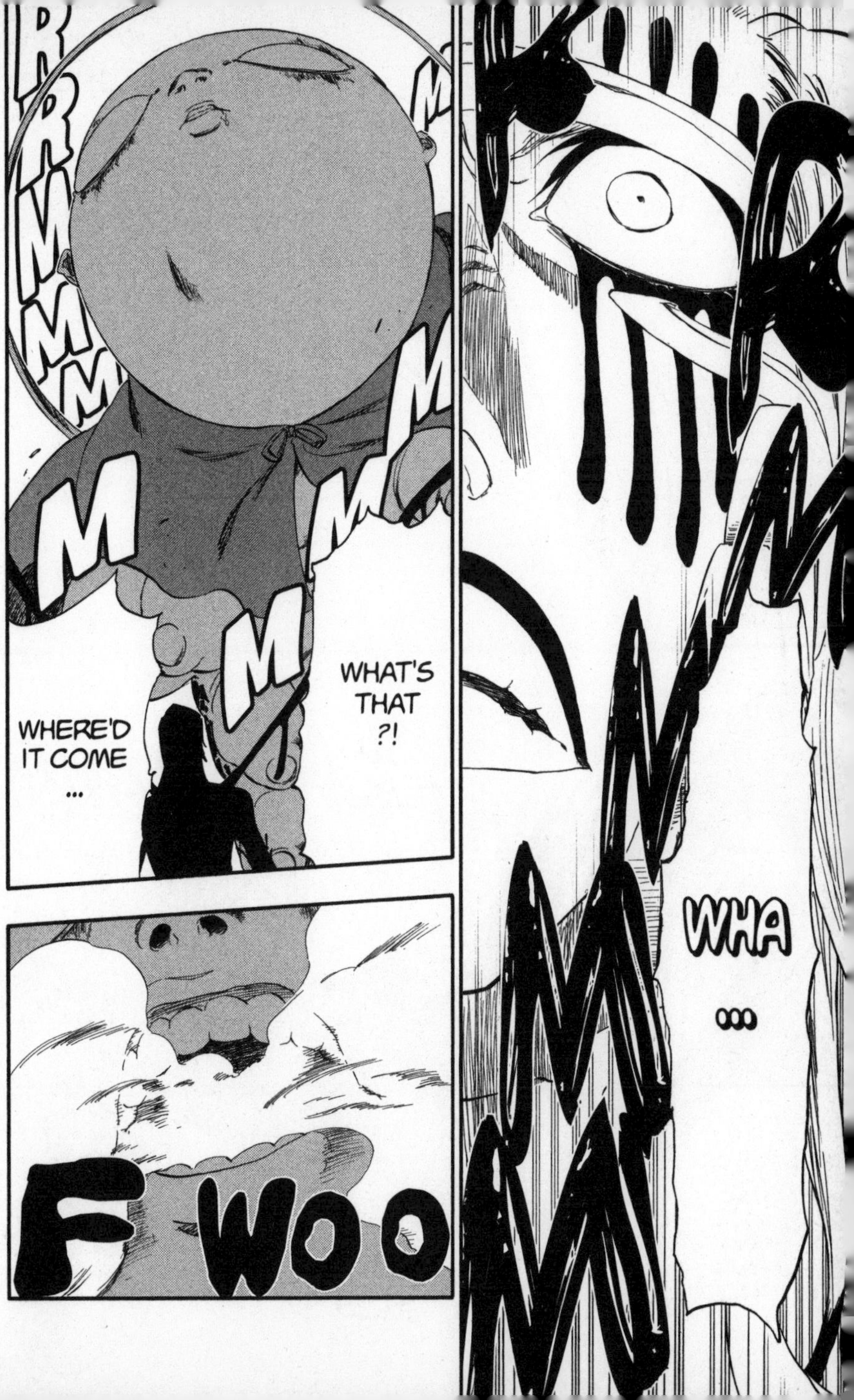
WHA ...
RRRMMMMM
MMMMM
WHAT'S THAT ?!
WHERE'D IT COME ...
FWOO

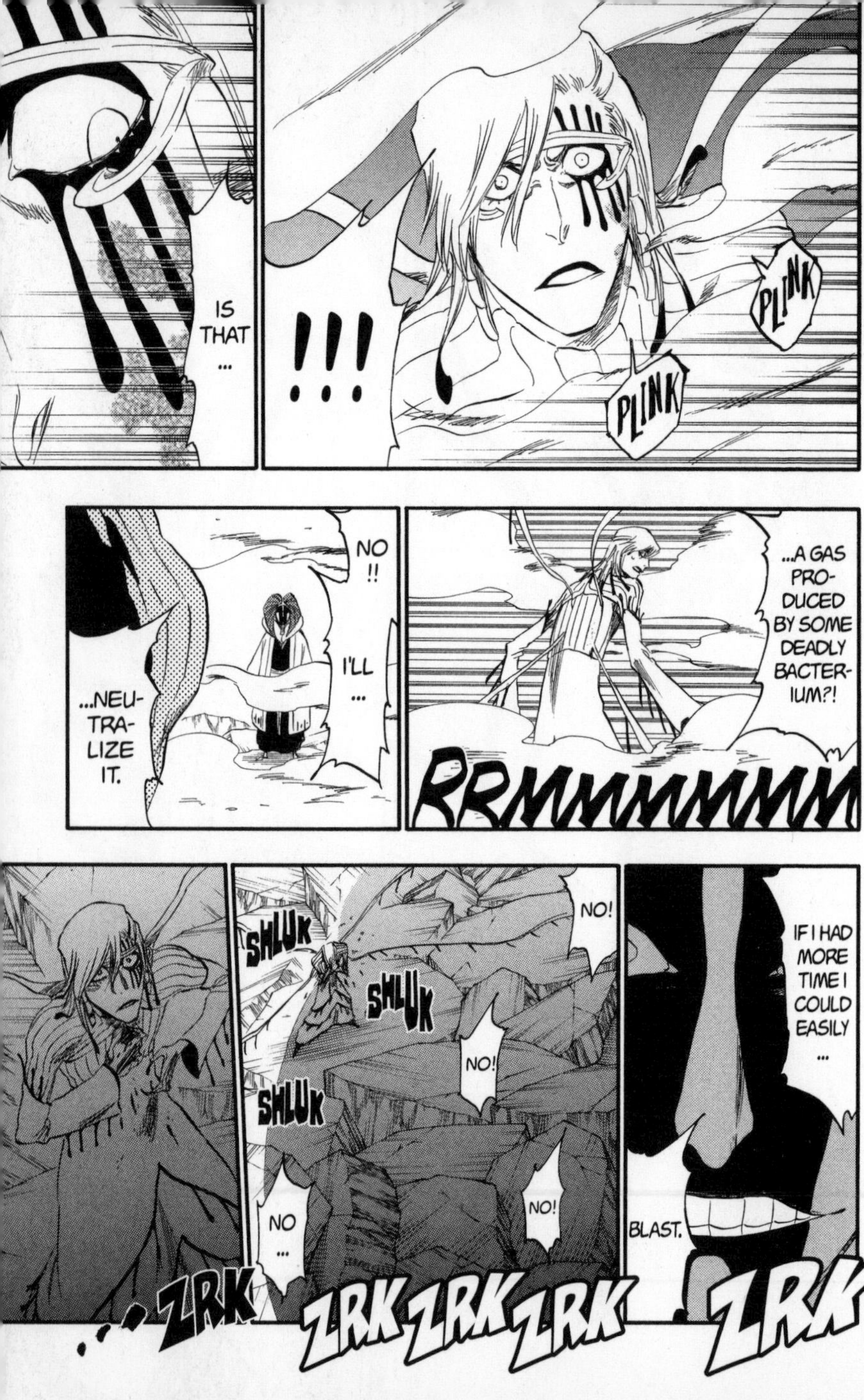
PLINK
PLINK
!!!
IS THAT ...
...A GAS PRODUCED BY SOME DEADLY BACTERIUM?!
RRMMMMMMMM
NO !!
I'LL ...
...NEUTRALIZE IT.
IF I HAD MORE TIME I COULD EASILY ...
BLAST.
ZRK
NO!
SHLUK
SHLUK
NO!
SHLUK
NO!
NO ...
ZRK ZRK ZRK
...ZRK

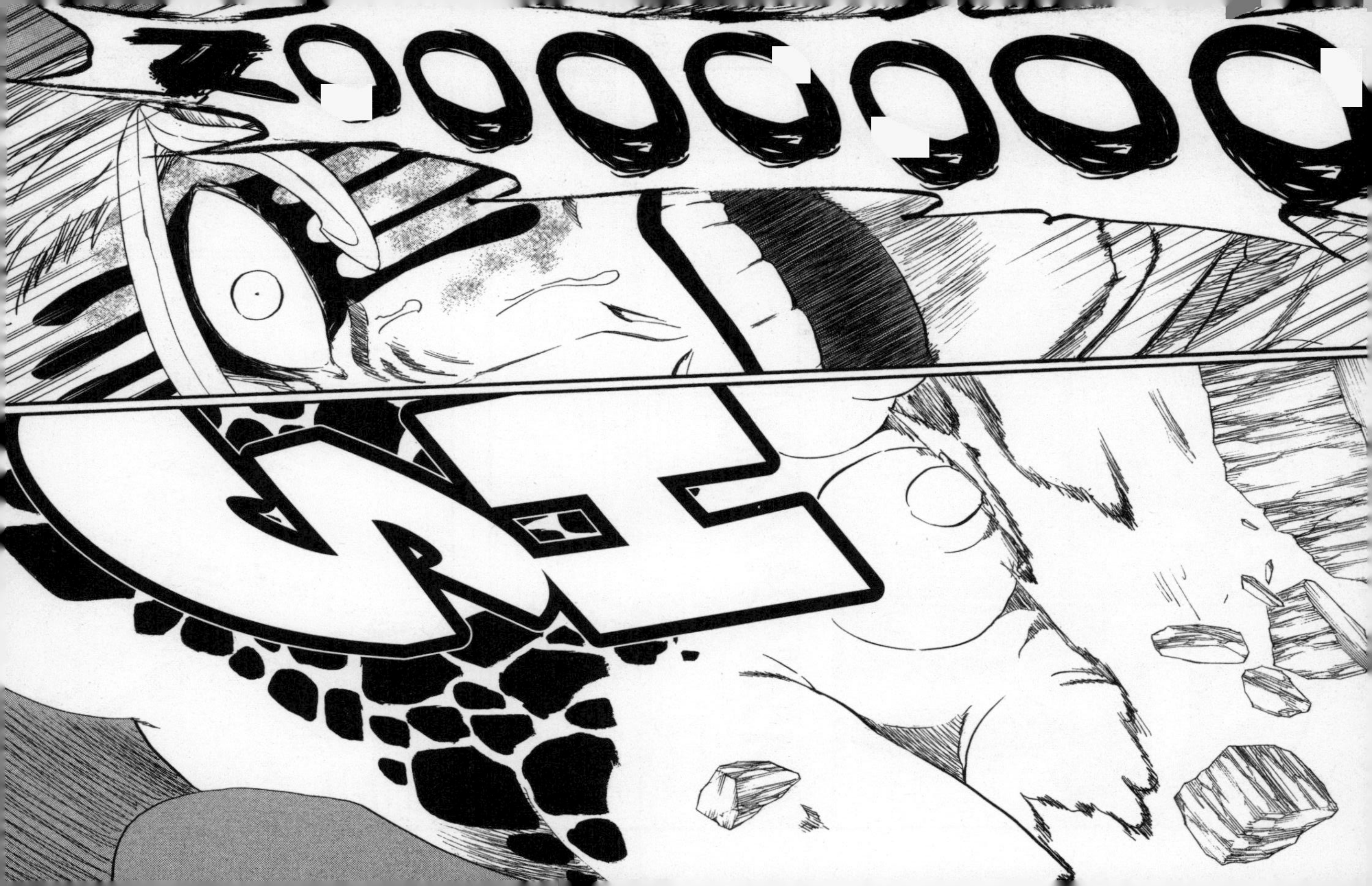
NOOOOOOO

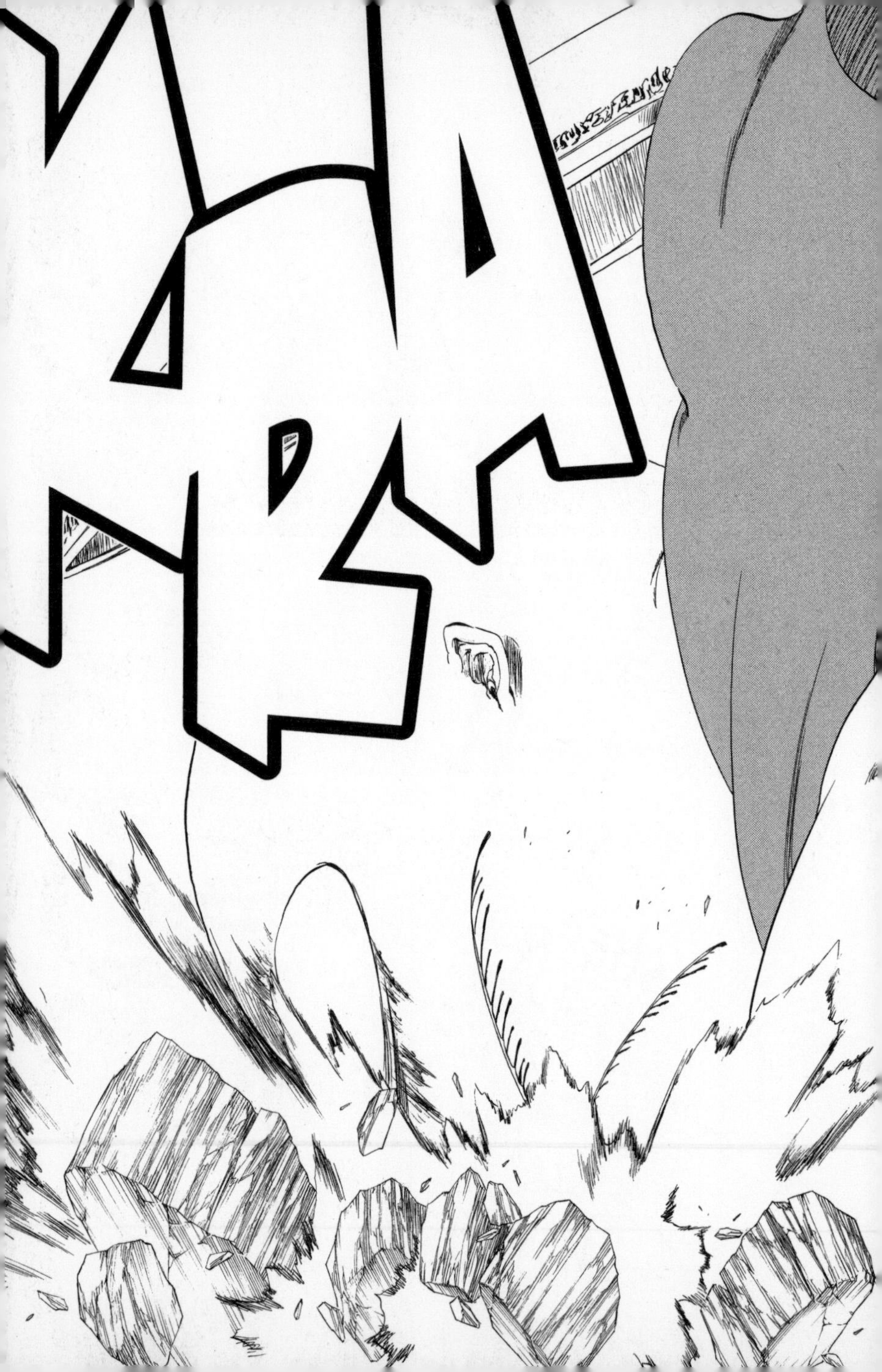

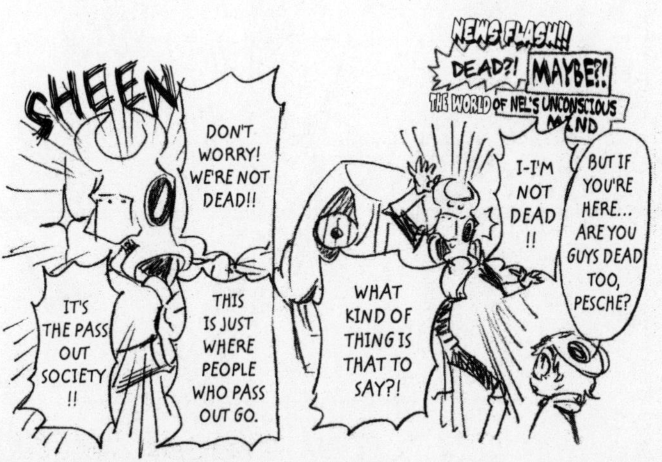NEWS FLASH!!
DEAD?! MAYBE?!
THE WORLD OF NEL'S UNCONSCIOUS MIND
BUT IF YOU'RE HERE... ARE YOU GUYS DEAD TOO, PESCHE?
I-I'M NOT DEAD!!
WHAT KIND OF THING IS THAT TO SAY?!
DON'T WORRY! WE'RE NOT DEAD!!
SHEEN
THIS IS JUST WHERE PEOPLE WHO PASS OUT GO.
IT'S THE PASS OUT SOCIETY!!

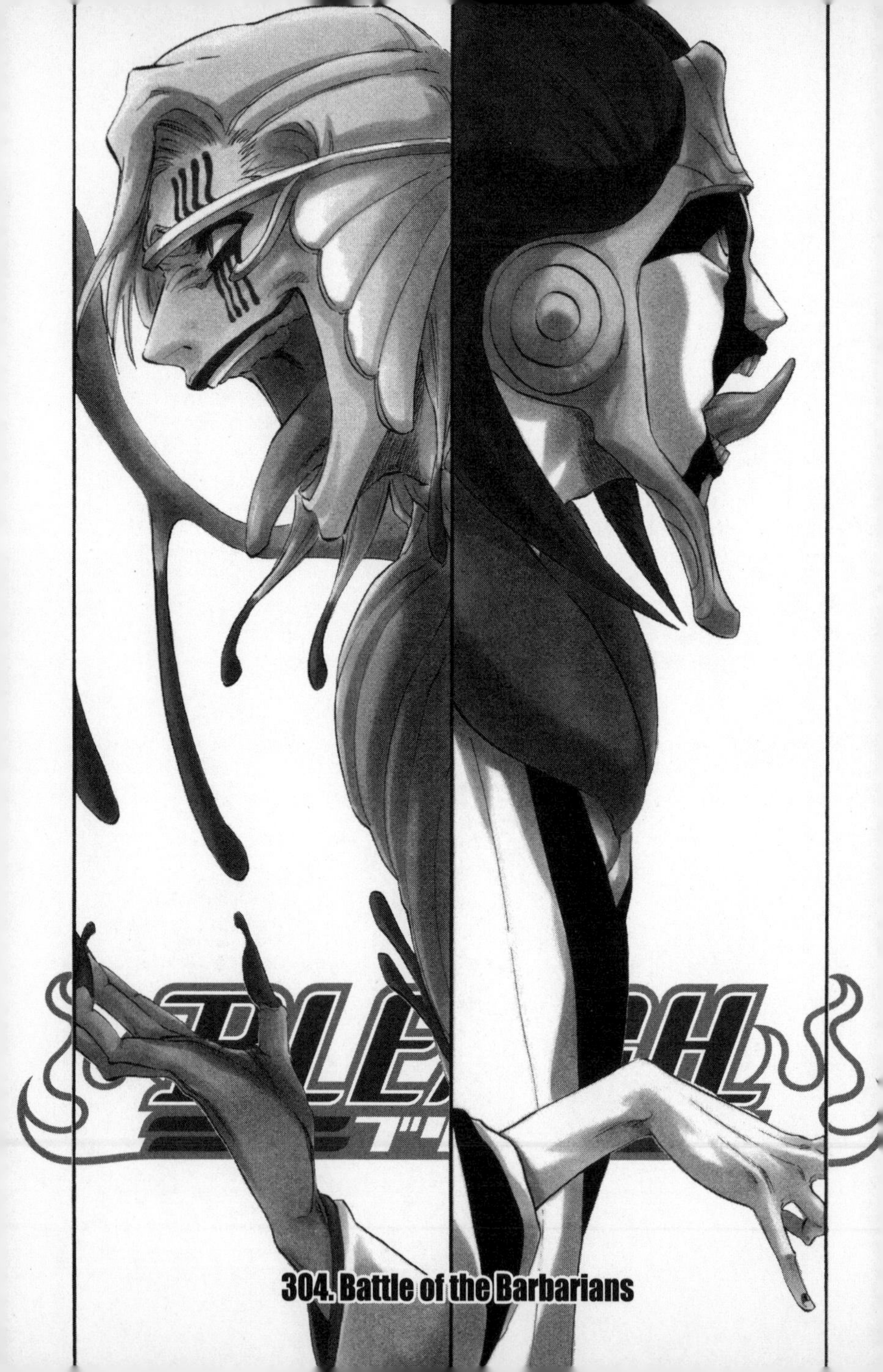

304. Battle of the Barbarians

BLEACH
ブリーチ

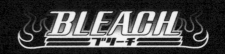

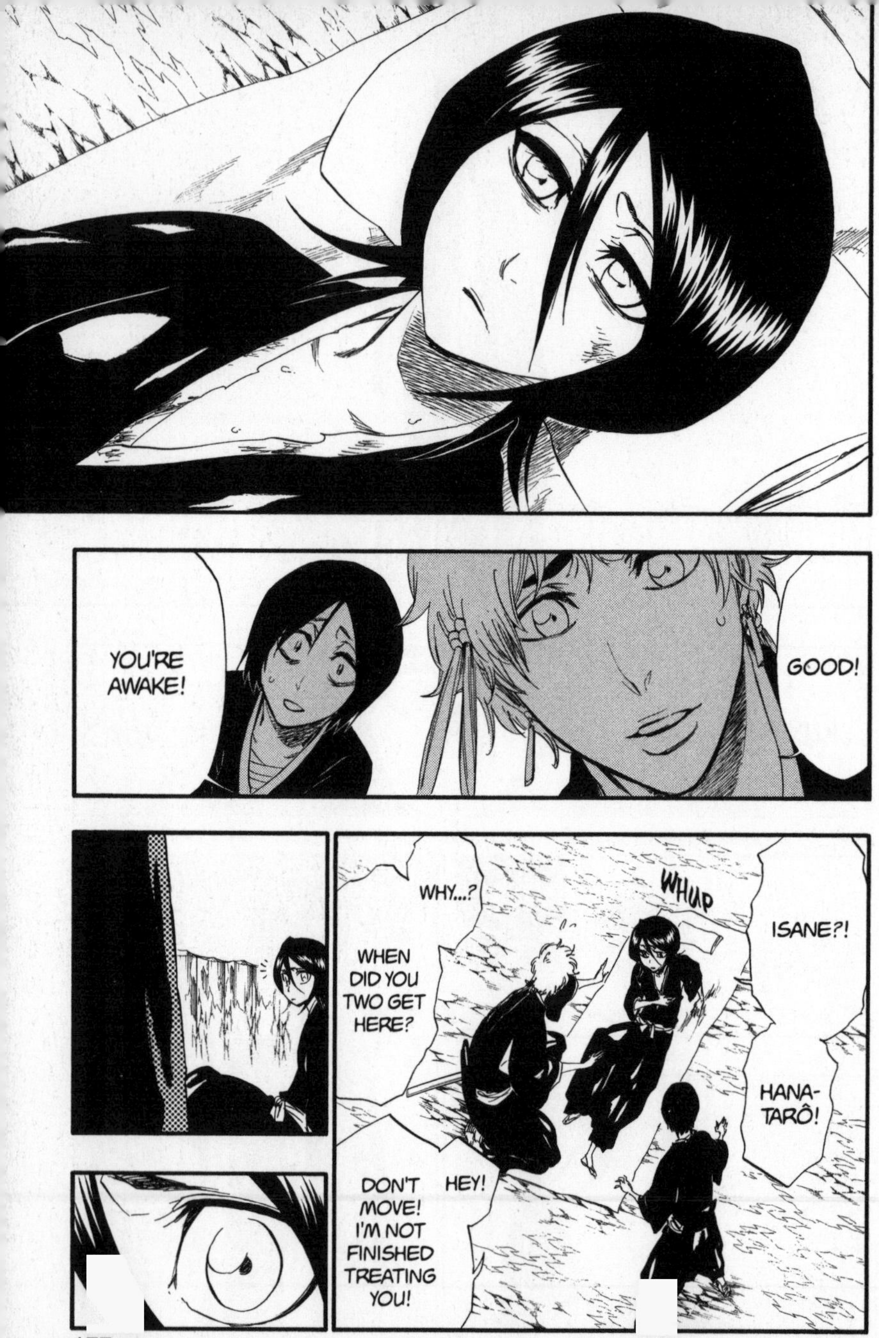
GOOD!
YOU'RE AWAKE!
ISANE?!
HANA-TARÔ!
WHUP
WHY...?
WHEN DID YOU TWO GET HERE?
HEY!
DON'T MOVE! I'M NOT FINISHED TREATING YOU!

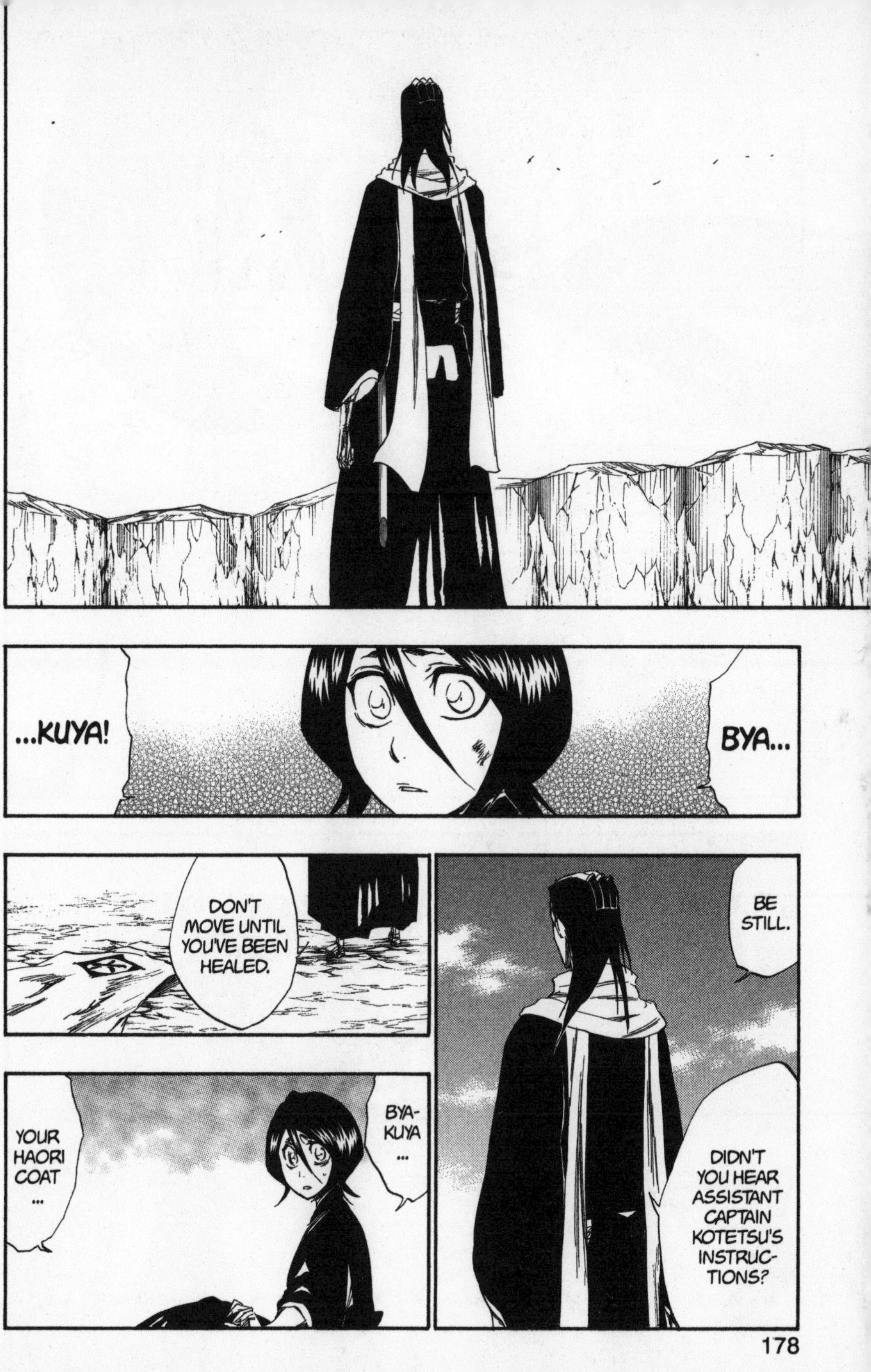
BYA...
...KUYA!
BE STILL.
DIDN'T YOU HEAR ASSISTANT CAPTAIN KOTETSU'S INSTRUC- TIONS?
DON'T MOVE UNTIL YOU'VE BEEN HEALED.
BYA- KUYA ...
YOUR HAORI COAT ...

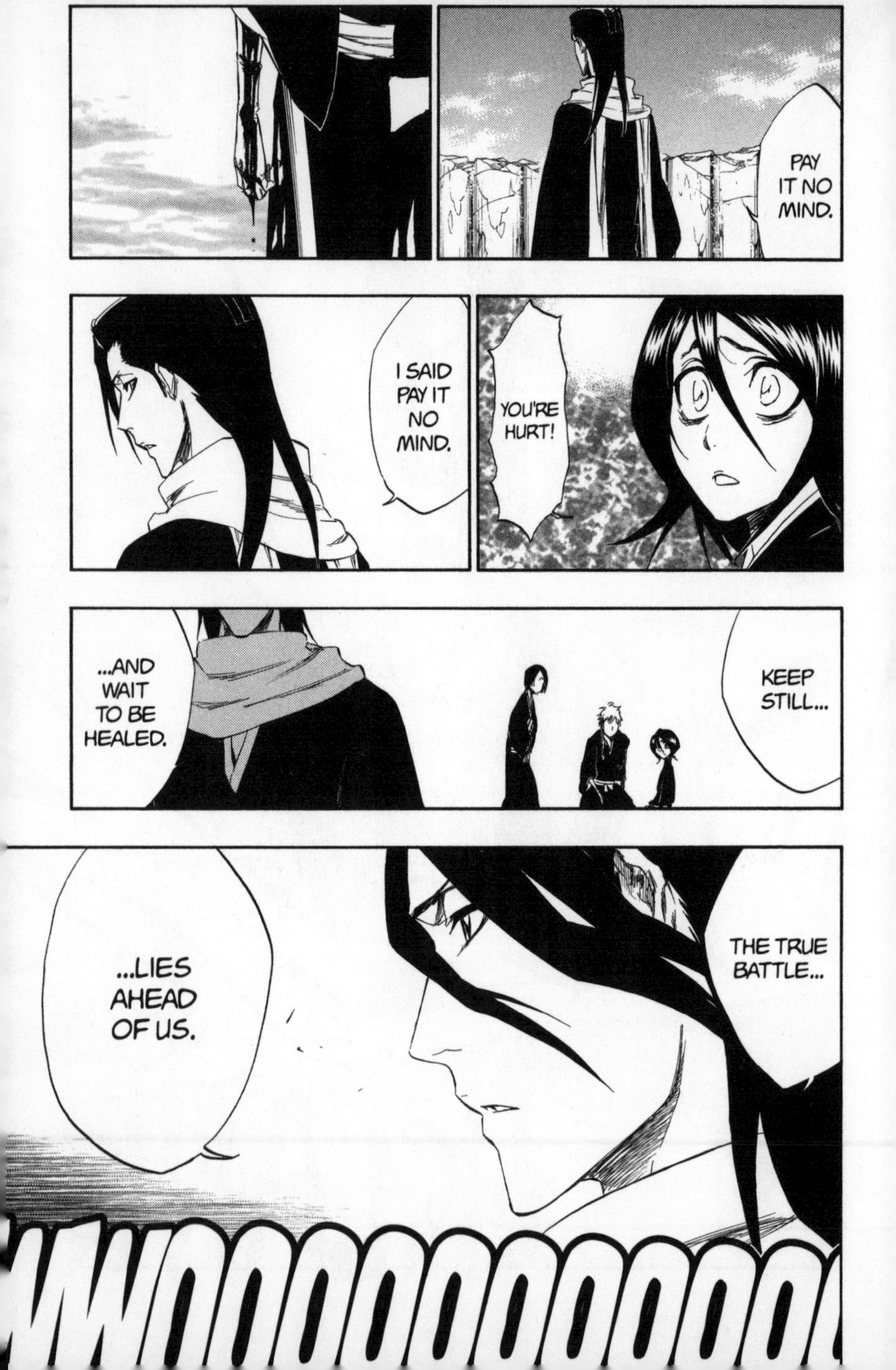
PAY IT NO MIND.
YOU'RE HURT!
I SAID PAY IT NO MIND.
KEEP STILL...
...AND WAIT TO BE HEALED.
THE TRUE BATTLE...
...LIES AHEAD OF US.

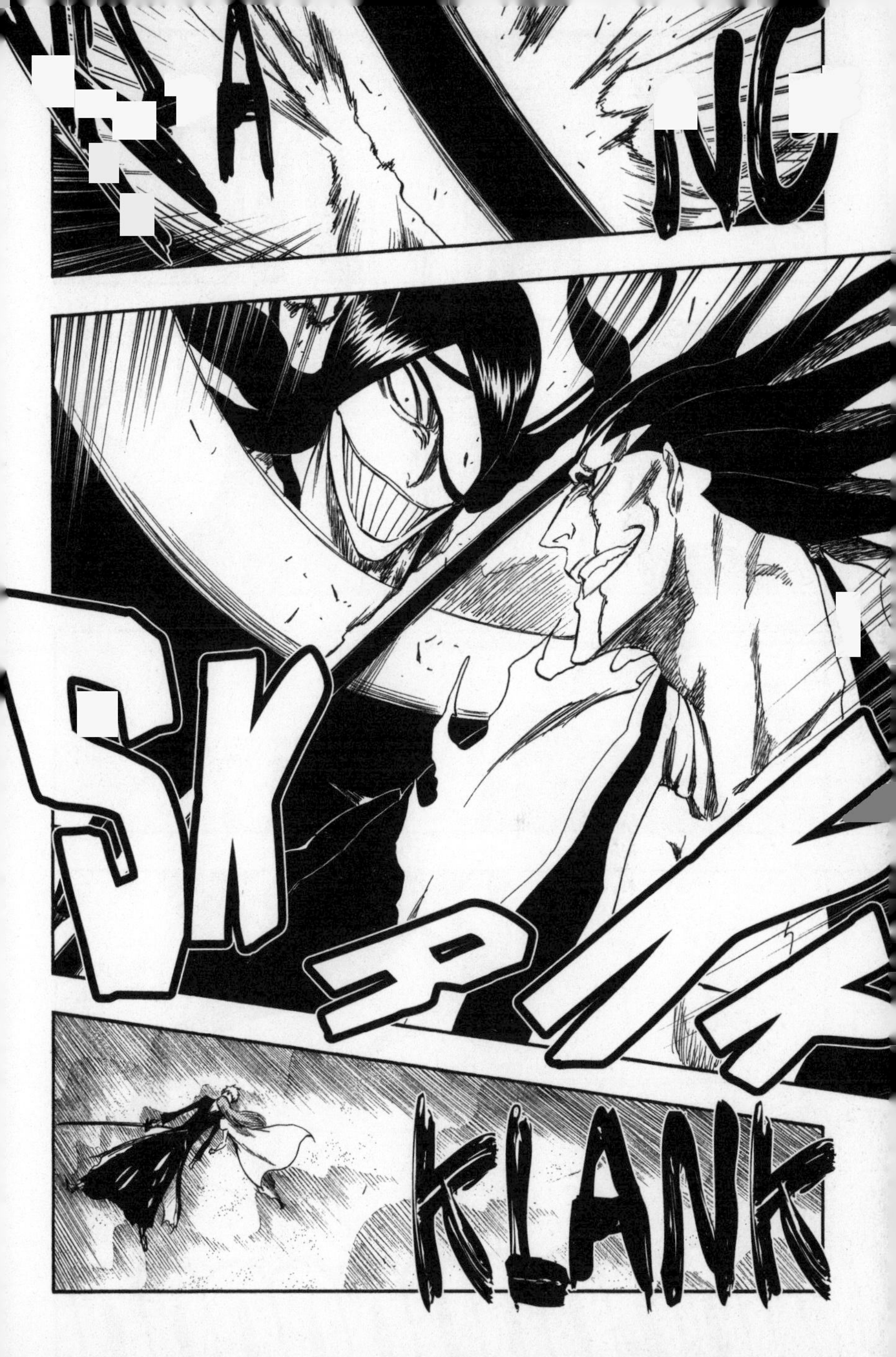
KLANK

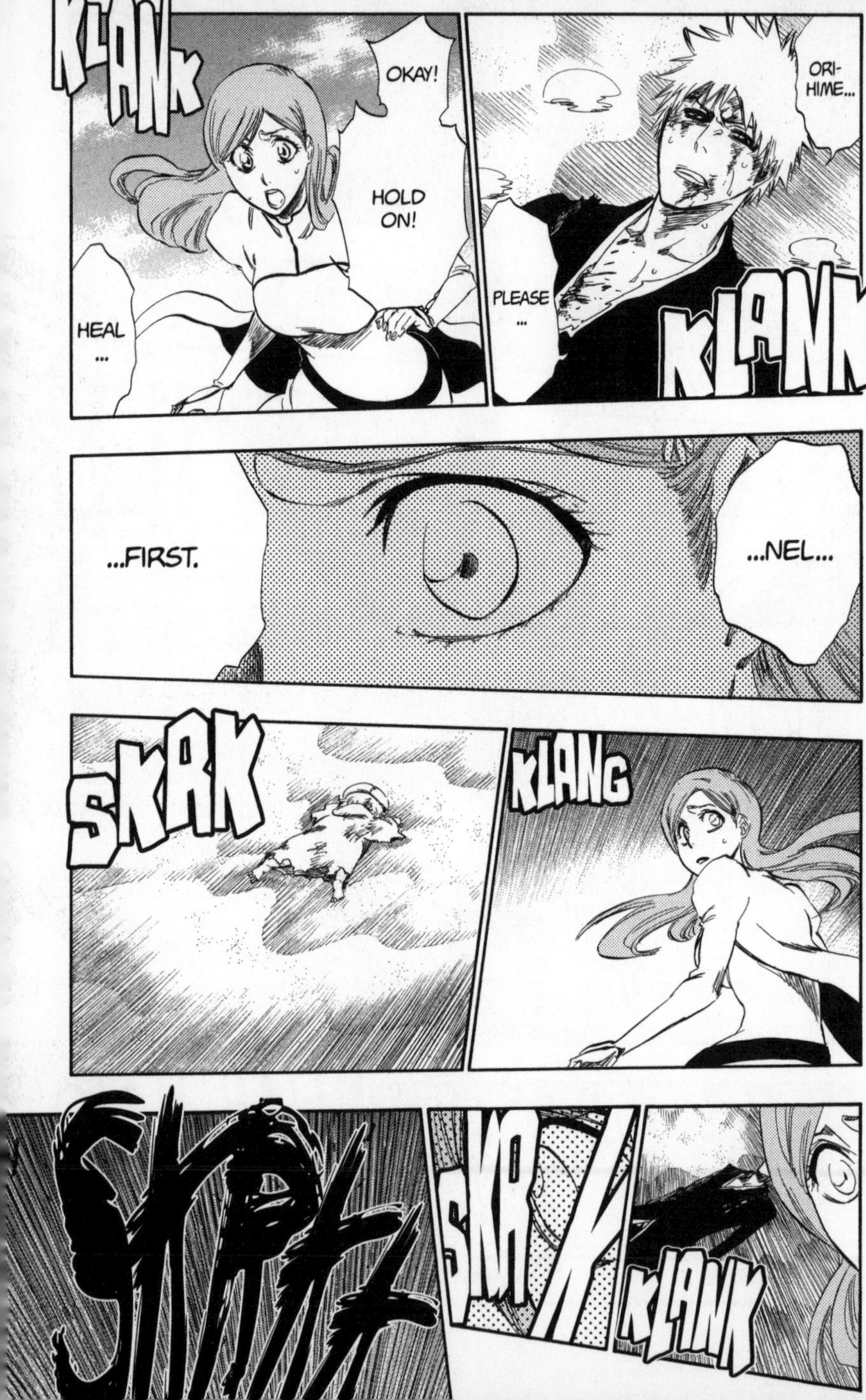
ORI-HIME...
PLEASE ...
KLANK
OKAY!
KLANK
HOLD ON!
HEAL ...
...NEL...
...FIRST.
KLANG
SKRK
KLANK
SKRK

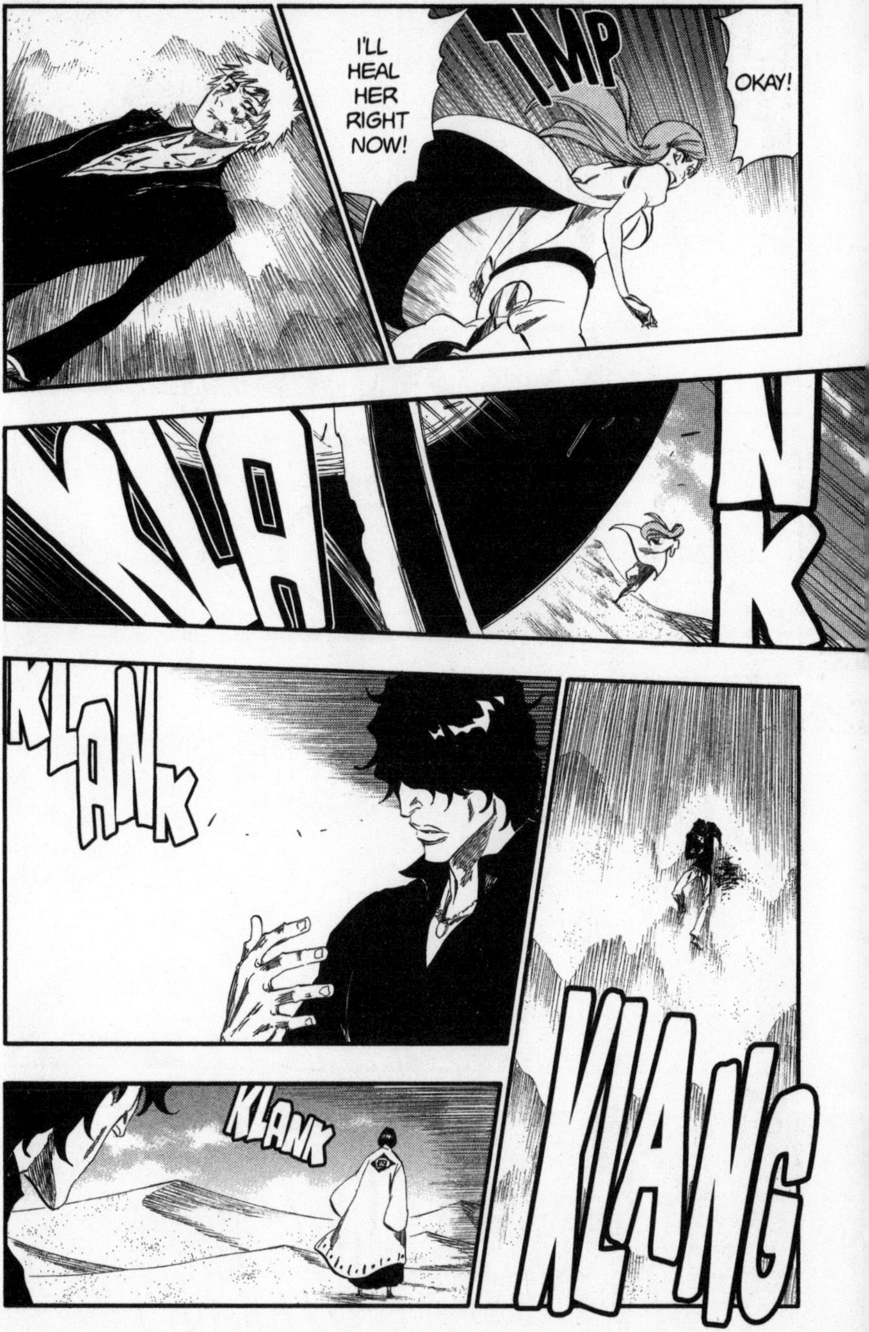
OKAY!
TMP
I'LL HEAL HER RIGHT NOW!
KLANG
KLANK
KLANK

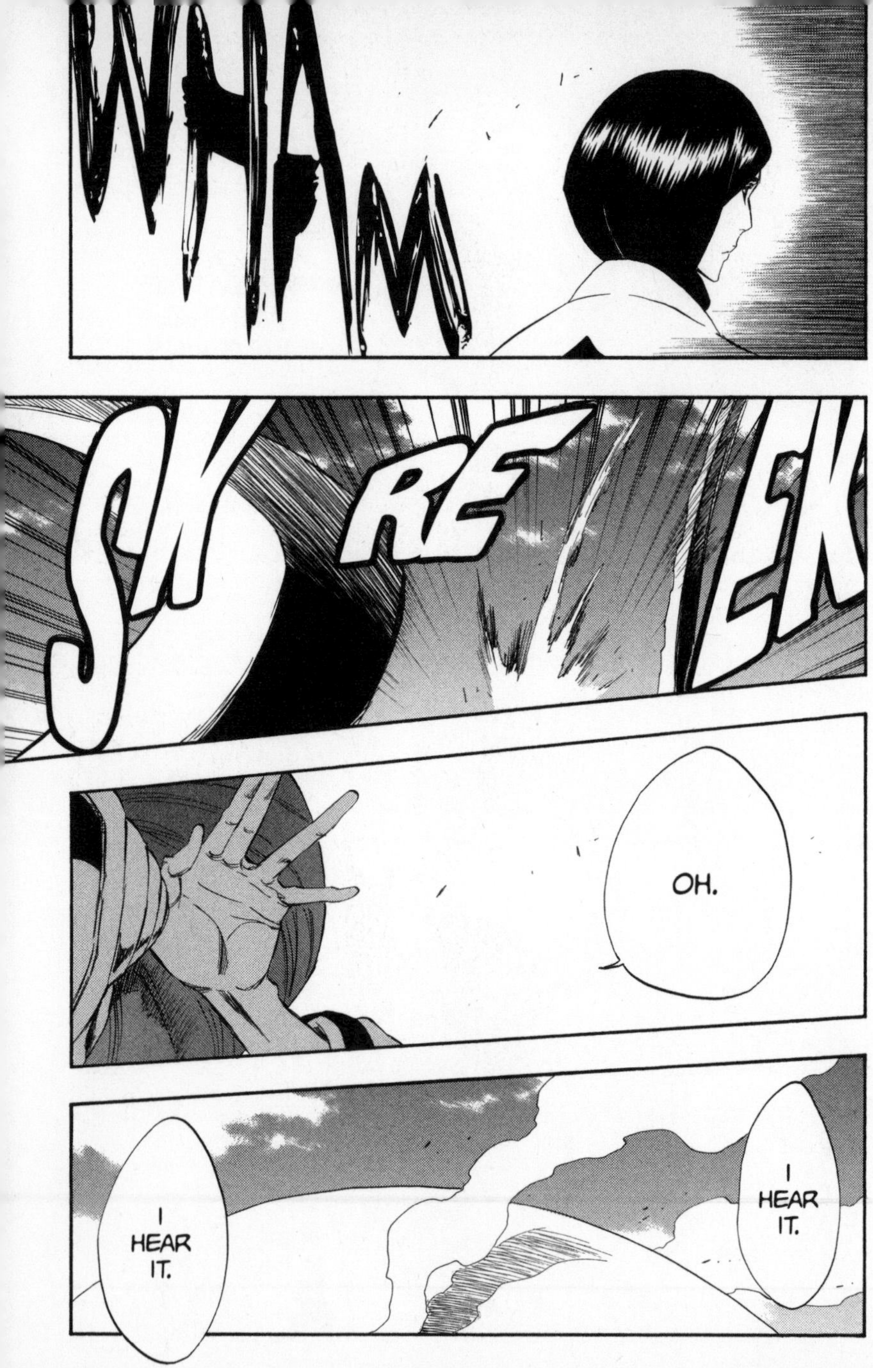
WHAM
SKREEK
OH.
I HEAR IT.
I HEAR IT.

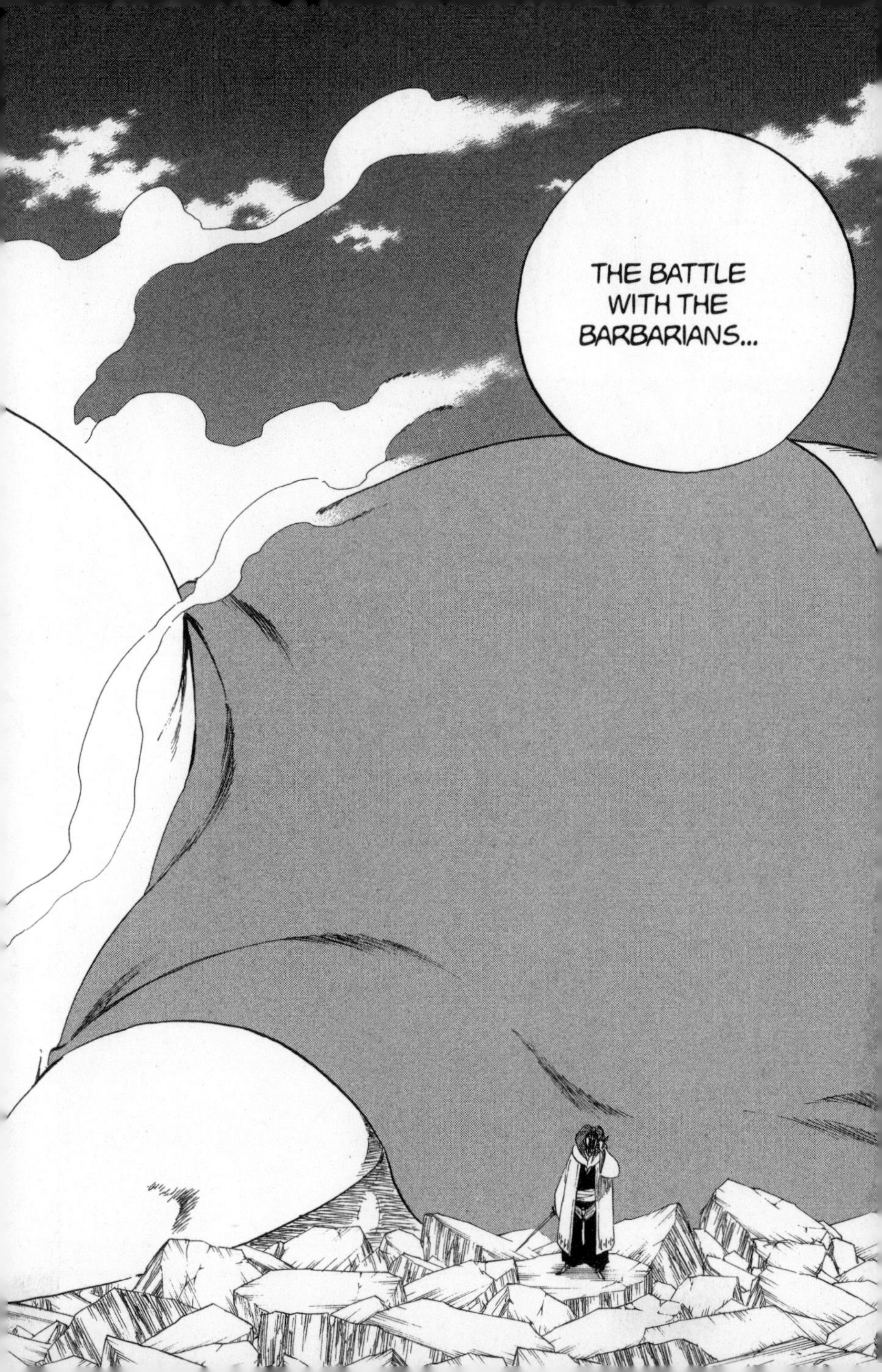
THE BATTLE WITH THE BARBARIANS...

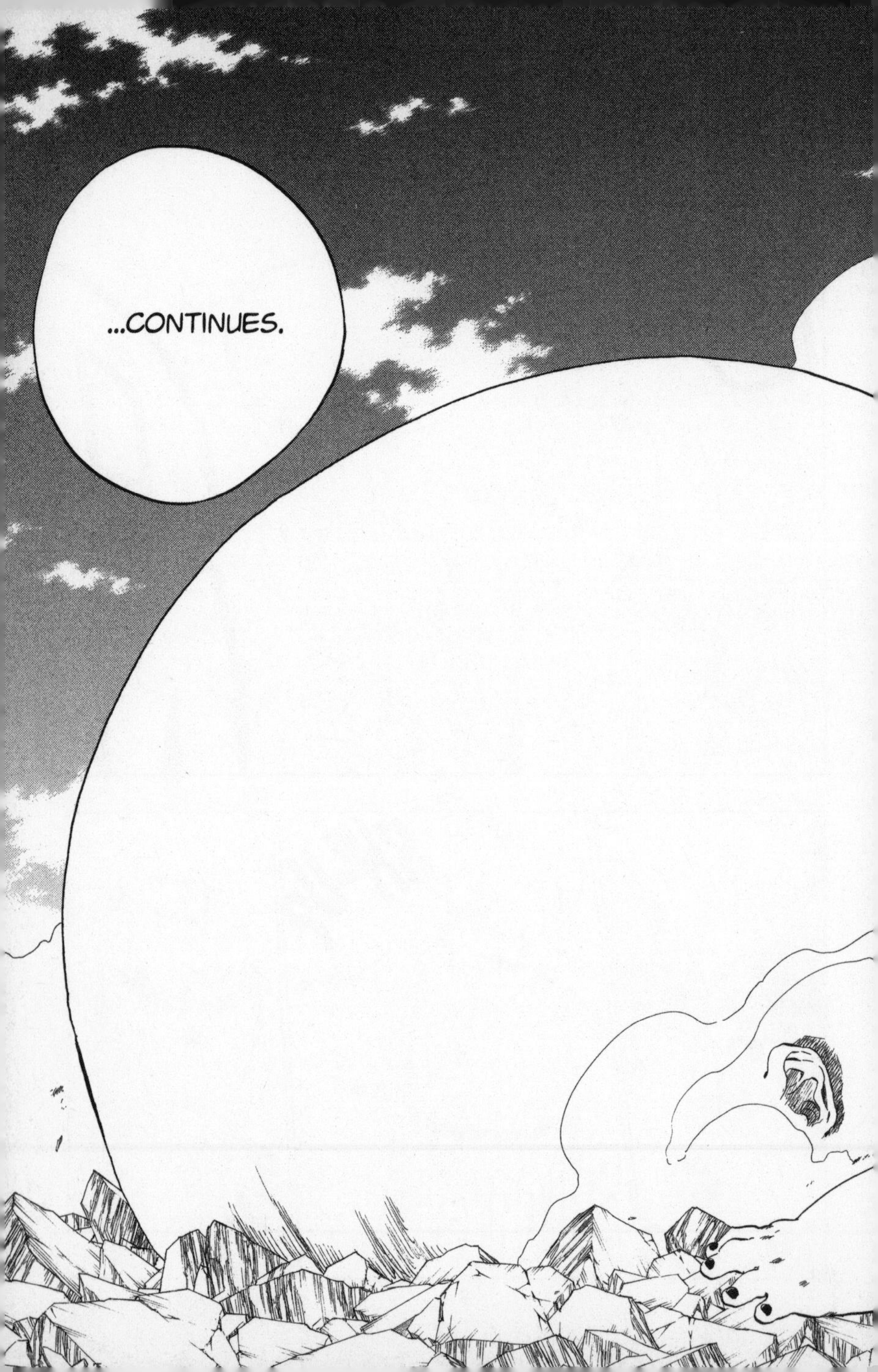
...CONTINUES.

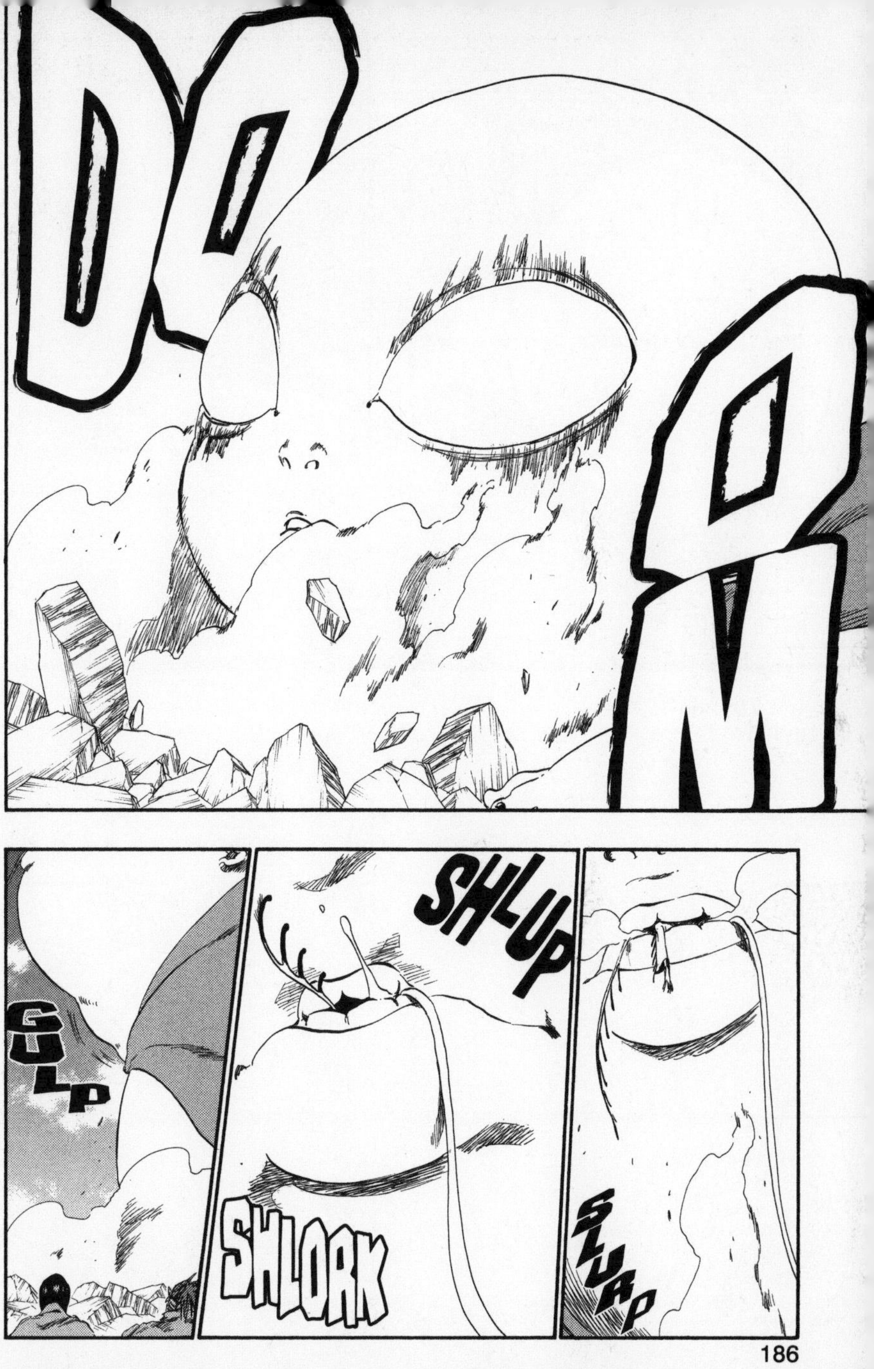
DOOM
SLURP
SHLUP
SHLORK
GULP

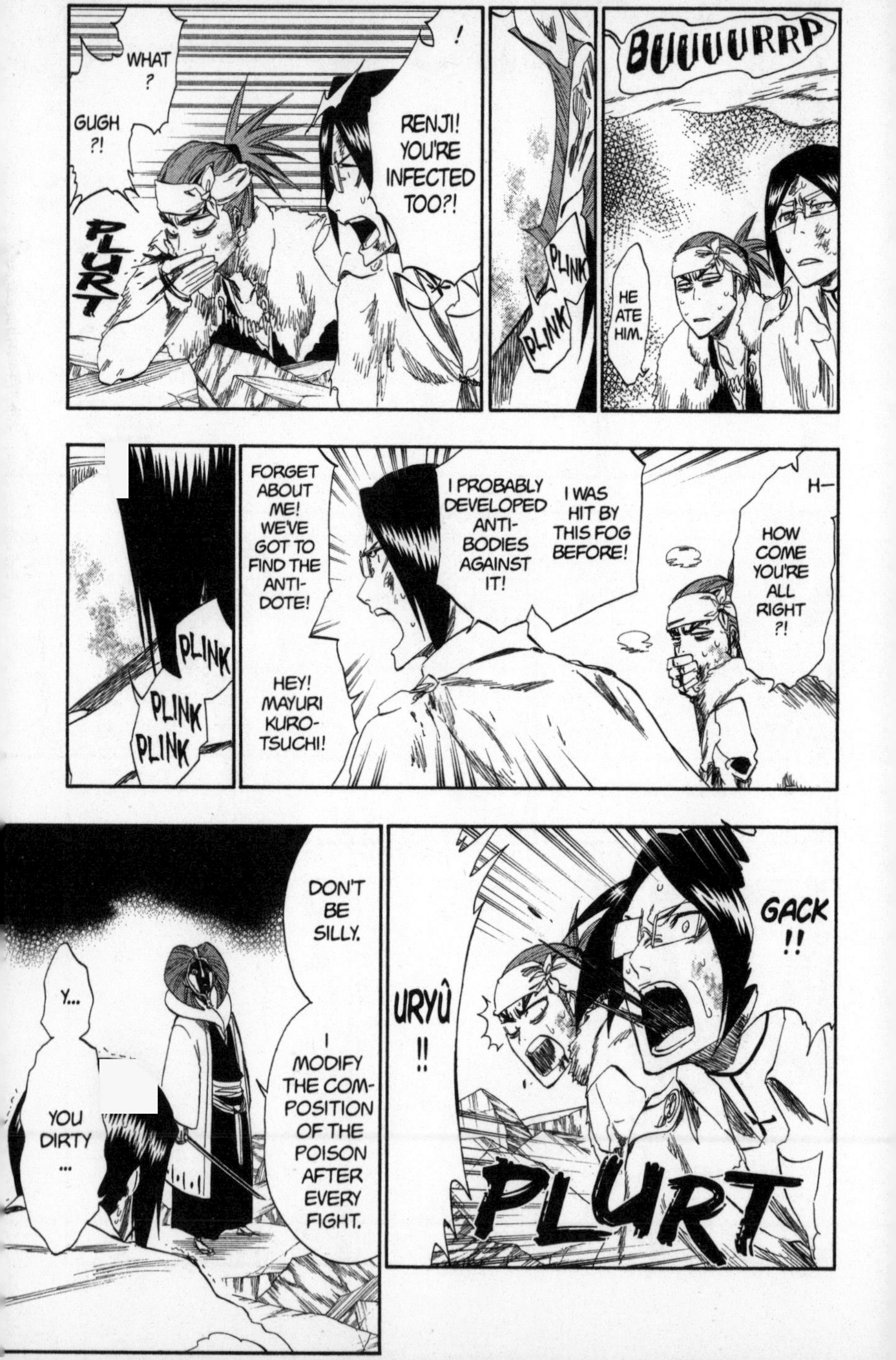
BUUUURRP
HE ATE HIM.
PLINK
PLINK
!
RENJI! YOU'RE INFECTED TOO?!
WHAT ?
GUGH ?!
PLURT
H—
HOW COME YOU'RE ALL RIGHT ?!
I WAS HIT BY THIS FOG BEFORE!
I PROBABLY DEVELOPED ANTI-BODIES AGAINST IT!
FORGET ABOUT ME! WE'VE GOT TO FIND THE ANTI-DOTE!
HEY! MAYURI KURO-TSUCHI!
PLINK
PLINK
PLINK
GACK !!
URYÛ !!
PLURT
DON'T BE SILLY.
I MODIFY THE COM-POSITION OF THE POISON AFTER EVERY FIGHT.
Y...
YOU DIRTY ...

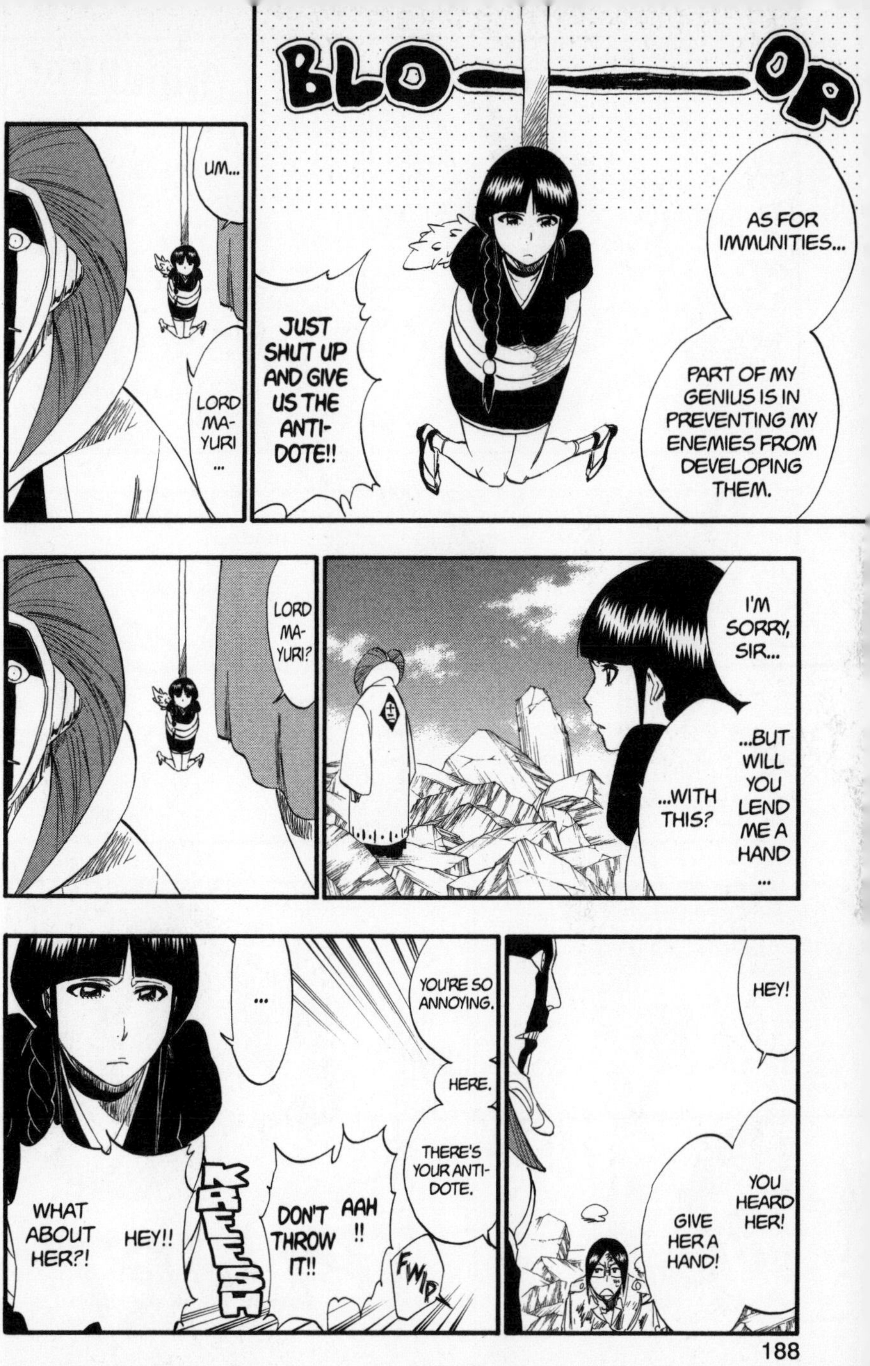
BLO—OP
AS FOR IMMUNITIES...
PART OF MY GENIUS IS IN PREVENTING MY ENEMIES FROM DEVELOPING THEM.
JUST SHUT UP AND GIVE US THE ANTI-DOTE!!
UM...
LORD MA-YURI ...
I'M SORRY, SIR...
...BUT WILL YOU LEND ME A HAND ...
...WITH THIS?
LORD MA-YURI?
HEY!
YOU HEARD HER!
GIVE HER A HAND!
...
YOU'RE SO ANNOYING.
HERE.
THERE'S YOUR ANTI-DOTE.
AAH !!
DON'T THROW IT!!
FWIP
HEY!!
WHAT ABOUT HER?!

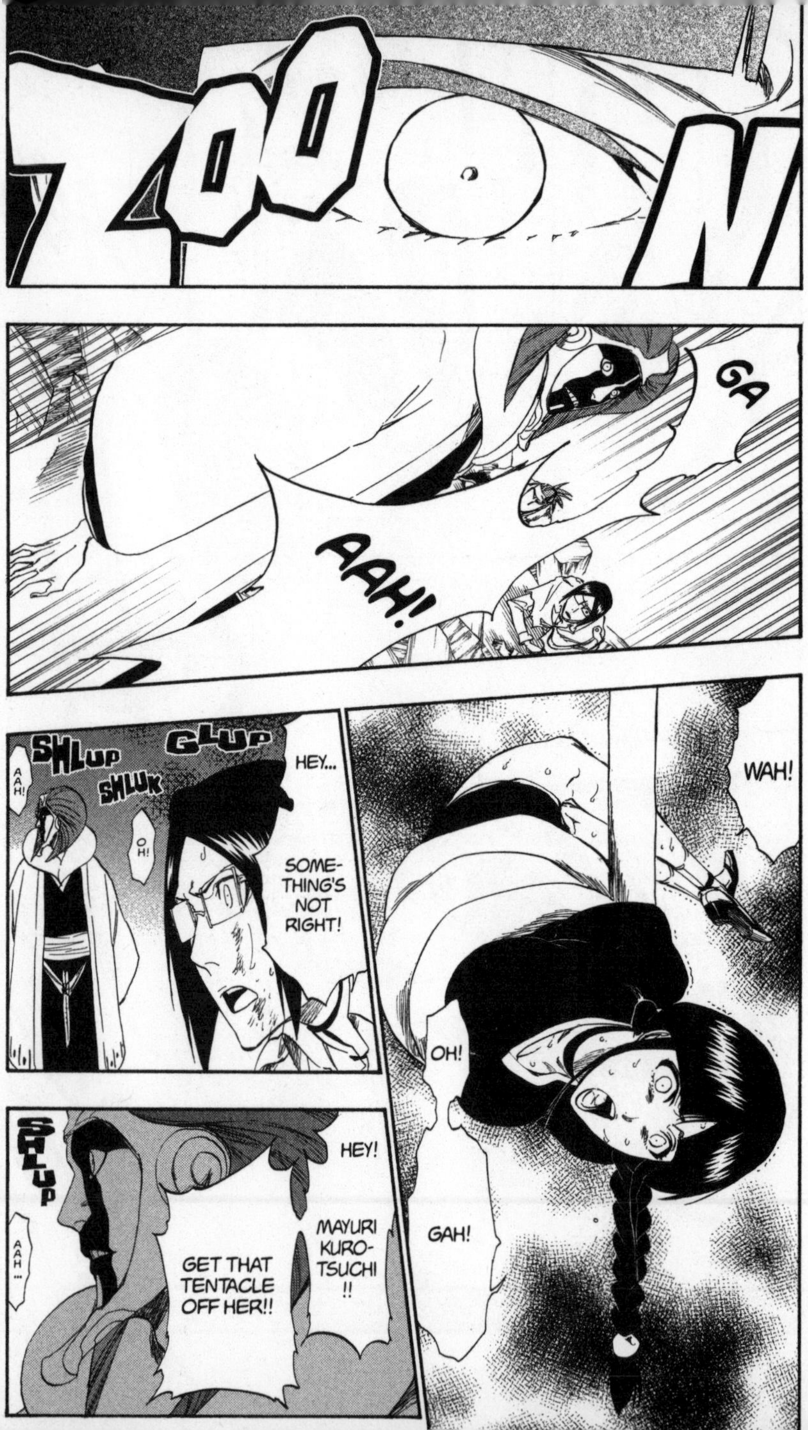
ZOOON
GA
AAH!
WAH!
OH!
GAH!
GLUP
HEY...
SOMETHING'S NOT RIGHT!
SHLUP
SHLUK
OH!
AAH!
HEY!
MAYURI KUROTSUCHI!!
GET THAT TENTACLE OFF HER!!
SHLUP
AAH...

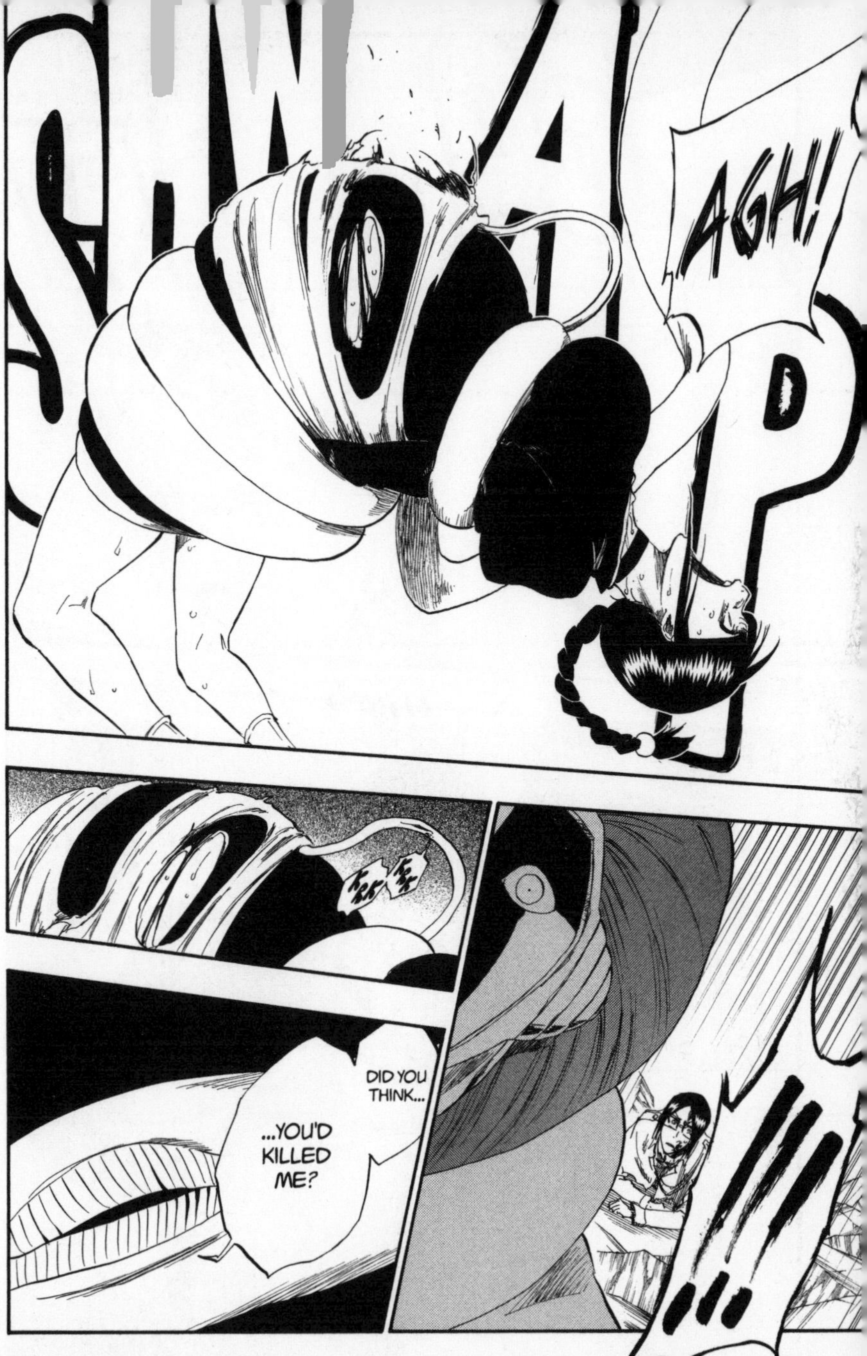
SWAP
AGH!
!!
KRK
KRK
DID YOU THINK...
...YOU'D KILLED ME?

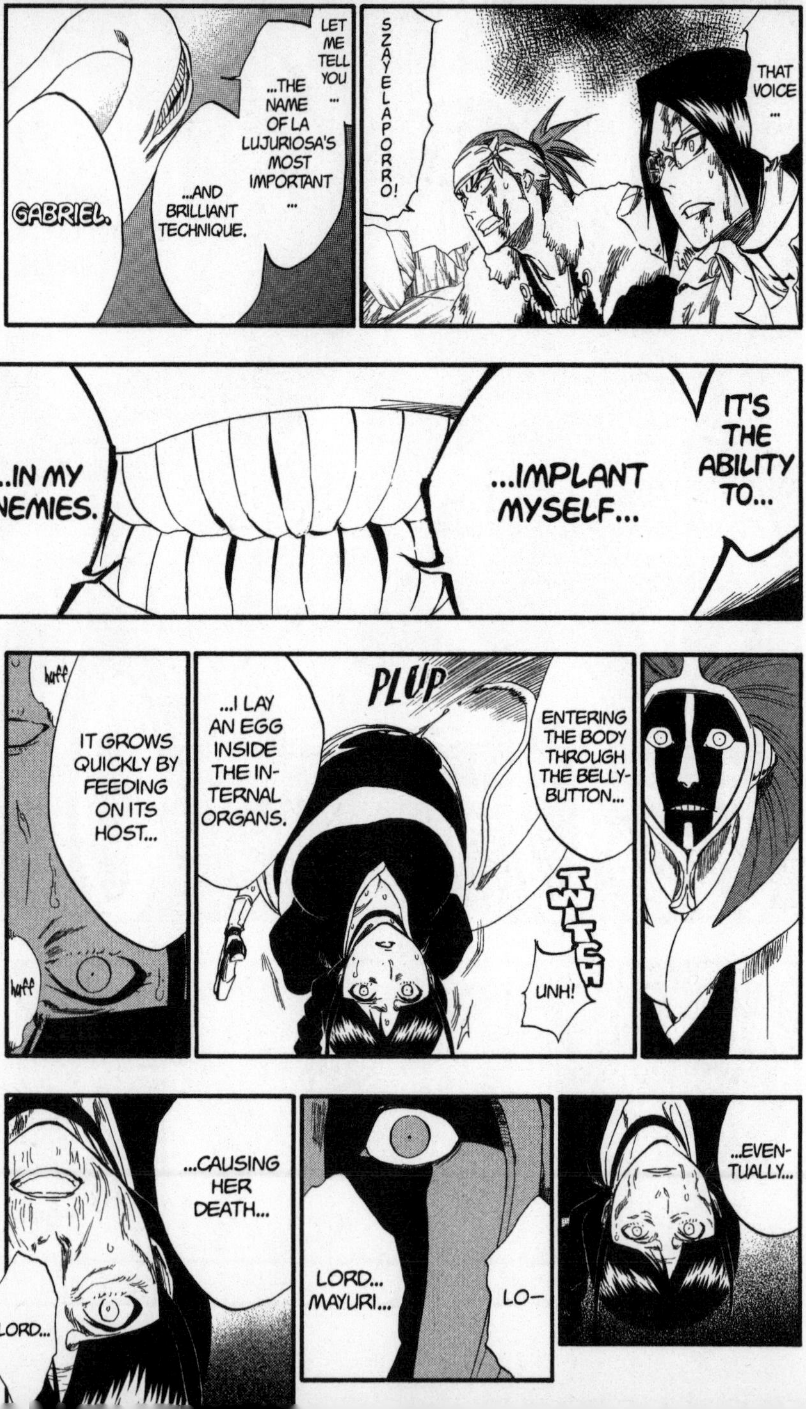
THAT VOICE ...
SZAYELAPORRO!
LET ME TELL YOU ...
...THE NAME OF LA LUJURIOSA'S MOST IMPORTANT ...
...AND BRILLIANT TECHNIQUE.
GABRIEL.
IT'S THE ABILITY TO...
...IMPLANT MYSELF...
...IN MY ENEMIES.
PLUP
ENTERING THE BODY THROUGH THE BELLY-BUTTON...
TWITCH
UNH!
...I LAY AN EGG INSIDE THE IN-TERNAL ORGANS.
huff
IT GROWS QUICKLY BY FEEDING ON ITS HOST...
huff
...EVEN-TUALLY...
LO—
LORD... MAYURI...
...CAUSING HER DEATH...
LORD...

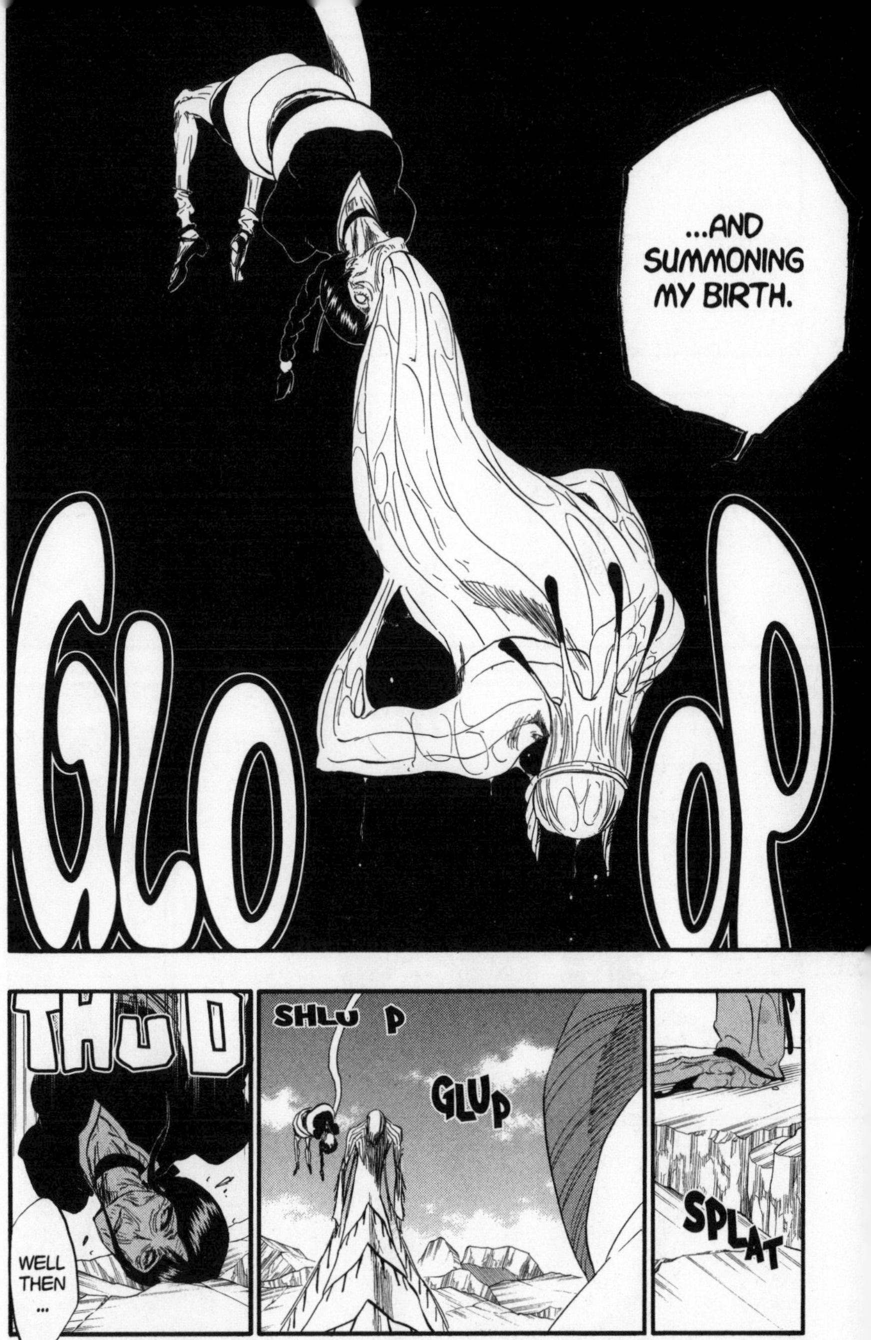
...AND SUMMONING MY BIRTH.
GLOOP
SPLAT
SHLUP
GLUP
THUD
WELL THEN ...

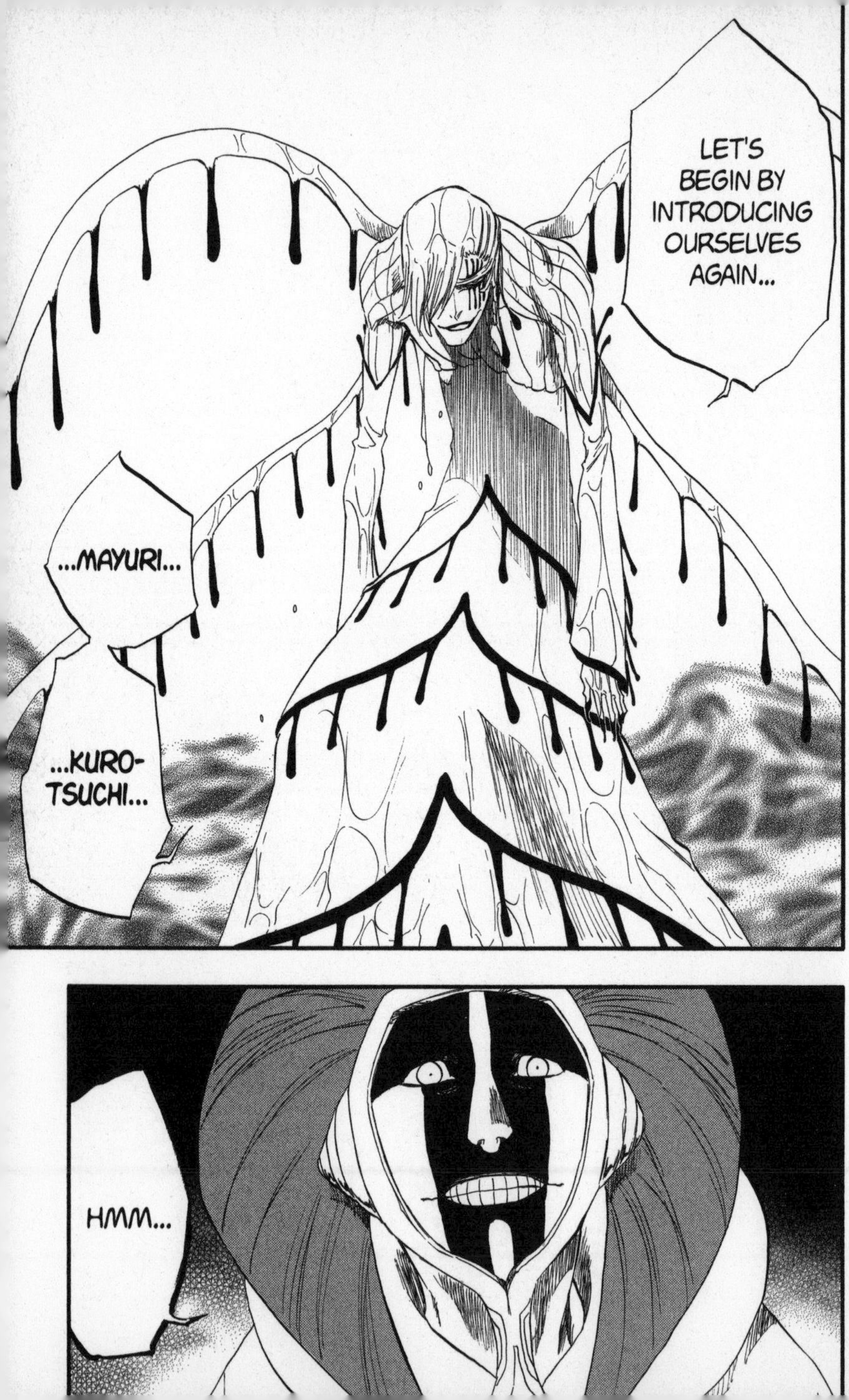
LET'S BEGIN BY INTRODUCING OURSELVES AGAIN...
...MAYURI...
...KURO-TSUCHI...
HMM...

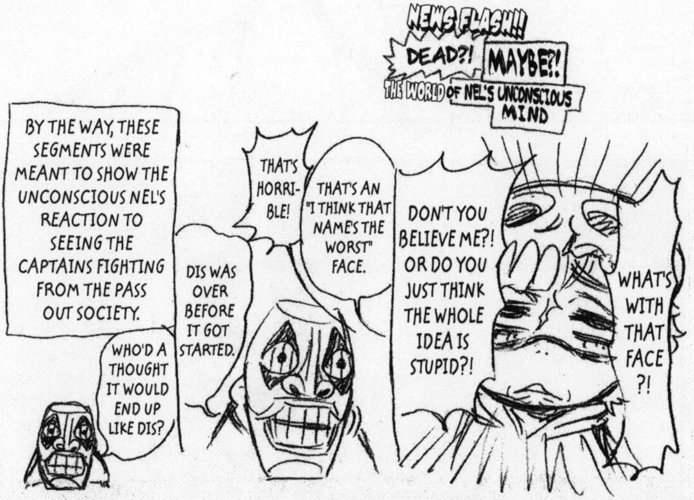
NEWS FLASH!!
DEAD?! MAYBE?!
THE WORLD OF NEL'S UNCONSCIOUS MIND
WHAT'S WITH THAT FACE?!
DON'T YOU BELIEVE ME?! OR DO YOU JUST THINK THE WHOLE IDEA IS STUPID?!
THAT'S AN "I THINK THAT NAME'S THE WORST" FACE.
THAT'S HORRI-BLE!
DIS WAS OVER BEFORE IT GOT STARTED.
BY THE WAY, THESE SEGMENTS WERE MEANT TO SHOW THE UNCONSCIOUS NEL'S REACTION TO SEEING THE CAPTAINS FIGHTING FROM THE PASS OUT SOCIETY.
WHO'D A THOUGHT IT WOULD END UP LIKE DIS?

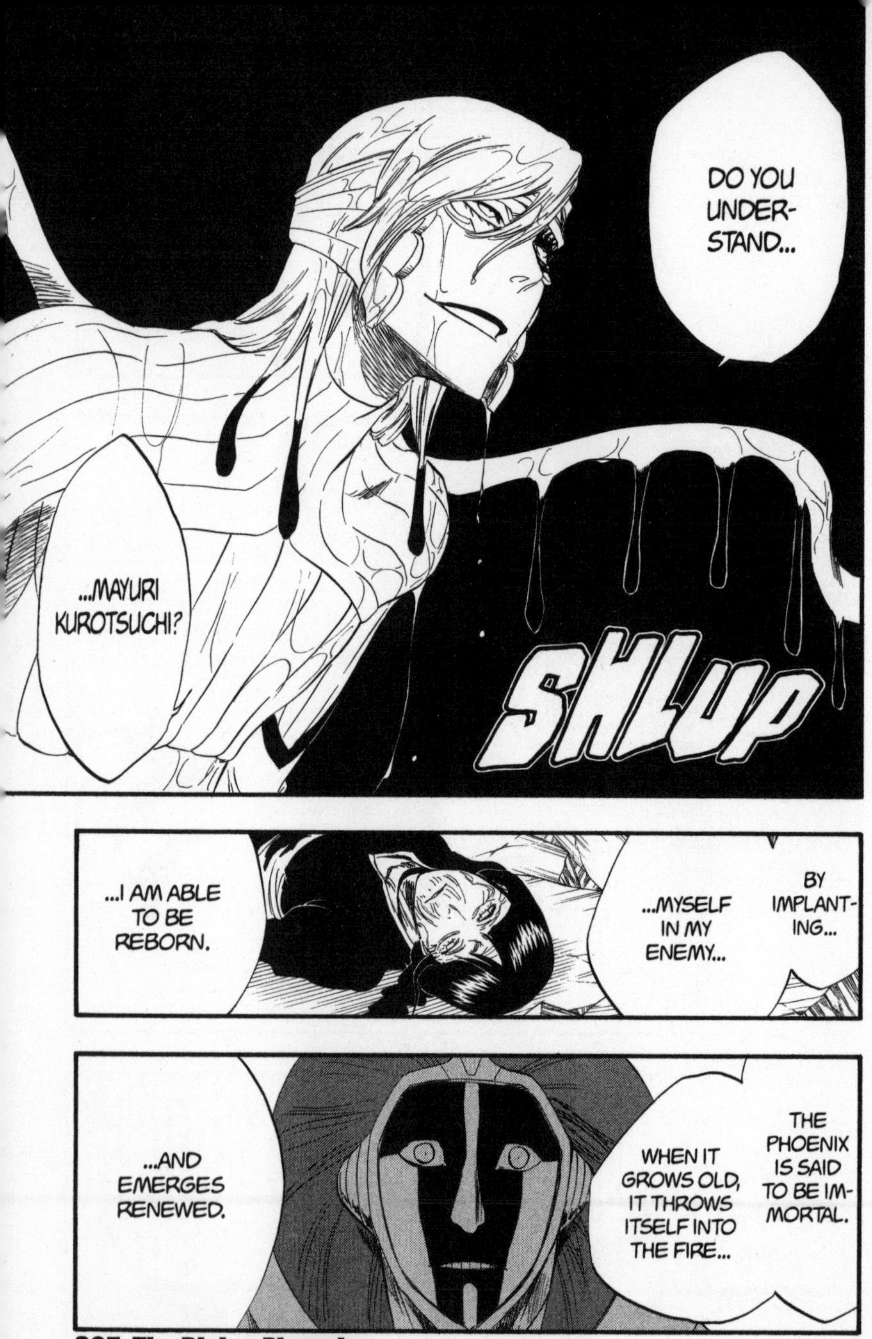
DO YOU UNDER-STAND...
...MAYURI KUROTSUCHI?
SHLUP
BY IMPLANT-ING...
...MYSELF IN MY ENEMY...
...I AM ABLE TO BE REBORN.
THE PHOENIX IS SAID TO BE IM-MORTAL.
WHEN IT GROWS OLD, IT THROWS ITSELF INTO THE FIRE...
...AND EMERGES RENEWED.

305. The Rising Phoenix

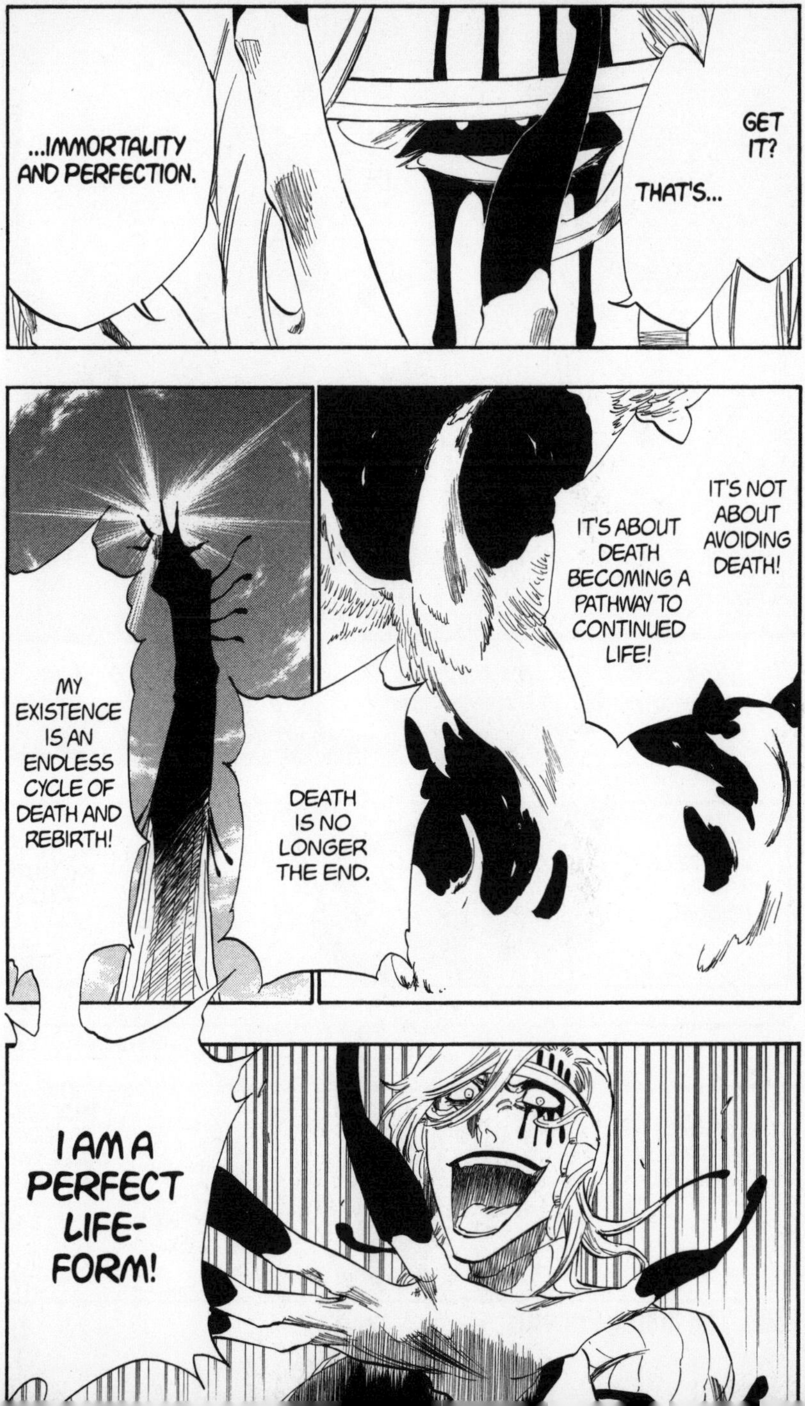
GET IT?
THAT'S...
...IMMORTALITY AND PERFECTION.
IT'S NOT ABOUT AVOIDING DEATH!
IT'S ABOUT DEATH BECOMING A PATHWAY TO CONTINUED LIFE!
DEATH IS NO LONGER THE END.
MY EXISTENCE IS AN ENDLESS CYCLE OF DEATH AND REBIRTH!
I AM A PERFECT LIFE-FORM!

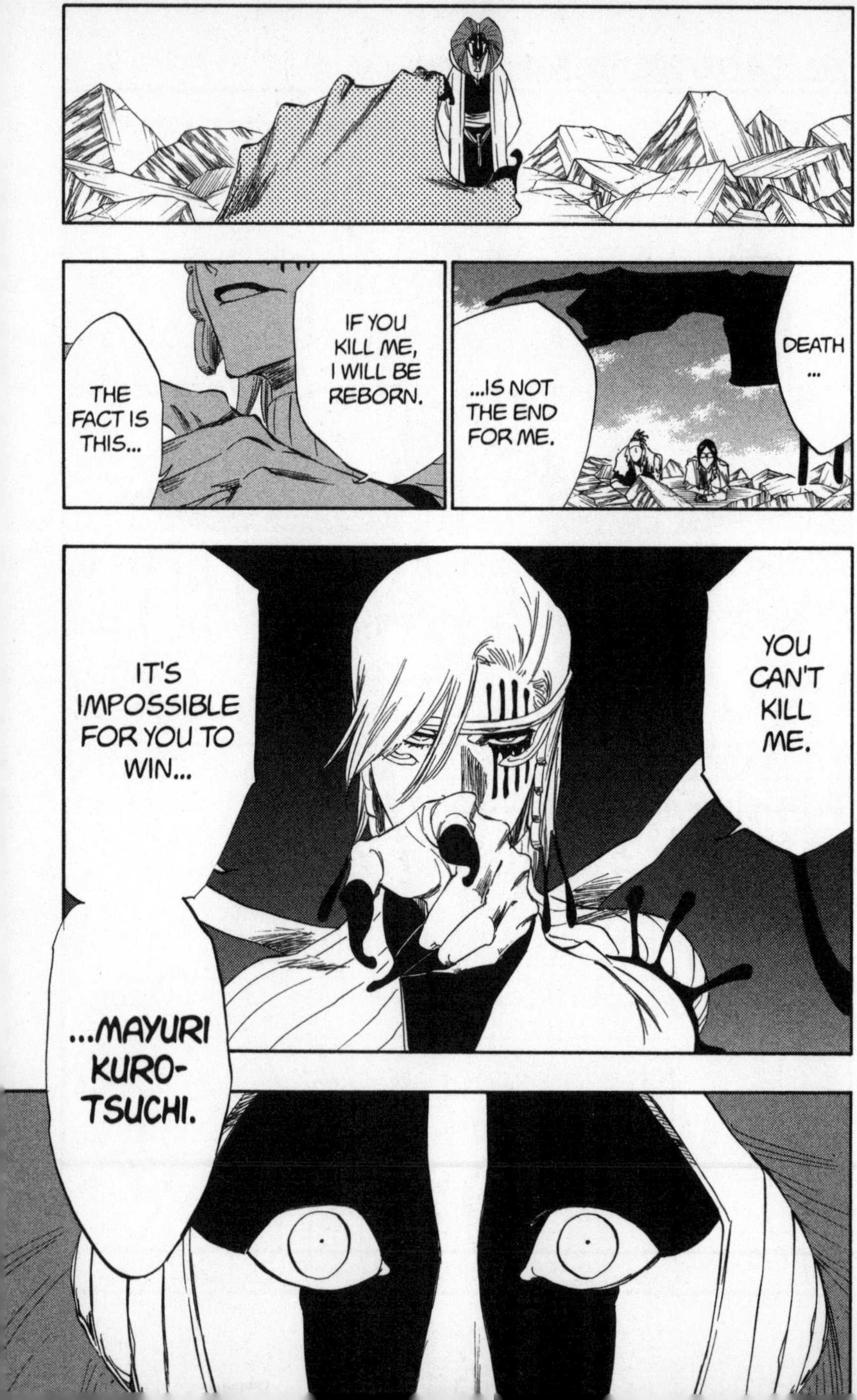
DEATH ...
...IS NOT THE END FOR ME.
IF YOU KILL ME, I WILL BE REBORN.
THE FACT IS THIS...
YOU CAN'T KILL ME.
IT'S IMPOSSIBLE FOR YOU TO WIN...
...MAYURI KURO-TSUCHI.

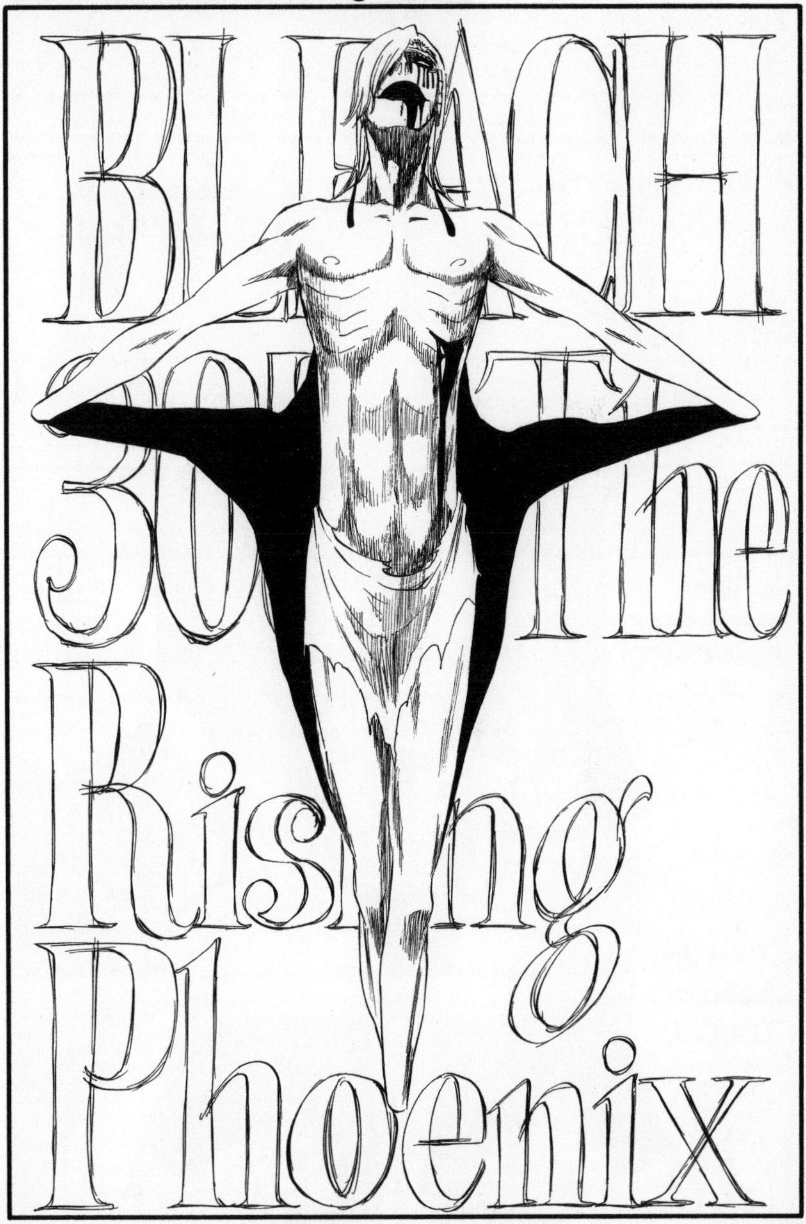
BLEACH
305. The
Rising
Phoenix

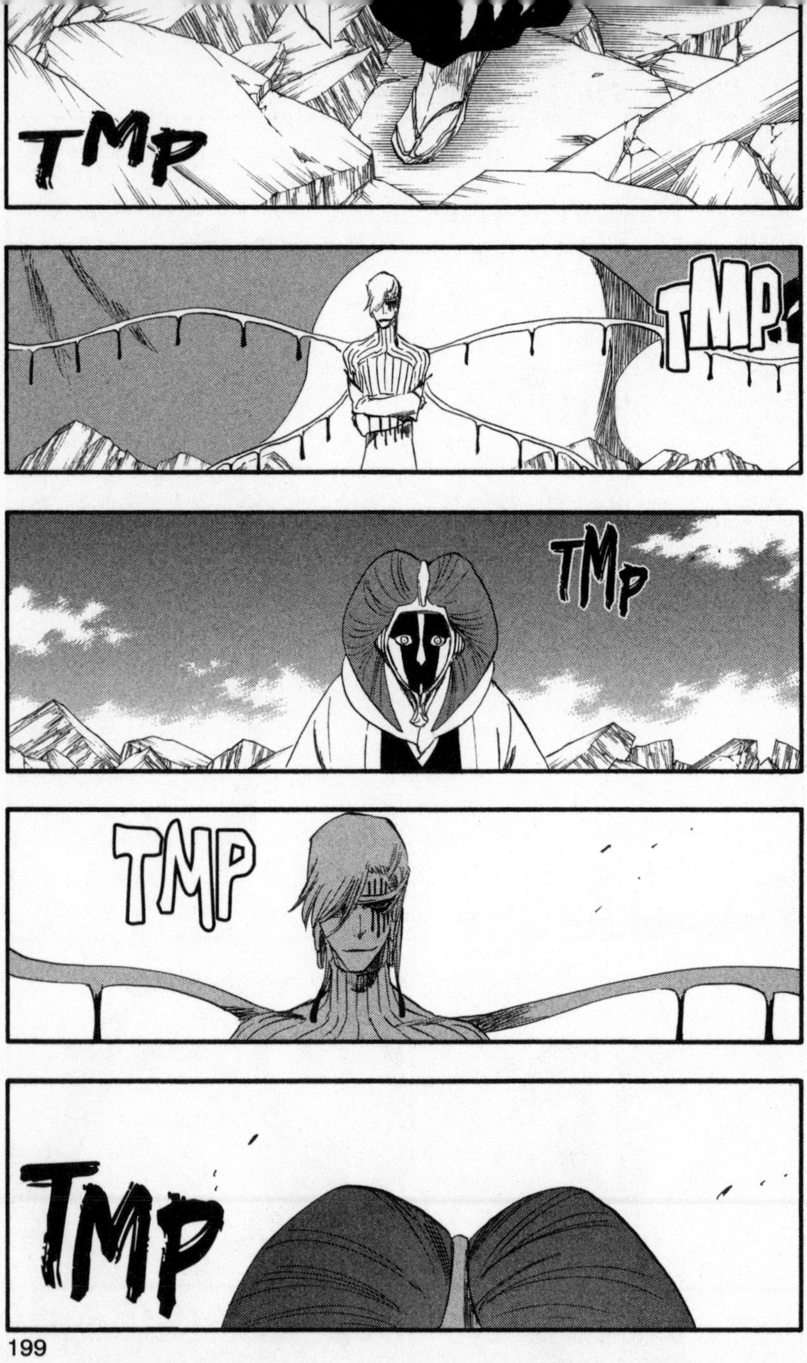
TMP
TMP
TMp
TMP
TMP

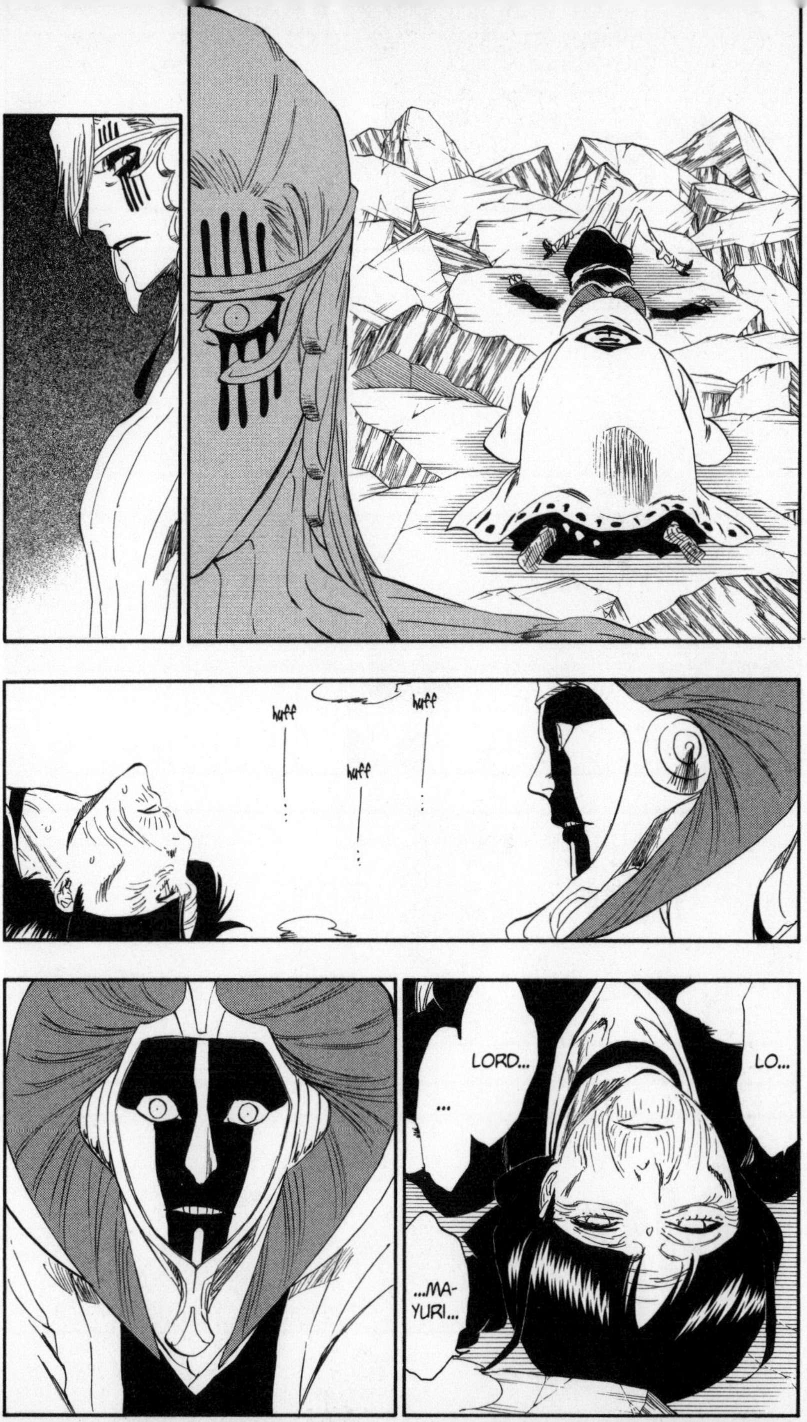
huff
huff
huff
LO...
LORD...
...
...MA-
YURI...

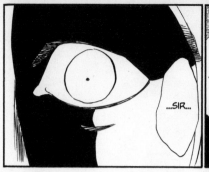

I'M...
...SO...
...SOR...
...RY...
...SIR...
WHAT'S WRONG?
ARE YOU STUNNED TO SEE YOUR ADJUTANT SO WITHERED?
YOU'RE MORE SEN-SITIVE...
...THAN I WOULD'VE GUESSED.
GIVE IT UP. SHE'S JUST SO MUCH DESICCATED MEAT NOW.
LET'S SEE...
...SHE MAY AS WELL BE BEEF JERKY.
TMP

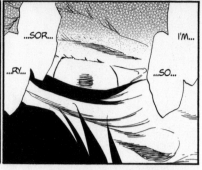

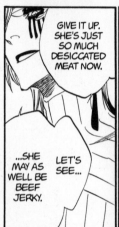

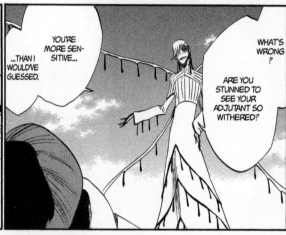

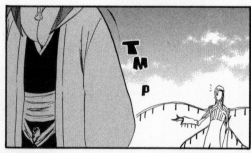

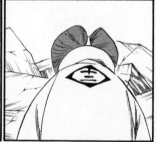

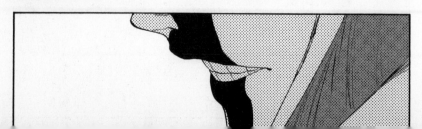

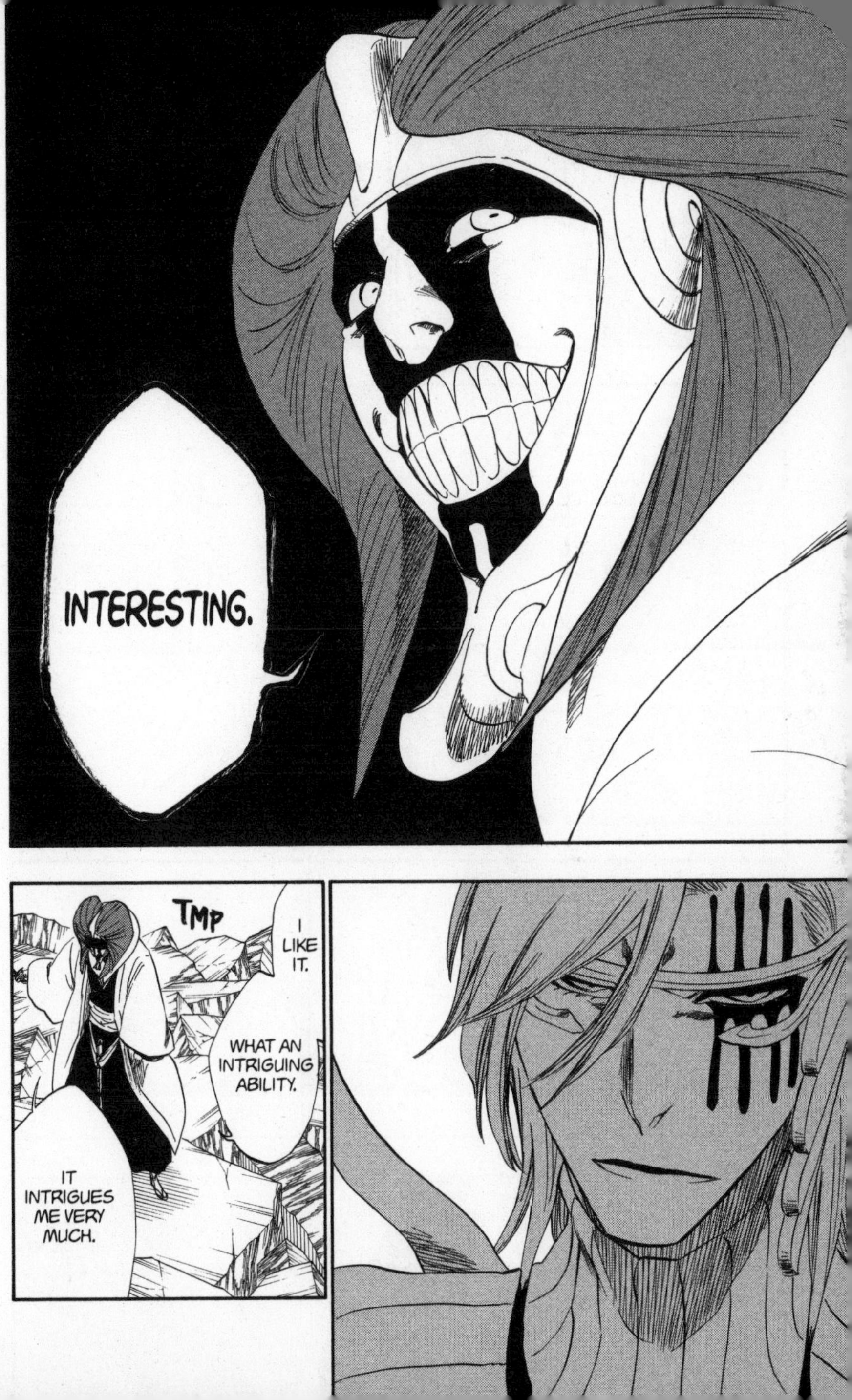
INTERESTING.
TMP
I LIKE IT.
WHAT AN INTRIGUING ABILITY.
IT INTRIGUES ME VERY MUCH.

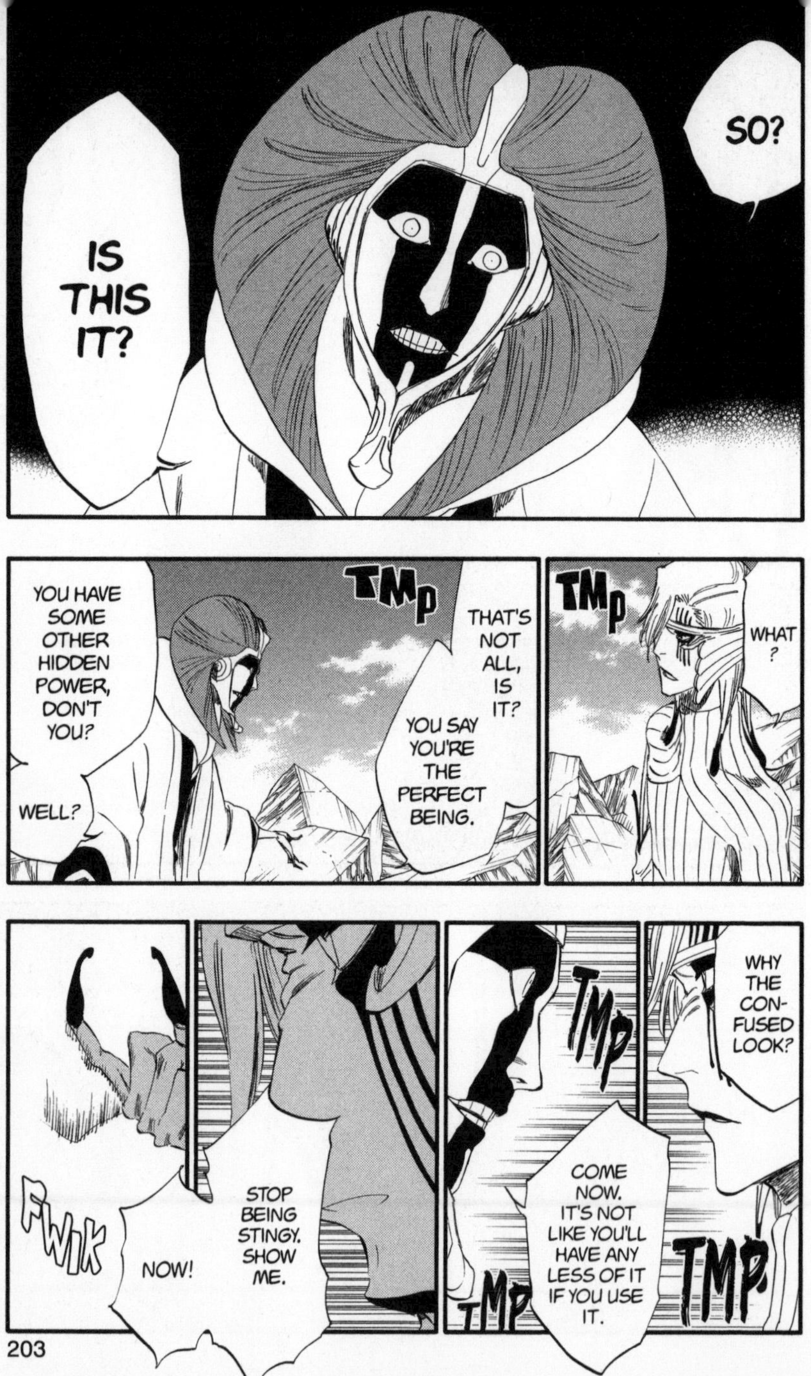
SO?
IS THIS IT?
TMp
WHAT?
TMp
THAT'S NOT ALL, IS IT?
YOU SAY YOU'RE THE PERFECT BEING.
YOU HAVE SOME OTHER HIDDEN POWER, DON'T YOU?
WELL?
WHY THE CON-FUSED LOOK?
TMP
COME NOW. IT'S NOT LIKE YOU'LL HAVE ANY LESS OF IT IF YOU USE IT.
TMp
TMP
STOP BEING STINGY. SHOW ME.
FWIK
NOW!

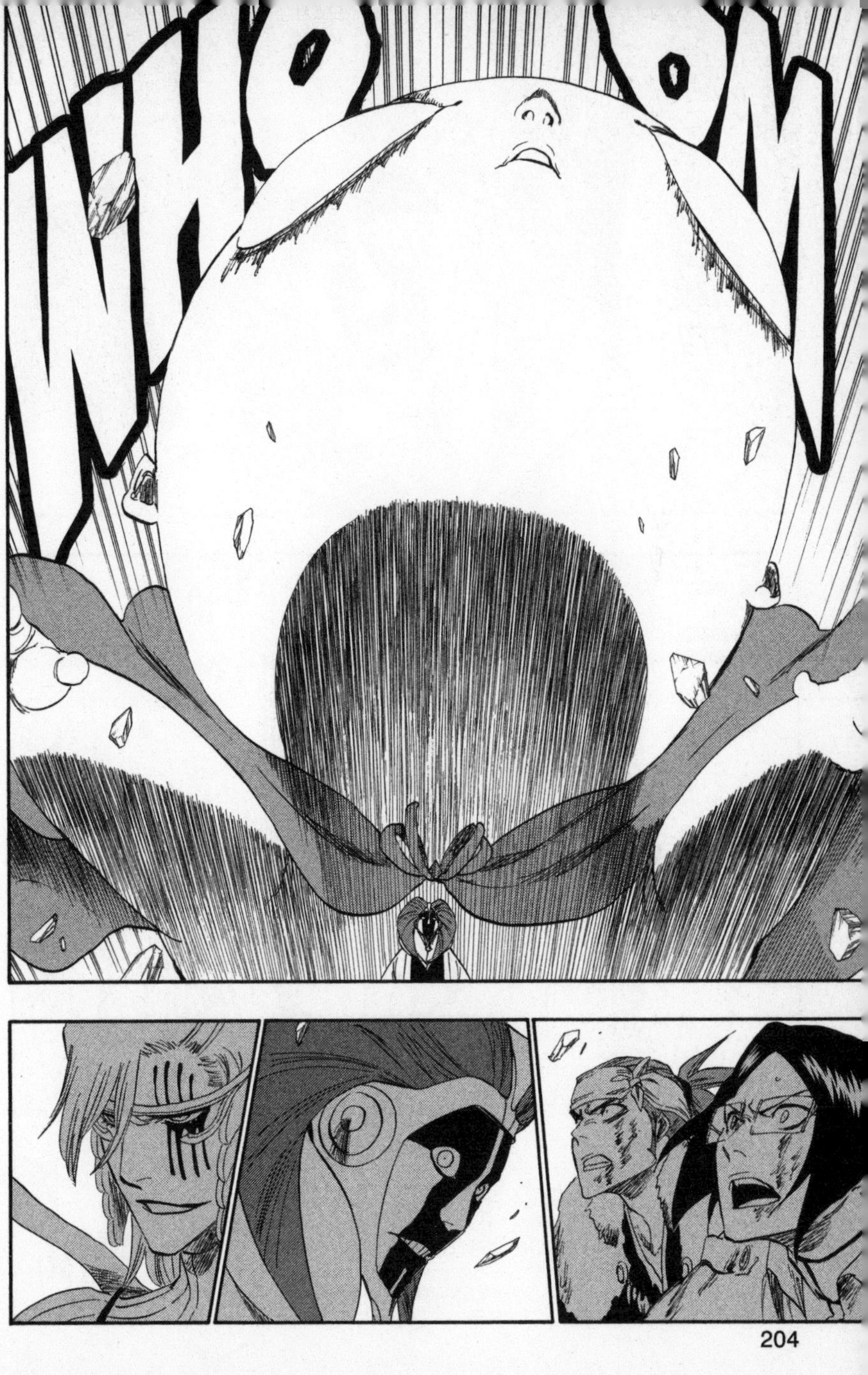
WHOOOM

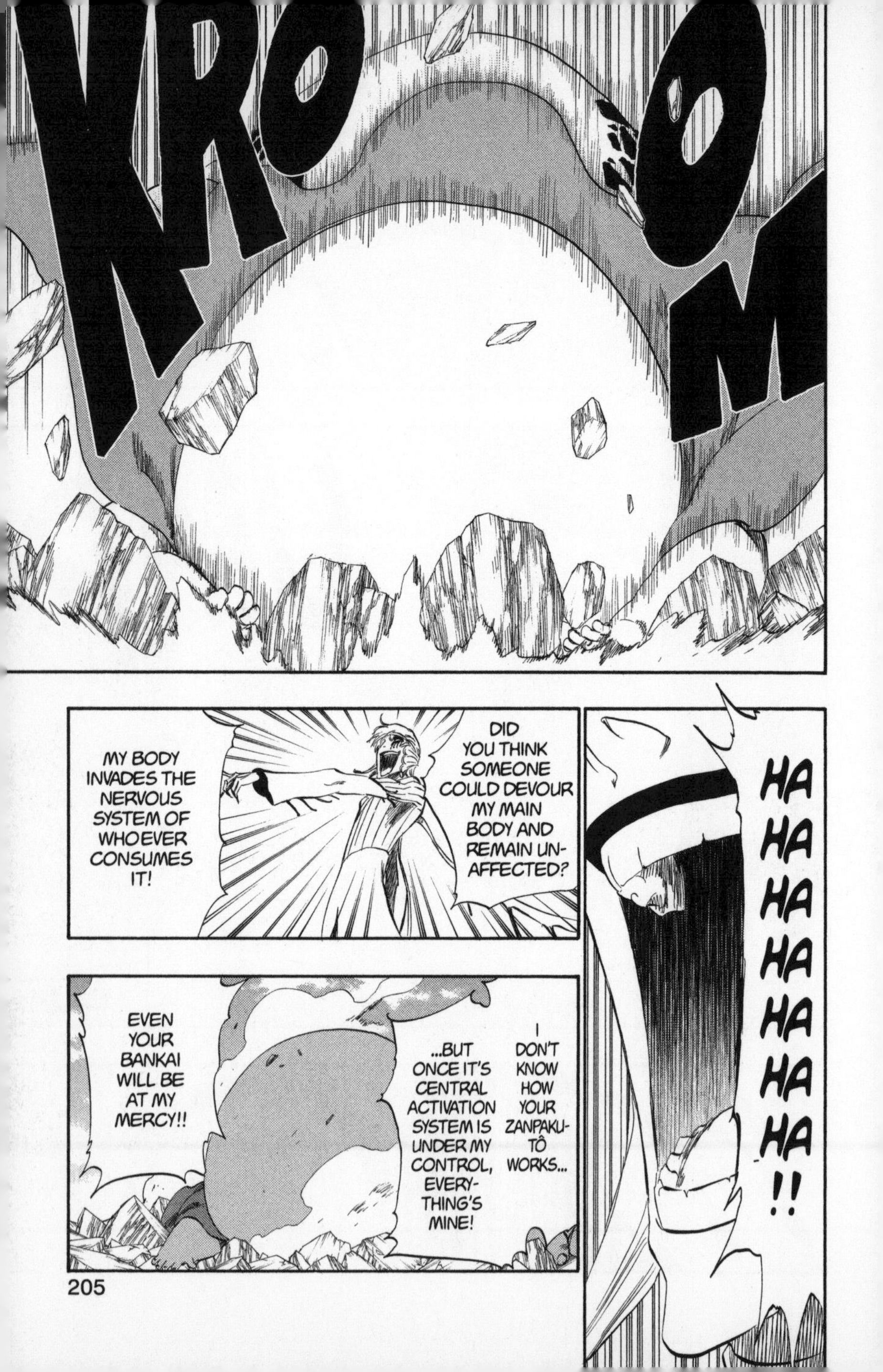
KROOM
HA HA HA HA HA HA HA HA HA!!
DID YOU THINK SOMEONE COULD DEVOUR MY MAIN BODY AND REMAIN UN-AFFECTED?
MY BODY INVADES THE NERVOUS SYSTEM OF WHOEVER CONSUMES IT!
I DON'T KNOW HOW YOUR ZANPAKU-TÔ WORKS...
...BUT ONCE IT'S CENTRAL ACTIVATION SYSTEM IS UNDER MY CONTROL, EVERY-THING'S MINE!
EVEN YOUR BANKAI WILL BE AT MY MERCY!!

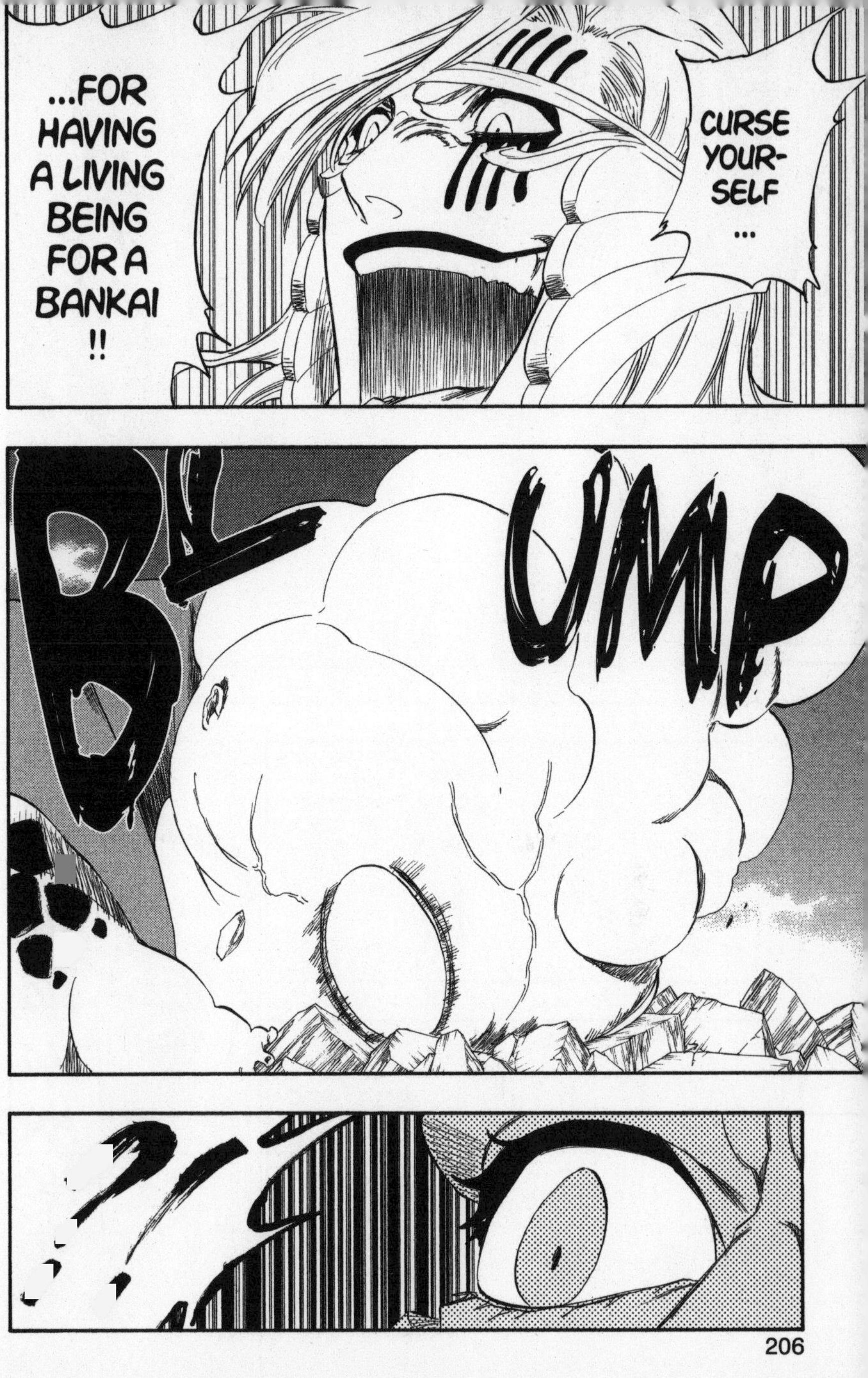
CURSE YOURSELF...
...FOR HAVING A LIVING BEING FOR A BANKAI!!
BLUMP

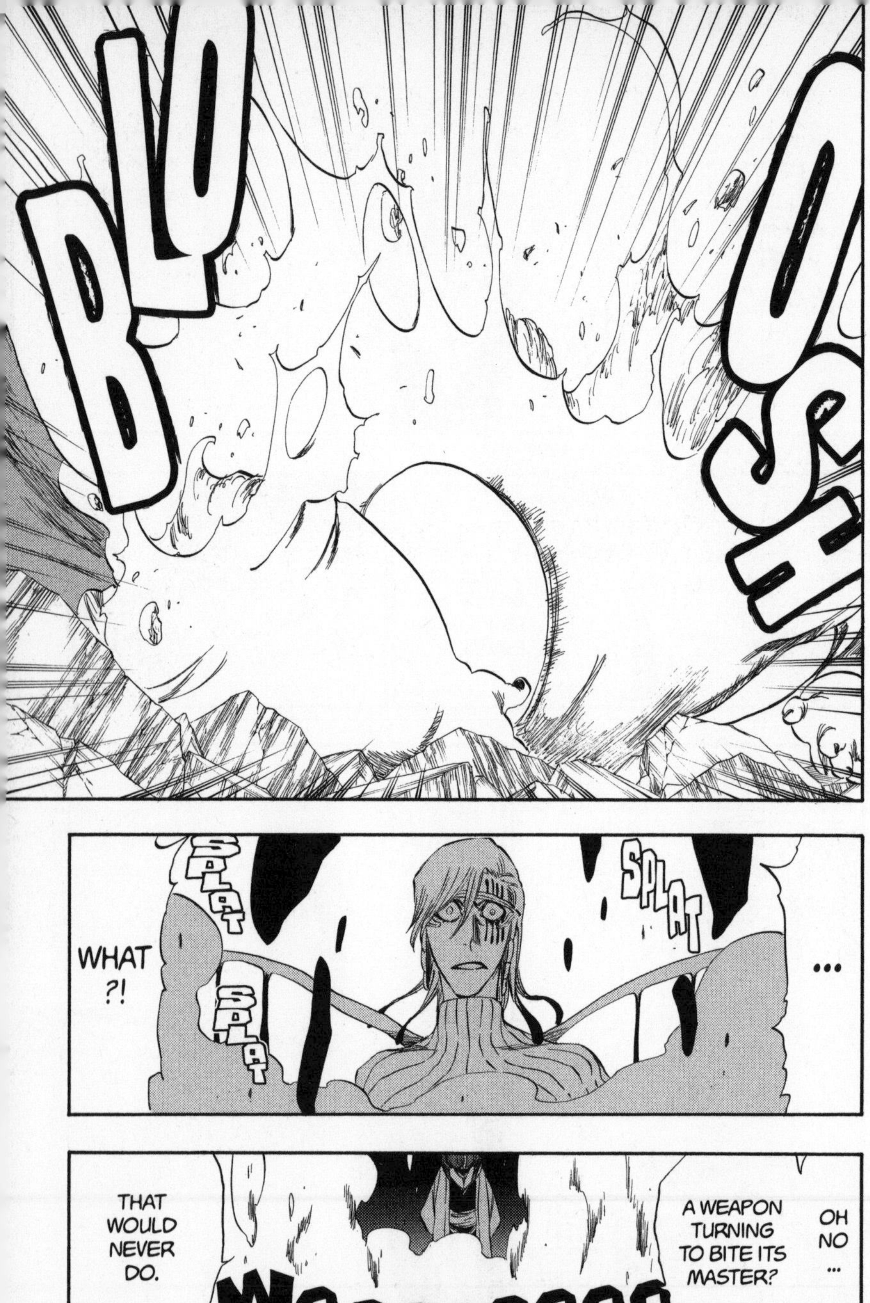
BLOOSH
...
SPLAT
SPLAT
WHAT ?!
SPLAT
OH NO ...
A WEAPON TURNING TO BITE ITS MASTER?
THAT WOULD NEVER DO.
WOOOOOOOO

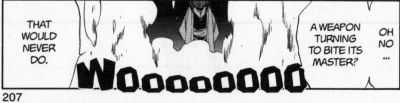

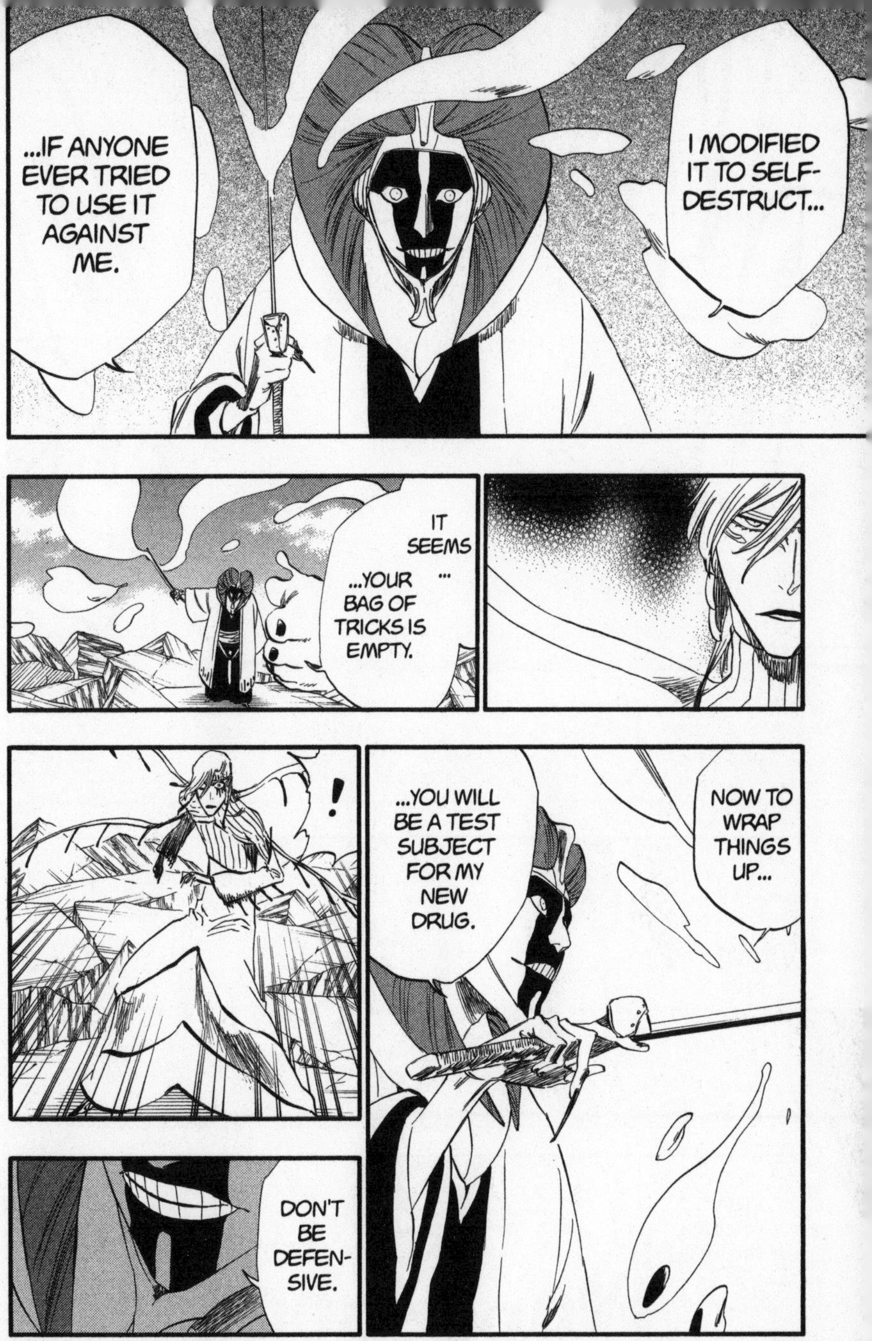
I MODIFIED IT TO SELF-DESTRUCT...
...IF ANYONE EVER TRIED TO USE IT AGAINST ME.
IT SEEMS...
...YOUR BAG OF TRICKS IS EMPTY.
NOW TO WRAP THINGS UP...
...YOU WILL BE A TEST SUBJECT FOR MY NEW DRUG.
!
DON'T BE DEFENSIVE.

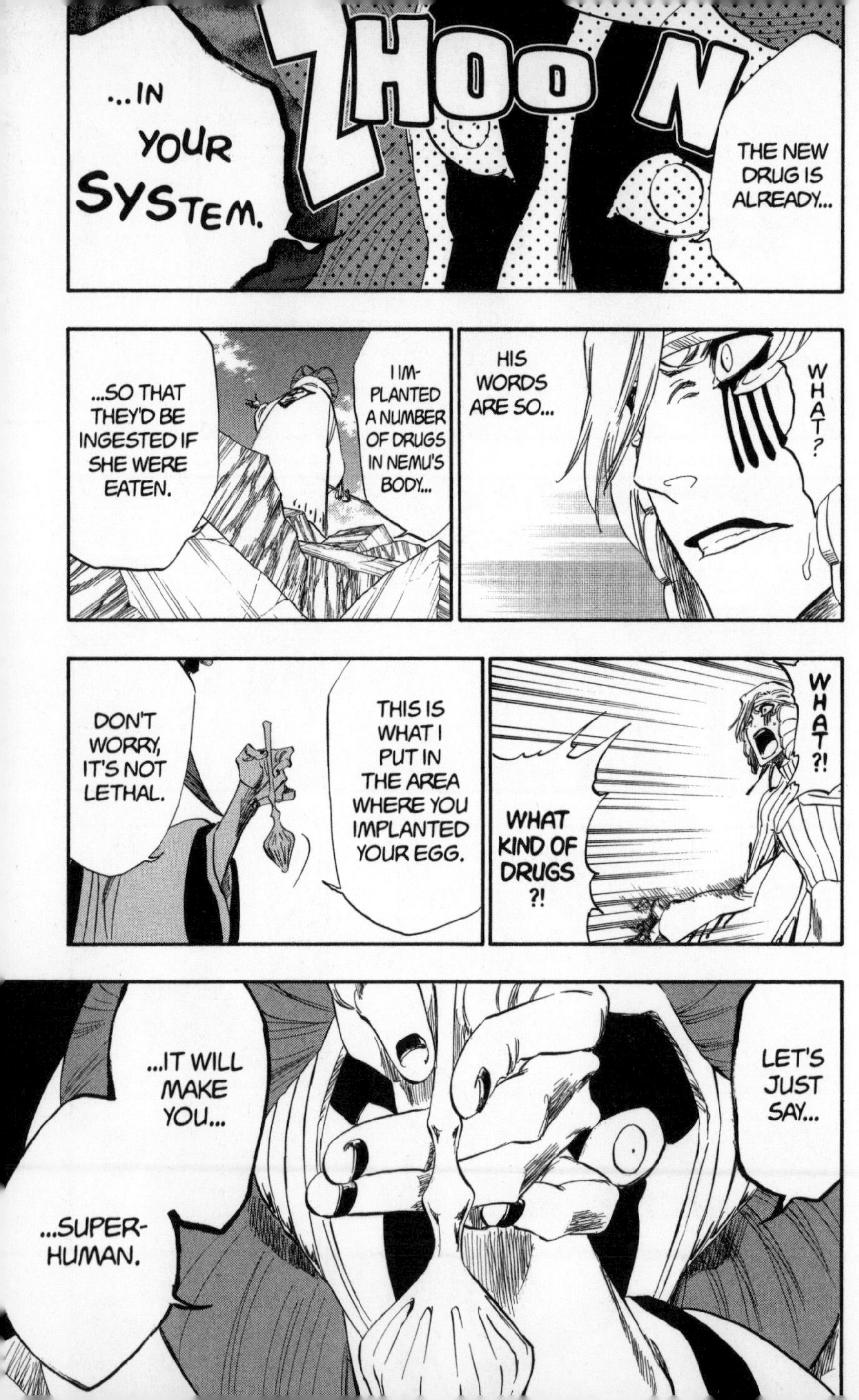
ZHOON
THE NEW DRUG IS ALREADY...
...IN YOUR SYSTEM.
WHAT?
HIS WORDS ARE SO...
I IM-PLANTED A NUMBER OF DRUGS IN NEMU'S BODY...
...SO THAT THEY'D BE INGESTED IF SHE WERE EATEN.
WHAT?!
WHAT KIND OF DRUGS?!
THIS IS WHAT I PUT IN THE AREA WHERE YOU IMPLANTED YOUR EGG.
DON'T WORRY, IT'S NOT LETHAL.
LET'S JUST SAY...
...IT WILL MAKE YOU...
...SUPER-HUMAN.

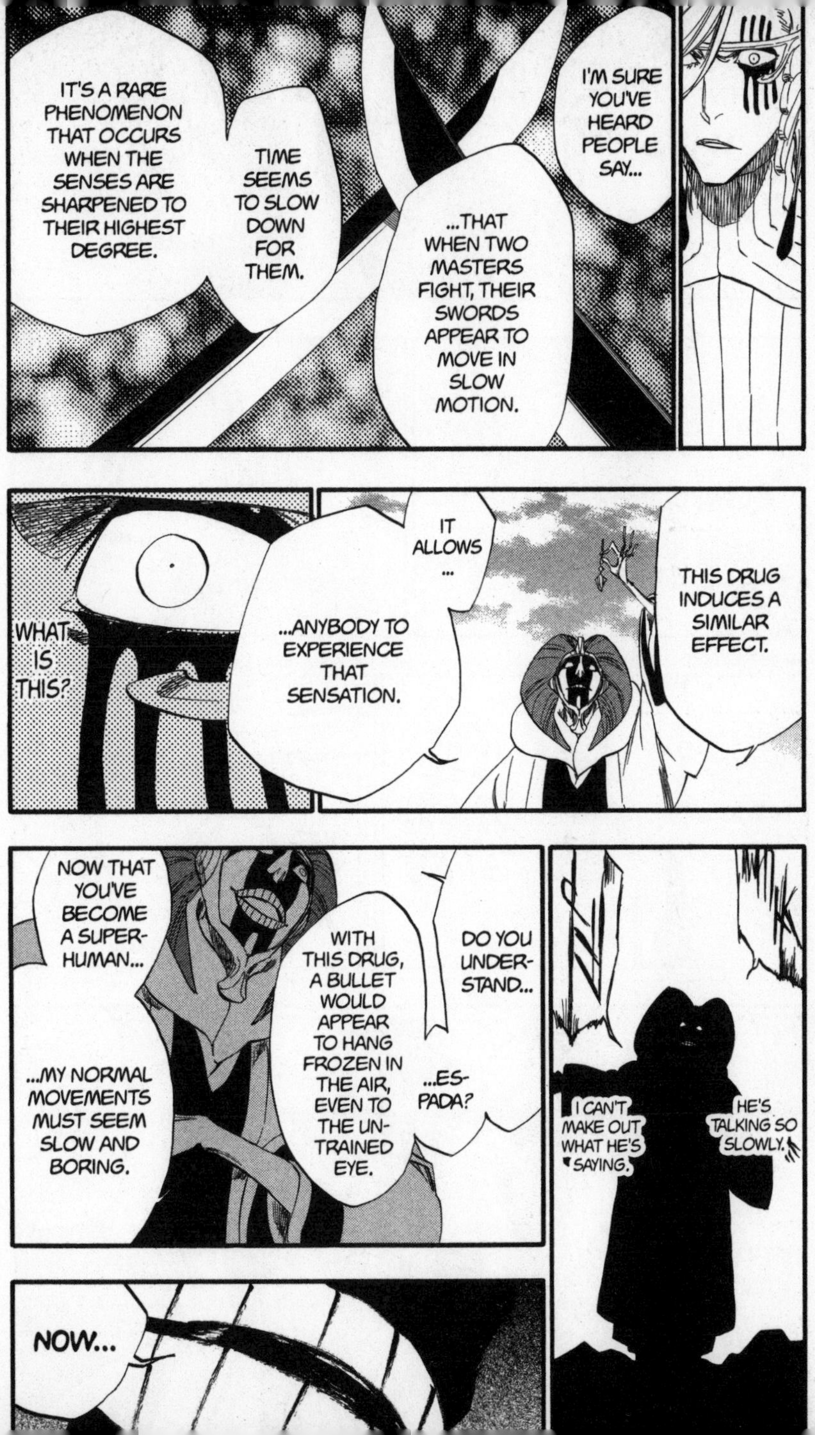
I'M SURE YOU'VE HEARD PEOPLE SAY...
...THAT WHEN TWO MASTERS FIGHT, THEIR SWORDS APPEAR TO MOVE IN SLOW MOTION.
TIME SEEMS TO SLOW DOWN FOR THEM.
IT'S A RARE PHENOMENON THAT OCCURS WHEN THE SENSES ARE SHARPENED TO THEIR HIGHEST DEGREE.
THIS DRUG INDUCES A SIMILAR EFFECT.
IT ALLOWS ...
...ANYBODY TO EXPERIENCE THAT SENSATION.
WHAT IS THIS?
HE'S TALKING SO SLOWLY.
I CAN'T MAKE OUT WHAT HE'S SAYING.
DO YOU UNDERSTAND...
...ES-PADA?
WITH THIS DRUG, A BULLET WOULD APPEAR TO HANG FROZEN IN THE AIR, EVEN TO THE UN-TRAINED EYE.
NOW THAT YOU'VE BECOME A SUPER-HUMAN...
...MY NORMAL MOVEMENTS MUST SEEM SLOW AND BORING.
NOW...

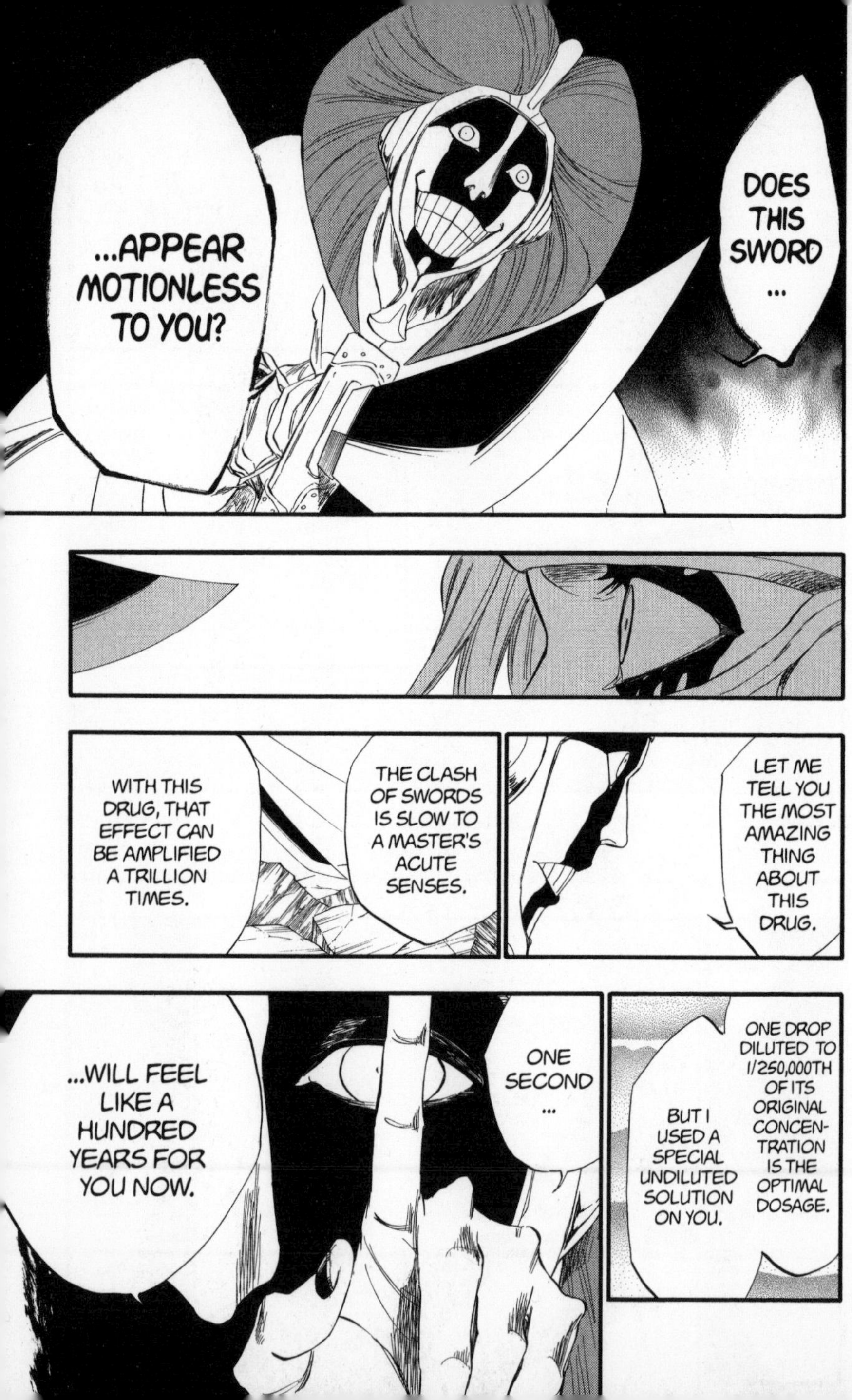
DOES THIS SWORD ...
...APPEAR MOTIONLESS TO YOU?
LET ME TELL YOU THE MOST AMAZING THING ABOUT THIS DRUG.
THE CLASH OF SWORDS IS SLOW TO A MASTER'S ACUTE SENSES.
WITH THIS DRUG, THAT EFFECT CAN BE AMPLIFIED A TRILLION TIMES.
ONE DROP DILUTED TO 1/250,000TH OF ITS ORIGINAL CONCENTRATION IS THE OPTIMAL DOSAGE.
BUT I USED A SPECIAL UNDILUTED SOLUTION ON YOU.
ONE SECOND ...
...WILL FEEL LIKE A HUNDRED YEARS FOR YOU NOW.

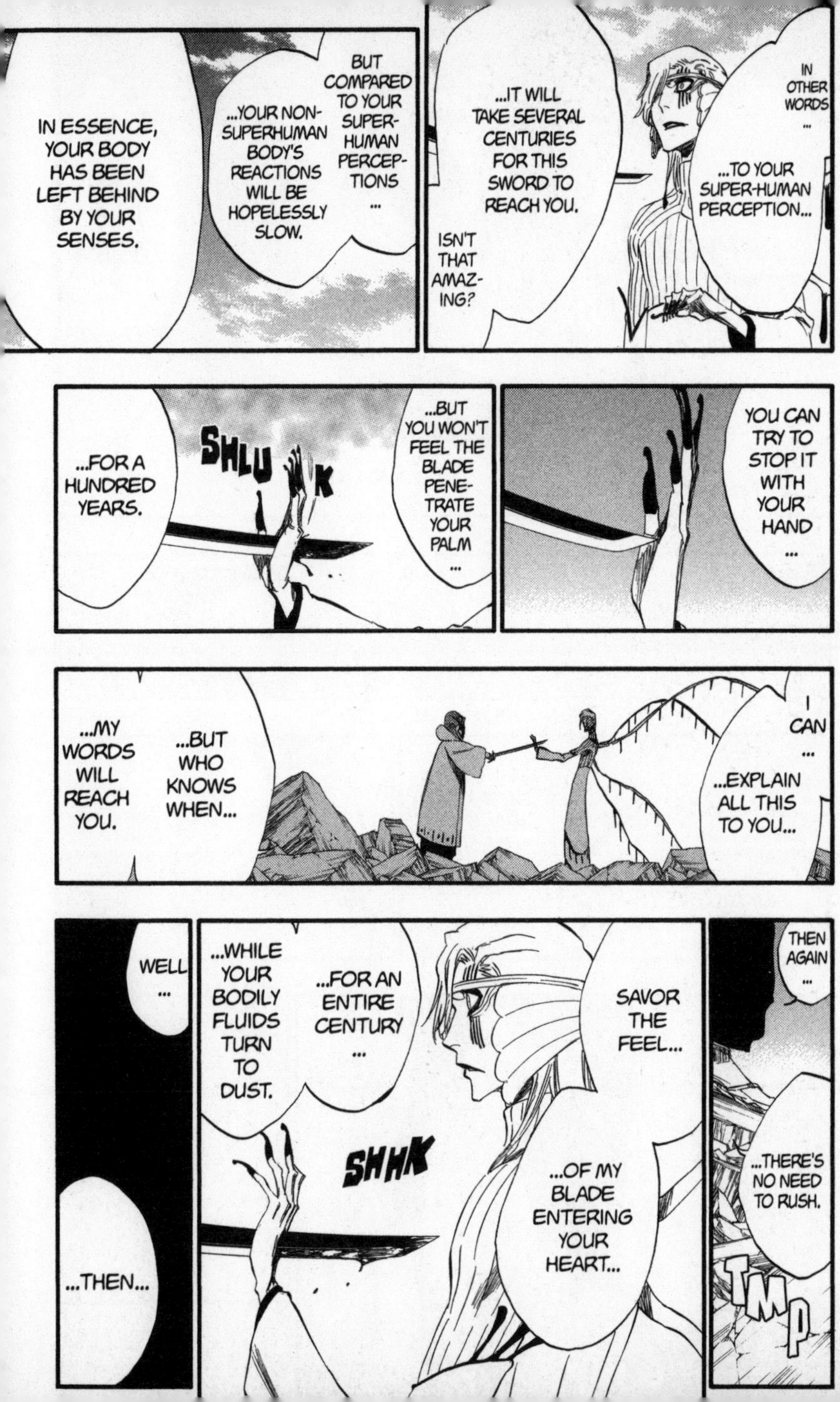
IN OTHER WORDS...
...TO YOUR SUPER-HUMAN PERCEPTION...
...IT WILL TAKE SEVERAL CENTURIES FOR THIS SWORD TO REACH YOU.
ISN'T THAT AMAZ-ING?
BUT COMPARED TO YOUR SUPER-HUMAN PERCEP-TIONS...
...YOUR NON-SUPERHUMAN BODY'S REACTIONS WILL BE HOPELESSLY SLOW.
IN ESSENCE, YOUR BODY HAS BEEN LEFT BEHIND BY YOUR SENSES.
YOU CAN TRY TO STOP IT WITH YOUR HAND...
...BUT YOU WON'T FEEL THE BLADE PENE-TRATE YOUR PALM...
SHLUNK
...FOR A HUNDRED YEARS.
I CAN...
...EXPLAIN ALL THIS TO YOU...
...BUT WHO KNOWS WHEN...
...MY WORDS WILL REACH YOU.
THEN AGAIN...
...THERE'S NO NEED TO RUSH.
TMP
SAVOR THE FEEL...
...OF MY BLADE ENTERING YOUR HEART...
...FOR AN ENTIRE CENTURY...
...WHILE YOUR BODILY FLUIDS TURN TO DUST.
SHHK
WELL...
...THEN...

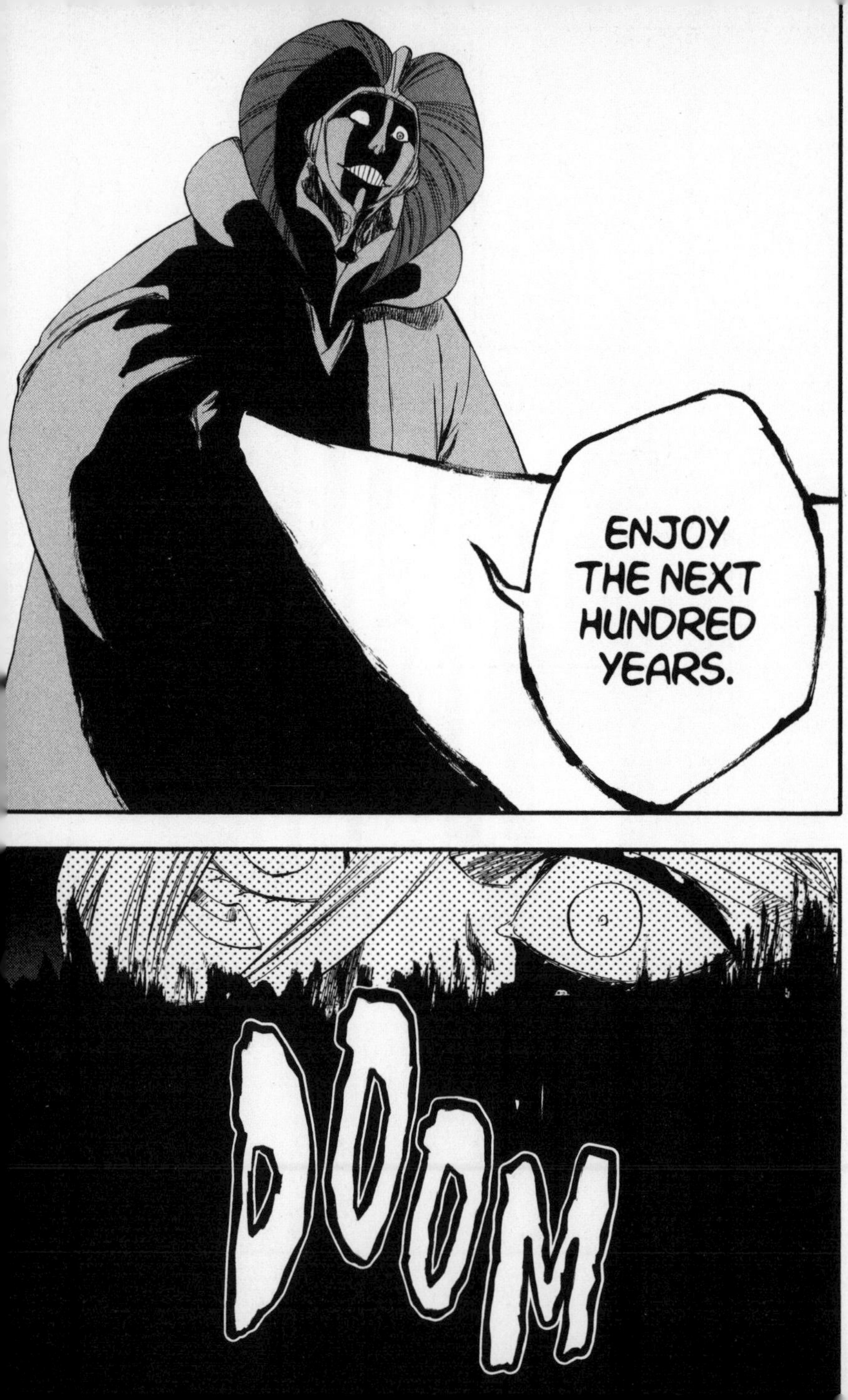
ENJOY THE NEXT HUNDRED YEARS.
DOOM

CONTI
NUED
IN
BLEACH
35

Next Volume Preview

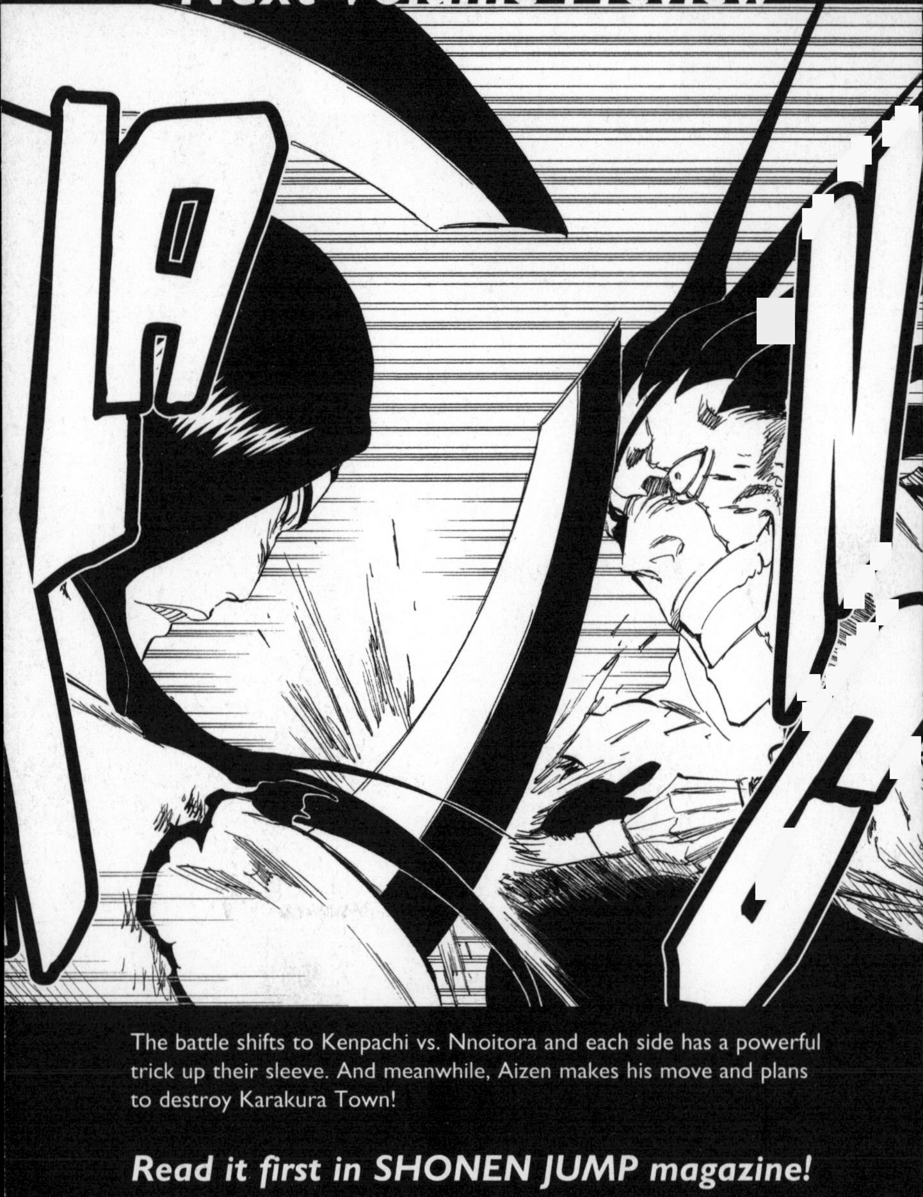

The battle shifts to Kenpachi vs. Nnoitora and each side has a powerful trick up their sleeve. And meanwhile, Aizen makes his move and plans to destroy Karakura Town!

Read it first in SHONEN JUMP magazine!

BONUS

WHAT SHOULD HAPPEN.

EEEEK!
THERE'S LOTS OF SCARY GUYS!
RIGHT?!
I THOUGHT THEY WERE THE VILLAINS!

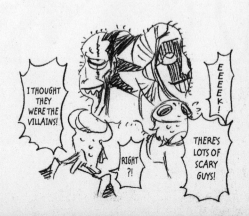